THE PSYCHOLOGY
OF LEARNING AND MOTIVATION

Advances in Research and Theory

VOLUME 27

THE PSYCHOLOGY
OF LEARNING AND MOTIVATION

Advances in Research and Theory

EDITED BY GORDON H. BOWER

STANFORD UNIVERSITY, STANFORD, CALIFORNIA

Volume 27

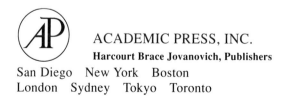

ACADEMIC PRESS, INC.

Harcourt Brace Jovanovich, Publishers

San Diego   New York   Boston
London   Sydney   Tokyo   Toronto

370.154

Copyright © 1991 BY ACADEMIC PRESS, INC.
All Rights Reserved.
No part of this publication may be reproduced or transmitted in any form or
by any means, electronic or mechanical, including photocopy, recording, or
any information storage and retrieval system, without permission in writing
from the publisher.

Academic Press, Inc.
San Diego, California 92101

United Kingdom Edition published by
ACADEMIC PRESS LIMITED
24-28 Oval Road, London NW1 7DX

Library of Congress Catalog Card Number: 66-30104

ISBN   0-12-543327-1   (alk. paper)

PRINTED IN THE UNITED STATES OF AMERICA
91 92 93 94   9 8 7 6 5 4 3 2 1

CONTENTS

Contributors ix
Preface xi

DERIVING CATEGORIES TO ACHIEVE GOALS

Lawrence W. Barsalou

   I. Introduction 1
  II. Structure of Goal-Derived Categories 6
 III. Goal-Derived Categories in Planning 22
 IV. Roles of Common Taxonomic and Goal-Derived Categories in
      the Cognitive System 45
   V. Conclusion 57
      References 58

LEARNING AND APPLYING CATEGORY KNOWLEDGE IN UNSUPERVISED DOMAINS

John P. Clapper and Gordon H. Bower

   I. Introduction 65
  II. Theoretical Issues 66
 III. A Model of Unsupervised Learning 69
 IV. Comparison to Alternative Approaches 76
  V. Experiments 77
 VI. Concluding Comments 104
      References 106

SPATIAL MENTAL MODELS

Barbara Tversky

I.	Overview	109
II.	Survey and Route Descriptions	111
III.	Spatial Frameworks	131
IV.	Summary	141
	References	143

MEMORY'S VIEW OF SPACE

Timothy P. McNamara

I.	Introduction	147
II.	Methods and Measures	148
III.	Structure and Content of Spatial Representations	157
IV.	Conclusions	179
	References	184

MADE IN MEMORY: DISTORTIONS IN RECOLLECTION AFTER MISLEADING INFORMATION

Elizabeth F. Loftus

I.	The Misinformation Effect	187
II.	Criticisms of the Modified Test	190
III.	Commitment to Misinformation	192
IV.	After the Modified Test, What?	199
V.	Implicit Tests and Misinformation	200
VI.	General Discussion	211
	References	212

COGNITIVE PROCESSES AND MECHANISMS IN LANGUAGE COMPREHENSION: THE STUCTURE BUILDING FRAMEWORK

Morton Ann Gernsbacher

I.	The Structure Building Framework	217
II.	The Process of Laying a Foundation	219
III.	Processes of Mapping and Shifting	229
IV.	Mechanisms of Suppression and Enhancement	238
V.	Individual Differences in General Comprehension Skill	248
VI.	Summary and Conclusions	254
	References	257

TEMPORAL LEARNING

John E. R. Staddon and Jennifer J. Higa

I.	Introduction	265
II.	Experimental Background: Performance on Patterned Interval Schedules of Reinforcement	268
III.	A Markovian Dynamic Hypothesis	272
IV.	A Diffusion-Generalization Model	277
V.	Conclusion	292
	References	293

BEHAVIOR'S TIME

Peter R. Killeen

I.	Introduction	295
II.	Contemporaneous Effects	296
III.	Retrospective Timing	305
IV.	Prospective Timing	313
V.	Time Horizons	320
VI.	Generalizations	323
VII.	Conclusions	329
	References	330

Index	335
Contents of Recent Volumes	347

CONTRIBUTORS

Numbers in parentheses indicate the pages on which the authors' contributions begin.

Lawrence W. Barsalou, Department of Psychology, University of Chicago, Chicago, Illinois 60637 (1)

Gordon H. Bower, Department of Psychology, Stanford University, Stanford, California 94305 (65)

John P. Clapper, Department of Psychology, Stanford University, Stanford, California 94305 (65)

Morton Ann Gernsbacher, Department of Psychology, University of Oregon, Eugene, Oregon 97403 (217)

Jennifer J. Higa, Department of Psychology, Duke University, Durham, North Carolina 27706 (265)

Peter R. Killeen, Department of Psychology, Arizona State University, Tempe, Arizona 85287 (295)

Elizabeth F. Loftus, Department of Psychology, University of Washington, Seattle, Washington 98195 (187)

Timothy P. McNamara, Department of Psychology, Vanderbilt University, Nashville, Tennessee 37240 (147)

John E. R. Staddon, Department of Psychology, Duke University, Durham, North Carolina 27706 (265)

Barbara Tversky, Department of Psychology, Stanford University, Stanford, California 94305 (109)

PREFACE

With publication of this Volume 27 of *The Psychology of Learning and Motivation*, I have decided to step down and bring to a close my editorship of the series. Having edited the last 25 volumes after contributing to the first two, I think it is time to bring some fresh, new talent to the editorship. The publisher's selection of Douglas Medin to be the new editor should achieve that goal brilliantly.

In retiring as editor, I was asked to write some brief reflections on the history of this series. The original idea for this annual publication of research reports on learning and motivation was conceived in 1964 by Kenneth Spence and Janet Spence. The objective of the series was

> to provide a forum in which workers in this field could write about significant bodies of research in which they were involved. The operating procedure has been to invite contributions from interesting, active investigators, and then allow them essentially free rein and whatever space they need to present their research and theoretical ideas as they see fit. The result of such invitations has been collections of papers which have been remarkable for the nature of their integrative summation . . . as presentations of a series of experimental results integrated around some particular problem or theory. (Spence & Bower, 1968, p. vii)

Kenneth and Janet had planned the chapters and contributors for the first two volumes just as Kenneth was becoming increasingly ill with cancer. Regrettably, he succumbed to cancer even before the first volume was published. Before his death, Kenneth and Janet asked me to carry on the editorship of the series, starting with the second volume. Janet helped me plan and edit Volume 3, teaching me how to get the job done. Thereafter, she cut me loose to run things on my own.

The Psychology of Learning and Motivation: Advances in Research and Theory has been a very successful series. It is one of the longest-running, best-selling *Advances* series produced by any scientific publisher in psychology. It has been remarkable for the consistently high quality of its authors and their contributed chapters. The quality is indicated by the prestigious reputation of the series as well as the high citation count of its articles.

Publishers have often inquired about the ingredients contributing to the success of the series. I believe that whatever success it has enjoyed may be attributed to several factors. First, I wanted to invite not only the big-name celebrities of psychology to write chapters but also to identify and invite younger, up-and-coming researchers who were not yet celebrities but who were doing research that impressed me as interesting and moving the field forward. This bias led to invitations to, and articles from, many young scientists who were most eager to have a forum in which to spread their wings and display their best ideas. For example, the incoming editor, Douglas Medin, was one such up-and-comer who contributed an invited chapter over 16 years ago (in 1975).

Second, since I was dealing with authors whose talent I trusted, I tried to curtail editorial hassling of them; that is, authors did not receive lengthy criticisms of their submitted manuscripts along with requests for revisions, entailing endless delays. Basically, contributors were told to take responsibility for what they displayed in public and to guard their own reputations. I also let contributors select their own schedules for submitting articles, a practice much loved by busy authors, which, however, produced rather unusual combinations in some volumes.

A third important factor underlying the success of the series is that the initial definition of the topics of *learning* and *motivation* was very broad, nearly all-encompassing. In her preface to Volume 1 of the series, Janet wrote

> For purposes of these volumes, learning research is broadly conceived, varying from studies of classical and instrumental or operant conditioning in human and animal subjects to investigations of complex learning, memorial processes, and problem-solving activities. Similarly, motivational research is intended to include the study of acquired and complex forms as well as simple, primary ones. (Spence, p.vii, 1967)

The breadth of this definition gave me license to follow whatever leads appeared promising or to flow with the trends, as the "animal learning theory" of the 1960s was modified by the conceptual revolutions of the 1970s and 1980s. In Volume 2, we had written

> A serial publication such as this must be prepared to move where the research workers of a field take it. It must be responsive to the diverse trends on the current research scene, and not become committed to a particular tradition or viewpoint regarding what are "important" scientific problems. The former and current editors are fully aware that conceptual revolution and change reflect the vitality of a science that is progressing, and that the important scientific problems of tomorrow will not be the same as those of yesterday. We cannot forecast whither this publication will be taken by its future contributors, but we shall always strive for contributions that are informative, provocative, and of first-class quality. (Bower & Spence, p. vii, 1968)

The series has been fortunate in attracting seminal contributions from many leading researchers so that our roster of authors reads like a *Who's Who* in the psychology of learning and cognition. I have tried throughout to provide a balanced distribution of articles from the several domains covered by our title—from studies of elementary associative learning in animals to the logic of inferences about mental representations, from mathematical analysis of learning by neural networks to experimental analysis of reinforcement schedules, from computer simulation models of language processing and learning to the analysis of problem-solving protocols produced by tutors or economic policy planners, from foraging and cache memory in birds to analytic studies of causal induction in humans. The diversity of topics has reflected the vitality of the research areas. One area which has been underrepresented in these volumes is studies of human motivation and emotion. Invitations to prospective writers on these topics have often been turned down on the grounds that the series primarily appealed to learning psychologists and would not draw the largest relevant audience for those writers—an example of a self-fulfilling prophecy. This is one of several areas in which the publisher and series editor would like to improve our coverage.

As I leave this editorship, it is with considerable pleasure and pride that I hand over the reins to my successor, Douglas Medin. Dr. Medin has a long, distinguished career of theoretical and experimental contributions in many domains, including animal learning, human memory, mathematical models, categorization, judgment, and problem-solving.

He has scholarly interests and contacts across a vast range of areas; and he is well positioned academically and nationally to be aware of new developments and newcomers to our field. Dr. Medin brings to this job an enviable record as a brilliant editor for several of the leading journals of our field—both experimental and theoretical, both animal learning and human cognitive psychology. Academic Press and I are fully confident that Dr. Medin will continue the leadership of this series' volumes at the forefront of the psychology of learning and motivation.

Gordon H. Bower
Stanford University

REFERENCES

Bower G. H., & Spence, J. T. (1968). Preface. In K. W. Spence & J. T. Spence (Eds.), *The pychology of learning and motivation* (Vol. 2). New York: Academic Press.
Spence, J. T. (1967). Preface. In K. W. Spence & J. T. Spence (Eds.), *The psychology of learning and motivation* (Vol. 1). New York: Academic Press.

THE PSYCHOLOGY
OF LEARNING AND MOTIVATION

Advances in Research and Theory

VOLUME 27

DERIVING CATEGORIES TO ACHIEVE GOALS

Lawrence W. Barsalou

I. Introduction

People often derive categories while constructing plans to achieve goals. In constructing the plan for a vacation to San Francisco, someone might derive the categories of *departure times that minimize work disruption, people to visit in California,* and *things to pack in a small suitcase.* An infinite number of goal-derived categories exist, including *foods to eat on a diet, clothing to wear while house painting, grocery stores that sell fresh herbs, activities to do on a vacation in Japan with one's grandmother,* and so forth. Many of these are ad hoc categories, not established in memory but derived impromptu to achieve a current and novel goal. Whereas some goal-derived categories become well established in memory from being processed on numerous occasions, many others are ad hoc, having never been relevant before. For example, *foods to eat on a diet* might be a well-established, goal-derived category for someone who diets often, but *activities to do on a vacation in Japan with one's grandmother* is probably an ad hoc category for most people. Although I only address the ad hoc categories that people derive while constructing plans to achieve goals, ad hoc categories also arise in other contexts, including decision making (Kahneman & Miller, 1986), metaphor (Glucksberg & Keysar, 1990), and comparative judgment (Čech, Shoben, & Love, 1990).

A. OVERVIEW

The central theme of this chapter will be that understanding the nature of categories depends on understanding their origins and roles in the cognitive system. If different types of categories have different origins and serve different roles, they are likely to develop different characteristics. In Section I,B, I contrast two fundamentally different ways in which categories originate: *exemplar learning* and *conceptual combination*. Much current work on categorization focuses on exemplar learning, addressing the induction of category knowledge from experiences with exemplars. Certainly, exemplar learning is central to the acquisition of many categories. For example, the acquisition of common taxonomic categories, such as *apple, bird, shirt,* and *chair,* relies heavily on experiences with exemplars. However, exemplar learning is not central to the acquisition of all categories. As we shall see, people often acquire goal-derived categories through conceptual combination, in the absence of exemplars. If the origins of categories determine their characteristics, then the disparate origins of common taxonomic and goal-derived categories should cause them to differ in important ways.

In Section II, I address the structure of common taxonomic and goal-derived categories. If these two types of categories have different origins, then their cognitive structures may differ. Much previous work has found that common taxonomic categories exhibit prototype structure, with some exemplars being more typical than others. Perhaps this structure reflects an outcome of exemplar learning, such as the abstraction of prototypical properties or the storage of prototypical exemplars. In contrast, the formulation of goal-derived categories through conceptual combination in the absence of exemplars should preclude the abstraction of prototypical information. Moreover, the conceptual combination that underlies goal-derived categories may produce definitions rather than prototypes to represent these categories. For these reasons, goal-derived categories may be equivalence classes that do not exhibit prototype structures. Even if prototype structures do exist in goal-derived categories, these structures may reflect fundamentally different factors than the prototype structures in common taxonomic categories, because of their different origins.

In Section III, I examine the role that goal-derived categories play in goal achievement and the conceptual combination that underlies their derivation. As protocol analyses of planning illustrate, people derive these categories while constructing plans to achieve goals. In the initial stages of planning, people retrieve an event frame and begin to instantiate its attributes. In planning a vacation, for example, people retrieve the frame for *vacation* and begin instantiating attributes such as *location* and *departure*. Goal-derived categories provide sets of potential instantiations for these attributes. For example, the goal-derived category of *vacation locations* provides potential instantiations of the *location* attribute in the *vacation* frame, perhaps including *Montana, Tahiti,* and *Paris.* To derive more specific, ad hoc categories that serve a plan in a particular context, people often integrate frame attributes with optimizations and constraints. For example, people might combine the frame attribute *location* with the optimization *inexpensive* and the constraint *enables snow skiing* to derive the ad hoc category of *inexpensive vacation locations that enable snow skiing*. Conceptual combination contextualizes categories, such that optimal and consistent instantiations can be found for frame attributes.

In Section IV, I examine further differences between common taxonomic and goal-derived categories, as well as relations between them. I first address the roles of common taxonomic and goal-derived categories in the time course of categorization. Whereas common taxonomic categories provide the primary categorizations of entities, goal-derived categories provide the secondary categorizations of entities. I suggest that this difference in temporal application produces different representations for common taxonomic and goal-derived categories, which serve different purposes in the cognitive system. I further suggest that this difference in temporal application results in lexicalization for common taxonomic categories but not for goal-derived categories, which often require more productive forms of linguistic expression. Finally, I propose a general framework for representing knowledge, in which common taxonomic and goal-derived categories play different but complementary roles. According to this framework, people use common taxonomic categories to build world models that represent the current state of the known environment. In contrast, people use goal-derived categories to interface world models with event frames for achieving goals. When trying to achieve a particular goal, people cannot succeed if attributes in the appropriate event frame do not map into a world model. Goal-derived categories provide the mappings from frame attributes to world models that make goal achievement possible.

B.   EXEMPLAR LEARNING AND CONCEPTUAL COMBINATION AS MODES OF CATEGORY ACQUISITION

Before proceeding to an examination of goal-derived categories, I address a distinction that will be central throughout this chapter. People can acquire categories in a variety of ways. At one extreme, people learn categories primarily through *exemplar learning,* inducing category knowledge from experiences with exemplars (e.g., Barsalou, 1990b; Brooks, 1978, 1987; Estes, 1986; Gluck & Bower, 1988; Hintzman, 1986; Homa, 1984; Jacoby & Brooks, 1984; McClelland & Rumelhart, 1985; Medin & Schaffer, 1978; Nosofsky, 1984; Posner & Keele, 1968; Rosch & Mervis, 1975). As people encounter a category's exemplars, they extract the exemplars' perceived characteristics and integrate them to form category knowledge. Upon encountering a new kind of bird, for example, people extract the physical and behavioral characteristics of its exemplars and integrate them into a new category representation. The representations that result from such learning can take the form of prototypes, exemplars, and/or definitions (Smith & Medin, 1981). In general, this kind of learning is relatively passive, bottom-up, and automatic, at least as many psychological theories characterize it. As perceptual systems provide information about exemplars, category knowledge accrues slowly. To the extent that perception and memory are accurate, exemplar learning provides a relatively veridical account of the physical world, although distortions and biases certainly occur.

Conceptual combination constitutes a very different way in which people can acquire knowledge of a category (Barsalou, in press-b; Hampton, 1987, 1988; Medin & Shoben, 1988; Murphy, 1988; Smith, Osherson, Rips, & Keene, 1988). In this form of category learning, people derive new categories by manipulating existing knowledge in memory. In extreme forms of conceptual combination, little experience with exemplars is necessary. For example, people can manipulate knowledge about *colors* and *natural earth formations* to derive new categories such as *purple oceans, orange rivers,* and *blue cliffs,* even though exemplars of these categories have never been experienced. In contrast to exemplar learning, conceptual combination appears to be relatively active, top-down, and effortful. By deliberately manipulating knowledge through reasoning, people produce new categories that serve their goals. As we shall see, conceptual combination often produces idealized knowledge about how the world should be rather than normative knowledge about how it is.

Knowledge of many categories may evolve through both exemplar learning and conceptual combination. For example, Murphy and Medin (1985) argue that people use intuitive theories to guide category learning (also see Keil, 1989; Markman, 1989; Wellman & Gelman, 1988). According to this view, people's intuitive theories about the world play central roles in the processing of exemplars, including the selection, interpretation, and integration of their perceived properties. In learning psychiatric disorders, for example, learners select, interpret, and integrate symptoms quite differently, depending on whether their clinical theory is psychodynamic or behaviorist. As people extract perceptual characteristics from exemplars, the mechanisms of conceptual combination integrate this information with intuitive theories and other background knowledge to develop increasingly articulated accounts of the category. Features do not simply accrue for categories as exemplars are experienced. Instead, background knowledge assimilates features and may be accommodated in the process.

Although exemplar learning and conceptual combination both play important roles in category learning, each appears more central to some categories than to others. For example, exemplar learning appears particularly important to the acquisition of common taxonomic categories such as *apple, bird, shirt,* and *chair*. Extensive literatures on conceptual and linguistic development document the simple fact that adults often point to exemplars, while uttering their category names, to help children acquire common taxonomic categories (Keil, 1989; Markman, 1989; Mervis, 1987). For example, an adult might use an encounter with a cat to teach a child the concept and name for *cat,* perhaps contrasting them with the concept and name for *dog*. Clearly, exemplars are central to children's acquisition of common taxonomic categories.

Exemplar learning also appears central to common taxonomic categories for another reason. As I propose in Section IV,A, common taxonomic categories serve to maintain accurate information about the kinds of entities in the world. For example, *chair* maintains accurate information about its exemplars, including their likely physical properties (e.g., *seat, back, legs*) and their standard function (e.g., *enables sitting*). For accurate information to accrue about common taxonomic categories, people must encounter their exemplars, or at least learn about them through hearsay, in which case the original source of the hearsay encountered exemplars. If the representations of common taxonomic categories do not reflect experiences with exemplars, then the information established for them is likely to be inaccurate. As we shall see in Section II,B, the presence of central tendency information in the representations of common taxonomic categories suggests that these categories maintain representative information about their exemplars.

In contrast, exemplar learning appears much less important for goal-derived categories. Consider *things to pack in a suitcase*. People do not establish this category from experiences with its exemplars. Upon encountering particular *shirts, novels,* and *toothbrushes* in the environment, people do not induce *things to pack in a suitcase*. Instead, reasoning and conceptual combination during planning are central to acquiring this category. Because transporting personal items is often necessary on trips, and because suitcases serve as conventional containers for transporting these items, people must combine concepts for *things, pack,* and *suitcase,* along with background knowledge about trips, to derive *things to pack in a suitcase*. Subsequently, people may search for exemplars, which may in turn influence the evolving category representation. Exemplars may suggest new properties that are relevant to the category and raise problems for existing properties. But because the role of these categories is to optimize a plan, reasoning about exemplars' ideal properties through conceptual combination may often be more important than acquiring central tendency information through exemplar learning. For example, people may derive the ideal weight of *things to pack in a suitcase* rather than inducing the average weight. Section III provides numerous examples of how people manipulate knowledge to produce goal-derived categories in the absence of exemplar learning.

II. Structure of Goal-Derived Categories

If common taxonomic and goal-derived categories arise through different mechanisms, their structures may differ. By *structure,* I do not mean the objective structures of categories in the environment or scientific theories about them (cf. Rey, 1983). Rather, I mean the cognitive representations of categories (Smith, Medin, & Rips, 1984). In this section, I review findings that bear on the structures of common taxonomic and goal-derived categories. Barsalou (in press-b) and Barsalou and Billman (1989) provide accounts of *structure* that differ considerably from those considered in this section.

A.   PROTOTYPE STRUCTURE IN COMMON TAXONOMIC CATEGORIES

Much work has shown that common taxonomic categories exhibit *prototype structure,* with some exemplars being more typical of a category than others. For example, *robin* is more typical of *birds* than is *falcon,* which is more typical than *chicken.* Similarly, *chair* is more typical of *furniture* than is *lamp,* which is more typical than *refrigerator.* Many theorists believe that an exemplar's typicality is a continuous function of its similarity to the prototypical information for its category (Barsalou, 1987, 1989; Hampton, 1979; McCloskey & Glucksberg, 1979; Reed, 1972; Rosch & Mervis, 1975; Smith, Shoben, & Rips, 1974; Tversky, 1977).[1] As an exemplar becomes increasingly similar to prototypical information, it becomes increasingly typical. Consider prototypical information for *birds,* such as *small, flies, sings,* and *lives in trees.* Exemplars similar to this information are typical (e.g., *robin, sparrow*); whereas exemplars dissimilar to this information are atypical (e.g., *ostrich, chicken*). The ordering of exemplars according to typicality that results from these similarity com-

---

[1] As we shall see in Section II,D,1, prototypical information can exist either in prototype or in exemplar representations of categories (Barsalou, 1990b).

parisons constitutes the category's prototype structure.[2] In addition, prototype structure extends into the complement of the category, with nonmembers varying in how typical they are of the complement (Barsalou, 1983; McCloskey & Glucksberg, 1979; Smith et al., 1974). For example, *butterfly, helicopter,* and *chair* are increasingly typical members of *nonbirds*.

Prototype structure does not appear to be a rigid structure stored in long-term memory (Barsalou, 1987, 1989). For example, the representation of *birds* probably does not specify explicitly that *robins, falcons,* and *chickens* decrease in typicality. Instead, prototype structure appears to be an implicit and emergent property that reflects the importance of prototypical information for a category, in conjunction with comparison and retrieval processes that utilize this information in various categorization tasks (e.g., classification, production, acquisition, reasoning). On a given occasion, the exemplars that are similar to prototypical information are processed more efficiently and confidently as category members than exemplars that are dissimilar. The implicit ordering of exemplars that emerges from this differential processing of exemplars constitutes prototype structure. Because the prototypical information for a category varies across individuals, tasks, and contexts, the prototype structures that emerge for a category vary considerably.

Prototype structure is central to how people represent and process categories. If one peruses reviews of the categorization literature, one sees that no other variable is as prevalent or robust in category processing as prototype structure (Medin & Smith, 1984; Mervis & Rosch, 1981; Oden, 1987; Smith & Medin, 1981). Prototype structure is central to the efficiency of classifying exemplars, with typical exemplars being classified faster and more accurately than atypical exemplars (e.g., McCloskey & Glucksberg, 1979; Smith et al., 1974). Prototype structure is central to the production of exemplars from categories, with people generating typical exemplars earlier and more often than atypical exemplars (e.g., Barsalou, 1983, 1985). Prototype structure is central to the acquisition of categories, with typical exemplars being acquired faster than atypical exemplars, and with typical exemplars facilitating category learning the most (e.g., Mervis & Pani, 1980). Prototype structure is central to reasoning about categories, with typical exemplars facilitating syllogistic reasoning more than atypical

---

[2] Elsewhere, I have referred to *prototype structure* as *graded structure* (Barsalou, 1983, 1985, 1987, 1989). However, I use *prototype structure* here to highlight the fact that the gradedness within categories reflects the typicality of exemplars, namely, their relation to the prototypical information of their category.

exemplars (Cherniak, 1984), and with typical exemplars producing stronger inductive inferences than atypical exemplars (Osherson, Smith, Wilkie, Lopez, & Shafir, 1990; Rips, 1975).

Yet some theorists have argued that prototype structure is unrelated to the essential structure of a category, as reflected in the formal bases of category membership. This is certainly true on occasion, as Armstrong, Gleitman, and Gleitman (1983) have shown for some categories (also see Rips, 1989). For example, *odd number* contains a prototype structure because people view some odd numbers as more typical than others. Yet this prototype structure has nothing to do with formal membership, which reflects a discrete, all-or-none rule (i.e., an odd number is any integer that produces a remainder of 1 when divided by 2). All odd numbers satisfy this rule equally, and thereby do not exhibit gradedness in formal membership.[3]

Certainly, prototype structure and formal membership are unrelated in some categories. But in many common taxonomic categories, formal membership is undefined. Rather than being clear and incontrovertable, membership is debatable and often undecidable. In these categories, membership typically varies continuously rather than being all-or-none. People are highly confident about the membership of some exemplars, somewhat confident about the membership of others, and not confident about the membership of others. In *furniture,* for example, people are confident that *chair* is a member, less confident that *rug* is a member, and still less confident that *refrigerator* is a member. Not only does membership vary reliably in these categories, typicality usually covaries with it. As an exemplar's membership increases, its typicality increases as well. In these categories, prototype structure reflects the ambiguous basis of membership. A variety of studies document this relationship between prototype structure and membership in common taxonomic categories (Chater, Lyon, & Myers, 1990; Fehr & Russell, 1984, Experiment 5; Hampton, 1979, 1988; McCloskey & Glucksberg, 1978).

B.   PROTOTYPE STRUCTURE IN GOAL-DERIVED CATEGORIES

As we just saw, common taxonomic categories exhibit prototype structure. What is the structure of goal-derived categories? Do they exhibit prototype structure as well? Or do these categories exhibit some other

---

[3] But note that prototype structure and the *cognitive* basis of membership are related, given that people classify typical odd numbers faster than atypical odd numbers (Armstrong et al., 1983). Because prototype structure is central to the efficiency with which people establish membership, prototype structure certainly plays some role in the cognitive realization of *odd number* (Barsalou & Medin, 1986).

kind of structure? Two factors suggest that goal-derived categories should not exhibit prototype structure. First, if people do not acquire goal-derived categories through exemplar learning, then they should not have the requisite opportunities for abstracting prototypical properties from category members. Nor should people be able to identify and store typical exemplars. As a result, people should not have a basis for judging some exemplars as more typical than others. Second, in the process of deriving a category through conceptual combination, people may deduce the necessary and sufficient conditions that enable its exemplars to achieve an associated goal (as in explanation-based learning; DeJong & Mooney, 1986; Mitchell, Keller, & Kedar-Cabelli, 1986). Moreover, because people define these categories a priori, they may be biased to represent them as simply and elegantly as possible, specifying properties true of all members (Medin, Wattenmaker, & Hampson, 1987). If all members of a goal-derived category are equivalent in enabling a common goal, then people may not have a basis for judging some exemplars as better members than others. Rather than perceiving prototype structure in goal-derived categories, people may perceive these categories as lists of equivalent entities that enable the achievement of particular goals.

In a variety of studies, my students and I have assessed whether goal-derived categories exhibit prototype structure. In these experiments, subjects receive goal-derived categories and judge the typicality of their exemplars. For example, subjects might receive *places to go on a vacation* and judge the typicality of *Montana, Tahiti, Paris,* and so forth. The key issue in these experiments is: Do people agree on their judgments of typicality for goal-derived categories? If these categories do not have prototype structures, then people should not respond systematically. Instead, people should either respond randomly or idiosyncratically, such that the average correlation between different judges approximates zero. On the other hand, if these categories have prototype structures, then the average correlation between the typicality judgments of different judges should be greater than zero.

In exploring this issue, we have observed significant agreement in subjects' judgments of typicality across a wide variety of goal-derived categories under diverse task conditions. For example, Barsalou (1983, Experiment 2) observed agreement for prototype structure in ad hoc categories. In this particular study, the ad hoc categories were rather bizarre, such as *ways to escape being killed by the Mafia* and *things that can fall on your head.* Nevertheless, subjects exhibited clear and reliable agreement in their judgments of typicality. For subjects who rated typicality, the average correlation between subjects' ratings for the exemplars in an ad hoc category was .56. For subjects who ranked the exemplars according to typicality, the average correlation between subjects' rankings was .54. Subjects performing both types of judgment agreed to a sizable extent in their assessments of prototype structure.

This agreement indicates that people construct similar prototype structures for a given ad hoc category. But because people rarely, if ever, consider these categories, how could they have acquired prototypical information for them? Moreover, why aren't these categories equivalence classes with respect to their associated goals? As we shall see in later sections, there is a single answer to both questions: People often establish goal-relevant information for these categories a priori that varies continuously across exemplars. In planning how to escape the Mafia, for example, people might reason that maximizing the *geographic distance* between themselves and the Mafia will optimize the chance of goal success. Because people derive this property a priori from background causal knowledge of the world, they do not have to experience exemplars to discover properties that define *ways to escape the Mafia*. Moreover, because *geographic distance* varies continuously, exemplars vary in how well they achieve the relevant goal (e.g., *moving to South America* is more optimal than *moving to Wyoming,* if one lives in Reno, Nevada). As an exemplar's *geographic distance* increases, its typicality and membership increase as well.

C. STABILITY OF PROTOTYPE STRUCTURE IN COMMON TAXONOMIC AND GOAL-DERIVED CATEGORIES

Earlier I suggested that the structures of common taxonomic and goal-derived categories should differ because they originate from different modes of category learning. But as we just saw, goal-derived categories exhibit the same prototype structure found in common taxonomic categories. This initial failure to identify a difference between these two category types led us to search further for differences. A second hypothesis we considered was that the prototype structures of common taxonomic categories are more stable than the prototype structures of goal-derived categories. Because lexemes such as *apple, chair,* and *dog* exist for common taxonomic categories, their meanings are conventional and impart a high degree of stability to prototype structure. Because goal-derived categories such as *things to pack in a small suitcase* arise idiosyncratically as individual persons pursue their daily goals, lexemes and conventional meanings do not develop for these categories, and their prototype structures vary widely across individuals and contexts.

In a number of studies, we have addressed the relative stability of prototype structures in common taxonomic and goal-derived categories (Barsalou, 1987, 1989; Barsalou, Sewell, & Ballato, 1986; also see Barsalou & Billman, 1989). Specifically, we have assessed the stability of *between-subject agreement, within-subject agreement,* and *contextual shift.* Because goal-derived categories are less conventional than common taxonomic categories, we expected the prototype structures of the former to exhibit less stability on all three measures. In performing these studies, we took care to sample a wide variety of categories, to sample exemplars representatively from categories, and to exhaust the range of typicality values within categories as much as possible. In general, the range of typicality values was the same for common taxonomic and goal-derived categories, such that differences in variability were not a factor. In addition, we assessed typicality with a variety of measures under a variety of task conditions, none of which altered our basic findings.

For between-subject agreement, we assessed the average correlation between all possible pairs of subjects in their judgments of typicality (as described in Section II,B). To the extent that subjects use the same prototypical information in judging typicality, correlations between subjects' judgments should be high. If the prototype structures of common taxonomic categories are more conventional than those of goal-derived categories, then between-subject agreement should be higher for common taxonomic categories.[4]

For within-subject agreement, subjects judged typicality in one session and returned 2 weeks later to judge typicality again for the same categories and exemplars. We then correlated each subject's judgments across the two sessions for each category to see how much their assessment of the category's prototype structure changed over time. To the extent that a subject uses the same prototypical information when judging typicality for a category on different occasions, the correlation between the subject's judgments in the two sessions should be high. If the prototype structures of common taxonomic categories are more stable than those of goal-derived categories, then within-subject agreement should be higher for common taxonomic categories.

To measure contextual shift, we had different subjects judge the typicality of the same categories in different contexts. In many of our experi-

---

[4] Rosch (1975) and Armstrong et al. (1983) reported between-subject agreement over .90 for typicality, suggesting that people are nearly unanimous in their perception of prototype structure. But as Barsalou (1987) notes, these previous studies used inappropriate measures of agreement, which estimate the stability of means rather than agreement between judges. These extremely high levels of agreement simply indicate that sample sizes were sufficiently large to ensure that mean typicality judgments were stable—they provide no information about between-subject agreement.

ments, we manipulated context by asking subjects to adopt different points of view while judging typicality. For example, we asked some subjects to judge the typicality of *birds* from the point of view of the average American but asked other subjects to judge the typicality of *birds* from the point of view of the average Chinese citizen. Of interest was the extent to which a category's prototype structure shifted from context to context. To what extent are typical exemplars in one context atypical in another? Most importantly, do goal-derived categories exhibit more contextual shift than common taxonomic categories? If the prototype structures of common taxonomic categories are more stable than those of goal-derived categories, then less contextual shift should occur for common taxonomic categories. To measure contextual shift, we correlated the average typicality ratings for the same category in two different contexts, corrected for the unreliability of the means, and assessed the extent to which the adjusted correlation differed from the correlation that would occur if point of view had no effect (Barsalou & Sewell, 1984; Barsalou et al., 1986). Values of our contextual shift measure that deviate reliably from zero in the positive direction indicate that a contextual manipulation alters prototype structure.

Table I summarizes the results that we obtained for between-subject agreement, within-subject agreement, and contextual shift across a variety of experiments. As can be seen, common taxonomic and goal-derived categories exhibit roughly equivalent stability for all three measures. Occasionally, a reliable difference favors common taxonomic categories. But these reliable differences occur relatively infrequently and are quite small in magnitude.

In a very different type of experiment, we actually found slightly higher agreement for the representations of goal-derived categories. In Barsalou, Spindler, Sewell, Ballato, and Gendel (1987, Experiment 1), we asked subjects to generate either average or ideal properties for common taxonomic and goal-derived categories. For example, subjects might generate *round* as an average property of *fruit* and *sweet* as an ideal. To measure between-subject agreement, we used the common element correlation to compute the average overlap in the properties that different subjects generated for the same category. The common element correlation is simply the number of properties common to two protocols divided by the geometric mean of the total properties in each (McNemar, 1969). To measure within-subject agreement, we used the common element correlation to compute the average overlap in the properties that the same subject generated for the same category on two different occasions. To measure contextual shift, we computed the difference in the common element correlations between subjects taking the same point of view vs. subjects taking differ-

TABLE I

AVERAGE MEASURES OF STABILITY FOR PROTOTYPE STRUCTURE*

Experiment	Between-subject agreement		Within-subject agreement		Contextual shift	
	Common taxonomic	Goal-derived	Common taxonomic	Goal-derived	Common taxonomic	Goal-derived
Barsalou (1983)						
Experiment 2 ratings	.50	.56	—	—	—	—
Experiment 2 rankings	.57	.54	—	—	—	—
Barsalou and Sewell (1984)						
Experiment 1a	.33	.36	—	—	.58	.64
Experiment 1b	.41	.40	—	—	.70	.86
Experiment 1c	.46[a]	.39[a]	—	—	.28[f]	.48[f]
Barsalou (1985)						
Experiment 1	.45[b]	.32[b]	—	—	—	—
Barsalou (1986)						
Experiment 1	.60	.49	.82[d]	.76[d]	.97	.88
Barsalou et al. (1986)						
Experiment 1	.57[c]	.44[c]	.81[e]	.76[e]	.04	.37
Experiment 3	.47	.40	.74	.74	−.20	−.08
Experiment 4	.49	.44	.85	.84	−.39	−.37
Experiment 7	.48	.42	.81	.82	.99	.64
Average	.48	.42	.81	.78	.28	.40

* Pairs of means indexed by the same superscript differ reliably at $p < .05$.

ent points of view (again, larger values indicate more shift). Table II illustrates that goal-derived categories generally exhibit more stability than common taxonomic categories, although these differences are small in magnitude and only reliable in a few cases.

The results from both sets of studies indicate that the category representations of goal-derived and common taxonomic categories do not vary noticeably in stability. When people judge typicality, the prototype structures that they produce for goal-derived categories are roughly as stable as those for common taxonomic categories. When people generate average and ideal information, they again exhibit equal stability. Contrary to our second hypothesis, the conventionality of common taxonomic categories does not make them more stable than goal-derived categories. At least two other factors may counteract conventionality. First, the causal principles that bear on goal achievement may often provide strong and salient constraints on the properties that can represent goal-derived categories. For example, causal principles relevant to human interactions specify that *geographic distance* is a relevant property for *ways to escape being killed*

TABLE II

Average Measures of Stability for Property Generation[*]

Condition	Between-subject agreement		Within-subject agreement		Contextual shift	
	Common taxonomic	Goal-derived	Common taxonomic	Goal-derived	Common taxonomic	Goal-derived
Average properties	.16	.18	.40	.42	.04	.03
Ideal properties	.20[a]	.25[a]	.42[b]	.47[b]	.05	.03

[*] All entries in this table are reliably greater than zero at $p < .05$, including the measures of contextual shift. Pairs of means indexed by the same superscript differ reliably at $p < .05$. From Barsalou et al. (1987).

by the Mafia. Even though a given goal-derived category may only occur to a few people on a few occasions, the causal principles that constrain it may be obvious and well known, such that different people construct similar representations. Second, the wide variability of exemplars that different people experience for common taxonomic categories may decrease their stability. For example, if people experience different distributions of exemplars for *furniture,* their prototypical knowledge may vary. Barsalou and Billman (1989, pp. 195–199) provide a more extensive list of factors that are likely to determine stability.

D.   Determinants of Prototype Structure in Common Taxonomic and Goal-Derived Categories

Thus far, we have seen no differences between common taxonomic and goal-derived categories. Contrary to our original predictions, goal-derived categories possess prototype structures, which are just as stable as those in common taxonomic categories. However, equivalent stability does not entail that prototype structures be identical. For prototype structures to be identical, the same determinants must produce them. Perhaps the determinants of prototype structure that develop for common taxonomic categories during exemplar learning differ from the determinants of prototype structure that develop for goal-derived categories during conceptual combination. I next review work that bears on this issue.

1.   Central Tendency

Following the classic work of Rosch and Mervis (1975), many researchers believe that similarity to central tendency constitutes the primary determinant of typicality in categories, where central tendency is the average or modal characteristics of a category's exemplars. According to this view, central tendency information constitutes the content of prototypes. For example, the prototype of *birds* might contain modal properties such as *small, flies, sings,* and *lives in trees.* As exemplars approximate this modal information, they become increasingly typical. Because *robin* has all of these properties, it is typical. Because *owl* has two of these properties, it is less typical. Because *ostrich* has none of these properties, it is atypical. Proximity to central tendency is essentially the prototype view that has appeared in the categorization literature for the last 20 years: The closer an exemplar is to the central tendency of a category—the prototype—the more typical it is. Many investigators have indeed found that proximity to central tendency does determine prototype structure in common taxonomic and artificial categories (e.g., Hampton, 1979, 1987, 1988; Homa, 1984; Posner & Keele, 1968; Reed, 1972; Rosch & Mervis, 1975; Rosch, Simpson, & Miller, 1976; Smith & Medin, 1981).

Actually, Rosch and Mervis (1975) viewed the role of central tendency in typicality somewhat differently. Following Wittgenstein (1953), Rosch and Mervis argued that an exemplar's *family resemblance* determines its typicality, where family resemblance is the average similarity of an exemplar to all other exemplars in the category. Some exemplar models of categorization account for prototype structure in this manner as well (e.g., Brooks, 1978, 1987; Estes, 1986; Hintzman, 1986; Medin & Schaffer, 1978; Nosofsky, 1984). For example, *robin* is typical of *bird,* because it has a high average similarity to all other birds, including *sparrow, pigeon, dove,* and so forth. In contrast, *ostrich* is atypical, because it has a low average similarity to all other birds. For most categories, an exemplar's similarity to central tendency is at least roughly equivalent to its average similarity to all other exemplars (Barsalou, 1985). This is analogous to the difference between a number and the average of several other numbers being equivalent to the average difference between the number and these other numbers (e.g., the difference between 10 and (4 + 5 + 6)/3 is the same as the average of $10 - 4$, $10 - 5$, and $10 - 6$). This equivalence becomes increasingly true for categories to the extent that a category's central tendency contains average or modal information about property co-occurrence—not just independent properties (Barsalou, 1990b).

Exemplar learning is closely related to the role that central tendency plays in determining prototype structure. If central tendency determines the prototype structure of a category, it follows that people must have knowledge of the category's central tendency in some form. Presumably, knowledge of central tendency often results from exemplar learning. In the process of experiencing a category's exemplars and extracting their properties, people might compute average and modal information, which later represents the category and determines prototype structure. Alternatively, people may not compute central tendency information explicitly, but may rely on its implicit presence across exemplars (i.e., family resemblance in an exemplar model). Either way, exemplar learning is essential to central tendency determining prototype structure. Some exposure to exemplars is necessary for information about central tendency to develop.

People may often acquire central tendency information without encountering exemplars directly. For example, people have roughly accurate, central tendency information about the relative sizes of African animals, even though they have never been to Africa and have rarely been to a zoo. Frequently, people acquire central tendency information through hearsay, receiving it from conversations, books, and other media. Under such conditions, central tendency information is likely to be somewhat distorted and stereotypical, but it may nevertheless often be reasonably accurate. Most importantly, exemplar learning must have occurred at some point for central tendency information to be transmitted by hearsay. Some person must have experienced exemplars directly, such that he or she could convey reasonably accurate central tendency information to someone else later. As we shall see next, another very different kind of category information—ideals—doesn't rely on exemplar learning either directly or through hearsay.

2. *Ideals*

Many researchers believe that central tendency is the exclusive determinant of prototype structure. Nevertheless, many other determinants are possible, such as ideals. An ideal is a characteristic that exemplars should have to serve a goal optimally. Consider the dimension of *calories* for the goal-derived category of *foods to eat on a diet*. Unfortunately for dieters, the central tendency of *calories* in this category is substantially higher than zero because most of its exemplars have a positive number of calories (e.g., one rice cake has 60 calories, one cup of nonfat yogurt has 130 calories). On the other hand, the ideal number of *calories* that exemplars should have is zero. The fewer calories a food has, the better it serves the goal of losing weight. Consequently, the central tendency and ideal value of *calories* differ for *foods to eat on a diet*. Most importantly, either could be prototypical. Exemplars could become increasingly typical as they approach the central tendency, the ideal, or both.

Whereas central tendency depends on exemplar learning, ideals do not. Instead, ideals arise from reasoning about categories with respect to goals. Consider the category of *food*. Outside the context of losing weight, *zero calories* does not become central to *food* through exemplar learning because few exemplars exhibit this property. Furthermore, *zero calories* is not an ideal but is instead a property of *food* to avoid, because people need calories to survive. But upon combining *food* with the goal of losing weight, *zero calories* acquires a new significance. Because *zero calories* epitomizes exemplars that enable weight loss, it becomes a salient ideal for the category. Frequently, ideals are central to category membership as well as to typicality. As exemplars approach the ideals of a category, they often become increasingly compelling category members.

Including ideals in prototypes extends prototypes in a nonstandard way because researchers typically assume that prototypes only contain central tendency information. But if a factor determines a category's prototype structure, it must exist in the category's representation. Consequently, ideals exist in the representations of categories whose prototype structures they predict (Medin & Barsalou, 1987). For this reason, assessing a category's prototype structure is useful, because it provides a methodology for revealing the current content of a category's representation (Barsalou, 1987, 1989). Further note that a prototype may contain multiple ideals that optimize multiple goals. For example, *minimal calories, maximal nutrition,* and *maximal taste* may exist simultaneously in the prototype for *foods to eat on a diet,* serving the goals of losing weight, staying healthy, and enjoying food.

3. Frequency

Most people who are not categorization experts believe intuitively that frequency determines prototype structure. According to this view, some exemplars are typical, because they occur frequently, whereas other exemplars are atypical, because they occur infrequently. In two studies, Rosch and her colleagues assessed the relationship between frequency and typicality and found none (Mervis, Catlin, & Rosch, 1976; Rosch, Simpson, & Miller, 1976). However, these tests of frequency were not strong, and subsequent researchers found effects of frequency on prototype structure, including Ashcraft (1978), Glass and Meany (1978), Hampton and Gardiner (1983), and Malt and Smith (1982). Consequently, frequency does contribute to prototype structure.

Two measures of frequency could determine prototype structure. First, an exemplar's overall *familiarity* could determine its typicality. As people acquire increasing knowledge about an exemplar and encounter it more frequently, its typicality in *any* category increases. According to this measure, if people are more familiar with *chairs* than with *logs,* then *chair* should be more typical in any category that contains both (e.g., *firewood*). Second, an exemplar's *frequency of instantiation* as a category member could determine its typicality. As people view an exemplar increasingly often as a member of a particular category, its typicality increases. According to this measure, if people encounter *log* more often than *chair* as a member of *firewood*, then *log* should be more typical. Familiarity, frequency of instantiation, or both could determine an exemplar's typicality. Because people acquire familiarity and frequency of instantiation from experiencing exemplars (or from hearsay about other people's experiences with exemplars), both measures reflect exemplar learning.

4. Assessing the Determinants of Prototype Structure

To what extent do central tendency, ideals, familiarity, and frequency of instantiation determine the prototype structure of categories? Which of these factors is most important? Does each factor have a unique effect on prototype structure, or are these factors redundant? Most importantly, are the determinants of prototype structure the same for common taxonomic and goal-derived categories? Although prototype structure may be equally stable in both category types, its determinants may differ.

Barsalou (1981, 1985) assessed the determinants of prototype structure in common taxonomic and goal-derived categories. One group of subjects judged the typicality of exemplars in categories of each type. Four other groups of subjects provided independent information about central tendency, ideals, familiarity, and frequency of instantiation. For central tendency, subjects received all possible pairs of exemplars for each category and judged the similarity of the exemplars in each pair. The similarity ratings involving a given exemplar were then averaged to obtain its average similarity to all other exemplars. As noted earlier, this family resemblance measure is essentially the same as the similarity of each exemplar to the category's central tendency. For ideals, one ideal value was selected for each category (e.g., *high calories* for *foods not to eat on a diet, tastes good* for *fruit*). Subjects then rated exemplars according to their values on the corresponding dimensions (e.g., *calories* for *foods not to eat on a diet, how much people like it* for *fruit*). In all cases, the ideal value was an extreme value of the dimension. For familiarity, subjects rated each exemplar for how familiar they were with that kind of thing. For frequency of instantiation, subjects rated each exemplar for how often they encountered that type of thing as a category member.[5]

---

[5] Subjects who rated frequency of instantiation could have simply rated typicality. If so, the correlation between frequency of instantiation and typicality should have approached 1 (or, more realistically, the average reliability of the means for these two measures; see the shift score of Barsalou & Sewell, 1984). But because these correlations were considerably lower, the ratings for frequency of instantiation were not typicality judgments. Perusal of the means for these measures in the appendix of Barsalou (1985) further suggests that subjects

TABLE III

CORRELATIONS OF CENTRAL TENDENCY, IDEALS, FREQUENCY OF
INSTANTIATION, AND FAMILIARITY WITH TYPICALITY[a]

Determinant	Factors partialed out	Category type	
		Common taxonomic	Goal-derived
Central tendency (CT)	None	.63*	.38*
	IDL, FOI	.71*	.05
Ideals (IDL)	None	.46*	.70*
	CT, FOI	.45*	.44*
Frequency of instantiation (FOI)	None	.47*	.72*
	FAM	.45*	.74*
	CT, IDL	.36*	.51*
Familiarity (FAM)	None	.19	.03
	FOI	−.11	−.16

[a] From Barsalou (1985, Experiment 1).

* Reliably greater than zero at $p < .05$.

Table III summarizes the results from this experiment. As can be seen, this table contains the raw correlations between each possible determinant and typicality, as well as partial correlations that remove the contributions of other predictors. Before turning to the central results of this study, I first address several preliminary points. First, familiarity did not predict typicality. Nor did familiarity contribute to frequency of instantiation's ability to predict typicality. Consequently, frequency of instantiation appears to be the critical measure of frequency that determines typicality—not familiarity. Second, this study underestimates the predictive power of ideals. Because only one ideal was assessed for each category, ideals may account for substantially more variance when all relevant ideals are assessed. Investigators who have measured ideals more exhaustively generally find that ideals account for much more variance than central tendency (Borkenau, 1990; Chaplin, John, & Goldberg, 1988; Loken & Ward, 1990; Read, Jones, & Miller, 1990). Third, the pattern of predictors for specific categories varied considerably (see Table 3 in Barsalou, 1985). For example, central tendency and ideals predicted typicality in *clothing*, but frequency

---

were judging frequency of instantiation, given many sensible departures of this measure from typicality. Finally, much work on frequency estimates indicates that people are quite sensitive to the frequency of events and can rate frequency reliably (e.g., Hasher & Zacks, 1979; Hintzman, 1976).

of instantiation did not (partial correlations of .71, .81, and −.10). In contrast, all three factors predicted typicality in *birds* (partial correlations of .75, .42, and .78). Fourth, the determinants of a category's prototype structure vary with context. Barsalou (1985, Experiment 2) found that central tendency determines the prototype structures of artificial categories in one context but that ideals determine them in another. As we saw earlier for contextual shift, the prototype structure of a category is highly malleable (Barsalou, 1987). Finally, these correlational studies must be interpreted with caution because correlations do not imply causation. However, additional research demonstrates that central tendency, ideals, and frequency causally determine prototype structure. Rosch and Mervis (1975, Experiments 5 and 6), Rosch, Simpson, and Miller (1976), Barsalou (1981, Experiment 3), and Barsalou (1985, Experiment 2) demonstrated that central tendency causally determines prototype structure in artificial categories. Barsalou (1985, Experiment 2) demonstrated that ideals causally determine prototype structure in artificial categories. Barsalou (1981, Experiment 3) and Nosofsky (1988) demonstrated that frequency causally determines prototype structure in artificial categories. As these experiments illustrate, all of these determinants bear a causal relation to prototype structure.

Turning to the results of primary interest, first consider the correlations in Table III for the common taxonomic categories. As can be seen, central tendency dominated the prediction of typicality, similar to the findings of Rosch and Mervis (1975). However, ideals and frequency of instantiation also accounted for unique typicality variance. By no means is central tendency the only determinant of prototype structure in common taxonomic categories. All factors together accounted for 64% of the typicality variance in common taxonomic categories.

In contrast, consider the results for the goal-derived categories in Table III. Ideals and frequency of instantiation each predicted typicality uniquely, with all factors together accounting for 69% of the typicality variance. Most importantly, central tendency accounted for no unique typicality variance in goal-derived categories. Although the raw correlation between central tendency and typicality was reliable, all of this variance was shared with ideals and frequency of instantiation. In Experiment 1 of Barsalou (1981), not even the raw correlation between central tendency and typicality exceeded zero for goal-derived categories (−.15). Here we have our first important difference between the two category types: Central tendency determines prototype structure in common taxonomic categories but not in goal-derived categories.

This difference indicates that exemplar learning is more central for common taxonomic categories than for goal-derived categories. Because exemplar learning is necessary for acquiring central tendency, and because central tendency determines the prototype structure of common taxonomic categories, exemplar learning is central to the acquisition of these categories. In contrast, exemplar learning is not as important to the acquisition of goal-derived categories because central tendency does not determine their prototype structures. Exemplar learning is of some importance to goal-derived categories because frequency of instantiation determines their prototype structures to a significant extent. Nevertheless, exemplar learning plays qualitatively different roles in common taxonomic and goal-derived categories: Whereas central tendency is by far the most significant determinant of prototype structures in common taxonomic categories, it plays no role in the prototype structures of goal-derived categories.

Interestingly, the importance of ideals for common taxonomic categories indicates that conceptual combination is important for these categories as well as for goal-derived categories. Consider the common taxonomic category of *fruit.* Because people eat fruit to achieve goals, ideals relevant to these goals become central to its representation (e.g., *tastes good*). Similarly, *high enjoyability* is an ideal for *sports,* and *high destructiveness* is an ideal for *weapons.* Other investigators have found much further evidence for the importance of ideals in category representations. Loken and Ward (1990) have found that ideals are far more important than central tendency in determining the prototype structures of consumer categories (e.g., *shampoos, stereos*). Researchers in social cognition have found that ideals are far more important than central tendency in determining the prototype structures of social categories (Borkenau, 1990; Chaplin et al., 1988; Read et al., 1990). Ideals are also important in the selection of names for cars, rock bands, and streets (Lehrer, in press). Lakoff (1987) reviews a variety of forms that ideals take in categories.

As these results illustrate, conceptual combination plays a central role in category formation. By no means does all category learning occur through the simple extraction of exemplar properties. Category representations not only contain exemplar properties; they also contain ideals derived through conceptual combination that serve goal achievement. As these results further illustrate, exemplar learning plays qualitatively different roles in common taxonomic and goal-derived categories. Whereas exemplar learning produces central tendency information for common taxonomic categories, it does not produce central tendency information for goal-derived categories. In the final section of this article, I return to this difference and propose that it reflects the different roles that common taxonomic and goal-derived categories play in the cognitive system. Whereas the role of common taxonomic categories requires that their representations contain central tendency information, the role of goal-derived categories does not. The role of a category in the cognitive system shapes the contents of its representation and therefore the determinants of its prototype structure.

III. Goal-Derived Categories in Planning

I turn next to a detailed analysis of the role that goal-derived categories play in the cognitive system. What specific functions do goal-derived categories serve in goal achievement? What is the nature of the conceptual combination the produces goal-derived categories during planning? What is the origin of the ideals that structure these categories? When Amy Rozett, Daniel Sewell, and I first considered these issues, we had few hypotheses about them. To gain an initial understanding, we performed exploratory studies to observe people's use of goal-derived categories. Because these categories appeared relevant to the plans that people construct for achieving goals, we asked subjects to plan various kinds of events, such as trips, purchases, repairs, and social gatherings. Typically, subjects spent anywhere from 5 to 15 min planning an event that would be plausible in the context of their lives. We tape recorded subjects' protocols and later performed coding analyses to identify the origins of goal-derived categories and the functions they serve. Table IV contains one subject's plan for a vacation.

In the remainder of this section, I review findings from these studies. I first describe the frames that guide planning and how people instantiate these frames to construct specific plans. I then describe how goal-derived categories provide sets of instantiations for frame attributes and how optimizations and constraints guide the selection of specific instantiations. As we shall see, optimizations produce the ideals that determine the prototype structures of goal-derived categories. Finally, I describe how people derive ad hoc categories from frames and how frames define large fields of categories relevant to achieving goals. Although I only describe people's plans for vacations from hereon, their plans for other types of events exhibit the same characteristics robustly. Barsalou, Usher, and Sewell (1985) and Barsalou and Hutchinson (1987) provide initial reports of this work.

A. FRAME INSTANTIATION

When beginning to plan a familiar type of event, such as a vacation, people retrieve a frame for it (see Barsalou, 1991-b, for a more thorough account

TABLE IV

Protocol of a Subject Planning a Vacation

Okay, well, given my monetary situation I think the first thing I would do is check how much money I have.

Just so I have a general feeling when planning whether I can afford anything at all.

Alright. Then, I think I would just sort of sit down . . . and think about the different places . . . I want to go.

There're obviously a lot of places I want to go to that I can't afford.

So . . . it'd have to be some place within a few hours of driving distance . . . from Atlanta.

That's the first thing.

So I'd just eliminate anything that I couldn't drive to in say . . . one day. Maybe eight or nine hours at the very most.

Alright, so, I'd have to drive.

And . . . if I wanted to relax, the only kind of vacation I could really relax on would be to get away from just about everybody I know here.

So, chances are I'd want to go alone, and just not . . . not go with anyone at all. So I'd probably just go by myself.

'Cause that's what I really need after being here for four months.

Um mm. And . . . so what would I do?

Well, I think . . . think I'd want to go camping.

Or go to some sort of rural or mountainous area.

Probably a park.

So probably . . . go to the library or book store and get books . . . and maps, guides to various parks and start reading about the different parks.

And what different, ah, facilities they have and what they're like.

And I'm not sure I'd know what I'd want, until I saw it. Just sort of looked through until I found something that looked good. Then I'd . . . then I'd pick that place to go.

After I picked what place I wanted to go to, then I'd have to think about what I was bringing.

Now, jumping back, I think I do know certain constraints that I would put on the place I go, like I'd probably want to go fishing.

I mean, that's something I really like to do.

So, I pick the place where I could go fishing.

And where there wasn't a lot of . . . sort of camping where people park their Winnebagos all over the place.

Some place where I could park but then, really in order to do any camping, you just have to hike a couple miles and just get away from anything.

So, and then I'd have to bring my fishing stuff.

And since it's really cold this time of year up in the mountains I'd have to bring a lot of really warm clothes.

And I'd have to bring my backpack and food, and this little Coleman stove I have . . . and probably . . . a book or two and some stuff to write with.

I'd just hike up into the mountains somewhere . . . find some place off in the middle of nowhere, go fishing all day, and sit around and read a book.

Although if it's really really cold (laugh) . . . I might not be able to read a book at all, because my hands will be so cold that . . . they'll freeze onto the pages and then I'd

(continued)

TABLE IV (*Continued*)

---

just have to wrap myself up in about ten layers of clothing and just fish or shiver or something.

Attempt to write with ah . . . three gloves on my hands or something!

But that's . . . that's the general plan I'd have.

Now let me think. Is there anything else I'd want to do.

Oh, I know. Aha! Well, before I even went, I'd want to check my car since it's sort of dying anyway. As a matter of fact it's sort of in bad shape, so I wonder whether if it would make it the whole way.

So I'd do, probably . . . probably do a complete checkup of the car and just figure whether it could make it on that distance trip.

And just check all the basic things like transmission fluid and oil and spark plugs and just everything.

Probably still something would go wrong, but (laugh) I'd check all those things . . . before I went.

And . . . hmm. Other than that . . . that's about it. I think I know exactly what I want. It's so . . . that . . . that is what I'd do.

---

of frames). Consider the partial frame for *vacation* in Fig. 1. As can be seen, this frame contains attributes that take different values across different vacations. For example, the *actors* who take a vacation vary from plan to plan, as do *vacation locations, things to take,* and so forth. As can also be seen, attributes form clusters. For example, the *expenses* cluster contains more specific attributes, such as *source of money* (i.e., the person who will pay for the vacation) and *total cost.* Similarly, the *activities* cluster contains more specific attributes, such as *preparations, not work* (i.e., the work from which the planner is taking a vacation), *not reside* (i.e., the planner's normal home), *travel* (i.e., transportation), *reside* (i.e., the vacation residence), and *entertainment.* Some of these more specific attributes constitute attribute clusters themselves. For example, the cluster for *travel* contains more specific attributes for *major travel* (e.g., flying from city to city), *minor travel* (e.g., getting from home to the airport), and *at location* (e.g., renting a car at the vacation location).

The nested sets of attributes in Fig. 1 form *attribute taxonomies* (Barsalou, in press-b). As the figure illustrates, the values of an attribute are often attributes themselves. For example, *departure, duration, return,* and *schedule* are all values of *temporal parameters.* But in turn, each of these values is an attribute that takes more specific values. For example, *departure* takes values such as *December, Spring Break, Memorial Day weekend,* and so forth. As each high-level attribute becomes increasingly differentiated in this manner, it forms an attribute taxonomy. Most of the highest level attributes in Fig. 1 occur across a wide variety of events. To a large

Fig. 1.   Attributes in a partial frame for *vacation*.

extent, the attributes for *actors, locations, temporal parameters, objects,* and *activities* recur frequently across events, with values of these attributes distinguishing specific types of events (Barsalou, 1988; Barsalou & Billman, 1989). Interestingly, these same attributes also occur ubiquitously as thematic roles in verb syntax, further implicating their centrality in events (Carlson & Tanenhaus, 1988; Fillmore, 1968, 1977; Jackendoff, 1987; Wilkins, 1988).

The *vacation* frame in Fig. 1 excludes much important structure. First, this frame omits many attributes that subjects mentioned. For example, *vacation location* often had attributes of *climate* and *health hazards,* and *companions* often had attributes of *convenient times for taking a vacation* and *preferred entertainment.* Second, this frame omits many attribute values. For example, people know possible values of *vacation location,* such as *Hawaii, Paris,* and *New York.* Similarly, people know possible values of *entertainment,* such as *swim, hike,* and *visit museums.* Third, this frame omits relations between attributes. For example, people know that actors cause *travel* to occur and that *travel* is typically from the *home location* to the *vacation location*. Fourth, this frame omits constraints between attribute values. For example, people know that if *snow ski* is the value of *entertainment*, then the value of *vacation location* must be a *mountainous region*. Similarly, people know that if the value of *travel* is *drive*, then the value of *total cost* is typically lower than if the value of *travel* is *fly*. Barsalou (in press-b) reviews the basic components of frames—attribute-value sets, relations between attributes, and constraints—and provides many examples of each, along with examples of other important properties of frames, especially recursion.

When people begin to construct a plan, they do not retrieve the entire event frame as a rigid structure in a single retrieval operation. We assumed in our analyses that subjects only considered a frame attribute in their plan if they mentioned it explicitly or implied its existence in a statement about some other attribute. On the basis of these criteria, no subject considered all of the attributes in the partial frame for *vacation* in Fig. 1. Instead, subjects varied in the attributes they considered, often failing to consider important attributes. For example, one subject failed to consider *reside, companions,* and *things to bring back;* whereas another subject failed to consider *temporal parameters, expenses,* and *things to bring back.* Subjects seemed aware of their failure to consider all attributes because they occasionally scanned the attributes that they had considered thus far, attempting to discover further attributes. Consider the following attribute scans:

Um . . . okay, so let's see . . . um, have I planned everything? Where, when, who, money, what I'm gonna do . . .

Well, after we have figured out the location, the time, and if we can afford it, then we'll plan what we're going to do.

Um . . . let's see, so once I had a time and an agreed upon group, then we'd work on the specific location.

Um . . . we'd be all set for the plane, for places to stay, travel while we're there, um . . . eating while we're there, um . . . what else . . . where to go while we're there . . . um . . . (whispered) God, I wonder if that's all there is to it?

As these examples illustrate, subjects were aware of the attributes that they had already considered and of further attributes that remained.

Further evidence that people do not retrieve frames rigidly comes from the orders in which subjects considered frame attributes. Subjects considered attributes in widely divergent orders. Although most subjects considered *vacation location* early in planning, the order in which they considered other attributes typically varied. For example, one subject considered *source of money* first, then *vacation location*, then *travel*, etc. Another subject considered *actors* first, then *vacation location*, then *temporal parameters*, etc. In addition, frame attributes sometimes appeared to be context-dependent. For example, subjects typically only considered *health hazards* when they had already selected a *vacation location* associated with health risks (e.g., *tropical locations*). For less risky *vacation locations*, subjects did not usually consider this attribute.

Because attributes are sometimes context-dependent, and because people vary in the attributes that they consider and in the order in which they consider them, frames are not rigid structures, as many theories in artificial intelligence assume (Barsalou, in press-b). Instead, frames are flexible, loosely organized bodies of knowledge. As Barsalou and Billman (1989) suggest, attributes vary in their likelihood of relevance for a frame across contexts, such that some attributes become more dominant than others. In the *vacation* frame, for example, *vacation location* appears more dominant than *health hazards* or *things to bring back*. In addition, a given attribute tends to covary with certain attributes and attribute values, such that relations and constraints develop between them. As a result, the activation of one part of a co-occurring pattern of attributes and values tends to activate the remaining parts of the pattern, similar to activation in a connectionist net (McClelland, Rumelhart, & the PDP Research Group, 1986; Rumelhart, McClelland, & the PDP Research Group, 1986).

As people retrieve a frame while planning, they begin to instantiate its attributes. By *instantiation,* I mean that people adopt particular values of an attribute for use in their current plan. When planning a vacation, for example, people consider values of *vacation location* and attempt to identify the specific location(s) that will instantiate this attribute. Similarly, vacation planners must instantiate other attributes, such as *departure, things to take, entertainment,* and so forth. This instantiation process appears to constitute the primary activity of early planning. Because our planners did not consider all attributes in the first 5–15 min of planning, many initial plans are probably quite sketchy. If people planned long enough, they might come closer to considering all relevant attributes. However, people often plan on instantiating some attributes during execution rather than during planning. For example, a planner might decide to instantiate *things to bring back* in an opportunistic manner once the vacation has begun (Hayes-Roth & Hayes-Roth, 1977). Nevertheless, planners often forget to instantiate key attributes in planning, such that minor and major disasters occur at execution. For example, someone on a foreign vacation might have forgotten to consider the attribute of *health hazards,* so that he or she does not have the necessary immunizations for entering a country.

When instantiating a frame's attributes, people do not proceed directly from considering an attribute to selecting a specific individual as its instantiation. For example, people often don't proceed directly from *vacation location* to the specific location that they plan to visit. Instead, people often *focus* their instantiations, beginning with a general class of instantiations and continually refining it down to more specific instantiations. For example, one subject's first instantiation of *departure* was *October,* followed later by *when the autumn leaves are at their peak color* and then *a weekend.* Typically, but not always, each more specific focusing inherits the properties of the previous, more general instantiation. For example, this subject's final departure was *a weekend in October when the autumn leaves are at their peak.* As this example illustrates, conceptual combination is central to the process of focusing instantiations because planners combine increasingly specific properties with the existing attribute description. The nature of this conceptual combination is the topic of later sections on optimization, constraint, and the derivation of ad hoc categories.

Often people are unable to instantiate an attribute because they have limited knowledge of its possible instantiations. For example, a subject planning a vacation in Paris had no idea of instantiations for *lodging.* Similarly, people are often only able to instantiate an attribute generally, because they lack knowledge of specific instantiations. For example, the subject who planned the backpacking trip in Table IV had a general idea of the type of location he wanted but did not know specific locations with these properties. Finally, people often do not know whether enabling states for particular instantiations are met. For example, subjects sometimes selected particular instantiations of *vacation location* or *entertainment* but did not know if their companions would approve of these selections.

Because of subjects' frequent inability to instantiate attributes, they spent much time planning *preparations,* namely, activities that must be performed prior to instantiating an attribute either at all or completely. In one study, four important types of preparations accounted for 84% of those mentioned. The most frequent type of preparation was *obtaining things* (34%). For example, one subject needed to obtain a swimsuit before taking a vacation to the beach. The other three most frequent types of preparations were *seeking information* (25%), *making decisions* (15%), and *verifying states* (10%). For example, one subject planned to *seek information* about lodging and then *decide* which lodging was best at a later time. Another subject planned to *verify* that her passport was still current. In general, preparations were oriented around the process of frame instantiation. Subjects realized that they couldn't instantiate an attribute completely during the current planning session and planned the necessary activities that would enable them to instantiate it later.[6]

Finally, subjects performed little scheduling of actions. This is of interest because most theories of planning and problem solving in psychology and artificial intelligence assume that the primary process in these activities is constructing a sequence of operators (Hayes-Roth & Hayes-Roth, 1977; Newell & Simon, 1972; Sacerdoti, 1975, 1979). But we observed very little sequencing in our planning protocols. Instead, subjects' primary activity was to instantiate frames in an optimal and coherent manner (cf. Stefik, 1981). Certainly, if subjects had planned long enough, they would have eventually planned sequences of actions necessary to preparing for their vacations and executing them. But this type of sequencing may often occur late in the planning process and during execution. In contrast, the early stages of planning focus primarily on frame instantiation. Much research on planning and problem solving finesses this phase because subjects or simulations receive fully instantiated frames prior to beginning the planning process. Because the actors, objects, locations, actions, and so forth are given in the problem statement, the only problem that remains is finding arrangements of them in time and space to achieve the goal.

B. ROLE OF GOAL-DERIVED CATEGORIES IN FRAME INSTANTIATION

Given that frame instantiation constitutes the primary activity in early planning, what role do goal-derived categories play? Essentially, these categories provide sets of instantiations for frame attributes. For example, when people instantiate the *location* attribute in the *vacation* frame, they typically have a category of *vacation locations* that they retrieve and consider. Similarly, when people instantiate *departure,* they typically have a category of *departure times* that they retrieve and evaluate. In this way, goal-derived categories support the instantiation of a frame's attributes during planning (cf. Byrne, 1977; Dougherty & Keller, 1985; Lucariello & Nelson, 1985).

Clearly, not all goal-derived categories exist prior to planning. Instead, many are ad hoc, being derived impromptu to instantiate an attribute in the plan for a novel goal. For example, people who work all of the time and never think about vacations, much less take one, may not have a well-established category of *vacation locations.* In attempting to instantiate this

---

[6] Preparations are similar to the procedural attachments in Winograd (1975).

attribute, these planners must derive an ad hoc category before they can consider and select instantiations. One strategy for constructing ad hoc categories under these conditions is the *generate-test procedure*. Using well-established knowledge of other categories, planners generate possible candidates for an ad hoc category and then test them for membership. For example, planners might generate candidates from their well-established knowledge of *continents* and *countries,* which they then test for the relevant properties of *vacation locations*. Later, we shall consider the processes that derive such categories in greater detail.

Once people derive an ad hoc category, they establish information about it in long-term memory. Because the processing that underlies the derivation of such categories is often deep, elaborative, and extended, information about them is likely to become transferred from working memory to a more permanent form of knowledge (cf. Crowder, 1976). If this same category is useful later for instantiating an attribute in another plan, planners may be able to retrieve it from long-term memory rather than having to construct it with the generate-test procedure in working memory. To the extent that the category receives frequent processing, it should become increasingly established, such that it is no longer ad hoc. As people become experts at planning a particular kind of event, the goal-derived categories that support frame instantiation become streamlined in memory. Rather than having to search for possible instantiations that are distributed throughout multiple sources of knowledge, people can retrieve a set of instantiations that have been stored together with the attribute as a byproduct of previous planning. Once planners have retrieved this set, they can search through it to find the most appropriate instantiations for the current plan. Depending on the familiarity of the planning situation, people may use either ad hoc or well-established goal-derived categories during frame instantiation.

C. FACTORS THAT GUIDE THE SELECTION OF INSTANTIATIONS

Given that goal-derived categories provide sets of instantiation for frame attributes, how do people select particular exemplars from them to instantiate an attribute?[7] Once people establish a goal-derived category of *vacation locations*—either ad hoc or well-established—how do they select specific exemplars for a particular vacation? Two important factors permeate people's selection of exemplars, as indicated by the ubiquitous discussion of these factors in subjects' planning protocols: *optimization* and *constraint*.

---

[7] Because the *exemplars* of a goal-derived category are also the *values* and *instantiations* of a frame attribute, I use *exemplar, value,* and *instantiation* interchangeably from hereon when discussing the members of goal-derived categories.

1. Optimization

Across a wide variety of events, people generally try to optimize a recurring set of background goals. For example, people generally try to preserve their health, obtain maximum enjoyment, minimize wasted time, conserve money, maximize the quality of possessions, avoid losing possessions, and so forth. When people plan events, these background goals interact with the goal-derived categories that instantiate frame attributes. Specifically, background goals establish ideals in category representations, with these ideals being specific characteristics that exemplars should have to produce optimal goal achievement. For example, if conserving money is important to someone planning a vacation, this goal may establish an ideal of *minimal cost* for the goal-derived category of *vacation lodgings*. These ideals are essentially the same as those we considered earlier as determinants of prototype structure.

Once ideals become established in the representation of a goal-derived category, they guide the selection of exemplars during frame instantiation. Exemplars in a goal-derived category that approximate its ideals are optimal candidates for a plan. Exemplars far from these ideals are poor candidates. Similar to making typicality judgments, people prefer the exemplars of a goal-derived category to the extent that they approximate its ideals. People often optimize more than one ideal for a given category. For example, optimizing only *cost* for *vacation lodgings* might produce unpleasant and inappropriate accommodations. Instead, people often optimize multiple ideals, such as *cost, facilities,* and *location.*

For one set of protocols on vacation plans, we performed an extensive analysis of the optimizations that subjects mentioned. The 16 subjects in this study produced a total of 66 unique optimizations, with many optimizations being produced by more than one subject. Table V summarizes the optimizations that subjects produced and provides 10 specific examples. As can be seen, the 66 optimizations reflected four general types of goals that subjects were trying to optimize. Subjects frequently tried to optimize the *achievements* or gains of their actions, they frequently tried to *preserve* goals that they had already obtained, they frequently tried to *conserve resources,* and they frequently tried to optimize *meta-planning.* These four types of goals are essentially the union of those suggested by Schank and Abelson (1977) and Willensky (1983). Each example of an optimization in Table V specifies the type of goal being optimized, the goal-derived category being instantiated, and the specific optimization. For example, the first entry in Table V describes subjects who tried to achieve knowledge by selecting values of *entertainment* that maximized the ideal of *educational value.* Similarly, some subjects tried to preserve their achievements at work (i.e., an abandoned system) by selecting *departures*

TABLE V

EXAMPLES OF OPTIMIZATIONS FROM SUBJECTS PLANNING A VACATION

Type of goal	Goal-derived category	Optimization
Achievement		
Knowledge	Entertainment	Maximize educational value
Enjoyment	Location	Minimize crowdedness
Preservation		
Abandoned system	Departure	Minimize work disruption
Comfort	Vacation location	Optimize temperature
Health	Actors	Maximize immunizations
Personal security	Things to take	Maximize emergency phone numbers
Resource		
Money	Transportation	Minimize cost
Time	Things to take	Minimize time to pack
Meta-planning		
Knowledge	Vacation location	Maximize amount of knowledge
Adaptability	Schedule	Maximize flexibility of schedule
Preparations	Lodging	Maximize timing of reservations

that minimized *work disruption*. Similarly, subjects sometimes tried to optimize their knowledge of *vacation locations* by planning to obtain as much knowledge about them as possible. As these examples illustrate, subjects considered a wide variety of optimizations instrumental to achieving a wide variety of goals. Much of the planning process centered around optimization, as subjects specified ideals for goal-derived categories and attempted to identify exemplars that approximated them.

2. Constraint

During frame instantiation, people frequently propagate constraints to ensure that the instantiations of different attributes are compatible. At most points in the planning process, planners have already determined instantiations of at least some frame attributes. When planners instantiate further attributes, they cannot ignore these prior instantiations. Imagine that earlier in planning, a planner decided that the instantiation of the *activity* attribute would be *snow skiing*. Further imagine that this planner is now trying to instantiate *location*. The planner can't select just any location, such as *La Jolla,* or the intended vacation might fail. Instead, the planner must select a location that is compatible with *snow skiing*.

For one set of protocols on vacation plans, we performed an extensive analysis of the constraints that subjects mentioned. The 16 subjects in this study produced a total of 78 unique constraints, with many constraints being produced by more than one subject. The six general relations that were sufficient to represent all 78 of the constraints were *requires, disallows, enables, prevents, leaves,* and *co-occurs*.[8] Every constraint that subjects mentioned contained at least one of these relations and no others.[9] The general relations are summarized below:

$$a–R \rightarrow b \qquad a \; requires \; b$$
$$a–D \rightarrow {}^\sim b \qquad because \; a \; requires \; b, \; a \; disallows \; {}^\sim b$$
$$b–E \rightarrow a \qquad b \; enables \; a$$
$$b–P \rightarrow a \qquad b \; prevents \; a$$
$$b–L \rightarrow {}^\sim a \qquad because \; b \; prevents \; a, \; b \; leaves \; {}^\sim a$$
$$a \leftarrow C \rightarrow b \qquad a \; co\text{-}occurs \; with \; b$$

Figure 2 provides specific examples of constraints containing these relations. Note that the verbal descriptions of the constraints in Fig. 2 are not direct quotes from the protocols but instead are redescriptions that capture what the subject said plus the surrounding context. Consider the first example for *requires*. This subject stated that a requirement for possible companions was that they be able to take time off from work at the time the subject wanted to vacation. The predicate notation (as just defined) beneath the verbal description captures this constraint more conceptually. The notation for the first example states that if the exemplar *(ex)* of *departure* is *my departure time,* then this requires that the exemplar of a companion's *departure* must also be *my departure time.* The remaining examples in Fig. 2 illustrate the complexity of the simplest constraints that subjects mentioned, namely, those containing a single relation.

---

[8] I do not assume that these relations are primitives because a given relation often takes a wide variety of forms (Winston, Chaffin, & Herrmann, 1987), and because frames typically represent such relations recursively (Barsalou, in press-b).

[9] Arguably, *disallows* and *leaves* are each composed of two of the other relations. Specifically, each *disallows* constraint could be represented as a constraint chain containing a *requires* relation and a *prevents* relation. Similarly, each *leaves* constraint could be represented as a constraint chain containing a *prevents* relation and an *enables* relation. But because these particular constraint chains seem to occur often, independent of specific domains, they seem to be fairly basic relations that people use in reasoning about constraints. For this reason, I treat *disallows* and *leaves* as single relations rather than as constraint chains, which tend to be more domain-specific (as discussed below).

Requires

Possible companions must be able to take off from work at the time I can go.

time (departure (ex = my_departure_time)) –R–> actor (companion (work (vacation_departure (ex = my_departure_time))))

The amount of luggage I take depends on how I travel.

activity (travel (major (ex = X (max_luggage = Y))) –R–> objects (things_to_take (amount ≤ Y))

Disallows

If my girlfriend goes with me (this requires romance with her), there can be no romances with strangers.

actor (self (goal = activity (entertainment (ex = romance (companion = girlfriend)))) & companion (ex = girlfriend)) –D–>
activity (entertainment (ex = romance (companion = stranger)))

If the vacation location is far (this requires long travel), I cannot drive.

location (vacation (ex = X (distance = far))) –D–> activity (travel (major (ex = car (rate = slow))))

Enables

I can go on vacation when I have saved enough money.

expenses (source = self (time = X, savings = Y > expenses (total_cost = Z))) –E–> time (departure (ex = X))

Being at the vacation location will enable visiting friends who live there, assuming they're home.

time (schedule (loc = X, time = Y)) –E–> activity (entertainment (ex = visit (time = X, loc = Y, obj = friends (loc = X, time = Y))))

Prevents

If I'm going to be flying, then I won't have my car at the vacation location.

activity (travel (major (ex = fly))) –P–> activity (travel (at_loc (ex = my car)))

If I'm only going to be there a short time, this makes renting a boat unfeasible.

time (duration (ex = X)) –P–> activity (entertainment (ex = rented_boat (required duration = Y > X)))

Leaves

Because I will be taking my car (this prevents distant vacation locations), I must go some place close to home.

activity (travel (major (ex = my_car)) –L–> location (vacation (distance_from_home = close))

Because I want to spend little money on accommodations (this prevents going at the peak season), I can only afford going in the off season.

location (vacation (accomodations (cost = low))) –L–> time (departure (ex = off_season))

Cooccurs

The amount of money I have available depends on the time of year.

expenses (source = self (available_money = X) <–C–> time (departure (ex = Y))

The climate a person wants to escape to depends on their current climate.

actor (companion (ex = X (like (obj = climate (ex = Y)))) <–C–> actor (companion (ex = X (climate (ex = Z)))

Fig. 2. Examples of constraints from subjects planning vacations. To verify attribute nestings, see the partial frame for *vacation* in Fig. 1. Note that verbal descriptions of the constraints are not direct quotes from the protocols. Instead they are redescriptions that capture the constraint directly and often incorporate surrounding context. In addition, these examples of primitive relations were sometimes extracted from constraint chains. Key: ex, exemplars; loc, location; obj, object.

Although many of the constraints that subjects mentioned only contained a single relation, many others were *constraint chains,* containing two or more relations. Of the 78 unique constraints that subjects mentioned, 17 were constraint chains of two relations, 3 were constraint chains of three relations, and 2 were constraint chains of four relations. On the surface, constraint chains often appear simple, stating only a single relation. For example, one subject noted that because he was going to the beach, he needed to take a swimsuit. But actually, he failed to state an intermediate step that is central to the pragmatic logic of this constraint: Going to the beach does not require taking a swimsuit. Instead, going to the beach *enables* going swimming, which in turn *requires* a swimsuit. Because people experience such patterns of constraint frequently, they streamline their knowledge about them. As a result, people quickly infer that taking a swimsuit is usually a good idea when going to the beach, without going through the intermediate step that concerns swimming. Figure 3 illustrates three of the more complex constraint chains in our data. Constraint chains reflect a mundane sort of domain-specific expertise about everyday events. As people become increasingly familiar with an activity, they compile repeated chains of constraints into simpler, more efficient rules (cf. Anderson, 1983).

D.   DERIVING AD HOC CATEGORIES

As we just saw, people use optimizations and constraints to select exemplars from goal-derived categories during frame instantiation. However, optimizations and constraints also play another important role in the planning process. Quite often, when people attempt to instantiate a particular attribute, they don't have any idea of the exemplars that could instantiate it. Planners don't know any exemplars for which optimizations and constraints could assist selection. Under these conditions, people often derive a conceptual description of the possible exemplars that could instantiate the attribute. In other words, they derive the description of an ad hoc category.

The protocol in Table IV provides an example of a subject deriving an ad hoc category in the absence of exemplars. Consider this subject's attempt to formulate his *vacation location.* At no point in this protocol does the subject ever specify particular exemplars that instantiate this attribute. But the subject does derive a description of this category. First, he notes that the *vacation location* must be *affordable* and *within a few hours driving distance.* Later he specifies that the *vacation location* must *allow*

If I'm going away for a long time, I should turn off the utilities at my house.

time (duration (ex = high)) <--C--> location (home (utilities (cost = high; necessity = low))) --E-->
actor (self (preparation = obtain (obj = home (utilities (status = off)))))

If I'm going to be flying, then I'll need to rent a car while I'm there to sightsee.

{{ activity (travel (major (ex = fly))) --P--> activity (travel (at_loc (ex = my car))) } & { activity (entertainment
(ex = sightsee (requirements = activity (travel (at_loc (ex = car))))) }} --R--> activity (travel (at_loc (ex = rental car)))

If I'm going with my grandmother, then we can only do things she's capable of doing.

actor (companion (ex = grandmother (age = old))) <--C--> actor (companion   --P--> activities (entertainment (required_physical_ability = high))
(ex = grandmother (physical_ability = low)))   --E--> activities (entertainment (required_physical_ability = low))

Fig. 3. Examples of constraint chains from subjects planning vacations. To verify attribute nestings, see the partial frame for *vacation* in Fig. 1. Note that verbal descriptions of the above constraints are not direct quotes from the protocols. Instead they are redescriptions that capture the constraint directly and often incorporate surrounding context. Key: ex, exemplars; loc, location; obj, object.

camping and be in a *rural or mountainous park*. Finally, he specifies that the *vacation location* must *have fishing*, must *not be crowded with Winnebagos*, and must *enable backpacking*. At this point the subject has derived the following ad hoc category:

> vacation locations
>> that are affordable and within a few hours driving distance,
>> that are in an uncrowded rural or mountainous park with
>>> few Winnebagos,
>> that allow camping, backpacking, and fishing.

As this example illustrates, planners combine the attribute being instantiated with the optimizations and constraints that bear on it to derive an ad hoc category. The subject has the background goals of optimizing *total cost* (inexpensive), *travel duration* (short), and *social isolation* (high); and he establishes constraints for *lodging* (camping, backpacking) and *entertainment* (fishing). If the subject attempts to instantiate *vacation location* without taking these optimizations and constraints into account, his plan will probably not achieve his goals. For this reason, he combines the optimizations and constraints with the attribute and derives the description of an appropriate category.

Subjects frequently derive ad hoc categories in this manner while planning. Often subjects don't know the possible instantiations of an attribute. Yet they do know the optimizations and constraints that bear on it. As an initial pass at instantiating the attribute, subjects combine it with relevant optimizations and constraints to derive a category description. This description serves subsequently to guide the search for exemplars that satisfy it and to select the best exemplar from those that do. Essentially, this description constitutes a prototype that produces prototype structure within the ad hoc category, as we saw in Section II. To the extent that exemplars approximate the description, they become increasingly typical and appropriate for the current plan. Table VI summarizes the process of deriving an ad hoc category.

The derivation of ad hoc categories from frames represents an extreme form of conceptual combination. People do not acquire these categories through exemplar learning because they do not know exemplars for them. Instead, people manipulate attributes, optimizations, and constraints in frames to derive novel conceptual combinations. It is unlikely that simple Boolean rules of intersection, union, and so forth account for step 5 of the derivation process in Table VI. Instead, the combination of attributes, optimizations, and constraints is likely to involve much background knowledge and proceed in complex manners. Frame modification, as discussed in Section III,E,3, appears to provide one workable account of this process (Barsalou, in press-a, Chaps. 7–9; Barsalou, in press-b; Murphy, 1988, 1990; Smith et al., 1988).

E. FIELDS OF GOAL-DERIVED CATEGORIES

Once exemplars of an ad hoc category are discovered, they are likely to become established in memory as a set. Consider the planner who produced the protocol in Table IV. If this subject pursued the planning process further, he would eventually identify specific exemplars of *vacation locations* that satisfy his optimizations and constraints. For example, this planner, who lived in Atlanta, might identify *Smokey Mountains National Park, Joyce Kilmer Wilderness,* and *Blue Ridge Parkway* as exemplars. As a result of the deep, elaborative, and extended processing that these exemplars receive, they are likely to develop representations in memory and become associated to the attribute for *location* in the *vacation* frame. Later, when attempting to plan another vacation, this subject might activate these exemplars when attempting to instantiate *location* again. Rather than having to derive an ad hoc category description and search for exemplars, the planner could instead examine previous exemplars and evaluate their appropriateness. To the extent that the current optimiza-

TABLE VI

A GENERAL PROCEDURE FOR DERIVING AN AD HOC CATEGORY

1. Select a frame.
2. Select an attribute in a frame.
3. Identify optimizations that bear on the attribute.
4. Identify constraints that bear on the attribute.
5. Combine the attribute with the optimizations and constraints that bear on it to form a category description.
6. Search for exemplars that satisfy the category description.
7. Order exemplars according to how well they satisfy the category description, i.e., prototype structure.
8. Store information about the category.

tions and constraints are the same as before, this prestored category should be useful. As the planner continues to process *vacation locations* and its exemplars on future occasions, it will become increasingly established in memory. As a result, the category will lose its ad hoc status and become a well-established category that supports expert planning. Gentner (1989), Kolodner (1988), Ross (1989), and Schank (1982) address a variety of issues that bear on people's use of previous plans to guide later planning by analogy.

1. Expert Planners

Imagine that a planner takes many vacations over the years that are of different types. In the process of planning this variety of vacations, she considers a disparate set of *vacation locations*. One possible account of her resulting representation for *vacation locations* is that all of the locations ever considered become associated with the *location* attribute in the *vacation* frame. As a result, this planner entertains the entire set of *vacation locations* every time she attempts to instantiate this attribute. Still more extremely, imagine that this planner eventually becomes an expert travel agent. From the process of planning several vacations a day for years, she develops an extensive set of exemplars associated with the *location* attribute in the *vacation* frame. To develop a vacation plan for a particular client, she might search through this set, attempting to find the most appropriate exemplars.

Simply associating exemplars with a frame attribute in this manner is actually an inefficient way to represent a goal-derived category. If this were how expert travel agents organized vacation locations, then every time they had to plan a vacation, they would have to search the entire category of *vacation locations* to find the appropriate exemplars for the current plan. One client might want to know about locations to snow ski in December, whereas another client might want to know about locations to snow ski in August. Similarly, another client might want to know about locations to sunbathe in December, whereas another might want to know about locations to sunbathe in August. In each case, the travel agent would have to search through the entire category of *vacation locations* to identify the relevant subset.

A much more efficient way for experts to organize their knowledge of vacation locations would be to form subcategories of locations that satisfy specific configurations of optimizations and constraints. If vacation locations were organized in this manner, then each request to plan a certain kind of vacation would access the relevant subset of *vacation locations* directly, assuming that the particular configuration of optimizations and constraints is familiar. For example, upon encountering a client who wanted to snow ski in August, a travel agent might immediately access a well-established, goal-derived category of *locations to snow ski in August*. Rather than having to derive an ad hoc category from *vacation locations*, the planner could access a well-established, goal-derived category directly, indexed by the current configuration of optimizations and constraints. Similarly, an expert might have well-established subcategories for *locations to snow ski in December, locations to sunbathe in August,* and *locations to sunbathe in December.* Once the attribute, optimizations, and constraints that define a subcategory are known, these cues converge directly on the relevant subset of *vacation locations* already established in memory. In a sense, this type of convergence is similar to constraint propagation in connectionist nets: Once part of a particular *vacation* pattern is known, the network fills in the rest of the pattern.

2. Frames as Specifying Fields of Goal-Derived Categories

We currently have no evidence that experts organize their goal-derived categories according to optimizations and constraints. But to the extent that this conjecture turns out to be true in future studies, the instantiations of a frame attribute would be organized as a *conceptual field* of goal-derived categories (Barsalou, in press-b). Specifically, optimizations and constraints serve as contrasts that provide the instantiations of a frame attribute with a field structure (Grandy, 1987; Kittay, 1987; Lehrer, 1974; Lyons, 1977; Miller & Johnson-Laird, 1976). In *vacation locations,* for example, optimizations of *expensive* and *inexpensive* contrast to form *expensive vacation locations* vs. *inexpensive vacation locations.* Similarly, the constraints of *snow skiing* and *sunbathing* contrast to form *vacation locations for snow skiing* vs. *vacation locations for sun bathing.* This is analogous to how the attributes of *gender* (*male* vs. *female*), *age* (*child* vs. *adult*), and *species* (e.g., *human* vs. *equine*) produce the well-known semantic field of *animals* (e.g., *woman, boy, mare, colt*). In each case, relatively orthogonal values on multiple attributes project a field structure onto a set of conceptually related entities.

Frames delimit the extent of these conceptual fields (Barsalou, in press-b). By specifying the possible contrasts within a field, a frame delimits the set of possible categories that can be derived within it. Consider the potential contrasts in the field for *vacation locations* in Fig. 4. As can be seen, the *activity* attribute takes a variety of values, as does the *departure* attribute and the *goal* attribute of the *actor*. The values of these attributes, along with still other attributes not shown, specify the contrasts that can occur within the field for *vacation locations*. Values of *goal* contrast different subsets of *vacation locations,* such as *locations that provide privacy* vs. *locations that provide aesthetic enjoyment.* Similarly, values

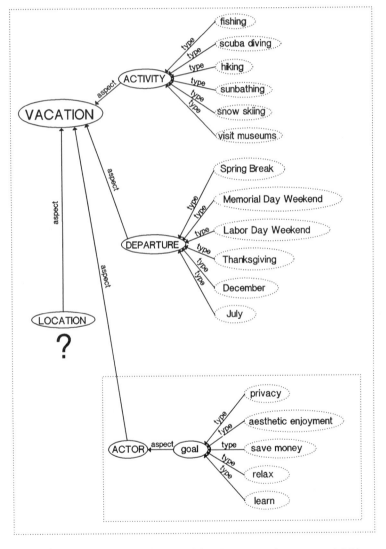

Fig. 4.   An example of a frame defining the extent of a conceptual field.

of *activity* and *departure* contrast other subsets, such as *locations for fishing* vs. *locations for scuba diving*. Each of these different *location* subsets constitutes a specific goal-derived category within the larger field.

The partial frame in Fig. 4 specifies a wide variety of possible goal-derived categories in the field for *vacation locations*. If only one value instantiates each attribute in a given plan, then combining all possible values across *activity, departure,* and *goal* produces 180 potential goal-derived categories (i.e., 6 activities × 6 departures × 5 goals). For example, one goal-derived category is *locations for fishing at Spring Break that provide privacy*. Another is *locations for sunbathing on Memorial Day weekend that provide aesthetic enjoyment*. By combining all possible constraints and optimizations in this manner, 180 such goal-derived categories result. If multiple values of an attribute can occur (or none at all), still more goal-derived categories are possible, including *locations for fishing and hiking*. Because Fig. 4 contains only four of the potential attributes for *vacation* as well as only a small subset of their potential values, 180 goal-derived categories greatly underestimates the number possible in the field for *vacation locations*. Because of the combinatorics involved, an indefinitely large number of goal-derived categories, well beyond the billions, is possible within this field. Most importantly, the frame for *vacation*—to the extent it can be fixed—specifies the space of possible categories. If the optimizations and constraints are known that bear on a field of goal-derived categories, they specify the categories within the field completely.

Clearly, not all possible combinations of optimizations and constraints are likely or even possible within a field (Barsalou, in press-b). For many combinations, the value of an attribute may not be optimal with respect to a background goal (e.g., wanting to save money and vacationing at the French Riviera). Similarly, many combinations of values do not satisfy constraints (e.g., snow skiing at La Jolla). In these ways, optimizations and constraints produce "conceptual gaps" in the field structure, namely, goal-derived categories that are unlikely to occur. Nevertheless, the number of feasible goal-derived categories is typically tremendous. Although we have only considered examples for the *location* attribute in the *vacation* frame, the same potential structure exists for any attribute in any frame.

3. Contextualization

As just noted, all possible optimizations and constraints specify all possible goal-derived categories within the field for a frame attribute. Conversely, a specific configuration of optimizations and constraints defines

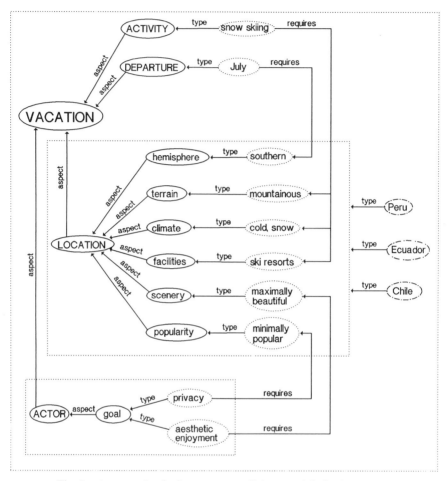

Fig. 5.   An example of a frame contextualizing a goal-derived category.

one particular goal-derived category within a field. For a given plan, existing optimizations and constraints contextualize a frame attribute by converging on a single goal-derived category. The contextualization of a frame attribute is essentially the derivation of an ad hoc category, as summarized in Table VI. In this section, I illustrate how frame modification underlies this process.

Consider the contextualization of the *location* attribute in Fig. 5. As can be seen, the optimizations projecting from *goal* to *location* are *privacy* and *aesthetic enjoyment*. Similarly, the constraints projecting from *activity* and *departure* to *location* are *snow skiing* and *July*, respectively. As Fig. 5 illustrates, these optimizations and constraints modify the *location* frame by setting values for its attributes. For example, the attribute of *hemisphere* is likely to be *southern*, the *terrain* must be *mountainous*, the *climate* must be *cold*, and so forth. As this example illustrates, optimizations and constraints contextualize *location* by setting values for attributes in its frame. Once these settings exist, they guide the subsequent search for possible exemplars and provide criteria for preferring one exemplar over another (i.e., the category's prototype structure).

If the optimizations and constraints in Fig. 5 were to change, they would contextualize the *location* frame differently. For example, if *departure* were *December*, the value for *hemisphere* might be *northern*, and exemplars of the category might be *United States, Canada,* and *France*. Similarly, if the *activity* were *sunbathing* and the *departure* were *December*, the values for most of the attributes in the *location* frame would be set differently, thereby producing another set of exemplars. As these examples illustrate, the current optimizations and constraints in a situation contextualize a frame attribute by modifying the attribute's frame, which in turn specifies a compatible set of category members. As optimizations and constraints change, the contextualization of the frame attribute and its accompanying goal-derived category change as well.

Before leaving this topic, it is worth noting that common taxonomic categories often appear to be contextualized in much the same manner. The only people who regularly consider categories like *clothing, fruit,* and *furniture* in their abstract, decontextualized senses may be categorization researchers! Under more normal conditions, people may typically contextualize these categories. For example, people usually think about *clothing* with respect to particular contexts, such that optimizations and constraints bear on it. Clearly, the optimizations and constraints that bear on *clothing* in the context of taking a walk on a Maine beach are very different from those in the context of taking a business trip to Tucson. In each context, attributes in the frame for *clothing* take different values, and the resulting exemplars vary. Contextualization—not decontextualization—may be the norm for categories of all types. People may even contextualize categories in minimally specified, laboratory contexts, thereby producing category representations that vary widely between and within individuals (Barsalou & Billman, 1989; Barsalou & Medin, 1986).

IV. Roles of Common Taxonomic and Goal-Derived Categories in the Cognitive System

In this section, I examine further differences and relations between common taxonomic and goal-derived categories. First, I explore the roles of common taxonomic and goal-derived categories in the time course of categorization. Whereas common taxonomic categories provide the primary categorizations of entities, goal-derived categories provide secondary categorizations. Second, I explore the relation between lexicalization and the time course of categorization. Because primary categories convey normative information that is relevant across contexts, lexemes develop for referring to this stable information. Because secondary categorizations convey goal-specific information that varies widely across contexts, too many lexemes would be needed to represent all possible categories. Instead, productive linguistic mechanisms generate complex phrasal constructions for goal-derived categories as needed. Finally, I propose a general framework for representing knowledge, in which common taxonomic categories compose world models, and goal-derived categories interface world models with event frames.

A. TIME COURSE OF CATEGORIZATION: PRIMARY VS. SECONDARY CATEGORIZATIONS

Whereas a *primary categorization* is a person's initial categorization of an entity, a *secondary categorization* is any subsequent categorization. For example, people might categorize something as a *chair* initially (the primary categorization) and later categorize it as *something to stand on to change a light bulb* (a secondary categorization).

People generally appear to use *basic level categories* and *subordinate categories*—two types of common taxonomic categories—for initial categorizations (Joliceur, Gluck, & Kosslyn, 1984; Murphy & Smith, 1982; Rosch, Mervis, Gray, Johnson, & Boyes-Braem, 1976). Tversky and Hemenway (1985) and Biederman (1987) suggest that this preference for basic level categories results from the diagnosticity of *shape* as a category cue, where *shape* refers more specifically to an entity's spatial configuration of physical parts. Because most members of a basic level category share a common shape, and because this shape does not occur in other categories, it provides a highly diagnostic cue for the category (Rosch, Mervis et al., 1976). Consider *chairs*. Because the shape of the average chair occurs for most chairs, and because this shape generally does not occur for other categories, an entity's possession of this shape strongly predicts that it is a chair. In contrast, shape is not a diagnostic cue for superordinate categories, because no shape is common to all category members (e.g., *animals*). Nor is shape a diagnostic cue for most subordinate categories, because different subordinate categories share the same global shape (e.g., *poodle, collie*).

The visual system's rapid analysis of shape information contributes further to the use of basic level categories as primary categorizations. Because the visual system extracts the low spatial frequency information for global shape faster than the high spatial frequency information for detailed stimulus properties, categories defined by shape are often the first to become available. In contrast, the information that specifies other categories is extracted more slowly, such that these categories are less likely to become available initially. For example, people categorize most kinds of birds initially as *bird*—not as *animal, robin, falcon, cardinal, blue jay,* etc.—because the shape information extracted from these entities accesses *bird* more rapidly than any other category. Because shape information is diagnostic for basic level categories, and because it becomes available so rapidly, these categories are more likely to be primary than other categories.

Interestingly, when an entity does not share the shape of its fellow exemplars in a basic level category, its subordinate category provides the primary categorization (Biederman, 1987; Joliceur et al., 1984; Murphy & Brownell, 1985). For example, people do not categorize chickens as *bird* initially because chickens do not share the common shape for *bird*. Instead, the shape of chickens is diagnostic for *chicken,* such that *chicken* is the primary categorization. Because shape is such a potent cue in initial categorization, categories for which shape is a diagnostic property provide primary categorizations. In other domains, such as audition, primary categorizations are likely to reflect whatever diagnostic information is extracted initially.[10]

In contrast, goal-derived categories generally appear to provide secondary categorizations. Once people categorize an entity with a basic level or subordinate category, they may categorize it subsequently in ways that are relevant to current goals. For example, someone might first categorize an entity as a *chair* but then categorize it subsequently into *things that can be stood on to change a light bulb*.

Goal-derived categories are not the only source of secondary categorizations. Many taxonomic superordinates, such as *furniture, animal,* and *clothing,* appear to provide secondary categorizations as well. First, some superordinates organize collections of basic level and subordinate entities in a particular context (Markman, 1979, 1989). For example, *furniture* might provide a secondary categorization for a collection of entities in a

---

[10] This account differs from the view of Rosch, Mervis et al. (1976), who argued that informativeness determines the basic level. Barsalou and Billman (1989, pp. 175–179) suggest that there may be multiple basic levels that operate in different task contexts. Specifically, a *perceptual basic level* may rely heavily on shape to produce primary categorizations during perception; whereas an *informational basic level* may provide secondary categorizations that carry optimal information during reasoning and communication.

particular room, including some chairs, a table, and a sofa. Similarly, *tools* might provide a secondary categorization for a collection of entities in a particular closet. Second, natural kind superordinates often integrate lower level categories that share a common intuitive theory (Barsalou & Billman, 1989, pp. 190–192). For example, *animal* is associated with an intuitive causal theory about certain categories of living things, specifying information about genes, birth, and so forth. Similarly, *fruit* represents an intuitive theory about other categories of living things, specifying information about plant growth and reproduction. These superordinates may provide secondary categorizations when achieving a goal requires understanding the underlying physical principles of a natural kind entity. Third, artifact superordinates often constitute goal-derived categories, containing instantiations of an attribute in an event frame (Barsalou & Billman, 1989, pp. 190–192). For example, *clothing* contains values of the *object* attribute in the frame for *wear*. Similarly, *tool* contains values of the *instrument* attribute in the frame for *make*. As these examples illustrate, superordinates play a variety of roles as secondary categorizations.

It is unlikely that people use goal-derived categories or superordinates without having made a basic or subordinate level categorization first. For example, it is unlikely that people would categorize a chair directly into *things that can be stood on to change a light bulb* without categorizing it first as a *chair*. Because the shape information that specifies *chair* is probably available before the information that specifies *things that can be stood on to change a light bulb,* it is likely that *chair* is the initial categorization. Even though primary categorizations may be irrelevant in goal contexts, the automatic application of basic and subordinate categories may be obligatory, given the consistent mappings of these categories and their associated shapes over extended experience (Schneider & Shiffrin, 1977; Shiffrin & Schneider, 1977). Moreover, primary categories may remain active as secondary categorizations are made, because they carry important information. For example, remembering an entity simply as *something to stand on to change a light bulb* loses important information about its other properties. Remembering it as a *chair* carries important information that may be useful for achieving later goals.

As I have noted, the early availability of shape information constitutes one important reason why basic and subordinate level categories provide primary categorizations. A second reason is that these categories typically convey correlated patterns of physical properties that are informative across a wide range of contexts (Billman & Heit, 1988; Rosch, Mervis et al., 1976). In contrast, goal-derived categories typically do not carry as much information about physical structure (Barsalou, 1983, 1985). To see this difference, imagine that a speaker says her garage contains a *chair.*

The listener can draw a wide variety of inferences about the entity's physical structure from the correlated properties that typically occur for *chair*. For example, the referent of *chair* is likely to have *legs*, a *seat*, and a *back* of certain sizes and in a particular configuration. Knowing these physical properties of the referent is relevant in a wide variety of contexts because these properties support a wide variety of goals (e.g., the entity has a flat horizontal surface that could support a can of paint; the entity has a flat vertical surface to which a paper sign could be attached; the entity has four supports that could penetrate through a coarse grate in the floor).

On the other hand, imagine that the speaker says her garage contains *something to stand on to change a light bulb*. The listener can draw many fewer inferences about the entity from this categorization than from *chair*. This categorizations only tells the listener that the entity is capable of supporting heavy weight at a certain height. Only physical properties relevant to the goal that the category serves are inferable. Much additional physical information about the parts of the entity and their configuration is not. Some inferences are possible, such as the entity being heavy enough to hold down a tarp. But because the categorization is so specific to the goal, drawing inferences beyond this context is limited.

A third reason that common taxonomic categories may be primary is that they convey information about standard functions (Rosch, Mervis et al., 1976). If a speaker says that she received a *chair* for her birthday, the listener can infer that the speaker will use it typically for sitting. Not only does *chair* convey information about correlated physical properties, it also conveys related information about the entity's standard function and the actions that people perform to achieve it. From knowing that the entity is a *chair*, the listener can infer what its standard function will be on many future occasions. The ideals associated with common taxonomic categories may often be associated with these standard functions (e.g., *comfortable* for *chair*).

Conversely, goal-derived categories do not typically specify the standard functions of their exemplars. If the speaker says that she received *something to stand on to change a light bulb* for her birthday, it is not safe for the listener to infer that this function will be the primary use of the entity. Instead, the entity is likely to have some more typical function that the listener cannot ascertain. From knowing this categorization, the listener has very limited knowledge of the entity's function.

The correlated physical properties of a category, along with its standard function, constitute central tendency information because they are the properties most likely to occur across exemplars. As we saw in Section II,D, central tendency information dominates the prototype structure of common taxonomic categories but plays no role in the prototype structure of goal-derived categories. Central tendency information may be central for common taxonomic categories because it enables them to provide maximal information about an entity following a primary categorization. Once the entity disappears from view, central tendency information associated with the primary categorization provides the best possible guess of what the entity's properties were. Any other information associated with the primary categorization would provide less accurate information on the average, by definition. Because common taxonomic categories provide the primary categorizations of entities, it is not surprising that central tendency represents them. By simply storing the basic or subordinate category of a perceived entity, and later retrieving the central tendency information for this category, a perceiver can retain maximal information about the entity without storing a detailed perceptual record of it or after forgetting it.

In contrast, central tendency should not be as important for secondary categorizations. Because secondary categorizations serve to categorize an entity with respect to particular goals, they do not need to convey central tendency information about their members. Instead, these categories must convey ideals that are relevant for achieving their associated goals. Whereas primary categorizations store normative information for an entity, secondary categorizations add information relevant to goals in particular contexts.

B. LEXICALIZATION AND THE TIME COURSE
    OF CATEGORIZATION

Typically, people refer to common taxonomic categories with lexemes, namely, a word or a short phrase that constitutes a conventional unit of vocabulary. For example, *cat, blue jay, kitten,* and *tom cat* are lexemes that refer to common taxonomic categories. In contrast, people typically refer to goal-derived categories with complex phrasal expressions, such as *expensive vacations that are relaxing* and *inexpensive vacations to go hiking.* As we saw in Section III,E, the linguistic mechanisms that produce these expressions are highly productive and contrastive, being capable of expressing tremendous numbers of goal-derived categories within a field. In the remainder of this section, I examine reasons for this difference between common taxonomic and goal-derived categories. As we shall see, this difference is closely related to the time course of categorization.

Before proceeding further, it is important to note that not all taxonomic categories are lexicalized and that some goal-derived categories are. As much work has illustrated, common taxonomic categories typically exhibit a field structure (Grandy, 1987; Kittay, 1987; Lehrer, 1974; Lyons, 1977; Miller & Johnson-Laird, 1976). Sometimes this field structure takes a matrix form, when various attributes are orthogonal to one another. For example, the orthogonal attributes of *gender, age*, and *species* provide a matrix structure in *animals*. Sometimes a field's structure takes a more hierarchical form, exhibiting superordinate, basic, and subordinate levels (Rosch, Mervis et al., 1976). For example, *fruit* descends into *apple, orange, melon*, and so forth, each of which may descend further (e.g., *apple* descends into *Granny Smith, Macintosh*, etc.). Within these field structures, lexical gaps exist at various intersections of attribute values. For example, the lack of lexemes for *neutered male cat* and *adult male robin* constitute lexical gaps in the field for *animal*. When taxonomic categories are rarely relevant to human activity, lexemes do not develop for them, and people must refer to them with complex phrasal constructions.

Conversely, some goal-derived categories are lexicalized, such as *buyer, payment, donor*, and *gift*. Each of these lexicalized goal-derived categories contains the instantiations of a frame attribute. Consider *payment*. This category contains instantiations of the *instrument* attribute in the frame for *buy*, including *cash, credit card*, and *loan*. Consider *gifts*. This category contains instantiations of the *object* attribute in the frame for *give*, including *flowers, clothing*, and *jewelry*. Certain goal-derived categories probably become lexicalized because they contain instantiations of frame attributes frequently relevant to human activity and communication.

Lexicalized goal-derived categories vary in the extent to which they are contextualized. *Gifts* is a contextualized form of the *object* attribute in the *give* frame because it does not contain all possible instantiations of the *object* attribute. When the *agent* of *give* is *police officer*, a *parking ticket* as the *object* is certainly not a *gift*. Instead, *gift* is a contextualized version of *object*, derived from optimizations and constraints in the *give* frame. When *gift* specifies the *object* of the *give* frame, the value of *time* is often *special occasion*, the value of *goal* is *provide unexpected pleasure to the recipient*, and so forth. In contrast, *payment* is a noncontextualized form of the *instrument* attribute in the *buy* frame. Any possible *instrument* for *buy* would also be a *payment*.

A surprising number of lexemes refer to goal-derived categories. One heuristic for generating these lexemes is as follows: Select a common verb and consider each of its central attributes, such as *agent, object, instrument, location, time*, and so forth. For each such attribute, search for a lexeme that refers to all of its instantiations or to a contextualized subset. Consider *eat*. *Food* is the object, *utensil* is the *instrument*, and *diner* is the *actor* contextualized by the constraint of *restaurant* for *location*. Consider *farm*. *Farmer* is the *agent*, and *crop* is the *object*. Consider *wear*. *Clothing* is a contextualized form of *object*, and *model* is a contextualized form of *agent*.

Even though some common taxonomic categories are not lexicalized and some goal-derived categories are, lexicalization appears closely related to the time course of categorization. Typically, lexicalized categories provide primary categorizations, whereas nonlexicalized categories provide secondary categorizations. For example, people might initially categorize an entity as a *chair* (lexeme) and later as *something that can be stood on to change a light bulb* (complex phrasal construction). Similarly, someone might initially categorize an entity as *celery* and later as *food to eat on a diet*. As we just saw, lexicalized goal-derived categories sometimes provide secondary categorizations, such as categorizing something initially as a *sweater* and then as a *gift*. But in general, lexicalized categories seem much more likely to provide primary categorizations.

The normativeness of primary categorizations vs. the goal-relevance of secondary categorizations may underlie this relation between lexicalization and the time course of categorization. Because the same primary category is used across a wide range of goal contexts, a single lexeme can convey its central tendency information in each. Even though chairs may occur in many goal contexts, such as changing light bulbs and holding doors open, the lexeme for *chair* conveys the same central tendency information across all of them. Because the purpose of primary categorizations is to provide the same central tendency information in all situations, a single lexeme can develop to convey this information.

In contrast, secondary categorizations of the same entity vary widely with context, such that no single linguistic expression can convey all of them. Instead, a different linguistic expression is necessary for each. To the extent that a particular secondary categorization occurs frequently, it may develop a lexeme (e.g., *gift*). But because most secondary categorizations only occur occasionally, their lexicalization would be inefficient. Too many lexemes would develop. Instead, it makes much more sense to allow the productive mechanisms of a language to express these categorizations in complex phrasal constructions. Although more cumbersome expressions result, people do not have to learn thousands of lexemes that they would use rarely.

In addition, it is necessary to have productive linguistic abilities that can express ad hoc categories the first time they become relevant. People could not refer to such categories with lexemes the first time they derive them because such lexemes would be unknown to listeners. For example, if someone referred to a newly constructed ad hoc category as *daxes,* it would be impossible to determine that it refers to *gifts for my granddaughter's birthday party*. Instead, the complex phrasal construction *gifts for my granddaughter's birthday party* is necessary. Conceivably, a culture could attempt to lexicalize this category. But doing so would be predicated on the belief that this category is important sufficiently often as a secondary categorization to warrant a lexical entry in the language. Most importantly, such lexicalization would typically occur *after* the use of a more complex, phrasal construction beforehand, when the category was derived initially. Even though some secondary categorizations become lexicalized, a language must still have productive mechanisms for expressing new categories.

C. Goal-Derived Categories as the Interface between Event Frames and World Models

In this final section, I propose a framework for knowledge that integrates findings from the previous sections. According to this framework, common taxonomic and goal-derived categories play different but complementary roles in the cognitive system. Whereas common taxonomic categories provide building blocks for world models, goal-derived categories provide interfaces between world models and event frames for achieving goals.

I define *world model* as a person's knowledge of locations in the environment, together with knowledge of the entities and activities that exist currently in these locations. A world model begins with a person's knowledge of his or her current location and of the entities and activities present. For example, someone's world model might represent that she is currently in her garage at home, between her car and the work bench, with a stack of boxes on the floor in front of her, and a dog sleeping behind her. A world model contains further knowledge about the current existence of locations, entities, and activities that are not immediately present. If people are at home, they know about locations, entities, and activities at work. If people are at work, they know about locations, entities, and activities in their home. Not only do world models contain information idiosyncratic to a particular individual, they also contain much culturally shared information, such as knowledge about neighborhoods, schools, parks, and rivers. In general, people have a tremendous amount of knowledge about the current state of the world, both immediately and more distantly.

By *world model* I do not mean general knowledge about the kinds of things in the world. For example, I do not mean people's general knowledge about *garages, cars, dogs, schools, parks,* and so forth. Instead, I mean specific knowledge and beliefs about the current state of the world. An extensive system of spatial frames for locations underlies a world model. As Minsky (1977) suggests, people have extensive systems for representing positions in space, which contain the specific entities and activities whose current positions are known. As entities and activities move about in the world, people move representations of them to new positions in their world models. Other transformations occur in world models as well, such as changes in the state of an entity (e.g., a car becomes broken, a roof develops a leak). To the extent that people are aware of changes in the world, their world model changes correspondingly. Researchers in artificial intelligence have often worried about world models in the context of the frame problem, truth maintenance systems, and nonmonotonic logics: Once a given change occurs in a data base, to what extent do other changes take place in the data base as well (e.g., Brown, 1987; Hayes, 1985; McCarthy & Hayes, 1969)? Little if any study has addressed the nature of world models in cognitive psychology. However, increasing work addresses the much more specific notion of situation models and their important roles in various tasks (e.g., Greeno, 1989; Johnson-Laird, 1983; Morrow, Bower, & Greenspan, 1989; van Dijk & Kintsch, 1983).

World models also provide natural representations of the past and the future. On this view, the system of spatial frames that organizes a world model also organizes long-term memory. To represent past events, previous states in a world model remain associated with the locations of their occurrence. To represent future events, envisioned states in a world model are similarly associated with their predicted locations. As the representation of an event unfolds over time within a world model, representations of its successive states become associated with the locations containing them. Not only do world models represent the present, they also represent the past and the future.

I propose that common taxonomic categories constitute the building blocks of world models. Upon perceiving an entity or activity in the environment, people categorize it with a basic level or subordinate category, storing this categorization at the position of the entity in their spatial reference system. For example, when people represent where things are in their homes, they represent the locations of particular *chairs, shirts, cups, apples, cats,* and so forth. People may generally use common taxonomic categories to construct world models because these categories describe entities independent of idiosyncratic goals. People often do not know what particular goals will become relevant to the entities that they encounter in the environment. They may therefore try to capture as much "objective" information as possible in primary categorizations to support a wide variety of idiosyncratic goals later.

Because common taxonomic categories maintain central tendency information about physical structure (Section IV,A), using them to build world models captures information about entities that is useful for achieving unanticipated goals. Imagine that a person's world model contains a desk at a location in an office building. Central tendency information about the physical structure of desks allows using this particular desk in a wide variety of unexpected ways. For example, if a person needs to blockade a door, he might consider this desk as a possible blockade because it is likely to have the *size, weight,* and *mobility* typical of desks. On another occasion, if this person needs to hide a birthday gift for a coworker, he might consider this desk as a possible hiding place because it is likely to have the drawers typically found in a desk. By building world models with common taxonomic categories, people establish central tendency information that supports achieving unanticipated goals as they arise.

Event frames complement world models, integrating the information that people must have to achieve familiar goals. When people want to buy groceries, their frame for *buy* must specify the relevant attributes that need to be instantiated. People must find a *location* that sells groceries, they must select a *time* to go shopping, they must have some form of *payment,* they must have a means of *traveling* to the grocery store, and so forth. As we saw earlier, knowledge about the attributes relevant to achieving goals resides in event frames. For each goal, an event frame specifies the particular attributes that must be instantiated to ensure successful goal achievement. Without knowledge of these attributes, planners would not know how to begin achieving the goal. Knowledge about optimizations and constraints in frames is also essential for successful goal achievement.

Successful goal achievement further requires a satisfactory interface between an event frame and a world model. If people cannot map the attributes in an event frame into their world models, they cannot achieve the respective goal. For example, if people need to buy groceries, the *buy* frame specifies that they must consider *location, payment, temporal parameters,* and so forth. But to actually achieve the goal, people must be able map these frame attributes into a world model. For example, people must be able to map the *location* attribute into particular *locations* in their world model that sell groceries. People must be able to map the *payment* attribute into the types of payment that they possess and that are acceptable at grocery stores. Knowing an event frame and having a world model is not enough. Instead, successful goal achievement requires an interface between these two systems of knowledge.

Mapping different event frames into the same world model defines different partitions on entities in the world model. Consider all of the geographic locations in a world model. Each event frame maps its *location* attribute into a different partition of geographic locations. To instantiate the *location* attribute in the *vacation* frame, people must partition geographic locations in their world model into *vacation locations* and *nonvacation locations.* In contrast, to instantiate the *location* attribute in the *buy* frame, when *groceries* is the value of *merchandise,* people must partition geographic locations quite differently. *Vacation locations* and *locations for buying groceries* constitute very different partitions on geographic locations in a world model. Similarly, as the value of *merchandise* in the *buy* frame varies from *groceries,* to *clothing,* to *cars,* the relevant partition of geographic locations continues to change.

Other frame attributes besides *location* must similarly map into world models for goals to succeed. *Object* attributes in frames must map into appropriate objects in world models, as must *agent* attributes, *instrument* attributes, *time* attributes, and so forth. Moreover, the partitions that these attributes produce on a world model change from frame to frame and from context to context. For example, the *object* attribute in the frame for *eat* produces a very different partition of objects in a world model than the *object* attribute in the frame for *wear* (i.e., *food* vs. *clothing*). Similarly, the *object* attribute for *eat* produces different partitions on objects as the *agent* of *eat* varies (e.g., *lions* vs. *birds*).

Essentially, each of these partitions constitutes a goal-derived category. For each attribute in each event frame, a goal-derived category contains the entities in the world model that can instantiate it. As people become familiar with achieving a particular type of goal, partitions on world models become increasingly established in memory. For example, when *groceries* instantiates *merchandise* in the *buy* frame, most people can immediately access a relevant partition on *locations* in their world model. Because people frequently process the *location* attribute in conjunction with particular grocery stores, the mapping between them becomes well established in memory as a goal-derived category. Similarly, when planning to see a movie, many people can immediately access a different partition on *locations* in their world model. As people become increasingly familiar with an activity, they develop direct mappings from frame attributes into world models, enabling the rapid retrieval of satisfactory instantiations. Without such interfaces between event frames and world models, goal pursuit would often be difficult, unsuccessful, and nonoptimal when successful. With such interfaces, people can quickly discover the parts of their world model relevant to a current goal. They do not need to perform the time- and resource-consuming operations that compute these mappings. Nor do they run the risk of miscalculating them.

As we saw earlier, expertise in planning develops as these mappings become sensitive to particular configurations of optimizations and constraints. Experts may often be able to use the optimizations and constraints in a situation to specify highly specialized partitions in their world model. In contrast, novices may often have trouble using optimizations and constraints to specify partitions. Instead, novices may use rigid partitions across contexts that ignore the full set of optimizations and constraints in a given context. Consequently, expertise at performing an activity may reflect a wide variety of mappings from frame attributes into a world model, each indexed by a different configuration of optimizations and constraints.

To the extent that this account is correct, common taxonomic and goal-derived categories play fundamentally different but complementary roles in the cognitive system. In perceiving the world and storing information about it, people use common taxonomic categories for primary categorizations, as they build and update their world models. These categories form the building blocks of world models because they specify central tendency information about entities that is useful across many contexts. Following primary categorizations, people use goal-derived categories for secondary categorizations that specify the relevance of entities to particular goals. By linking entities in a world model to attributes in event frames, people store information that will later facilitate their ability to construct plans. Because common taxonomic and goal-derived categories play these very different roles in the cognitive system, the information that develops to represent them adapts to these functions. Central tendency information becomes established for common taxonomic categories to optimize the applicability of information in world models, whereas ideals become established for goal-derived categories to support frame instantiation during goal achievement. Similarly, ideals become established for common taxonomic categories to support the optimization of their standard functions, and frequency of instantiation becomes established for goal-derived categories to provide base rates about the previous use of particular exemplars for achieving goals. As this analysis of common taxonomic and goal-derived categories illustrates, understanding the nature of categories depends on understanding their roles in the overall activity of the cognitive system.

V. Conclusion

Much work on categorization focuses on the issue of access: Given a featural description of an entity, how does an intelligent system access a correct category in memory? Prototype models, exemplar models, and connectionist models are all attempts to address this issue. Certainly, the issue of access is important and challenging, and solving it will have significant implications for both theoretical and applied research.

Yet much of the work on access fails to consider *why* access is important (Barsalou, 1990a). Why would an intelligent system want to know the category of an unfamiliar entity? Sometimes models of categorization seem to view categorization as an end in itself. Yet clearly, the purpose of categorization is not to know an entity's category. Instead, the purpose of categorization is to identify information in memory that provides useful inferences. Upon accessing a category for an entity, a tremendous amount of knowledge becomes available that is useful in a variety of ways. This knowledge may specify the origins of the entity, its physical structure, its probable behavior, its implications for the perceiver's goals, or actions for interacting with it successfully. Accessing a category is not an end in itself but is instead the gateway to knowledge for understanding an entity and interacting with it appropriately.

I have focused on the roles that categories play in the cognitive system following their access. For example, I have proposed that goal-derived categories provide sets of instantiations for frame attributes during planning and that common taxonomic categories constitute the building blocks of world models. Much of the evidence I present is not as rigorous as experimental psychologists prefer, and some of my proposals do not rest on any sort of systematic data collection. Moreover, the framework I present is far from being a fully developed formal or computational theory. Much progress certainly remains to be made in all of these regards. Nevertheless, one should not be afraid to ask new questions for fear of being unable to utilize methodological tools of the utmost technical sophistication. Otherwise, the science of categorization has little hope for initiating progress on numerous daunting issues that dwarf those we understand currently. To make significant progress, it will be necessary to explore important issues for which meticulous answers do not exist initially but exist eventually.

ACKNOWLEDGMENTS

Work on this chapter was supported by National Science Foundation Grant IRI-8609187 and Army Research Institute Contract MDA903-90-K-0112. I am grateful to Gordon Bower for the opportunity to write this article and am deeply indebted to him for his contributions to my career. I am also grateful to Boaz Keysar, Barbara Malt, Robert McCauley, Douglas Medin, Gregory Murphy, and Brian Ross for helpful comments and discussion regarding this chapter.

REFERENCES

Anderson, J. R. (1983). *The architecture of cognition*. Cambridge, MA: Harvard University Press.
Armstrong, S. L., Gleitman, L. R., & Gleitman, H. (1983). On what some concepts might not be. *Cognition, 13*, 263–308.
Ashcraft, S. L. (1978). Property norms for typical and atypical items from 17 categories: A description and discussion. *Memory & Cognition, 6*, 227–232.

Barsalou, L. W. (1981). *Determinants of graded structure in categories.* Unpublished doctoral dissertation, Stanford University, Stanford, CA.

Barsalou, L. W. (1983). Ad hoc categories. *Memory & Cognition, 11,* 211–227.

Barsalou, L. W. (1985). Ideals, central tendency, and frequency of instantiation as determinants of graded structure in categories. *Journal of Experimental Psychology: Learning, Memory, and Cognition, 11,* 629–654.

Barsalou, L. W. (1986). Unpublished study.

Barsalou, L. W. (1987). The instability of graded structure: Implications for the nature of concepts. In U. Neisser (Ed.), *Concepts and conceptual development: Ecological and intellectual factors in categorization* (pp. 101–140). New York: Cambridge University Press.

Barsalou, L. W. (1988). The content and organization of autobiographical memories. In U. Neisser (Ed.), *Remembering reconsidered: Ecological and traditional approaches to the study of memory* (pp. 193–243). New York: Cambridge University Press.

Barsalou, L. W. (1989). Intra-concept similarity and its implications for inter-concept similarity. In S. Vosniadou & A. Ortony (Eds.), *Similarity and analogical reasoning* (pp. 76–121). New York: Cambridge University Press.

Barsalou, L. W. (1990a). Access and inference in categorization. *Bulletin of the Psychonomic Society, 28,* 268–271.

Barsalou, L. W. (1990b). On the indistinguishability of exemplar memory and abstraction in category representation. In T. K. Srull & R. S. Wyer, Jr. (Eds.), *Advances in social cognition: Content and process specificity in the effects of prior experiences* (Vol. 3, pp. 61–88). Hillsdale, NJ: Erlbaum.

Barsalou, L. W. (in press-a). *Cognitive psychology: An overview for cognitive scientists.* Hillsdale, NJ: Erlbaum.

Barsalou, L. W. (in press-b). Frames, concepts, and conceptual fields. In E. Kittay & A. Lehrer (Eds.), *Frames, fields, and contrasts: New essays in semantic and lexical organization.* Hillsdale, NJ: Erlbaum.

Barsalou, L. W., & Billman, D. O. (1989). Systematicity and semantic ambiguity. In D. Gorfein (Ed.), *Resolving semantic ambiguity* (pp. 146–203). New York: Springer-Verlag.

Barsalou, L. W., & Hutchinson, J. W. (1987). Schema-based planning of events in consumer contexts. In P. F. Anderson & M. Wallendorf (Eds.), *Advances in consumer research* (Vol. 14, pp. 114–118). Provo, UT: Association for Consumer Research.

Barsalou, L. W., & Medin, D. L. (1986). Concepts: Fixed definitions or context-dependent representations? *Cahiers de Psychologie Cognitive, 6,* 187–202.

Barsalou, L. W., & Sewell, D. R. (1984). *Constructing categories from different points of view* (Emory Cognition Rep. No. 2). Atlanta, GA: Emory University.

Barsalou, L. W., Sewell, D. R., & Ballato, S. M. (1986). *Assessing the stability of category representations with graded structure.* Unpublished manuscript.

Barsalou, L. W., Spindler, J. L., Sewell, D. R., Ballato, S. M., & Gendel, E. M. (1987). *Assessing the stability of category representations with property generation.* Unpublished manuscript.

Barsalou, L. W., Usher, J. A., & Sewell, D. R. (1985). *Schema-based planning of events: The origins of goal-derived and ad hoc categories.* Paper presented at the meeting of the Psychonomic Society, Boston, MA.

Biederman, I. (1987). Recognition by components: A theory of human image understanding. *Psychological Review, 94,* 115–147.

Billman, D. O., & Heit, E. (1988). Observational learning from internal feedback: A simulation of an adaptive learning method. *Cognitive Science, 12,* 587–626.

Borkenau, P. (1990). Traits as ideal-based and goal-derived social categories. *Journal of Personality and Social Psychology, 58,* 381–396.

Brooks, L. R. (1978). Non-analytic concept formation and memory for instances. In E. H. Rosch & B. B. Lloyd (Eds.), *Cognition and categorization* (pp. 169–211). Hillsdale, NJ: Erlbaum.

Brooks, L. R. (1987). Decentralized control of categorization: The role of prior processing episodes. In U. Neisser (Ed.), *Concepts and conceptual development: Ecological and intellectual factors in categorization* (pp. 141–174). New York: Cambridge University Press.

Brown, F. M. (Ed.). (1987). *The frame problem in artificial intelligence.* Los Altos, CA: Morgan Kaufmann.

Byrne, R. (1977). Planning meals: Problem-solving on a real data-base. *Cognition, 5,* 287–332.

Carlson, G. N., & Tanenhaus, M. K. (1988). Thematic roles and language comprehension. In W. Wilkens (Ed.), *Syntax and semantics: Thematic relations* (Vol. 21, pp. 263–288). San Diego, CA: Academic Press.

Čech, C. G., Shoben, E. J., & Love, M. (1990). Multiple congruity effects in judgements of magnitude. *Journal of Experimental Psychology: Learning, Memory, and Cognition, 16,* 1142–1152.

Chaplin, W. G., John, O. P., & Goldberg, L. R. (1988). Conceptions of states and traits: Dimensional attributes with ideals as prototypes. *Journal of Personality and Social Psychology, 54,* 541–557.

Chater, N., Lyon, K., & Myers, T. (1990). Why are conjunctive categories overextended? *Journal of Experimental Psychology: Learning, Memory, and Cognition, 16,* 497–508.

Cherniak, C. (1984). Prototypicality and deductive reasoning. *Journal of Verbal Learning and Verbal Behavior, 23,* 625–642.

Crowder, R. G. (1976). *Principles of learning and memory.* Hillsdale, NJ: Erlbaum.

DeJong, G., & Mooney, R. (1986). Explanation-based learning: An alternative view. *Machine Learning, 1,* 145–176.

Dougherty, J. W. D., & Keller, C. M. (1985). Taskonomy: A practical approach to knowledge structures. In J. W. D. Dougherty, (Ed.), *Directions in cognitive anthropology.* Urbana: University of Illinois Press.

Estes, W. K. (1986). Array models for category learning. *Cognitive Psychology, 18,* 500–549.

Fehr, B., & Russell, J. A. (1984). Concept of emotion viewed from a prototype perspective. *Journal of Experimental Psychology: General, 113,* 464–486.

Fillmore, C. J. (1968). The case for case. In E. Bach & R. Harms (Eds.), *Universals in linguistic theory* (pp. 1–88). New York: Holt, Rinehart & Winston.

Fillmore, C. J. (1977). The case for case reopened. In P. Cole & J. M. Sadock (Eds.), *Syntax and semantics: Vol. 8. Grammatical relations* (pp. 59–81). San Diego, CA: Academic Press.

Gentner, D. (1989). The mechanisms of analogical reasoning. In S. Vosniadou & A. Ortony (Eds.), *Similarity and analogical reasoning* (pp. 199–241). New York: Cambridge University Press.

Glass, A. L., & Meany, P. J. (1978). Evidence for two kinds of low-typical instances in a categorization task. *Memory & Cognition, 6,* 622–628.

Gluck, M. A., & Bower, G. H. (1988). Evaluating an adaptive network model of human learning. *Journal of Memory and Language, 27,* 166–195.

Glucksberg, S., & Keysar, B. (1990). Understanding metaphorical comparisons: Beyond similarity. *Psychological Review, 97,* 3–18.

Grandy, R. E. (1987). In defense of semantic fields. In E. Le Pore (Ed.), *New directions in semantics* (pp. 259–280). San Diego, CA: Academic Press.

Greeno, J. G. (1989). Situations, mental models, and generative knowledge. In D. Klahr & K. Kotovsky (Eds.), *Complex information processing: The impact of Herbert A. Simon* (pp. 285–318). Hillsdale, NJ: Erlbaum.

Hampton, J. A. (1979). Polymorphous concepts in semantic memory. *Journal of Verbal Learning and Verbal Behavior, 18,* 441–461.

Hampton, J. A. (1987). Inheritance of attributes in natural concept conjunctions. *Memory & Cognition, 15,* 55–71.

Hampton, J. A. (1988). Overextension of conjunctive concepts: Evidence for a unitary model of concept typicality and class inclusion. *Journal of Experimental Psychology: Learning, Memory, and Cognition, 14,* 12–32.

Hampton, J. A., & Gardiner, M. M. (1983). Measures of internal category structure: A correlational analysis of normative data. *British Journal of Psychology, 74,* 491–516.

Hasher, L., & Zacks, R. T. (1979). Automatic and effortful processes in memory. *Journal of Experimental Psychology: General, 108,* 356–388.

Hayes, P. J. (1985). The second naive physics manifesto. In J. R. Hobbs & R. C. Moore (Eds.), *Formal theories of the commonsense world.* Norwood, NJ: Ablex.

Hayes-Roth, B., & Hayes-Roth, F. (1977). Concept learning and the recognition and classification of exemplars. *Journal of Verbal Learning and Verbal Behavior, 16,* 321–328.

Hintzman, D. L. (1976). Repetition and memory. In G. H. Bower (Ed.), *The psychology of learning and motivation: Advances in research and theory* (Vol. 10, pp. 47–91). New York: Academic Press.

Hintzman, D. L. (1986). "Schema abstraction" in a multiple-trace memory model. *Psychological Review, 93,* 411–428.

Homa, D. (1984). On the nature of categories. In G. H. Bower (Ed.), *The psychology of learning and motivation: Advances in research and theory* (Vol. 18, pp. 49–94). Orlando, FL: Academic Press.

Jackendoff, R. (1987). The status of thematic relations in linguistic theory. *Linguistic Inquiry, 18,* 369–411.

Jacoby, L. L., & Brooks, L. R. (1984). Nonanalytic cognition: Memory, perception, and concept learning. In G. H. Bower (Ed.), *The psychology of learning and motivation: Advances in research and theory* (Vol. 18, pp. 1–47). San Diego, CA: Academic Press.

Johnson-Laird, P. N. (1983). *Mental models: Towards a cognitive science of language, inference, and consciousness.* Cambridge, MA: Harvard University Press.

Joliceur, P., Gluck, M., & Kosslyn, S. M. (1984). Pictures and names: Making the connection. *Cognitive Psychology, 16,* 243–275.

Kahneman, D., & Miller, D. T. (1986). Norm theory: Comparing reality to its alternatives. *Psychological Review, 93,* 136–153.

Keil, F. C. (1989). *Concepts, kinds, and cognitive development.* Cambridge, MA: MIT Press.

Kittay, E. F. (1987). *Metaphor: Its cognitive force and linguistic structure.* Oxford: Oxford University Press.

Kolodner, J. (Ed.). (1988). *Proceedings of the Case-Based Reasoning Workshop.* San Mateo, CA: Morgan-Kaufman.

Lakoff, G. (1987). *Women, fire, and dangerous things: What categories reveal about the mind.* Chicago, IL: University of Chicago Press.

Lehrer, A. (1974). *Semantic fields and lexical structure.* New York: American Elsevier.

Lehrer, A. (in press). Names and naming: A frame approach. In E. Kittay & A. Lehrer (Eds.), *Frames, fields, and contrasts: New essays in semantic and lexical organization.* Hillsdale, NJ: Erlbaum.

Loken, B., & Ward, J. (1990). Alternative approaches to understanding the determinants of typicality. *Journal of Consumer Research, 17,* 111–126.

Lucariello, J., & Nelson, K. (1985). Slot-filler categories as memory organizers for young children. *Developmental Psychology, 21*, 272–282.

Lyons, J. (1977). *Semantics* (Vol. 1). New York: Cambridge University Press.

Malt, B. C., & Smith, E. E. (1982). The role of familiarity in determining typicality. *Memory & Cognition, 10*, 69–75.

Markman, E. (1979). Classes and collections. *Cognitive Psychology, 11*, 395–411.

Markman, E. (1989). *Categorization and naming in children*. Cambridge, MA: MIT Press.

McCarthy, J., & Hayes, P. (1969). Some philosophical problems from the standpoint of artificial intelligence. In B. Meltzer & D. Michie (Eds.), *Machine learning* (Vol. 4). Edinburgh: Edinburgh University Press.

McClelland, J. L., & Rumelhart, D. E. (1985). Distributed memory and the representation of general and specific information. *Journal of Experimental Psychology: General, 114*, 159–188.

McClelland, J. L., Rumelhart, D. E., & the PDP Research Group. (1986). *Parallel distributed processing: Explorations in the microstructure of cognition: Vol. 2. Psychological and biological models*. Cambridge, MA: MIT Press.

McCloskey, M., & Glucksberg, S. (1978). Natural categories: Well-defined or fuzzy sets? *Memory & Cognition, 6*, 462–472.

McCloskey, M., & Glucksberg, S. (1979). Decision processes in verifying category membership statements: Implications for models of semantic memory. *Cognitive Psychology, 11*, 1–37.

McNemar, A. (1969). *Psychological statistics* (4th ed.). New York: Wiley.

Medin, D. L., & Barsalou, L. W. (1987). Categorization processes and categorical perception. In S. Harnad (Ed.), *Categorical perception: The groundwork of cognition*. New York: Cambridge University Press.

Medin, D. L., & Schaffer, M. M. (1978). A context theory of classification learning. *Psychological Review, 85*, 207–238.

Medin, D. L., & Shoben, E. J. (1988). Context and structure in conceptual combination. *Cognitive Psychology, 20*, 158–190.

Medin, D. L., & Smith, E. E. (1984). Concepts and concept formation. *Annual Review of Psychology, 35*, 113–138.

Medin, D. L., Wattenmaker, W. D., & Hampson, S. E. (1987). Family resemblance, conceptual cohesiveness, and category construction. *Cognitive Psychology, 19*, 242–279.

Mervis, C. L. (1987). Child-basic object categories and early lexical development. In U. Neisser (Ed.), *Concepts and conceptual development: Ecological and intellectual factors in categorization* (pp. 201–233). New York: Cambridge University Press.

Mervis, C. L., Catlin, J., & Rosch, E. (1976). Relationships among goodness of example, category norms, and word frequency. *Bulletin of the Psychonomic Society, 7*, 283–284.

Mervis, C. L., & Pani, J. R. (1980). Acquisition of basic object categories. *Cognitive Psychology, 12*, 496–522.

Mervis, C. L., & Rosch, E. (1981). Categorization of natural objects. *Annual Review of Psychology, 32*, 89–115.

Miller, G. A., & Johnson-Laird, P. N. (1976). *Language and perception*. Cambridge, MA: Harvard University Press.

Minksy, M. L. (1977). A framework for representing knowledge. In P. H. Winston (Ed.), *The psychology of computer vision* (pp. 211–277). New York: McGraw-Hill.

Mitchell, T. M., Keller, R. M., & Kedar-Cabelli, S. T. (1986). Explanation-based generalization: A unifying view. *Machine Learning, 1*, 47–80.

Morrow, D. G., Bower, G. H., & Greenspan, S. L. (1989). Updating situation models during narrative comprehension. *Journal of Memory and Language, 28*, 292–312.

Murphy, G. L. (1988). Comprehending complex concepts. *Cognitive Science, 12*, 529–562.

Murphy, G. L. (1990). Noun phrase interpretation and conceptual combination. *Journal of Memory and Language, 29,* 259–288.

Murphy, G. L., & Brownell, H. H. (1985). Category differentiation in object recognition: Typicality constraints on the basic category advantage. *Journal of Experimental Psychology: Learning, Memory, and Cognition, 11,* 70–84.

Murphy, G. L., & Medin, D. L. (1985). The role of theories in conceptual coherence. *Psychological Review, 92,* 289–316.

Murphy, G. L., & Smith, E. E. (1982). Basic-level superiority in picture categorization. *Journal of Verbal Learning and Verbal Behavior, 21,* 1–20.

Newell, A., & Simon, H. A. (1972). *Human problem solving.* Englewood Cliffs, NJ: Prentice-Hall.

Nosofsky, R. M. (1984). Choice, similarity, and the context theory of classification. *Journal of Experimental Psychology: Learning, Memory, and Cognition, 10,* 104–114.

Nosofsky, R. M. (1988). Similarity, frequency, and category representations. *Journal of Experimental Psychology: Learning, Memory, and Cognition, 14,* 700–708.

Oden, G. C. (1987). Concept, knowledge, and thought. *Annual Review of Psychology, 38,* 203–227.

Osherson, D. N., Smith, E. E., Wilkie, O., Lopez, A., & Shafir, E. (1990). Category based induction. *Psychological Review, 97,* 185–200.

Posner, M. I., & Keele, S. W. (1968). On the genesis of abstract ideas. *Journal of Experimental Psychology, 77,* 353–363.

Read, S. J., Jones, D. K., & Miller, L. C. (1990). Traits as goal-based categories: The importance of goals in the coherence of dispositional categories. *Journal of Personality and Social Psychology, 58,* 1048–1061.

Reed, S. K. (1972). Pattern recognition and categorization. *Cognitive Psychology, 3,* 382–407.

Rey, G. (1983). Concepts and stereotypes. *Cognition, 15,* 237–262.

Rips, L. J. (1975). Inductive judgments about natural categories. *Journal of Verbal Learning and Verbal Behavior, 14,* 665–681.

Rips, L. J. (1989). Similarity, typicality, and categorization. In S. Vosniadou & A. Ortony (Eds.), *Similarity and analogical reasoning* (pp. 21–60). New York: Cambridge University Press.

Rosch, E. H. (1975). Cognitive representations of semantic categories. *Journal of Experimental Psychology: General, 104,* 192–233.

Rosch, E. H., & Mervis, C. B. (1975). Family resemblances: Studies in the internal structure of categories. *Cognitive Psychology, 7,* 573–605.

Rosch, E. H., Mervis, C. B., Gray, W. D., Johnson, D. M., & Boyes-Braem, P. (1976). Basic objects in natural categories. *Cognitive Psychology, 8,* 382–439.

Rosch, E. H., Simpson, C., & Miller, R. S. (1976). Structural bases of typicality effects. *Journal of Experimental Psychology: Human Perception and Performance, 2,* 491–502.

Ross, B. H. (1989). Remindings in learning and instruction. In S. Vosniadou & A. Ortony (Eds.), *Similarity and analogical reasoning* (pp. 438–469). New York: Cambridge University Press.

Rumelhart, D. E., McClelland, J. L., & the PDP Research Group. (1986). *Parallel distributed processing: Explorations in the microstructure of cognition: Vol. 1. Foundations.* Cambridge, MA: MIT Press.

Sacerdoti, E. D. (1975). *A structure for plans and behavior* (Tech. Note No. 109). Menlo Park, CA: Stanford Research Institute.

Sacerdoti, E. D. (1979). *Problem solving tactics* (Tech. Note No. 189). Menlo Park, CA: Stanford Research Institute.

Schank, R. C. (1982). *Dynamic memory: A theory of reminding and learning in computers and people*. New York: Cambridge University Press.

Schank, R. C., & Abelson, R. P. (1977). *Scripts, goals, plans, and understanding: An inquiry into human knowledge structures*. Hillsdale, NJ: Erlbaum.

Schneider, W., & Shiffrin, R. M., (1977). Controlled and automatic human information processing: I. Detection, search, and attention. *Psychological Review, 84*, 1–66.

Shiffrin, R. M., & Schneider, W. (1977). Controlled and automatic human information processing: II. Perceptual learning, automatic attending, and a general theory. *Psychological Review, 84*, 127–190.

Smith, E. E., & Medin, D. L. (1981). *Categories and concepts*. Cambridge, MA: Harvard University Press.

Smith, E. E., Medin, D. L., & Rips, L. J. (1984). A psychological approach to concepts: Comments on Rey's "Concepts and stereoptypes." *Cognition, 17*, 265–274.

Smith, E. E., Osherson, D. N., Rips, L. J., & Keane, M. (1988). Combining prototypes: A selective modification model. *Cognitive Science, 12*, 485–528.

Smith, E. E., Shoben, E. J., & Rips, L. J. (1974). Structure and process in semantic memory: A featural model for semantic decisions. *Psychological Review, 81*, 214–241.

Stefik, M. J. (1981). Planning with constraints. *Artificial Intelligence, 16*, 111–140.

Tversky, A. (1977). Features of similarity. *Psychological Review, 84*, 327–352.

Tversky, B., & Hemenway, K. (1985). Objects, parts, and categories. *Journal of Experimental Psychology: General, 113*, 169–193.

van Dijk, T. A., & Kintsch, W. (1983). *Strategies and discourse comprehension*. The Hague, Netherlands: Mouton.

Wellman, H. M., & Gelman, S. A. (1988). Children's understanding of the non-obvious. In R. Sternberg (Ed.), *Advances in the psychology of human intelligence* (pp. 99–135). Hillsdale, NJ: Erlbaum.

Wilkins, W. (Ed.). (1988). *Syntax and semantics: Vol. 21. Thematic relations*. San Diego, CA: Academic Press.

Willensky, (1983). *Planning and understanding: A computational approach to human reasoning*. Reading, MA: Addison-Wesley.

Winograd, T. (1975). Frame representations and the declarative-procedural controversy. In D. G. Bobrow & A. M. Collins (Eds.), *Representation and understanding: Studies in cognitive science*. New York: Academic Press.

Winston, M. E., Chaffin, R., & Herrmann, D. (1987). A taxonomy of part-whole relations. *Cognitive Science, 11*, 417–444.

Wittgenstein, L. (1953). *Philosophical investigations* (G. E. M. Anscombe, Trans.). Oxford: Blackwell.

LEARNING AND APPLYING CATEGORY KNOWLEDGE IN UNSUPERVISED DOMAINS

John P. Clapper
Gordon H. Bower

I. Introduction

In order to behave intelligently, people need internal models of their environment and how their actions will modify it (see Craik, 1943; Gentner & Stevens, 1983; Johnson-Laird, 1983). In this article, we focus on how people discover regularities among the objects, events, and situations they encounter, and how they create general categories to capture these consistent patterns. By partitioning their experiences into distinct categories, people can build up a collection of internal models that apply to many similar objects or events, allowing them to use their past experience to interpret and respond adaptively to the currrent situation. We are also concerned with the way that such categories, once formed, affect how further instances are encoded into memory and how such encodings serve as a basis for discovering further subcategories within a given domain. Much previous research indicates that learning to recognize recurrent patterns (categories) within a stimulus domain improves the efficiency of encoding and representing specific instances (e.g., Chase & Simon, 1973; de Groot, 1965, 1966); this, in turn, should facilitate the discovery of new, more specific subcategories within that domain.

Our analysis presupposes a broad definition of categories that focuses on their role in allowing a knowledgeable subject to predict the features of

65

specific instances. Here, a *category* is defined as any collection of features or components that occur together with relatively high consistency across different contexts (instances). Such correlation of elements or constituent features provides the learner with predictive power: Given that enough features are observed in a specific instance to match it up with the appropriate category, the category can be used to predict or imply the presence of other features not directly observed. This broad definition admits many types of "categories" that are not always studied or thought of as such, including recurring temporal patterns, chess board configurations, mental models of standard electrical circuits, and so on, as well as familiar "natural kinds" such as cats, birds, or medical diseases. While there may be real differences between different types of categories, e.g., between those with a clear object–property structure as opposed to, say, recurring temporal patterns in a musical score, those differences are beyond the scope of the present analysis.

II. Theoretical Issues

A. Induction of Categories from Instances

A large experimental literature has accumulated regarding the acquisition of concepts, much of it following in the tradition of studies by Bruner, Goodnow, and Austin (1956; see, e.g., Millward, 1971, for a review). Most of that laboratory research focused on *supervised* learning of categories, in which an external tutor informs the subjects what classifications are to be learned (i.e., category labels are provided by the tutor) and provides feedback relative to a specific criterion for the current learning task. By contrast, many categories that people acquire in real life are learned in untutored, observational conditions. Such *unsupervised* learning occurs in the absence of predefined categories and without feedback from any tutor. For example, much of what we know about the perceptual properties and behavior of physical objects, social interactions, linguistic classes and rules, and everyday tasks and procedures is probably learned in this manner (Billman & Heit, 1988). Any learning of a pioneer in a novel environment is unsupervised. For example, botanists classifying new plants from a newly discovered island, geologists classifying rocks from a new planet, or medical pathologists inspecting histological sections of tissues infected with various diseases have no one to tell them how to group the specimens in different subclasses. Pioneers must create their own groupings that are sensitive to the salient regularities detectable in the domain.

Curiously, little psychological research or theorizing has been devoted to the topic of unsupervised learning. This paucity of research is surprising in light of the pervasiveness of unsupervised learning in everyday life. More to the point, unsupervised learning seems to involve somewhat different principles from those that characterize concept learning with a tutor. For example, in an unsupervised task the learner must decide whether, and how, to create new concepts to describe stimuli that fit poorly into existing categories. This issue does not arise in supervised classification tasks because the tutor essentially tells the learner when to set up a new category and assign a given exemplar to it. In addition, unsupervised tasks provide opportunities to study people's *incidental* learning of concepts; by studying when certain concepts spontaneously "pop out" of the learner's stream of experience, we may discover the kinds of regularities that people's inductive machinery is designed to detect naturally, in contrast to the regularities whose learning requires a tutor's feedback.

B. REPRESENTATION OF CATEGORIES IN MEMORY

For centuries philosophers have debated the mental representation of concepts. One view proposes that learners abstract summary representations of categories (e.g., prototypes or schemas; see Kant, 1787/1963; Posner & Keele, 1968, 1970; Rumelhart & Ortony, 1977); a contrasting view proposes that people merely store in memory collections of instances from which generalizations about the category can be computed as they are needed (e.g., Hintzman, 1986; Hume, 1748/1960; Medin & Schaffer, 1978). This debate has proven difficult to resolve because the range of inferences derivable from unrestricted computation over a collection of stored instances is greater than that provided by summary statistics, such as mean and variance, computed from these instances. In other words, any generalization or inference about a category (e.g., boundary conditions for membership) that could be stored in a summary representation could also be computed during testing from memories of specific instances. For this reason, it is difficult to obtain strong evidence for summary models merely by examining the pattern of classification responses people give to a particular set of test stimuli.

Although instance storage theories can easily mimic the inferential power of summary representations, the two positions differ in their assumptions about (1) how knowledge of categories, subcategories, and individual exemplars is organized in memory and (2) people's ability to use their experience with a category to improve their interpretation, analysis, and encoding of specific novel cases. These differences mainly influence measures of processing or encoding in various tasks rather than the semantic content of subjects' inferences. For example, different theories of memory organization make different predictions about which factors affect the speed and accuracy of verifying facts from memory, even though the theories may agree on what features subjects would attribute to a given category or instance.

In the experiments to be described, we investigated how knowledge of a category affects the learning of new instances. Many of the patterns of learning and memory organization observed in our experiments appear incompatible with current formulations of instance theories. We do not take such results as implying that people never retain specific instances or make inferences based on them; rather, we interpret out results as showing that under appropriate conditions people are also quite capable of learning and applying generalizations about members of a category.

C.   CATEGORY-BASED PROCESSING OF INSTANCES

Considerable research suggests that concept models (e.g., spatial models, temporal scripts) play a key role in how people process instances. This role is illustrated in studies comparing experts to novices in processing problems in their domain. These studies show that experts are able to represent information about their domains more efficiently than novices, resulting in much improved memory and problem-solving performance (e.g., Chase & Simon, 1973; de Groot, 1965, 1966). This efficient compacting of information by experts is seen in domains as diverse as chess, electronic circuitry, baseball, and culturally specific scripts. Experts' advantage rests on their stockpile of categories for recognizing recurrent situations in their domains, so that such situations can be represented and reasoned about with familiar ideas.

Interestingly, the experimental literature on concept learning has largely ignored the way that concepts, once formed, alter the processing of later instances. The traditional research agenda has been driven by another issue, i.e., how to characterize the essentially "bottom-up" process by which people acquire generalizations about categories from descriptions of specific instances (e.g., Hunt, 1962; Millward, 1971). This learning orientation may be contrasted to the "top-down" process by which people use their category knowledge to guide their processing of instances. Consistent with this traditional emphasis, concepts have tended to be regarded as *decision rules* for classifying new stimuli, but not as active processing structures that determine how particular stimuli are represented and acted on.

Much of the existing research on how general models of categories affect the interpretation and processing of specific situations has used social-ethnic stereotypes (e.g., Srull & Wyer, 1989), personality stereotypes (e.g., Cantor & Mischel, 1979), or situational scripts for routine activities (e.g., the restaurant script of Schank & Abelson, 1977). An example of the latter type of experiment is one by Bower, Black, and Turner (1979), which examined how subjects' memory for text statements describing a routine activity varied with whether a given event was predictable or deviated from the script. At best, however, such experiments yield only imprecise measures of processing; their obvious imprecision arises from the experimenter's ignorance of the structure, properties, and training history of these familiar concepts for each subject. For valid generalizations, we prefer to investigate the way subjects learn and use artificial concepts that have been designed to precise laboratory specifications.

III. A Model of Unsupervised Learning

To guide our research, we have developed a tentative model describing how people might learn categories in unsupervised environments and use them to guide the encoding of specific instances. The learners in this model are assumed to be engaged in unguided exploration of a given domain of objects, i.e., learning is unsupervised and learners are simply attending to the features of individual objects without explicitly searching for categories among them. Importantly, human learners have a limited attentional capacity with which to carry out such exploration. This capacity limitation presents them with the problem of selecting appropriate features of their environment to attend to and record into memory. When the environment provides direct reinforcement (e.g., a tutor's feedback in a supervised classification task), subjects will learn to attend to features that are correlated with this reinforcement. In the absence of such explicit consequences, we assume that people use heuristic strategies for allocating attention that help them (1) encode instance representations with the greatest efficiency, given their limited attentional capacity, and (2) maximize the likelihood of discovering useful patterns or regularities, i.e., new subcategories, without explicitly searching through the space of possible categories within a given domain. We hypothesize that such heuristics require that subjects use existing categories to evaluate new stimuli and distinguish informative from uninformative features, and then selectively attend to the informative features. In the present treatment, we are particularly concerned with statistical, inductive determinants of informativeness, i.e., the relative likelihoods of different features within a category. We do not dispute that other factors may influence perceived informativeness in addition to the inductive criteria that we emphasize, e.g., theoreti-

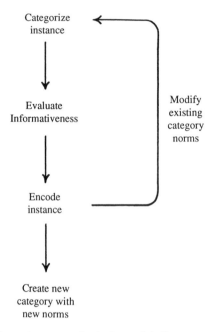

Fig. 1.   Information processing in the model of unsupervised learning.

cal knowledge, but those factors are beyond the scope of the present treatment. An informal description of this model is shown schematically in Fig. 1.[1]

A. REPRESENTATION

Stimuli are described in terms of *features,* which are specific values of *attributes,* e.g., size, color, or shape. Thus, brown and blue would be possible values of the attribute of eye color. We imagine that the attributes with which real objects are described would depend on the objects' current categorization; since a stimulus could be categorized differently in different contexts, in principle the attributes used to describe it are to some extent mutable and dependent on the other stimuli with which it is

---

[1] We have composed a computer program that implements most of the assumptions of this model; however, we are more committed to the heuristic principles that the model implements than to any specific computational instantiation. The experiments described in this article investigate qualitative predictions of the model and do not require a complete description of the simulation program for their motivation. Therefore, only an informal verbal description of the model is provided here.

contrasted. In practice, an experimenter will usually define a set of canonical attributes by which a stimulus set is generated and/or described, with each instance from that set represented as a vector of specific values. Within such a stimulus set, different subcategories are distinguished by clusters of correlated (consistently co-occurring) attribute values. For example, a geneticist might describe a collection of fruitflies in terms of several attributes such as size, wing shape, eye color, and so on. If it was then noticed that most individuals with long wings were also large and had red eyes, whereas those with short wings were medium-sized and had white eyes, these patterns of co-occurrences would form an inductive basis for distinguishing two different families or categories within that population. Importantly, this characterization of categories does not imply that the interfeature correlations must be perfect; in principle, a category would have positive utility as long as at least some features of instances could be predicted with greater-than-baseline reliability. Thus, the present characterization of categories admits "fuzzy" categories with probabilistic features and does not require categories to be defined by necessary and sufficient features. Moreover, not all the attributes of an instance would necessarily be highly correlated with its category; within any category, different attributes will take on predominate values with different reliabilities across different instances.

We assume that a learner's knowledge of a specific category is represented in long-term memory as a schema that specifies a set of attributes in terms of which instances will be described, and specific values of each. Norms for each attribute are represented by a collection of *strengths* of association between the category and each value of the attribute. These strengths represent the relative expectedness or availability from memory of each value of each attribute, e.g., their frequency and recency among previous category members.

B. STEP 1: CATEGORIZE THE INSTANCE

A basic tenet of our approach (see Fig. 1) is that a stimulus event evokes its own frame of reference, i.e., it is automatically classified in the best-fitting category available from memory. This category then provides a familiar framework within which the stimulus can be further interpreted and reasoned about. A stimulus is categorized by matching a sample of its features (i.e., specific values of attributes) to the attribute norms for each candidate category, and then selecting the best match. An instance will be assigned to that category with which it shares the largest proportion of highly expected values and the fewest surprising or unusual values.

C. STEP 2: EVALUATE THE INSTANCE

With respect to the norms of a particular reference category, the features of a given stimulus will vary in how typical or expected they appear. This typicality in turn determines which features are considered most informative for describing that particular instance. Although several definitions of "informativeness" are plausible, all capture the intuition that the informativeness of a stimulus value increases with its unpredictability or surprisingness in a given context. Importantly, this principle implies that consistent, highly expected values of an attribute (referred to as *defaults*) will be considered as uninformative, whereas features that are unusual or not specified in advance by the schema will be judged as informative.

A simple way to conceptualize a value's informativeness is in terms of its strength (availability) in the attribute norm for a given category. The greater a value's strength, relative to alternative values of the same attribute, the more expected and less informative it should appear. Assuming that a value's strength increases with its relative frequency within a category, the strength view is equivalent to equating a value's informativeness with its improbability of occurrence within the category.

This view of informativeness is broadly consistent with a rational encoding strategy for an "ideal learner," and with intuitions about the kinds of events that people find interesting and to which they pay attention. An efficient learning mechanism should attempt to maximize the new (previously unknown) information it acquires about a stimulus within the encoding capacity avaiable for a given task. Thus, an ideal learner should avoid expending limited resources recording facts about an exemplar that are already predictable from categorical knowledge; rather, the optimal strategy is to focus on features that are unpredictable, surprising, and informative.

Just as people tend to focus on informative features when recording a given experience, so do they also focus on similarly distinctive, informative properties when communicating to others. This injunction is embodied in one of Grice's "maxims of conversation," namely, that speakers should be informative and not convey known, redundant information to listeners (Grice, 1975). For example, uninteresting truisms are not normally uttered in conversation; rather, people abide by the rule of describing objects, situations, and events in terms of their more distinguishing or informative properties. Thus, people might describe their car as a "blue Chevy" but not as a "Chevy with four wheels"; they refer to penguins as "flightless birds" but not to dogs as "flightless mammals," although both statements are equally accurate. When describing criminal suspects, police bulletins and news programs highlight any unusual features the suspect might possess, such as scars and tattoos, rather than features the suspect shares with the general population.

D. STEP 3: ENCODE THE INSTANCE

After categorizing the instance and assigning informativeness to each of its attribute values, the next step is to record the instance into memory. The features of an instance compete for fixed attentional or encoding resources, which are assumed to be distributed among the features so as to maximize the total informativeness of the features encoded. The model assumes that the resources allocated to a given attribute value are proportional to its informativeness relative to that of the other attributes of the stimulus. This rule ensures that the learner encodes the maximum of distinguishing information about an instance given the attentional resources available to process it.

The episodic memory representation of the instance that results from this encoding process can be thought of as a set or vector of features, each with a specific strength of association to that instance. A feature's strength in this record depends on how much attention it received at encoding, which depended in turn on its informativeness. The instance's categorization at the time of encoding is presumed also to be stored with that instance in memory.

E. STEP 4: UPDATE CATEGORY NORMS

The model assumes that people incrementally update their norms for the activated concept after each presented instance. Two cases are distinguished according to whether the current instance is adequately covered by a previous category or, due to its novelty, requires the creation of a new category.

1. Assimilation to a Previous Category

Normally, instances are assimilated to the category used to evaluate and encode them. The attribute norms of this category are adjusted by increasing the strength of each observed value in proportion to the amount of attention it received during encoding. As the same value of an attribute is repeated over a series of instances, it becomes less informative and learners should pay progressively less attention to it. This process is analogous to habituation to a constant stimulus repeated within a particular context, except that the context in this case is given by category membership. Due to this habituation of the constant features, more attentional resources are left over to process the remaining, unpredictable features of each instance.

2. Create a New Category before Assimilating

Learners are assumed to create new categories in response to the failure of old ones. Specially, in exploring a domain, learners use a "surprise heuristic" to indicate when they should invent a new category. According to this heuristic, when an instance contains sufficient features that are surprising (highly informative) with respect to its assigned category, a new category is created to describe the unusual stimulus. This strategy for creating new categories is similar to the "failure-based generalization" of Schank (1982). By creating new categories only when an instance violates prior norms, subjects can learn categories in a domain without explicitly searching through the entire space of possible categories within that domain, i.e., keeping track of all possible feature correlations. For complex domains characterized by vast numbers of possible categories, such an explicit search strategy might be unrealistic for human learners (but see Billman & Heit, 1988, for a different approach to solving this search problem).

The model assumes that if a new category is triggered by an unusual instance, then that instance will be assimilated to the new category; thus, the unusual instance will not affect norms for the prior concept from which it deviated. This segregation principle allows people to accommodate highly unusual instances without discarding beliefs that have proven generally useful and reliable in the past. To illustrate, if zoologists discovered an unusual elephant that had thick fur and no tail, they probably would not abandon their belief that elephants are generally hairless with tails. Instead, they would assume that they had discovered a new subspecies of elephant, closely related to, but distinct from, the familiar species.

In the model, the schema for the new category is created by modifying the schema for the "source" category (that to which the instance was originally assigned) in order to describe the deviant instance. In doing this, we assume that learners believe that all their norms about the source category that are not specifically violated by the triggering instance can be transferred to the new category created around that unusual instance. New norms are created only for those attributes whose exceptional values triggered the formation of the new category. To return to our example of the furry, tailless elephant, in creating a new category around this stimulus the model would transfer all its prior beliefs about elephants to the new category (e.g., that they are plant eaters, have trunks and lungs, etc.), except those relating to the "fur" and "tail" attributes. New norms, based on the triggering instance, will be created for these unusual attributes; prior norms concerning these attributes for ordinary elephants would not apply to this new subspecies. By conforming to this transfer rule, learners need to make the fewest possible changes to their existing taxonomy to handle the deviant instance. Thus, existing knowledge is exploited to the fullest to conserve computational resources in forming the new concept.

F. STEP 5: RETRIEVING FEATURES FROM INSTANCE MEMORIES

When people attempt to remember the features of an instance, limited retrieval resources (e.g., spreading activation) are divided among the features in its underlying memory representation. The activation received by each feature increases with its strength divided by the combined strength of all features of that instance. This rule implies that the more features that are strongly associated with an instance, the more difficult it should be to retrieve any particular one. This fact has received extensive empirical validation in analogous memory experiments; the more independent facts that people learn about a particular topic or item, the more time they require to verify any one of them from memory (see Anderson, 1976, 1983, for reviews of this research). This phenomenon is known as the *fan effect* or as associative interference.

The model's assumptions about encoding and retrieval imply differences in the way predictable vs. unpredictable features of an instance are remembered. Because of their low informativeness, the highly predictable features of an instance will be only weakly associated, if at all, to the instance. As a first approximation, we will simply assume that subjects omit these category defaults from their memory representations of specific instances. Rather, the default values would merely be noted as properties of the general category, and hence inferable for specific instances by property inheritance. In such a memory organization, the default properties of an instance would be effectively segregated from its distinctive or variable features. The instance with its distinctive features would be recorded as a "subnode" in memory pointing to the category node with its associated defaults (see Fig. 2). As a result, when retrieving the fact that an instance has a specific distinctive feature, the system avoids associative interference (the fan effect) from the category defaults. Besides economizing on learning and storage that results from the encoding process, this "subnoding" maneuver confers a major advantage on this memory organization for later information retrieval. The memory organization helps solve the so-called paradox of interference, which is that experts with vast domain knowledge do not suffer the massive slowdown in retrieval that interference principles alone would have expected (Smith, Adams, & Schorr, 1978). The subnoding solution is similar to earlier solutions of the paradox proposed by Reder and Ross (1983) and Anderson (1983).

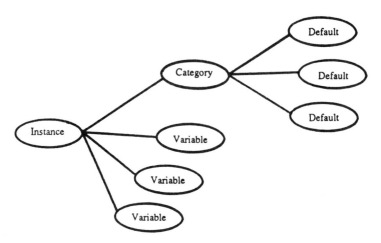

Fig. 2. Network representation depicting the organization of instance and category knowledge in memory.

IV.   Comparison to Alternative Approaches

The model we have proposed differs in several respects from previous models of unsupervised learning. One advantage of the present model is that it makes explicit the role of generic concepts in the interpretation, analysis, and recording of novel cases; in turn, the model shows how the processing of specific instances affects the learning of category level expectations. Most previous models of category formation are strictly "bottom-up" in the sense that they specify how instance information is used to form concepts but not how the concepts in turn determine the encoding and representation of further instances. By exploring these issues experimentally, we hope to shed light on how concepts economize the processing of later exemplars.

Most previous models of concept learning were formulated to deal primarily with the classification of instances into categories, and not with the problem of storing those instances in memory for later reproduction. Consequently, they assume that learners become more likely to attend to attributes whose values consistently co-occur across category members (i.e., that are diagnostic of category membership). While this process is acceptable for partitioning a stimulus set into categories at one level of specificity, it is not adequate for learning and retrieving descriptions of specific instances or for building hierarchies of categories and subcategories at multiple levels of specificity. A classification model that increasingly focused attention on category diagnostic features would learn progressively less about the distinguishing features of specific instances. Similarly, a learning process that focuses solely on known category defaults would be completely blocked or very slow in learning specific subcategories that might be differentiated within more general categories. For example, once having learned to differentiate oak trees from maple trees, people operating under this limitation would be unlikely to attend to subtler properties that differentiate among subspecies of oaks because they would be focusing instead only on features common to all oaks. Such a focus contrasts with more naturalistic learning, in which people consider known categories as "background" and proceed to focus on subtler distinctions among instances that might form a basis for learning more differentiated categories.

V. Experiments

A. EXPERIMENT 1: ATTRIBUTE LISTING TRACKS UNSUPERVISED LEARNING

In a first experiment, we explored a new task designed to investigate the evolution of subjects' category level norms as they examined successive instances from a single category. The objective of this task was to provide a trial-by-trial index of subjects' evolving beliefs about the informativeness of each attribute and its specific values. According to the model, subjects should learn to discriminate among the features of instances according to their informativeness within the reference category. Category defaults should be considered uninformative and receive low priority, while exceptional or highly variable features should receive high priority. These biases should develop gradually as subjects accumulate experience with instances of a given category. If an index could be found for the informativeness of each feature in a series of training instances, this index could be used to trace "learning curves" for norms about the experimental categories. By studying the properties of such learning curves and how they are affected by task structure and stimulus design, much fundamental knowledge could be acquired about unsupervised learning.

In this experiment, subjects were shown a series of training instances from a single category and were asked to list the distinguishing features of each. The distinguishing features were portrayed for the subject as those characteristics that would be most helpful in discriminating that instance from others of the same general type on a multiple-choice recognition test. The stimuli were line drawings of fictitious insects (see Fig. 3). The insects were composed of a consistent base structure, consisting of parts such as

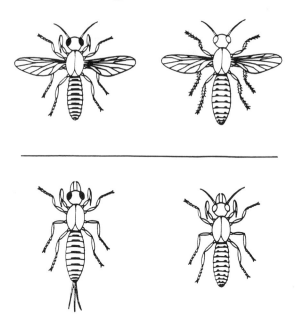

Fig. 3.   Insect stimuli used in Experiment 1.

head, thorax, abdomen, eyes, and so on, plus nine binary attributes that could be varied to generate distinct instances (e.g., presence or absence of wings, color of eyes, and so on). From nine binary attributes, a population of $2^9 = 512$ stimulus patterns can be composed. For presentation to a particular subject, a subset of this stimulus population was selected such that four of the nine attributes had a constant (default) value across all the instances, whereas the remaining five varied randomly. (That is, each value of the variable attributes occurred in a randomly ordered one-half of the presented instances, and the different attributes varied independently of each other). Thus, a single category was generated in which four attributes had highly predictable (default) values, while five other attributes varied freely across different instances. Several training sets were constructed and presented to different subgroups of subjects to ensure that the assignment of attributes to conditions (consistent or variable) was properly balanced.

Subjects received test booklets in which a single insect picture appeared on each page; below each picture was a space for subjects to write their feature lists. The instructions on each page told subjects to list only those features of each insect that would help distinguish it from others of the same general type. The first seven training instances were always standard instances, in which all defaults were present as described above. After these initial training trials, however, subjects would occasionally see a deviant instance in which a particular default was violated (e.g., if all the standard bugs had wings, one of the deviant bugs would be wingless). Out of a total of 40 instances presented over the course of the experiment, subjects saw two such deviant instances, each of which violated a different default.

The dependent measure of interest was the proportion of subjects that listed each of the nine experimental attributes on each trial. The probability of reporting the presented value of an attribute should depend on how informative subjects consider it to be for discriminating that instance from other category members. Thus, such listing provides an index of changes in subjects' learning about that attribute at each point in the training sequence.

Turning to the results, as expected subjects' reporting of default values declined rapidly over the first few trials, from about 54% on the first trial to 10% on the fifth, where it remained thereafter (see Fig. 4). The linear component of this decreasing trend was statistically significant at the .01 level [$t(24) = 5.69$], and the quadratic component was marginally significant [$t(24) = 1.79$, $p < .10$]. Subjects' reporting of variable attributes averaged about 75% and was fairly constant over trials. By the end of the training phase, the variable attributes were being reported nearly 65% more than the default attributes, a highly significant difference ($p < .01$). This pattern of results indicates that subjects rapidly learned that the presence of defaults could be taken for granted and that only the variable features provided differentiating information about each instance.

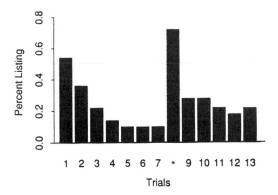

Fig. 4.   Percent listing of defaults in Experiment 1. The instance with a missing default occurred on the trial marked with an asterisk.

A second result of interest was that subjects were very likely to notice and report the absence of default features in the two deviant instances. The increase in listing, from 10% on the preceding trial to 72% on the deviant trial (marked with an asterisk in Fig. 4), was highly significant [$t(24) = 8.40, p < .01$]. Listing of the default value dropped significantly on the following, normal, trial [$t(24) = 5.52, p < .01$], but for several trials remained higher than it had been previously. This result suggests that the missing default caused subjects to temporarily "dishabituate" to that attribute, much as an unexpected change in a stimulus produces an orienting reflex and temporarily releases previous habituation to that stimulus.

These results indicate that the attribute listing task is sensitive to manipulations of feature informativeness and that the patterns of attribute listing are consistent with the model of unsupervised learning. The findings suggest that attribute listing is a useful method for tracing learning curves for subjects' attribute norms as successive instances are assimilated to a single category. Thus, the method should prove useful for investigating many variables that influence unsupervised learning.

B. Experiment 2: Learning Two Blocked Categories

The next experiment proposes extending the attribute listing procedure to a situation in which subjects would learn two contrasting categories in an unsupervised environment. This would require that subjects learn the category level discrimination built into the stimulus set and that they reflect this learning in their patterns of attribute listings. That is, subjects should learn to selectively report the values of attributes that are variable within each category, while omitting values shared by instances within a category (but that differ between the two categories). Such a response pattern would indicate that subjects had learned to evaluate a value's informativeness within the specific category to which the current instance belongs rather than evaluating its informativeness across the stimulus set as a whole. Hopefully, the results would show separate learning curves for the attribute norms of each category. If successful, the method would enable investigation of variables that facilitate or interfere with the discovery of distinct categories, thus permitting evaluation of different models of how such discoveries arise.

The stimuli were similar to those used in Experiment 1, i.e., line drawings of fictitious insects (see Fig. 3) that varied along dimensions such as wing type, eye color, length of legs, and so on. Two distinct categories were defined by collections of correlated values on several attributes. For example, for a given subject all of the insects in the A category might have wide wings, a fat body, fuzzy antennae, large pincher mouthparts, and black eyes, whereas members of the B category would have opposite values on each of these five attributes. A total of eight attributes in this stimulus set could be varied to create different instances. Of these eight, five were assigned a consistent default value within each category, whereas the remaining three were free to vary across instances. Within categories, each variable attribute had two values (a different two for each category) that occurred equally often across different instances and varied independently of each other. Two different stimulus sets were created and shown to different groups of subjects to ensure that the assignment of attributes to the variable vs. default conditions was properly balanced.

The procedure and instructions to the subjects were similar to those of Experiment 1. The stimuli were presented in booklets with one insect per page and a space at the bottom for subjects to write their feature lists. The instances were presented blocked by category. Sixteen instances of the A category were presented first, followed by 16 instances from the B category. Such blocking should increase the probability that subjects would create two distinct categories rather than assimilating both A and B instances to a single omnibus concept. Following the two same-category blocks, a final block of eight trials was presented in which instances of the two categories were intermixed in a random sequence. This mixed block was included to check whether the discrimination learned during the blocked trials would be maintained when instances of the two categories were presented in random order.

Consistent with the results of Experiment 1, subjects learned the defaults of the A category as they examined the first several instances, gradually reducing their listing of the default features of category A. Starting from a high rate of listing of 58% on the first trial, listing of default values gradually decreased over trials until it reached about 16% on trial 10, where it remained until the first B instance was presented (see top panel of Fig. 5). This decreasing trend in subjects' listings of A defaults was highly significant [$t(15) = 4.29$, $p < .001$]. By contrast, the A variables (bottom panel of Fig. 5) were listed with an average rate of 94%, significantly exceeding that of the defaults [$t(15) = 12.87$, $p < .001$]. Upon encountering the first instance of the B category, subjects dramatically increased their listing of the contrasting defaults for that new category (Fig. 5, top panel). The 55% jump in listings was highly significant [$t(15) = 7.00$, $p < .001$]. Over the next several trials, however, subjects gradually reduced their reporting of these newly constant defaults and reverted to a strategy of listing mainly the variable features of each instance. This decreasing trend was significant at the .001 level [$t(15) = 4.39$]. These listing patterns reveal orderly learning curves for the acquisition of the two concepts.

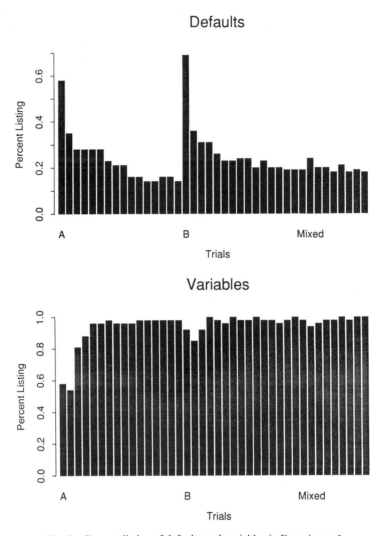

Fig. 5.   Percent listing of defaults and variables in Experiment 2.

Another important result is that listing of defaults for either category A or B did not significantly increase during the final, mixed block of instances, when compared to the final block of immediately preceding instances [$t(15) = 0.32$, $p > .50$]. Had listings increased at this point, a skeptic could have argued that the earlier suppression during the blocked trials might have reflected not the learning of two distinct categories but rather the assimilation of all instances to a single, overarching category.

On that account, the gradual decrease in listings in both blocks would reveal merely localized habituation within a single category due to lengthy "runs" of similar instances. In other words, during the series of B instances, subjects would have gradually modified their attribute norms so that the earlier A defaults were now overshadowed by the more recent B defaults. Were this the correct account, subjects should have dramatically increased their listing of these attributes when they encountered the first A instance during the mixed block (since the A defaults would now be considered exceptional). Moreover, by this alternate account, if default attributes began to appear highly variable throughout the mixed trials, then they should have been listed at the same frequency as the variables in earlier trials. The fact that subjects continued to list the A category (and B category) defaults with low frequency during the mixed block indicates that they had acquired two distinct, stable concepts during the blocked trials.

The results of this experiment demonstrate that the attribute listing task can trace the discovery and learning of distinct categories in an unsupervised task. The pattern of learning observed in this experiment is consistent with the predictions of the information-processing model described earlier. This task may therefore have considerable potential for exploring variables that affect category discovery and modification, allowing tests of the basic model.

C. EXPERIMENT 2A: LEARNING TWO CATEGORIES WITH MIXED SEQUENCES

Experiment 2 demonstrated that subjects could learn to discriminate categories based on contrasting defaults without supervision from an external tutor, and that the attribute listing task could be used to index this learning. A possible criticism of that experiment, however, is that the training instances were artificially sequenced by categories to maximize the probability of successful discrimination learning. Perhaps such learning would not have occurred with a less contrived, random sequence of A and B exemplars. In defense of Experiment 2, it was explicitly designed to demonstrate that subjects could detect contrasting categories without supervision when the exemplars were optimally sequenced and that such learning would be reflected in their attribute listings. Experiment 2 did not explore the boundary conditions under which such learning would be possible. We wanted to demonstrate in the next experiment (2A) that unsupervised learning could occur even with intermixed training sequences.

The information-processing model sketched in the Introduction predicts that subjects could learn to discriminate contrast categories in a randomly intermixed sequence, but that in some cases this learning would be considerably impaired relative to a blocked-sequence condition. Such interference is expected on the model's assumption that new categories are created in response to expectation failures (surprise); for the defaults of a B instance to appear surprising, however, they must violate strong default expectations already acquired for category A. It is easy to understand how such surprise would arise in Experiment 2, since strong expectations would be acquired during the A block before the first B instance was encountered. However, when a randomized training sequence is used, only a small number of A instances (perhaps one or two) would be encountered prior to the first B instance, providing little opportunity to learn strong A defaults. According to our theory, violations of weak expectations are less informative (surprising) than violations of strong ones; thus, the new value may not appear sufficiently surprising to trigger the creation of a new category. Instead, the two types of instances might be assimilated together into a single, encompassing category that summarized the stimulus set as a whole. In such a case, the default values of each category would be encoded as alternative values of variable attributes, i.e., since the correlations among the default values would not be captured by having separate categories, subjects would be unaware of them and would consider the values uncorrelated. Once the categories were initially aggregated together in this manner, it might be difficult to later "unlearn" this overgeneralized framework and correctly discriminate the two categories. Indeed, an analogous effect on supervised category learning was demonstrated by Holstein and Premack (1965), who found that an initial period of random feedback substantially retarded learning of a simple classification of the same stimuli.

Experiment 2A was similar in most respects to Experiment 2 except that the stimuli were presented in an intermixed sequence rather than blocked by category. A total of 48 instances was presented, designed according to the same specifications as in Experiment 2. The order of instances was randomized, except that runs longer than three instances from the same category were disallowed. As before, five attributes of the stimuli had correlated values that served as defaults for the two categories, while the remaining three varied independently across different instances. Two different stimulus sets were constructed, each with a different assignment of attributes to default vs. variable status, to ensure that any attribute-specific effects would be properly counterbalanced. In addition, two other stimulus sets were constructed in which all eight attributes varied independently. These fully variable "control sets" allowed us to compare listing performance in structured vs. unstructured stimulus sets, and to ensure that less listing of defaults expected in experimental groups would not simply be an artifact of their having fewer total values than defaults. (Recall, default attributes took on only two values within a set, one for each category, whereas variable attributes took on four different values, with two different values for each category). Unlike the previous two experiments, which used Stanford undergraduates as subjects, the subjects in Experiment 2A were recruits from Lackland Air Force Base.

As shown in Fig. 6, evidence of subcategory learning was obtained in the experimental groups. Subjects tended to reduce their listing of defaults and increase their listing of variables as more stimuli were encountered. When listing of defaults is subtracted from listing of variable attributes, it can be seen that the learning effect in these conditions is quite substantial; the difference in responding increased from -2% on the first trial to 48% in the last trial (see Fig. 6, third panel). The increasing trend in this index is statistically significant $[t(19) = 2.84, p < .02]$. By contrast, no such trend appeared for subjects exposed to the fully variable, "control" stimuli. When listing of defaults (two-valued attributes) was subtracted from that of variables (four-valued attributes) for control subjects, no significant learning effect was observed $[t(23) = 0.92, p > .20]$. Moreover, in direct comparisons, defaults were listed an average of 25% less often by the experimental subjects than were the corresponding features by the control subjects $[t(46) = 22.39, p < .001]$. Thus, despite the intermixed sequence of training instances, significant learning, reflecting correlations in the default values defining the two categories, occurred in this experiment.

These results may be compared to those of Experiment 2 to examine how the different sequencing of training instances affected learning. Comparing the learning curves obtained in these two experiments (Fig. 6 vs. Fig. 5), learning occurred far faster and more clearly in Experiment 2 than in 2A. In addition, the asymptotic listing of defaults is far greater in Experiment 2A than in Experiment 2. Comparing the listing of defaults in the final, mixed, block in Experiment 2 (trials 32–40) to default listing in the same trials from Experiment 2A, listing was 16% higher in the mixed sequence compared to the blocked sequence. Comparison of the two experiments, matched by trials, yielded a significant difference $[t(7) = 9.63, p < .001]$.

Unfortunately, this difference cannot be interpreted as unambiguous evidence for interference in the mixed condition. Technically, it is inappropriate to compare data across different experiments conducted at different times with different groups of subjects. This problem arises in this comparison because the subjects in Experiment 2 were Stanford undergraduates whereas those in Experiment 2A were Air Force recruits. The different levels of learning could have been due to different average

Defaults

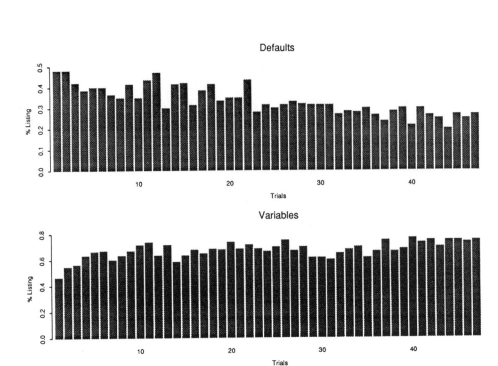

Variables

Differences

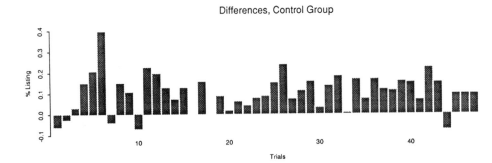

Differences, Control Group

learning abilities in these two subject populations, as well as the training sequences. Obviously, a more appropriate procedure would be to compare blocked and intermixed conditions within one population and experiment. (We should note, however, that several pilot versions of this mixed-sequence experiment were presented to Stanford undergraduates as we were developing the version administered to Air Force recruits, and learning by these pilot subjects always appeared much poorer than was observed in Experiment 2). In light of the absence of a direct comparison between different sequencing conditions to substantiate the interference hypothesis, the conservative conclusions from this experiment are that subjects clearly can learn contrasting categories even from mixed training sequences and that attribute listing provides a useful index of this learning.

D. EXPERIMENT 3: UNSUPERVISED LEARNING OF A HIERARCHY OF CATEGORIES

In accumulating knowledge about a domain, people often develop a set of related categories at multiple levels of specificity. Many real-world domains, such as categories of animals, plants, automobiles, jet aircraft, or medical diseases, are partitioned at more than one level as some form of default hierarchy. One way domain experts differ from nonexperts is by the rich conceptual hierarchies of interrelated subcategories they have acquired, as well as their facility in using this knowledge to improve their processing and retrieval of new information in the domain (e.g., Holland, Holyoak, Nisbett, & Thagard, 1986). Given the prevalence and importance of such conceptual hierarchies, it is odd that prior research on category learning has usually examined single-level categories. There have been few demonstrations of learning of multilevel categories or even reliable methods for observing such learning (but see Murphy & Smith, 1982).

Experiment 3 was intended to demonstrate that subjects could spontaneously induce categories in a multilevel domain and that the attribute listing procedure could track this learning. In contrast to previous categorization models suited only for learning single-level partitions, our theory can apply to the progressive learning of categories and subcategories at multiple levels of specificity. Multilevel learning is possible because the model assumes that once defaults at a given level are learned, the subject will take them as "background" and proceed to focus on other aspects of

Fig. 6. Percent listing of defaults and variables from the experimental group in Experiment 2A. The third panel shows the difference in listing between defaults and variables on each trial for the experimental group, while the bottom panel provides the corresponding index for the control group.

the stimulus. Such refocusing is conducive to finding previously unnoticed, correlated attributes of the stimuli, leading the model to attend to features that might form a basis for learning more differentiated subcategories.

Experiment 3 was similar to Experiment 2 except that instead of two contrasting categories, four categories of exemplars were presented in blocked sequence. Instances of the first insect category—call it A1—were presented for the first 10 trials, followed by 10 A2 instances, then 10 B1s, and 10 B2s. Each insect varied in eight attributes. The default values characterizing the four categories can be denoted as follows: A1 = 111111XX, A2 = 111222YY, B1 = 222333QQ, and B2 = 222444RR, where X, Y, Q, and R denote different pairs of values of variable attributes occurring in each of the four categories. The superordinate defaults (A vs. B) occur on the first three attributes, whereas the subordinate defaults are defined by the values of the fourth, fifth, and sixth attributes. (The blocked sequence was intented to facilitate the learning of the category discriminations in this initial demonstration experiment; later studies can examine the boundary conditions of such learning.) For testing purposes, following the four training blocks, a mixed block was finally presented in which instances of all four categories were presented in random sequence. (A control condition was also included; subjects in this group received stimuli constructed from random combinations of the two-, four-, and eight-valued attributes). The listing task was similar to those of previous experiments, except that subjects were explicitly told to limit the number of features listed by imagining that each listed feature would cost them 25 cents, whereas each incorrect identification (based on their lists) on a final recognition test would cost them one dollar.

Turning to the results, the pattern of responding generally conformed to the model's predictions (see Fig. 7). For superordinate defaults (top panel of Fig. 7), listing decreased from 49 to 9% as successive A1 instances were encountered, and decreased further during the A2 block. This decreasing trend occurred for 10 of 11 subjects, and was significant at the .01 level by a sign test. Presenting the first A2 instance caused an abrupt drop in listing from a low level of around 9% to near zero. This drop may reflect attentional competition at this point, since the surprising features of the first A2 instance may have shaken subjects out of a routine pattern of listing some A defaults unnecessarily. A 15% increase in listing of superordinate de-

Fig. 7.   Percent listing of superordinate defaults, subordinate defaults, and variables from Experiment 3.

Superordinate Defaults

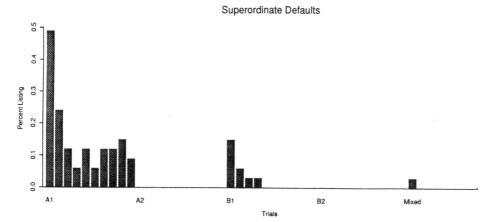

Subordinate Defaults

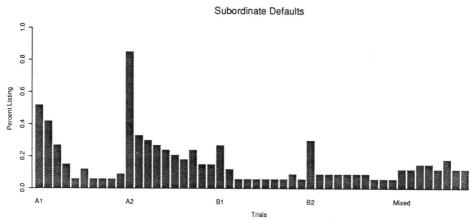

Variables

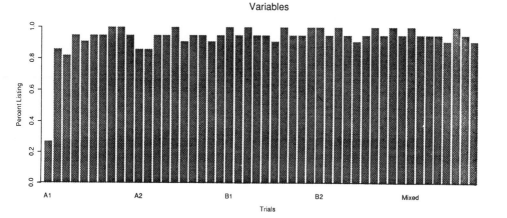

faults was then observed on the first B1 instance [marginally significant, $t(10) = 2.18$, $p < .10$], followed by a rapid decline back to the zero baseline [$t(10) = 2.23$, $p < .05$]. Listings did not increase significantly on the first trial of the mixed block [$t(10) = 1.0$, $p > .20$]; this indicates that subjects had learned stable discriminations at the superordinate level during the earlier training blocks.

Listings for subordinate defaults were also consistent with the model (see middle panel of Fig. 7). Listings declined significantly from 52 to 9% over trials for the A1 category [$t(10) = 4.31$, $p < .01$] and then increased sharply on the first instance of each of the following categories. These increases were statistically significant for A2 [from 9 to 85%, $t(10) = 11.69$, $p < .001$] and B2 [6 to 30%, $t(10) = 2.66$, $p < .05$], but not for B1 [15 to 27% $t(10) = 1.31$, $p > .20$]. The lack of significance for B1 may have been due to the fact that defaults at both levels (attributes 1–6) shifted on this trial, and this competition may have reduced the number of defaults at each level that might otherwise have been reported. As expected, on the first trial of the mixed block, reporting of default values did not increase [$t(10) = 1.49$, $p > .10$]. Moreover, listing of these values by this time was 80% lower than listing of variable attributes [$t(10) = 17.53$, $p < .001$]. Throughout the mixed block, listing of defaults was far lower than that of comparable four-valued attributes in the random control group [by 62%, $t(7) = 9.59$, $p < .001$].

Thus, subjects seem to have learned stable discriminations at both the superordinate and subordinate levels. Moreover, subjects apparently transferred superordinate defaults learned for A1 to A2, and for B1 to B2, since no increase in listing of superordinate values was observed when instances of the latter subordinate categories were first introduced. The only unexpected result was the higher listing of variable attributes than of default violations on the first trial of the later blocks (B1 and B2). Possibly subjects developed a fixed routine of listing selected variable attributes during these early blocks and simply continued this routine into later blocks. Since the variable attributes were uniquely identifying in this experiment (i.e., variable values predicted categorization since a different pair of values were used for each category), such selection would be a reasonable listing strategy.

Setting aside this small discrepancy, the results clearly show that subjects could learn without supervision to distinguish multiple categories in a hierarchically organized domain. More research will be required to characterize details of how this knowledge is organized in subjects' memories, and to identify the boundary conditions and major variables that influence such learning.

E. EXPERIMENT 4: SIMILARITY RELATED TO
   ATTRIBUTE SALIENCE

A basic assumption of our approach is that attentional salience will be controlled by informativeness. Subjects' patterns of attribute listings in the preceding experiments could be interpreted as an index of attentional salience, but subjects in those experiments were directly instructed to report the most discriminating features of the instances. While subjects' listings provide a good record of changes in their beliefs about a category, it is not obvious that they provide an index of salience that would generalize to other situations. A more valid measure of attentional salience per se might be provided by people's judgments of the similarity of two patterns from the same general class. In applying our model to predict similarity ratings, we will assume that presented stimulus pairs are first encoded into working memory, and that these working memory representations constitute the input to the comparison process. Because informative features are expected to have high salience in such memory representations, they should exert a strong effect on ratings of similarity. In general, subjects' judgments of how similar two patterns are should be dominated by the instances' variable or exceptional features, whereas category defaults should have little impact on subjects' comparisons.

The hypothesis that learning category defaults reduces their impact on similarity judgments leads to the seemingly paradoxical implication that two instances of a category may become more dissimilar as people become increasingly familiar with that category. A moment's thought reveals that this is actually a commonplace phenomenon associated with expertise: people who become very expert about a particular domain (e.g., expert botanists, wine tasters, dog-show judges, etc.) become highly sensitive to differences among the objects in that domain while taking for granted their well-known commonalities. For instance, a black oak and a red oak are much less alike to an expert botanist than they are to most nonexperts. In fact, people's tendency to take for granted what they know about a general domain and to focus attention on the novel aspects of instances is probably what allows experts to discover progressively more specific subcategories within that domain. It may also be a powerful factor that promotes perceptual learning, i.e., improvements in perceptual judgments and discriminations that accompany experience in a given domain (see e.g., Gibson, 1963, 1969).

Another implication of this analysis is that when an instance violates a default expectation of its category, that violation should be highly salient and have a strong impact on similarity. We can use this hypothesis to predict circumstances in which *decreasing* the number of common features shared by two stimuli leads paradoxically to *increased* similarity—an implication in direct contradiction to results ordinarily obtained in similarity experiments (e.g., Gati & Tversky, 1984). If presence and absence are conceptualized as two alternative values of a binary attribute, then as one value occurs more frequently within a category, its informativeness is decreased whereas the informativeness of the other value is increased. Thus, the absence of a highly expected default from a given instance should appear more informative than its presence. If this surprising absence occurred in two instances being judged for similarity, it would have the paradoxical effect of increasing the salience of their "common" features. By similar reasoning, deleting a default feature from one instance but not from another would result in an unusually salient difference between them, greatly reducing the similarity between the exceptional and unexceptional instances.

The experiment to test these implications consisted of a series of similarity judgments in which college student subjects rated the similarity of pairs of instances on a 20-point scale. The stimuli were realistic line drawings of fictitious insects ("bugs"), similar to those used in the attribute listing experiments described above. Several features (e.g., wings, tails, antennae) could be added or removed to construct different instances. Two of these features were consistently presented in all instances (defaults), and two others were presented half the time (variables); in addition, instances were varied along several other attributes to increase the perceived variability of the category. We expected that after having seen several pairs of bugs (with no category feedback whatever), subjects would learn structural norms for the consistently correlated features, treating them as a category of stimuli. These norms would specify which features were correlated (expected defaults) and which tended to vary across instances. In the midst of this uniform training series, stimulus pairs were occasionally presented in which one or both insects violated the category expectations; such bugs would either be missing an expected default or possess an extra feature not seen in any of the other instances. We were interested in how subjects would rate the similarity of two bugs that were deviant in the same way, in contrast to the way subjects rated matched, "normal" pairs of bugs.

As expected, the results showed that subjects' expectations influenced their similarity judgments. However, violations of defaults had a much larger effect when they served as distinctive features (differences) than when they served as common features. As predicted, pairs in which one member was missing an expected feature (or in which a previously unencountered feature was added) were rated significantly less similar than pairs that differed by a variable feature. To illustrate, if one insect had wings and the other did not, the effect of this difference on perceived similarity was greater if subjects expected all instances to have wings (2.60 points) than if they expected wings to be present or absent equally often (1.42 points); the difference between these two effects was statistically significant [$t(21) = 3.20$, $p < .01$]. However, contrary to predictions, when both test instances were missing an expected feature, their similarity was *not* increased by this shared anomaly; such pairs with missing defaults were rated as equally similar as pairs in which the defaults were present [$t(21) = 0.48$, $p > .50$]. To illustrate, if wings were an expected default, then two bugs that had wings were rated as similar as two bugs that did not. But for subjects who learned wings as a variable feature, pairs that shared this attribute appeared slightly more similar (by 0.22 point) than pairs in which it was absent [$t(21) = 2.84$, $p < .01$].

Although these results clearly showed that subjects' category norms influenced their judgments, we were disappointed that pairs lacking expected defaults were not rated as more similar than normal pairs. Perhaps this was due to subjects' weighing distinctive features more than common features in their pairwise similarity judgments [over six times as much, $t(21) = 10.80$, $p < .001$]. This greater weighting of distinctive features is the typical result with pictorial stimuli (see Gati & Tversky, 1984). Indeed, subjects' reports (and other data) indicated that most of our subjects were computing similarity of two bugs by simply counting the features that *differed* between the bugs, and largely ignoring their common features. Such a difference-counting strategy would, of course, wash out the impact of our manipulation of common features. To circumvent this strategy, we designed a second study in which we could pursue the "common deviation" effect in a situation that minimized those strategic factors that mitigated its appearance in Experiment 4.

F. Experiment 5: Similarity of Memorized Instances

In this experiment, subjects were asked to rate from memory the similarity of instances, given only verbal labels designating the bugs they had learned earlier. We expected this modified procedure to have several advantages over similarity ratings of explicitly displayed instances. First, due to memory limitations it should be more difficult for subjects to use an artificial, attribute-by-attribute, differencing strategy, as they apparently did in Experiment 4. Instead, subjects should be more likely to make their ratings intuitively, from a wholistic impression of the instances' similarity. Second, because people's memories of instances tends to be dominated by their unusual, unexpected features, similarity judgments from memory may be more influenced by such exceptional features than would judgments of displayed stimuli. Third, comparisons from memory are arguably more natural and interesting in some respects than comparisons between displayed instances. Similarity in memory is probably an important factor controlling categorization, spontaneous remindings across separate episodes (see Ross, 1984; Schank, 1982), and the formation of novel subcategories based on informative commonalities between specific instances (Malt, 1989).

This experiment consisted of two phases. In Phase 1, subjects learned to associate a specific label (a CVC nonsense syllable) with each of 10 instances from a single category of insects. The insects were constructed from the same materials used in Experiment 4. For each subject, eight of the presented instances possessed a target default value, whereas this value was absent from the remaining two instances. To balance stimulus-specific effects, four different stimulus sets were constructed and presented to different groups of subjects. Each set had a different default feature that was absent from 2 of the 10 instances. Thus, the influence on similarity judgments of presence vs. absence of a default feature was compared for four defaults across the experiment as a whole. Subjects were taught the names of the 10 instances by a cued recall procedure. They were first shown a given stimulus, were asked to label it, and were then told its correct label. This training continued until subjects could correctly name all the instances, or until they had completed 20 cycles through the 10 instances.

In Phase 2, subjects rated the similarity of specific pairs of insects learned earlier, referred to only by their CVC labels. Ratings were made on a 20-point scale, where 1 indicated very low similarity and 20 indicated very high similarity. Two of these pairs referred to the two deviant instances that were lacking a given target default. For each such target pair, another pair was presented that was identical to the target pair except that the target default was present in both instances. Several filler pairs were also included, which varied in their number of mismatching attributes. If subjects were attending to the task and rating similarity in a manner consistent with previous research, pairs would be rated as more similar the fewer the differences between the two insects.

As predicted, the results showed that increasing the number of mismatching attributes in a pair reduced similarity, $t(16) = 10.42$, $p < .01$. Each mismatch between the two members of a pair decreased their rated similarity by an average of 3.52 points on the 20-point scale. Thus, the effects of mismatching attributes demonstrated that the rating-from-memory procedure produced an overall pattern of results comparable to those found in standard similarity experiments.

The more interesting data concern the similarity of pairs for which the default attribute is absent. As predicted, removing a default from both members of a pair increased their rated similarity by an average of 3.35 points above the rating given to control pairs in which that default value was present—a statistically significant effect, $t(16) = 2.67, p < .02$. Thus, the predicted effect of surprising attribute values (absence in this case) on similarity was confirmed by these data.

One difficulty with the similarity-from memory procedure, however, is that it is not clear to what extent outcomes reflect the way in which instances are *encoded* during the training phase, in contrast to the way in which they are later retrieved and *compared* during the similarity rating phase. For example, our model predicts that subjects would learn each instance by recording its category membership and then learning mainly features that are highly informative with respect to that category (i.e., variables and missing defaults). However, if subjects focused on absent defaults in learning the unusual instances, they might have allocated correspondingly less attention to the variable features of these instances (relative to the amount of attention these features would receive in normal instances). In fact, subjects need not have learned all the variable features of the unusual instances, since the necessary discriminations could have been acquired by learning only the absent default plus a single variable feature to distinguish between the two unusual instances. Thus, it is not clear whether the greater similarity of pairs sharing an absent default was due to the greater salience of this unusual value at the time of comparison or to fewer differences between the pair members available from memory.

One way to eliminate this ambiguity would be to use a training procedure that forced subjects to learn *all* the features of each instance sufficiently well to ensure that they would be available from memory during the similarity ratings. This could be accomplished by using a training procedure in which subjects recalled all the features of instances when cued with their names, rather than the reverse, recalling the name to the presented bug, as in the present experiment. Such a modification would force subjects to learn all the features of each instance. If later similarity ratings still showed an effect of shared absence, it could not be explained by fewer differences between the unusual pairs available from memory. If the shared-absence effect was eliminated by such a learning regimen, then shared absence would be considered an encoding effect rather than reflecting comparison strategies per se. But because such encoding biases are assumed to influence much of people's learning of real-world stimuli, they could indirectly affect many phenomena related to similarity, such as remindings, the discovery of new subcategories, and generalization of learning. Our model is quite compatible with an encoding explanation as well as a salience-in-comparison explanation of the shared-absence effect.

G. EXPERIMENT 6: INSTANCES STORED IN RELATION
TO CATEGORIES

The aim of the next experiment was to study the impact of a category schema on learning and memory performance in processing specific instances. According to our theory, people should be biased to record into memory new instances of a well-known category by learning primarily their informative features, while bypassing their uninformative defaults. By storing the two types of features at separate locations in memory (defaults associated with the schema, nondefaults with individual instances), the two feature bundles would not interfere with each other's retrieval. Presumably, such learning benefits are a major reason that experts in a given domain can process and remember stimuli in that domain much more efficiently than nonexperts (e.g., Chase & Simon, 1973; de Groot, 1965, 1966).

The experiment conducted to demonstrate these advantages due to schema-based encoding consisted of three phases. In Phase 1, subjects were pretrained on the features characteristic of several categories. The categories were types of astronomical stars, supposedly differentiated by their chemical compositions. That is, a category (e.g., blue stars, red stars) was coordinated with a list of chemical elements characteristically found in that type of star. Attempting to simulate the easy command people have of their knowledge of everyday categories, we trained subjects on these feature lists until they could remember them very easily. In Phase 2, the subjects learned several named instances of each category (stars such as Rigel and Vela). These named instances were described solely in terms of their chemical constituents, which contained all the features true of the general category to which they belonged, plus one or more variable features distinctive to that instance. The number of default features in a given category (two to four) was orthogonally varied along with the number of extra variable features attributed to particular instances (one or three). In Phase 3, subjects were tested on their knowledge of (1) the features associated with particular named instances and (2) the categories to which such instances belonged. The testing was a speeded verification task, in which instance questions (e.g., "Rigel contains hydrogen") had to be judged *true* or *false* as rapidly as possible while maintaining accuracy. Reaction times were the major dependent measure of interest.

Our main predictions were based on the familiar "fan effect" (see Anderson, 1976), which implies that the more features associated with the tested instance, the longer subjects should take to verify any particular one. The predictions can be easily understood by referring to Fig. 8, which illustrates two possible memory organizations in terms of an associative network notation. In Fig. 8B, the categorization of the instances is directly

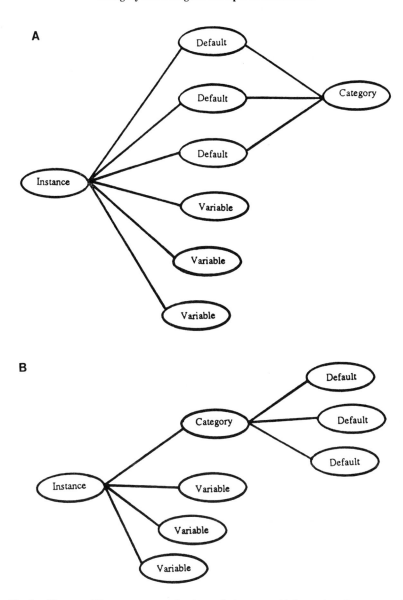

Fig. 8. Two possible memory organizations relating general information about categories to specific information about instances.

encoded, but no direct associations have been formed between the instances and the category defaults. However, those defaults are still accessible from the instances via indirect retrieval (inference) through the category. The key predictions of this model concern the effects of the number (fan) of default vs. variable features on verifying variable-feature probes. Because of the partitioning of subnodes in Fig. 8B, the number of defaults should exert no fan effects on the retrievability of instance-to-variable feature associations. By contrast, the time to verify a variable feature should increase with the fan of variable features associated to the instance.

Figure 8A shows an alternative hypothesis that assumes that subjects store common features of the category redundantly and directly with each of its instances. This is a necessary assumption of pure exemplar-storage models, which assume that people represent category knowledge merely by storing instances and then compute generalizations about the category from those instances as needed. In such a representation, default properties of a category could only be inferred if they were stored in a large proportion of its memorized instances. According to this hypothesis, category defaults will be directly associated with the instance, so they should produce fan effects on verifying variable features. That is, increasing default fan should cause the same slowdown in verifying variable features as would increasing variable fan, in contrast to the segregated organization illustrated in Fig. 8B.

Turning to the reaction time results, a robust fan effect on verifying variable features was demonstrated as a function of the fan of variable features associated with the tested instance. That is, the time to verify an instance-to-variable feature question increased in the predicted manner with the instance's number of variable features [$F(1, 14) = 28.56$, $p < .0001$]. However, the number of default features inherited from the category had no significant effect on the speed with which variable-feature probes were verified [$F(2, 28) = 0.84$, $p > .25$]. It is remarkable that increasing the number of category defaults produced an insignificant slowdown in retrieving variable features because these defaults were verified at least as fast as the variable features, and hence (according to the theory in Fig. 8A) should have produced equally strong interference if they had been directly associated with the instances. In a direct comparison, the 588-msec variable fan effect on verifying variable features was reliably greater than the nonsignificant 215-msec default fan effect, $t(14) = 2.27$, $p < .05$ (reaction times to confirm variable features averaged 2634 msec in this experiment). Moreover, greater default fan did not significantly slow down recognition of instance-to-default probes [$F(2, 28) = 0.98$, $p > .25$], whereas increasing variable fan did slow down recognition of the instance-to-default probes [$F(1, 14) = 5.94$, $p < .05$], further confirming the dissociation between default and variable fan effects. Also, subjects were over 800 msec faster to verify the categorization of instances than either instance-to-category feature or instance-to-variable feature probes [$F(2, 28) = 36.70$, $p < .0001$], even though they had never been explicitly taught this information. This result suggests that subjects noticed, rehearsed, and made strong use of category membership in encoding the original instance information, as predicted.

The results of this experiment are consistent with the assumption that people can learn summary models of categories, and that these models play a strong role in determining the encoding of instances and their organization in memory. The results are incompatible with extreme versions of exemplar-storage theories, which assume that both default and variable features are stored together in association with specific instances (see Fig. 8A). In addition, the results validate the utility of the fan effect technique for investigating issues related to the abstraction and organization of category knowledge.

H. EXPERIMENT 7: DEFAULTS IMPROVE LEARNING OF VARIABLES

Experiment 6 provided evidence that people encoded instances in terms of their category membership, which would have produced the memory structure depicted in Fig. 8B, rather than recording a full listing of their features, which would have created the structure depicted in Fig. 8A. But the subjects in that experiment were directly taught the generalizations they had to know for later use. It is important to check whether similar encoding processes occur when the general schemas are being learned concurrently with the instances. Therefore, a second memory task was developed to observe how people learn and apply category models for themselves, using only instances without prior explicit category training. In this experiment, subjects induced for themselves the shared properties that defined categories of stimuli. We then examined the organization of the resulting memory and how the categories were used for encoding new instances.

The procedure involved presenting a training instance on each trial on a CRT screen. An instance consisted of a series of letters; for example, a particular instance might contain the letters B, D, Q, and N. This feature list remained on the computer screen for a brief period (1 sec per feature) during which the subject was asked to study and try to memorize it. After this brief study period, the letter string disappeared from the screen and was followed by a short distractor task to reduce short-term memory. This distractor task consisted of a single arithmetic problem (e.g., 8 + 7 = ?), which subjects solved in their heads and then answered on the computer terminal keyboard. Following the distractor task, the subject tried to free-recall in any order all of the letters in the most recently studied list. Recall was recorded by the subject typing the letters on the terminal keyboard in any order.

The training instances (letter sequences) fell into three distinct categories, two of which were characterized by correlated elements and the third of which was a "junk category" consisting of randomly generated sequences of different lengths. For the two categories with correlated features, there was a specific set of letters that consistently appeared in the same positions in every instance, with different consistent letters for each category. As in Experiment 6, the fans of default and variable elements were independently manipulated across different instances. Instances of one category had three consistent default letters while instances of the other category had four defaults. In addition to the default letters, each instance contained either one or two extra, variable letters. For purposes of comparison, an equal number of randomly constructed control stimuli were presented as a junk category. These control stimuli were matched with those from the correlational categories in their number of letters but had neither of the default letter clusters. Subjects were not told which category each instance belonged to, or even that there were separate categories in the experiment.

The training instances and categories in this experiment were designed in a similar manner to those in the previous experiments, except that the stimuli were letter strings rather than pictures of objects (insects) or lists of verbal descriptors. Letter string stimuli allow subjects to conveniently record their instance memories on the computer keyboard. From the perspective of our model, the use of letter strings as stimuli should make little difference because they are as easily described in terms of attributes (serial positions) and values (the specific letters appearing at each position) as other types of category materials. Moreover, categories are characterized in exactly the same way as in previous studies, namely, in terms of intercorrelated, mutually predictable features. Furthermore, letter sequences have often been used as materials in standard studies of classification learning (e.g., Bower & Trabasso, 1964; Hunt, 1962; Rosch & Mervis, 1975), and generally behave much the same as other types of stimuli used in artificial category experiments.

We expected that after repeated experience with the training instances, subjects would learn which groups of features consistently co-occurred across instances. Once an instance was recognized as containing a familiar cluster of correlated features, i.e., as belonging to the category characterized by those default features, subjects could concentrate on encoding the unpredictable variables while retaining their ability to recall the defaults. By contrast, if subjects did not learn the correlational patterns, the defaults would not be predictable, so that instances from the correlational categories should be remembered the same as control instances of the same length.

Turning to the results, as expected, subjects showed significantly better memory for the features of category members (89% correct recall) than for control stimuli of the same length [81% recall, t (51) = 10.49, $p < .0001$]. This result clearly showed that subjects were able to induce category level knowledge and use it to improve their memory performance.

Technically, any difference in recall between the control stimuli and instances of the correlational categories could be taken as evidence of some degree of category acquisition. However, the major difference between the two theories depicted in Fig. 8 is the predicted effect of category learning on memory for an instance's *variable* features—those that cannot be directly recovered from defaults of the category. The model depicted in Fig. 8A predicts that category learning will not improve memory for variable features, relative to the control condition. This full-storage theory implies only that the subject can reconstruct the instance's category defaults from general knowledge at the time of testing, thus improving memory for those defaults. In contrast, the schema-encoding theory depicted in Fig. 8B does predict better memory for variable features because once the category defaults are learned the subject can attend more to variable features during encoding. In addition, the variable features stored with each instance should suffer less competition from other features during the memory retrieval process. In accordance with the schema-encoding theory, our subjects showed significantly better recall for variable features of category members (85%) than for the corresponding features of control stimuli [80%, $t(51) = 4.68$, $p < .0001$].

The schema theory also predicts that increasing the number of variable features in the instances (from one to two) should increase the overall difficulty of learning an instance more than would increasing its number of defaults by the same amount (from three to four). This prediction arises because variable features require more attention than default features during encoding, thus reducing attentional resources available to encode the remaining features of the instances. Consistent with this prediction, adding a variable feature reduced overall recall by an average of about 4%, significantly more than the 1% reduction due to adding a default feature, $t(12) = 2.71$, $p < .05$.

The results of this experiment support the schema hypothesis that people learn instances in terms of a category model. The results are consistent with those from Experiment 6, which showed that variable features were encoded mainly as distinctive properties of specific instances whereas defaults were stored with the generic schema for a given category. They provide further evidence against pure exemplar-storage models which assume that subjects must encode and store both the default and variable properties of category members. Furthermore, the success of the experimental task provides opportunities for detailed investigation of the structure of these category models, how they are learned, and the strategies by which they are applied.

I. EXPERIMENT 8: VARYING RELIABILITY OF DEFAULTS

In most realistic learning situations, the data on which learners must base their generalizations contain errors and exceptions. Many beliefs about natural categories are violated by specific instances. For example, the ability to fly is a default property of birds in general, but several birds (e.g., ostriches, kiwis, penguins) violate this default. The notion that natural categories can be defined in terms of necessary and sufficient features has come under vigorous attack (see Rosch, 1975, 1977; Smith & Medin, 1981), and the view that categories are "fuzzy" with probabilistic features has been promoted. Therefore, it is important to ask whether the outcomes of our previous experiments would hold for situations in which category defaults occurred with moderate to high degrees of unreliability. The purpose of the following experiment was to study peoples' ability to learn and apply schemas based on "noisy" input data, for which generalizations would be somewhat unreliable in that usually consistent features would sometimes be replaced or missing from particular instances.

A recall procedure similar to that in Experiment 7 was used. The stimuli were sequences of six letters; each position in the sequence can be thought of as an attribute, and the letters filling that position serve as the alternative values of the attribute. Three possible letters could occur at a given position, providing 3^6 possible stimulus patterns. On each trial, subjects were presented with a single instance (six-letter string) for a brief study period, followed by a 15-sec distractor task to reduce short-term memory (adding or subtracting digits from a running total). They then tried to recall in any order the six letters presented on that trial. Each subject was presented with instances of a single category, characterized by both consistent and variable attributes. For the consistent attributes, one value occurred more frequently than the other two; this was the modal (default) value of that feature. In contrast, all three values of the variable attributes occurred equally often. The major independent variables were (1) the probability of the modal value of the default attributes (60, 70, 80, or 90%)

and (2) the ratio of default to variable attributes characterizing the concept (four defaults and two variables vs. two defaults and four variables). A control condition was also included in which all six attributes were completely variable. Thus, a total of nine conditions were tested in a between-subjects experiment design. The subjects were 227 Air Force recruits from Lackland Air Force Base, who were randomly assigned to nine experimental groups.

We were interested in how default reliability, and the ratio of default to variable attributes, would affect people's ability to learn and apply default schemas. We predicted that subjects would be able to learn such schemas even when they were fairly unreliable (i.e., at lower levels of default probability and default/variable ratios). However, the degree to which subjects could use the schema to improve their learning of its instances should depend on several factors. First, the proportion of attributes with strong defaults should determine how much attentional capacity can be allocated to encode the remaining, nondefault values. Second, as the probability of a category's defaults is decreased, their strength in the category norms also declines. As a result, their perceived informativeness will increase, attracting more attention. This increases competition for attention among the other features, reducing the benefits of schema abstraction for recall. Third, the poorer the fit of an instance to its schema, i.e., the more exceptions it contains, the less the schema will facilitate learning of that instance. Each exception draws more attention than the default it replaced, increasing its share in the competition for attentional resources. To summarize these considerations, the schema theory predicts that performance should be highest for subjects whose instances display the highest level of predictability (i.e., instances with no exceptions, a high ratio of defaults to variables, and default values occurring with 90% probability), and performance should decrease as predictability is decreased. The poorest performance should occur, of course, for control subjects who see only randomly generated letter strings.

The results of Experiment 8 strongly supported these implications. Taking the highest predictability group as a reference standard, all three independent variables significantly affected recall. Increasing the number of exceptions per instance significantly decreased the recall of both variable and default features [$F(2, 424) = 12.35$, $p < .01$, $F(1, 212) = 25.39$, $p < .01$, respectively; see Fig. 9, left panel]. The higher the default probability, the higher the recall of variable features [$F(4, 60) = 8.65$, $p < .01$] and defaults [$F(4, 60) = 11.56$, $p < .01$; see Fig. 9, right panel]. The ratio of the number of defaults to variable features also affected average recall. When default values were 90% reliable, variable features were recalled 10% better in the high-ratio condition than in the corresponding low-ratio

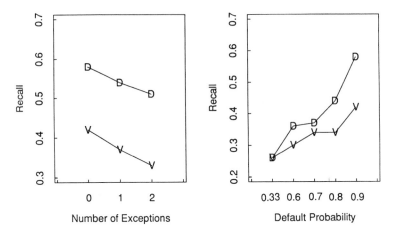

Fig. 9.   Two graphs illustrating the effects of the number of exceptions (left) and default probability (right) on recall of defaults (D) and variables (V). For both graphs, the reference standard is the zero exceptions, 90% probability, high default-to-variable ratio condition. The graphs show the effects of manipulating number of exceptions and default probability; the remaining factors are held constant for each graph.

condition [$t(24) = 2.42, p < .05$]; defaults were also recalled about 10% better in the high-ratio group [$t(24) = 1.97, p < .10$]. As predicted, the data indicate that subjects learned default expectations and used them to facilitate recall even for noisy input data. For example, although recall of defaults in the high-ratio groups declined with decreasing default probability, even the 60% group showed evidence of improved recall due to schema learning relative to the control group that saw only random letter sequences [a 10% difference, $F(21) = 1.91, p < .10$].

These results confirm several predictions of the schema model and show its applicability to categories with probabilistic features. The fact that variable features as well as defaults were better recalled at high levels of predictability suggests that category knowledge had a top-down influence on encoding process beyond simply helping subjects to guess default values on the recall test (see discussion in Experiment 7). The results are incompatible with strictly bottom-up learning theories, such as pure exemplar storage models.

VI.   Concluding Comments

Overall, the studies yielded results highly consistent with the proposed theoretical framework. The attribute-listing experiments revealed patterns of unsupervised learning characterized by initial discovery of categories based on featural contrasts with previous default expectations, gradual learning of defaults within a new category, and an overall bias to report informative (exceptional and variable) features of the instances. The task also reveals the distinct stages in learning categories in hierarchical domains. Norms about a prior source category transferred to new derivative categories when they were applicable. The attribute-listing task shows promise as a useful paradigm within which unsupervised learning can be studied in complex, hierarchically organized domains, and in which detailed theories may be tested and refined.

The similarity experiments provided independent confirmation of the proposed attentional biases toward surprising features. In particular, the similarity-from-memory procedure appears promising for investigating factors determining perceived informativeness. Such tasks may provide greater insights into comparative judgments themselves, by suggesting constraints regarding the representation of stimuli in such tasks.

The memory studies provide further support for the model's attentional assumptions, and explicate their impact on encoding processes, organization of category and instance information in memory, and later retrieval of facts about instances. The results of those experiments disconfirm an assumption of simple exemplar storage theories, i.e., that both predictable defaults and informative nondefaults are encoded together as properties of individual instances. In concert with our earlier tasks, the memory paradigms may prove useful for investigating fundamental issues related to domain expertise and its cognitive benefits. The results of such experiments also suggest how people's prior stereotypes influence their processing of and memory for events and objects they encounter.

We have attempted to sketch a general model of learning that describes the abstraction of observations into general concepts and then the utilization of these concepts to encode later instances. Since top-down (conceptually driven) and bottom-up (data-driven) components are closely intertwined in human learning, this approach has some advantages compared to strictly bottom-up or top-down approaches. Equally important as our specific theoretical formulation are the general methods or paradigms developed to investigate an important set of new issues. For example, unsupervised learning, especially in multilevel domains, has been little investigated in previous research; also little prior research has analytically examined schema-based effects on new instance learning by synthesizing and manipulating schematic knowledge in the laboratory.

Many extensions of the methods discussed may be suggested. For example, variants of the attribute-listing task could provide further converging observations of unsupervised learning and shifts in attentional biases under various task constraints. Variants might include (1) asking subjects to rate directly the surprisingness or distinctiveness of each attribute on each trial; (2) recording how much time a person devotes to looking at each instance and correlating this with the number of informative values the instance contains; (3) using text descriptions of the instances, recording line-by-line reading times, and relating those to the predicted informativeness of each statement with respect to a general schema; or (4) requiring two subjects to communicate with one another about successive instances (Krauss & Weinheimer, 1966) and noting how their referential descriptions of stimuli change as they acquire shared knowledge of the stimulus defaults. But confining ourselves to the present set of tasks, we have only begun to investigate many relevant variables, such as interference among related categories and variations in feature distributions, that could provide further tests of our model of unsupervised learning. Such issues should provide fruitful topics for future investigation.

ACKNOWLEDGMENTS

This research was supported by the Air Force Office of Scientific Research Grant #87-0282. We express our appreciation to the personnel at the Air Force's Learning Abilities Measurement Program (LAMP) at Brooks Air Force Base in San Antonio, Texas, for the use of their facilities and subject pool in running several of these experiments.

REFERENCES

Anderson, J. R. (1976). *Language, memory, and thought*. Hillsdale, NJ: Erlbaum.
Anderson, J. R. (1983). A spreading activation theory of memory. *Journal of Verbal Learning and Verbal Behavior, 22*, 261–295.
Billman, D., & Heit, E. (1988). Observational learning from internal feedback: A simulation of an adaptive learning method. *Cognitive Science, 12*, 587–625.
Bower, G. H., Black, J. B., & Turner, T. J. (1979). Scripts in memory for the text. *Cognitive Psychology, 11*, 177–220.
Bower, G. H., & Trabasso, T. R. (1964). Concept identification. In R. C. Atkinson (Ed.), *Studies in mathematical psychology* (pp. 32–94). Stanford, CA: Stanford University Press.
Bruner, J. S., Goodnow, J. J., & Austin, G. A. (1956). *A study of thinking*. New York: Wiley.
Cantor, N., & Mischel, W. (1979). Prototypes in person perception. In L. Berkowitz (Ed.), *Advances in experimental social psychology* (Vol. 12). New York: Academic Press.
Chase, W. G., & Simon, H. A. (1973). The mind's eye in chess. In W. G. Chase (Ed.), *Visual information processing*. New York: Academic Press.
Craik, K. (1943). *The nature of explanation*. Cambridge, UK: Cambridge University Press.
de Groot, A. D. (1965). *Thought and choice in chess*. Mouton: The Hague.
de Groot, A. D. (1966). Perception and memory versus thought. In B. Kleinmuntz (Ed.), *Problem-solving*. New York: Wiley.
Gati I., & Tversky, A. (1984). Weighting common and distinctive features in perceptual and conceptual judgements. *Cognitive Psychology, 16*, 341–370.

Gentner, D., & Stevens, A. L. (1983). *Mental Models.* Hillsdale, NJ: Erlbaum.

Gibson, E. J. (1963). Perceptual learning. *Annual Review of Psychology, 14,* 29–56.

Gibson, E. J. (1969). *Principles of perceptual learning and development.* New York: Appleton.

Grice, P. H. (1975). Logic and conversation. In P. Cole & J. L. Morgan (Eds.), *Studies in syntax* (Vol. 3) New York: Academic Press.

Hintzman, D. L. (1986). Schema abstraction in a multiple trace memory model. *Psychological Review, 93,* 411–428.

Holland, J. H., Holyoak, K. J., Nisbett, R. E., & Thagard, P. R. (1986). *Induction: Processes of inference, learning, and discovery.* Cambridge, MA: MIT Press.

Holstein, S. B., & Premack, D. (1965). On the different effects of random reinforcement and presolution reversal on human concept identification. *Journal of Experimental Psychology, 70,* 335–337.

Hume, D. (1960). *A treatise of human nature.* Oxford: Claredon Press. (Original work published 1748).

Hunt, E. B. (1962). *Concept learning: An information processing problem.* New York: Wiley.

Johnson-Laird, P. N. (1983). *Mental models: Towards a cognitive science of language, inference, and consciousness.* Cambridge, MA: Harvard University.

Kant, I. (1963). *Critique of pure reason.* New York: Macmillan/St. Martin's Press. (Original edition 1787)

Krauss, R. M., & Weinheimer, S. (1966). Concurrent feedback, confirmation, and the encoding of referents in verbal communication. *Journal of Personality and Social Psychology, 4,* 343–346.

Malt, B. C. (1989). An online investigation of prototype and exemplar strategies in classification. *Journal of Experimental Psychology: Learning, Memory, and Cognition, 15,* 539–555.

Medin, D. L., & Schaffer, M. M. (1978). A context theory of classification learning. *Psychological Review, 85,* 207–238.

Millward, R. B. (1971). Theoretical and experimental approaches to human learning. In J. W. Kling & L. A. Riggs (Eds.), *Experimental psychology* (3rd ed., pp. 905–1017,). New York: Holt, Rinehart & Winston.

Murphy, G. L., & Smith, E. E. (1982). Basic level superiority in picture categorization. *Journal of Verbal Learning and Verbal Behavior, 21,* 1–20.

Posner, M. I., & Keele, S. W. (1968). On the genesis of abstract ideas. *Journal of Experimental Psychology, 77,* 353–363.

Posner, M. I., & Keele, S. W. (1970). Retention of abstract ideas. *Journal of Experimental Psychology, 83,* 304–308.

Reder, L. M., & Ross, B. H. (1983). Integrated knowledge in different tasks: The role of retrieval strategy on fan effects. *Journal of Experimental Psychology: Learning, Memory, and Cognition, 9,* 55–72.

Rosch, E. (1975). Cognitive representation of semantic categories. *Journal of Experimental Psychology: General, 104,* 192–233.

Rosch, E. (1977). Human categorization. In N. Warren (Ed.), *Advances in cross cultural psychology* (Vol. 1). New York: Academic Press.

Rosch, E., & Mervis, C. B. (1975). Family resemblance studies in the internal structure of categories. *Cognitive Psychology, 7,* 573–605.

Ross, B. H. (1984). Remindings and their effects in learning a cognitive skill. *Cognitive Psychology, 16,* 371–416.

Rumelhart, D. E., & Ortony, A. (1977). The representation of knowledge in memory. In R. C.

Anderson, R. J. Spiro, & W. E. Montague (Eds.), *Schooling and the acquisition of knowledge*. Hillsdale, NJ: Erlbaum.

Schank, R. C. (1982). *Dynamic memory*. Cambridge, UK: Cambridge University Press.

Schank, R. C., & Abelson, R. P. (1978). *Scripts, plans, goals, and understanding: An inquiry into human knowledge structures*. Hillsdale, NJ: Erlbaum.

Smith, E. E., Adams, N., & Schorr, D. (1978). Fact retrieval and the paradox of interference. *Cognitive Psychology, 10*, 438–464.

Smith, E. E., & Medin, D. L. (1981). *Categories and concepts*. Cambridge, MA: Harvard University Press.

Srull, T. K., & Wyer, R. S. (1989). Person memory and judgement. *Psychological Review, 96*, 58–83.

SPATIAL MENTAL MODELS

Barbara Tversky

I. Overview

There are many simple, everyday tasks, such as following road directions, using instructions to assemble a bicycle, reading a novel, or helping to solve your child's geometry homework, that seem to entail constructing a spatial mental model from a description. In order to comprehend *Go straight till the first light, then turn left, go down about three blocks to Oak, and make a right,* it is useful to have a spatial representation. Of course, the gist of the message could be remembered instead, but incorporating the instructions into a mental model helps, especially when things don't quite turn out as expected, such as encountering a "No Left Turn" sign at the light. Indeed, there is evidence that people do construct such spatial models. The nature of such models is the topic of this article.

Ample research in memory and comprehension of text supports the assertion that listeners or readers form not only representations of the language of the text—of sound or graphemic properties, of actual words or sentences, of gist—but also of the situation described by the text (Bransford, Barclay, & Franks, 1972; Garnham, 1981; Johnson-Laird, 1983; van Dijk & Kintsch, 1983; among others). Because they are familiar, universal, and objective, we have chosen to investigate descriptions of spatial environments. People have considerable experience converting spoken or written communications about environments into mental representations, and then acting on them. People then get feedback—they either get lost or find their way—and can correct their models. In addition, there is a large body of data on how people learn and remember environments from experience or from maps that can be compared to acquiring environments from descriptions. Just as for maps, learning environments from narratives can be assessed by measuring speed and accuracy to make judgments of spatial relations, distance, and direction, as well as by style and accuracy to make productions, such as maps.

We have developed two separate but related experimental paradigms to investigate spatial mental models constructed from text. In the first paradigm, we vary characteristics of the descriptions and observe the consequent mental models. This work has been done with Holly Taylor. In the second paradigm, we examine in great detail the spatial characteristics of a particular but very common situation, the one people are in most of the time, of having objects at different places around them. Much of this work has been done with Nancy Franklin and, more recently, David Bryant.

This research program has several goals. The first is to demonstrate that the mental models constructed from text with neither visual displays nor special instructions to image nevertheless reflect spatial properties described in the text. Many of the early and elegant demonstrations of imagery and spatial thinking per force used contrived situations. Now that a body of techniques for exploring spatial thinking has been developed, such techniques can be applied to more natural situations, and especially to cases where neither visual information nor instructions to image are given. Another aim is to discover which spatial properties are preserved, and how they are organized and accessed, and to investigate the effects of discourse organization and spatial organization on that. Studies by Denis and Denhiere (1990), Foos (1980), Mani and Johnson-Laird (1982), Ehrlich and Johnson-Laird (1982), and Perrig and Kintsch (1985) have shown that when descriptions are complete and coherent, readers' mental models preserve information about the spatial relations among the objects in a described scene. Studies by Denis and Cocude (1989), Franklin (1991), Glenberg, Meyer, and Lindem (1987), Morrow, Bower, and Greenspan (1989), Morrow, Greenspan, and Bower (1987), and Wagener-Wender and Wender (1990) indicate that some distance information described in text is preserved in mental models. The first set of studies addresses the issue of the generality and perspective of spatial mental models constructed from different text perspectives. Specifically, are they like structural descriptions (e.g., Marr, 1982; Minsky, 1975; Palmer, 1977; Pinker, 1984; Ullman, 1989), i.e., perspective-free representations of the spatial relations of parts of a scene that allow viewers to take different perspectives on them? Or are they like images (e.g., Kosslyn, 1980; Shepard & Podgorny, 1978), i.e., internalized perceptions, representing a scene from a particular viewpoint, namely, the one described in the text? The second set of studies investigates representation and access of particular spatial relations from particular perspectives.

II. Survey and Route Descriptions

When tourists visit a new place, they often buy guidebooks to let them know what is worth seeing and doing, and how to get there. An informal review of guidebooks reveals that they tend to adopt one of two perspectives on the place described. Some take the reader on a mental tour or *route* through the environment. A route description of the Smithsonian in Washington, D.C. might proceed:

> As you leave the Capitol going along the Mall, the first building you pass on your right is the East Wing of the National Gallery. Continuing on, you come to the main building of the National Gallery. On your left, across the Mall, you can see the Air and Space Museum . . . until you reach the Washington Monument.

Another perspective commonly adopted is to give the reader a bird's eye view or *survey* of the place. A survey description of the same scene might proceed:

> At the east end of the Mall stands the Capitol and at the west end, the Washington Monument. Along the north side of the Mall, the eastern-most building is the East Wing of the National Gallery. Just west of it is the National Gallery. . . . On the south side of the Mall, the eastern-most building is the Air and Space Museum, directly south across the Mall from the National Gallery.

Survey descriptions take a perspective from above and describe the locations of landmarks relative to one another in canonical direction terms: north, south, east, and west. In addition, survey descriptions are often hierarchical, beginning with an overview of boundaries of large-scale regions, and becoming more specific. Route descriptions take the perspective of a moving observer in the environment, typically addressed as *you,* and describe the locations of landmarks relative to your (the observer's) changing position in terms of left, right, in front, and behind. Route descriptions are typically at a single level of analysis whose sequence is determined by the particular path. Thus, the description perspectives differ in spatial terminology, and whether locations of landmarks are described with respect to other landmarks or with respect to the location of an observer.

The initial question Taylor and I (in press) asked is: Do route and survey descriptions lead to different mental representations? That is, do the representations generated by each perspective preserve that perspective, or are they perspective-free? The question of perspectives of narratives and of mental representations is of more generality than just spatial models, as route-like and survey-like descriptions are appropriate for other topics as well, e.g., descriptions of time. Here we focus on spatial descriptions only.

Previous research on narrative comprehension and on learning actual environments suggests that different perspectives yield different representations. Readers remember details relevant to their own perspective better than those relevant to an alternate perspective for both physical (Abelson, 1975; Perrig & Kintsch, 1985) and character perspective (Anderson & Pichert, 1978; Bower, 1978). Some information about actual environments is better acquired by studying maps, such as Euclidean distance and direction, whereas other information is better acquired from actual navigation, such as traversal distance (Evans & Pezdek, 1980; Sholl, 1987; Streeter, Vitello, & Wonsiewicz, 1985; Thorndyke, 1981; Thorndyke & Hayes-Roth, 1982). Narratives, however, cannot easily present the continuous information available from maps and navigation. Narratives can easily convey categorical information: north, south, east, west, and right, left, front, back. Considerable research has shown that spatial information acquired from both maps and actual traversal is distorted toward these and other major spatial categories, though, of course, some more detailed information is retained and used (e.g., R. W. Byrne, 1979; Chase, 1983; Hirtle & Jonides, 1985; Maki, 1981; McNamara, 1986; Moar & Bower, 1983; Stevens & Coupe, 1978; Tversky, 1981; Wilton, 1979). In this research on narratives, we can only assess the global, categorical spatial relations easily conveyed by language.

A.   EXPERIMENT 1: ROUTE VS. SURVEY DESCRIPTIONS

1.   Task

Taylor and I (in press) developed four fictitious environments: two large-scale—one county-sized and the other a small town—and two small-scale—a zoo and a convention center—containing from 11 to 15 landmarks each. Depictions of these environments are in Figs. 1–4, but subjects in the initial experiments did not see these maps.

We wrote a survey and a route description of each environment. The

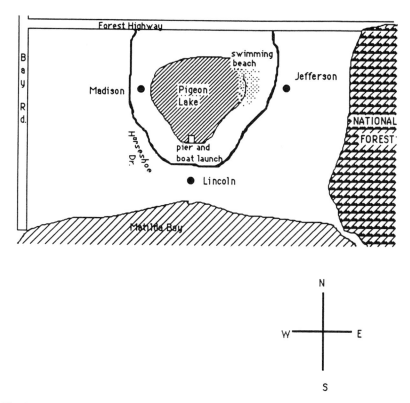

Fig. 1.   Map of resort area. From Taylor and Tversky (in press). Reprinted by permission.

survey descriptions took a perspective from above, used a hierarchical organization, and adopted canonical direction terms to describe landmarks relative to each other in terms of north, south, east, and west. The route descriptions took a perspective from within the environment, used a sequential organization, and adopted egocentric direction terms to describe landmarks in relation to a moving ego, in terms of left, right, and front.

While we wished to make the alternative descriptions equally coherent, there is no widely applicable measure of discourse coherence. Coreference, i.e., linking sentences in sequence by referring to the same thing, has sometimes been suggested (Johnson-Laird, 1983; van Dijk & Kintsch, 1983). Coreference may be appropriate for route or sequential organizations, but not for hierarchical descriptions, where a new descriptive part will refer back to the overview but not to the previous sentence. Lacking an objective measure, we asked a group of pilot subjects to evaluate the coherence of the texts, and they reported that the two types of

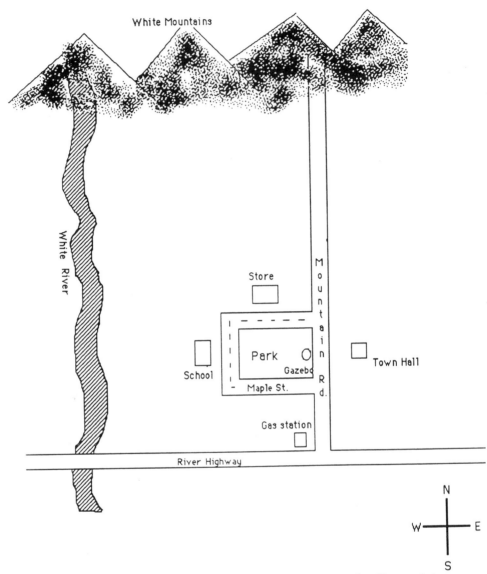

Fig. 2.   Map of town. From Taylor and Tversky (in press). Reprinted by permission.

descriptions were equally coherent. We also pretested the descriptions to make sure that readers could correctly place all landmarks in sketches, i.e., that the information was in fact complete and determinate. In addition to the locative information, each description contained nonlocative information, e.g., relating activities that could be performed in different parts of

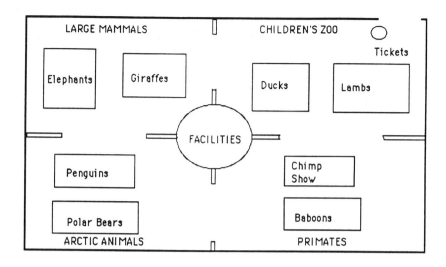

Fig. 3.   Map of zoo. From Taylor and Tversky (in press). Reprinted by permission.

the environment, or giving elaborative details about landmarks. This information was identical for route and survey descriptions. As examples, the route and survey text for the resort area are presented as follows:

Survey Description of Resort Area

The Pigeon Lake resort area is well situated for people who are interested in a variety of outdoor activities. The resort area is bordered by four major landmarks: the National Forest, Matilda Bay, Bay Rd., and the Forest Highway. The eastern border is made up of the National Forest. The National Forest has facilities for camping, hiking, and rock climbing. The southern border is made up of Matilda Bay. Two major roads, Bay Road and the Forest Highway, form the other two borders of the region. Bay Rd., runs north–south along the western border of this region. Bay

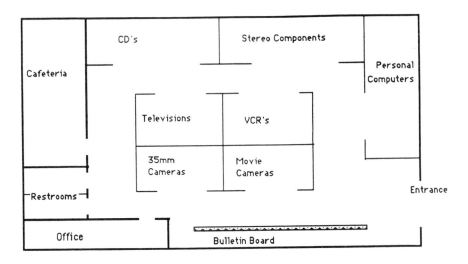

Fig. 4. Map of convention center. From Taylor and Tversky (in press). Reprinted by permission.

Rd. is the main access to the many recreational areas on Matilda Bay. Bay Rd. is also the main route in and out of this region. The Forest Highway forms the northern border and provides the 120-mile link between Bay Rd. and the National Forest. Pigeon Lake is a large recreational lake in the center of the region. There are many activities that center around Pigeon Lake. People enjoy boating, water skiing, and swimming on the lake. There is a fishing pier and boat launch at the southernmost point of the lake. Since this is the only place to launch boats, there is usually quite a bit of traffic near the launch site. On the east shore of the lake there is a swimming beach. In the busy summer tourist season, there are lifeguards on the beach. Horseshoe Drive follows the rounded outline of the lake and is connected at both ends to the Forest Highway. Horseshoe Drive begins about 40 miles east of Bay Rd. and ends about 40 miles west of the national forest. There are three small towns within the Pigeon Lake region that all lie along Horseshoe Drive. Madison lies on the west shore between the lake and Horseshoe Drive. Madison is directly across the lake from the swimming beach. Madison is the site of the annual seafood festival where the main event is the fishing contest. Jefferson lies on the east side of the lake on the National Forest side of Horseshoe Drive. Jefferson is the main center for hiking and cycling. Lincoln lies on the south side of the lake midway between Horseshoe Dr. and the Bay. Lincoln is considered by tourists to have the best location in the region because of its close proximity to the bay.

Route Description of Resort Area

The Pigeon Lake resort area is well situated for people who are interested in a variety of outdoor activities. To reach the Pigeon Lake region, drive south along Bay Rd. until you reach, on your left, the point where the Forest Highway dead-ends into Bay Rd. From this intersection, you can see in the distance that Bay Rd. continues to Matilda Bay and its many recreational areas. You turn left onto the Forest Highway and travel about 40 miles until, on your right, you reach Horseshoe Drive. Horseshoe Dr. is the only road that you can take to get into the Pigeon Lake region. Turning right onto Horseshoe Drive, from the Forest Highway, you see, on your left, Pigeon Lake. Pigeon Lake is a large recreational lake in the center of this region. There are many activities that center around Pigeon Lake. On the lake, people enjoy boating, water skiing, and swimming. After you drive for ten miles along Horseshoe Drive, you see, on your left, the small town of Madison. Madison is the site of the annual seafood festival where the main event is the fishing contest. As you continue along Horseshoe Drive, you notice that the road follows the rounded outline of the lake. Twenty miles after you leave Madison, you see, off Horseshoe Dr. on your right, the little town of Lincoln. From your position, only a short distance beyond Lincoln you can see Matilda Bay. Because of its close proximity to the bay, Lincoln is considered, by tourists, to have the best location in the region. From your position with Lincoln on your right, you see, on your left, the fishing pier and boat launch for Pigeon Lake. Since there is only one boat launch for Pigeon Lake, there is usually quite a bit of traffic near the launch site. Continuing around the shore of the lake on Horseshoe Dr., you drive about twenty more miles until you come to the swimming beach and the town of Jefferson. On your left is the swimming beach. In the busy summer tourist season, there are lifeguards on the beach. From your position with the swimming beach on your left, you see, on your right, the town of Jefferson. Jefferson is the main center for hiking and cycling for the area. You drive for another ten miles on Horseshoe Dr. until you return to the Forest Highway. To your right, about forty miles away, you can see the National Forest. The National Forest has facilities for camping, hiking, and rock climbing. Turning left onto the Forest Highway, you travel about 40 miles and again see, on your left, the beginning of Horseshoe Dr. Continuing along the highway, you return to Bay Rd., which leads you out of the region.

We modeled the design and memory tasks on those of Perrig and Kintsch (1985), who tested a similar hypothesis. Their results were inconclusive, partly because their descriptions were too difficult, hence poorly learned, and partly because their survey description's organization was derived from that of the route description and was consequently awkward as well as indeterminate, i.e., the locations of some of the landmarks could not be determined from the description. Our subjects read two route and two survey descriptions, one large-scale and one small-scale environment for each description type. Across subjects, each environment was presented equally often as a route and as a survey description. Subjects could read each description up to four times. Reading time was self-paced, and total times were recorded.

After reading each description, subjects were presented with statements to verify as true or false; reaction time and errors were recorded. Some statements tested the nonlocative information. Perspective should make no difference on performance on these questions. Other statements tested the locative information. The verbatim locative statements were taken directly from the texts. The inference locative statements were from the same perspective of the texts and contained information that could be inferred from the text but was not directly given in the texts. Half of both the verbatim and inference locative statements were from a route perspective and half from a survey perspective. Of the inference statements, half were true, half false. A true route inference statement from the convention center was: *Walking from the Personal Computers to the Televisions, you pass, on your right, the Stereo Components.* A false route inference statement from the resort area was: *Driving from Jefferson to Lincoln, Pigeon Lake is on your left.* A true survey inference statement from the town was: *The Gas Station is east of the river and south of Maple St.* A false survey inference statement from the zoo was: *The Giraffes' Cage is west of the Polar Bears' Cage and south of the Baboon Colony.* Readers answered all questions regardless of perspective read. Thus, a verbatim statement from a different perspective was in effect an inference statement for that reader. Following the questions, readers drew a map of each environment. This served to check that readers were able to form integrated and correct spatial models from the text, and to check if one type of description (or environment) had an advantage.

2. Predictions

Previous research indicates that readers form multiple representations of text and may verify statements against any or all of those representations. If readers use representations of the language of the text to answer the questions, verbatim questions should be faster and more accurate than inference questions. When verification statements are verbal, comparison to linguistic or propositional information is faster than to images or mental models (e.g., Kosslyn, 1976). Inference statements, on the other hand, cannot be verified directly by comparison to a representation of the language of the text. They can be verified either by comparison to a representation of the text plus rules of spatial inference, or by comparison to a mental model of the situation described by the text. Using descriptions of spatial arrays similar to but simpler than the present ones, R. M. D. Byrne and Johnson-Laird (1989) showed that readers verify by comparison to mental models rather than by applying spatial inference rules to representations of text. If the situation models readers construct depend on the particular perspective of the narrative, then readers should respond faster and more accurately to inference statements from the perspective read than to inference and verbatim statements from the other perspective. If, however, readers construct the same spatial mental models irrespective of the perspective of the text, then there should be no differences in speed or accuracy on the inference questions that depend on perspective read.

3. Results

Route maps took slightly but significantly longer to read. Subjects made more map errors on route descriptions (1.31) than on survey descriptions (0.68), but there were very few errors made on maps altogether, indicating that readers formed highly accurate situation models from the texts. The data of primary interest are the reaction times and error rates to the different types of questions, presented in Fig. 5. As in the case of the maps, overall performance was excellent. First, there were fewer errors and faster reaction times to verify the nonlocative statements than the locative statements. As expected, perspective had no effect on performance on nonlocative statements. We would not like to claim that nonlocative infor-

Barbara Tversky

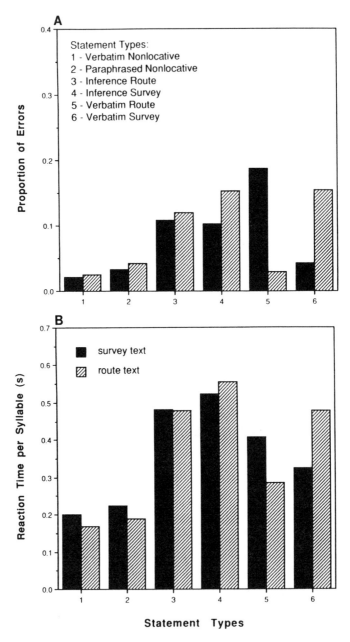

Fig. 5.   Experiment 1. A, errors to question types by description type. B, reaction times to question types by description type. Adapted from Taylor and Tversky (in press). Reprinted by permission.

mation is generally easier than locative; surely one could write nonlocative statements that would be very difficult to remember. One possibility is that nonlocative statements can be verified by reference to a representation of the language of the text, which is faster than verification by reference to a mental model.

As for locative statements, the only differences to be found are in the verbatim statements. Subjects were faster and more accurate verifying statements that they had actually read than statements about inferences from information presented in the descriptions. Verbatim statements can also be verified more efficiently by reference to a representation of the language of the text than by reference to a mental model. For inference statements, however, perspective read made no difference. In other words, subjects were as fast and accurate on inference statements from the perspective read than from the other perspective, for both perspectives.

4. *Discussion*

Consistent with previous research, the present results support the establishment of multiple mental representations from text. The rapid and accurate performance on nonlocative and verbatim statements suggests that they were verified by comparison to a representation of the language of the text. How abstract that representation (or representations) is we cannot determine from these results. In contrast to verbatim and nonlocative statements, inference statements were verified more slowly and less accurately, suggesting that these are verified against a mental model of the situation described by the text.

The lack of any differences in verification time or accuracy of survey and route inference statements as a consequence of perspective of description read suggests that the situation model constructed does not depend on the perspective of the text. Because readers are just as good taking a new perspective as taking a previous perspective, their mental models must be general enough to allow the taking of different perspectives with equal ease. Readers of route and survey descriptions appear to have formed the same mental models of the spatial relations of landmarks regardless of perspective of text. Because this finding is on the surface contrary to previous work and because it is a null finding, we replicated it in three more experiments that also allowed exploration of the phenomenon.

B. EXPERIMENT 2: VERBATIM VS. PARAPHRASED STATEMENTS

In the first experiment, readers were faster and more accurate verifying statements previously read than inference statements. Does the advantage to verbatim statements depend on the exact wording of the sentences or the gist of the information conveyed by them? The second experiment addressed this question by adding paraphrased statements to the set of statements readers were asked to verify. The paraphrased route and survey statements were exactly that, reversals of order of clauses. This was the only possible paraphrasing because there are no adequate synonyms for either the direction terms or the names of places. There was one other change in this experiment, the reason for which will become clear later; the descriptions were changed so that the orders of mentioning landmarks in survey and route versions were quite different. These new narratives were used in all subsequent experiments.

1. Results

All of the previous findings were replicated, as is evident in Fig. 6. Readers took longer to study route texts and made more errors on maps drawn from them. Performance was excellent, both in map drawing and in statement verification. Nonlocative statements were verified more quickly and accurately than locative statements. Subjects were equally fast and accurate with both types of inference locative statements regardless of perspective read. However, subjects were faster and more accurate with verbatim and paraphrased statements than with inference statements from either perspective; furthermore, there were no differences between verbatim and paraphrased sentences.

2. Discussion

Verbatim statements appear to be verified by comparison to a representation of the text, in contrast to inference statements, which took longer and appear to be verified by comparison to a representation of the situation described by the text, or a mental model. Like verbatim statements, paraphrased statements are verified more quickly and accurately than inference statements, and thus appear to be verified against a representation of the language of the text. Because only changes in word order and minor changes in wording could be used as paraphrases, no broad conclusions can be drawn about the nature of the representation of the language of the text beyond concluding that representation is not sensitive to large changes in word order and minor changes in wording.

C. EXPERIMENT 3: TEXTS VS. MAPS

Is the mental representation of spatial relations induced by the two types of descriptions similar to that induced by studying a map? If so, then subjects

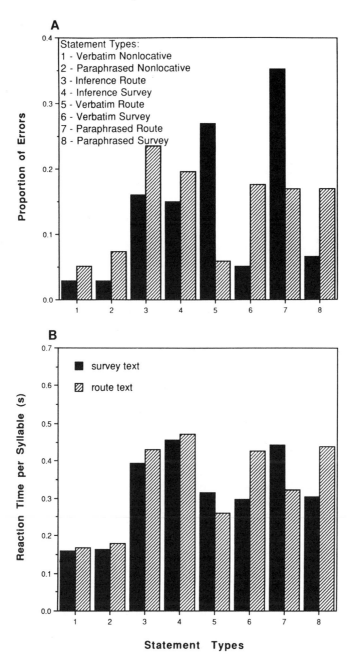

Fig. 6. Experiment 2. A, errors to question types by description type (paraphrased questions). B, reaction times to question types by description type (paraphrased question). Adapted from Taylor and Tversky (in press). Reprinted by permission.

who study a map should, like subjects who studied texts, do equally well on survey and route questions. On the other hand, a map, even more than a survey description, presents a survey perspective. Thus, if perspective is preserved in mental models of spatial relations, then subjects who study maps should perform better on survey than on route statements. This experiment was a replication of the first experiment with the addition of a second group of subjects who studied the maps presented in Figs. 1–4 in lieu of reading descriptions, for up to 10 min per map.

When the results of this experiment were analyzed, the main results of Experiment 1 were replicated a third time, as can be seen in Fig. 7. Locative statements were slower and less accurate than nonlocative statements. Route texts took longer to read, and subjects' maps of route texts were slightly less accurate than those of survey texts. The maps drawn by subjects who studied maps were the most accurate of all. For text subjects, verbatim sentences were faster and more accurate than inference statements, and there were no effects of perspective read on verification of inference statements.

As for map subjects, their pattern of reaction times to the statement types was comparable to that of text subjects. They responded equally quickly to both route and survey statements, indicating that their mental models were not biased toward either perspective. The pattern of errors for map subjects were slightly more complex. For route questions, accuracy of map subjects was at the level of survey text subjects and at that of inference questions for route text subjects, again supporting the claim that map subjects' mental models of spatial relations were comparable to those of text subjects. However, on survey questions, map subjects were more accurate than route subjects (though, again, note that the overall error rate is low). However, we are reluctant to take that as evidence that a survey perspective is inherent in the mental representations of map subjects for several reasons. First, there was no comparable effect for verification time, and second, map subjects' performance was highly similar to text subjects' performance. An explanation we prefer for the especially high accuracy of map subjects on survey statements is that the information required to verify these statements was given directly by the maps, whereas the information required to verify route statements was not. Thus, for map subjects, survey statements are analogous to verbatim statements, and route statements are analogous to inference statements. Such a stance seems to imply that just as there are multiple representations for text, for example, representations of the language of the text and representations of the situation described by the text, so there may be multiple representations of depictions, some closer to the actual visual

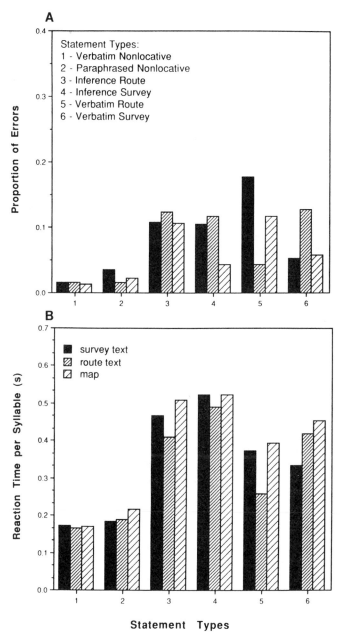

Fig. 7. Experiment 3. A, errors to question types by description type (text and map conditions). B, Reaction times to question types by description type (text and map conditions). Adapted from Taylor and Tversky (in press). Reprinted by permission.

display, and some more abstract representations constructed from integrating over the display.[1]

D. EXPERIMENT 4: SINGLE TRIAL

In the previous experiments, subjects studied four texts (or maps) and knew that they would be asked to draw a map after each one. Furthermore, after the first trial, they knew that they would be asked to verify statements from both perspectives. Perhaps these expectations led them to construct mental models more abstract than they otherwise would. For this reason, another experiment was run in which subjects studied only a single text, and were told to study the text so that they could answer questions about the information presented in it. They were not told ahead of time about the map task, though they were asked to draw maps after the verification task.

The results of this experiment showed no differences in study time or in map accuracy due to text perspective. Otherwise the main results were replicated a fourth time, and are displayed in Fig. 8. Verification of nonlocative statements was faster and more accurate than that of locative statements. Performance was very high in both statement verification and map drawing. Verbatim statements were faster and more accurate than inference statements. There were no effects of perspective on inference statements despite no expectations of map drawing or of questions from a different perspective.

E. SPATIAL MENTAL MODELS

In four experiments, subjects read a route or a survey description of an environment. Route descriptions took readers on a mental tour and described environments in terms of left, right, front, and back, relative to a moving observer, addressed as "you." Survey descriptions described the environments from above, relating locations of landmarks to one another in terms of north, south, east, and west. After each description, subjects verified verbatim and inference statements from both perspectives for each of up to four environments. Following the verification task, subjects drew sketch maps of the environments. The maps subjects drew contained very few errors, indicating that readers formed accurate mental representations of the envioments from text alone. Readers were faster and more accurate to verify verbatim statements than inference statements, indicat-

---

[1] Data on eye movements indicate that a pictorial display is scanned part by part (e.g., Noton & Stark, 1971). This in turn suggests that complex visual displays such as maps and pictures are not encoded wholistically as snapshops but rather are encoded piecemeal and integrated.

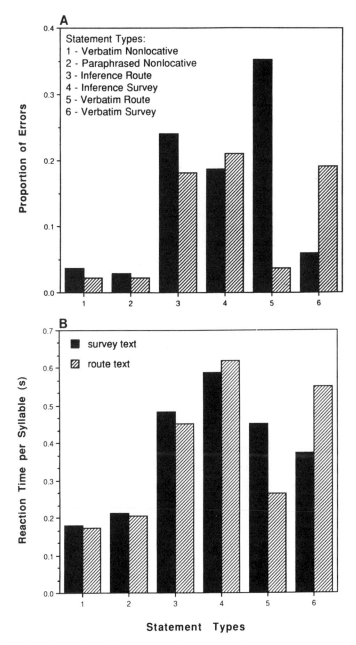

Fig. 8.   Experiment 4. A, Errors to question types by description type (single description). B, Reaction times to question types by description type (single description). Adapted from Taylor and Tversky (in press). Reprinted by permission.

ing that verbatim statements were verified by comparison to a representation of the language of the description. For inference statements there was no effect of perspective read. That is, readers were as fast and as accurate with statements in the other perspective as in the read perspective. This finding was obtained four times under varying conditions. Inference statement verification and map drawing seem to have been done from mental models of the situation described in the texts, of the spatial relations between landmarks.

The simplest account of these findings (an account quite similar to that of Johnson-Laird, 1983) is that for this type of text and environment, spatial mental models induced by the two text perspectives are functionally the same, and perspective-free. Perspective is represented, but in representations of the language of the text, not in representations of the situation described by the text. What might such a spatial mental model look like? Taylor and I (in press) speculated that it might not look like anything that can be visualized. Rather, it might be something analogous to an architect's 3-D model of a town that can be viewed or visualized from many different perspectives, but cannot be viewed or visualized as a whole. In fact, answering the locative questions required taking a particular perspective, either from above or from within. Moreover, the questions required subjects to call up only a small part of the representation, typically about three landmarks, rather than the entire scene. To verify a route statement seemed to require imagining being in a particular location in the environment, facing a specific landmark and surrounded by others, and checking that the landmarks were in the proper directions—front, back, left, right—relative to the imagined viewpoint. To verify a survey statement seemed to require focusing on the locations of a particular set of landmarks as if from above to ascertain if they were in the proper relations—north, south, east, west. Subjects' mental models were abstract enough to allow either type of judgment with equal ease. These speculations correspond to many peoples' introspections about spatial environments they know very well: their homes, workplaces, neighborhoods. That is, they do not have a single mental representation of them but many, and they can adopt many different points of view on such well-known environments.

As such, the spatial mental models constructed by readers of route and survey texts are like structural descriptions of objects. Structural descriptions specify the spatial relations among parts of an object. Rather than being viewer-centered, they are object-centered (e.g., Marr & Nishihara, 1978), that is, perspective-free. That construct, structural description, was developed to account for our ability to recognize objects from many different perspectives. Both mental models and structural descriptions differ from the representations proposed in the classic work on imagery (e.g., Finke & Shepard, 1986; Kosslyn, 1980; Pinker, 1984; Shepard & Podgorny, 1978), which are perception-like and from a particular point of view. As Johnson-Laird (1983, p. 157) put it, "images correspond to views of models."

Of course, these speculations about spatial mental models apply only for the simple categorical spatial relations among landmarks that can be easily specified in descriptions and were tested in these experiments, and not for the more continuous information that can be acquired from maps and navigation. Distances were not specified, nor were directions specified in terms of degrees, so we could not expect these spatial mental models to contain that information. Similarly, we do not mean to imply that all of what has been termed "cognitive maps," whether formed from descriptions, maps, or actual navigation, have this same abstract character, but of course it is possible that some of them do.

F. NEW DIRECTIONS: DRAWING ORDER

From the first experiment a serendipitous finding emerged that Taylor and I have begun to chase. Taylor noticed that in producing maps, subjects seemed to draw the landmarks in the order of their mention in the descriptions. Halfway through the study, she began recording the drawing order, and analysis of those data confirmed her observation. To make absolutely sure there was no bias, two new experimenters and a new set of subjects were recruited. The experimenters were told to record the order of drawing the landmarks, but they did not know which type of description subjects read each trial or the general hypothesis. Some of the descriptions were rewritten to make the route and survey orders as different as possible. The results of this study (Experiment 3) confirmed those of the first. The correlation between order of mentioning landmarks in descriptions and order of drawing them in maps was very high ($r = .72$), significantly higher than the correlation between the other description order and map drawing order ($r = .22$). Approximately the same correlations were found in Experiment 2, where drawing orders were also recorded by experimenters blind to the hypothesis.

At first, finding correspondences between description order and map-drawing order may seem contrary to the findings for speed and accuracy in verifying locative statements from the two types of text, where we found no differences save faster times for paraphrased statements. Now, for maps, we find a large difference in drawing order due to description in a task that seems to depend on drawing a mental image or a cognitive map. It is that latter assumption that we question. We proposed earlier that the mental representations subjects construct from these types of narratives do not seem like images but rather like structural descriptions of the spatial relations between the landmarks of the scene. As such, unlike a mental image, they cannot be visualized as a whole. They can be imagined from particular perspectives. Moreover, because they contain a relatively large number of landmarks and spatial relations, they may not be imagined in whole, but rather in parts. So, we conjecture, when subjects are asked to draw a map of the described environments, they do so by reconstructing their mental models part by part, and they reconstruct the mental model of the environment in the same order as they originally constructed it, i.e., in the order of the description they read. Thus, this finding is indirect evidence in support of the contention that readers' mental models are not image- or map-like. If they were, there should be no differences in drawing order depending on description perspective; rather, drawing order should depend on characteristics of the image or map alone (e.g., Novick & Tversky, 1987).

G.   New Directions: Descriptions and Depictions

Order of output has often been used as a clue to mental organization in unconstrained tasks (see, e.g., Tulving, 1962). With this in mind, we examined the order of drawing landmarks in the subjects in Experiment 3 who learned the environments from maps rather than descriptions. Their drawing orders contrasted the drawing orders of those who had read descriptions, whose orders corresponded to the order of mention in the descriptions. Subjects who had studied maps tended to draw maps in a hierarchical fashion, beginning with borders or large entities and working inward or toward smaller objects and parts. This pattern could be due to memory organization, i.e., spatial memory may be hierarchically organized (e.g., McNamara, 1986; Stevens & Coupe, 1978), or it could be due to demands of the drawing task, where borders and larger elements set the scale for internal and smaller elements, or both. It is also possible that in describing environments, subjects are implicitly aware that they are constructing mental models in the minds of their readers or listeners, and that many of the constraints of model construction are similar to those of actual construction (Novick & Tversky, 1987).

In another study of organization of descriptions and depictions of environments (Taylor & Tversky, 1990), subjects were asked to study one of three maps—a large-scale (town), a medium scale (a new map of an amusement park), or a small-scale (convention center)—in anticipation either of reproducing the map or of writing a description from memory. In fact, subjects were asked to do both, in counterbalanced order. Neither expectations nor order had effects on either descriptions or depictions. In both cases, almost all subjects recalled all or almost all of the landmarks.

Interestingly, there was a high correspondence between order of drawing landmarks and order of mentioning landmarks both within and across subjects, irrespective of the perspective of the description. Linde and Labov (1975) studied people's descriptions of their apartments, and Levelt (1982) studied people's descriptions of street map-like networks. Both studies found that subjects' descriptions took consistent perspectives on the environments. These descriptions for the most part took listeners on mental tours of the environments, i.e., subjects gave route descriptions. Linde and Labov, and Levelt, attributed this to the linear characteristic of language as opposed to pictures and environments. Language must serialize a two- or three-dimensional array, and the most natural way to serialize is to take a path through an environment.

Linde and Labov's and Levelt's findings and contentions notwithstanding, the descriptions our subjects produced used both route and survey perspectives (and no other perspective), both purely and in mixtures. About half of the subjects used a route perspective for the convention center; of the other half, a small proportion used a survey perspective, and the rest used mixed perspectives. The mirror image of this pattern emerged for the town: about half used a survey perspective, and of the other half, a small portion used a route perspective, and the rest used both. The amusement park, the medium scale environment, elicited a pattern in between that of the convention center and that of the town. Although all environments yielded route, survey, and mixed descriptions, the large-scale environment tended to elicit more survey descriptions and the small-scale environment more route descriptions. Several factors may contribute to this. The larger scale environment contained both large- and small-scale features, encouraging a hierarchical description. The large-scale environment had more than one route through it, and the small scale only a single route. In the real world, people are more likely to interact with a large-scale environment via many routes, and more likely to interact with a small-scale environment by a single path. It may be possible to disentangle these factors—features at more than one scale, single vs. multiple paths, and typical mode of interaction—using specially designed maps. Overall, these findings suggest that the spatial organization is primary for descriptions, and the linguistic devices, such as those used to establish perspective, are secondary.

III.   Spatial Frameworks

In the research reviewed in Section II of this article, Taylor and I studied the spatial mental models constructed from route or survey descriptions of environments. We found evidence that such models captured the spatial relations of the parts of an environment in a perspective-free manner. However, we asserted that verifying statements required taking specific perspectives, and other research has shown that language induces specific spatial perspectives (e.g., Bly, 1989; Bower, 1978). In experiments to be reviewed now, Franklin, Bryant, and I have begun to examine specific spatial relations and specific perspectives in detail (Bryant, Tversky, & Franklin, in press; Franklin & Tversky, 1990a, 1990b).

The basic situation we chose to study is the one we humans find ourselves in for most of our lives, of being surrounded by objects, and keeping track of the directions of those objects from our bodies as we change position. Not only is this situation familiar, it also serves as the basis for techniques as old and revered as the method of loci for memorization, and as contemporary and popular as computer adventure games. Unlike most imagery tasks, it also has the interesting property of being three-dimensional, not in the sense of depth of field in front of the observer (as in the tasks of Pinker, 1980), but in the sense of surrounding the observer, where not all of the field can be "viewed" from any given position.

A. TASK

As before, the scenes were described rather than actually viewed. Also as before, readers were not given any instructions to image (except in one study directed at that), or any diagrams or special training. The mental models constructed seem to be a natural consequence of instructions to comprehend and learn the narratives. In the first set of experiments, Franklin and I (1990b) developed 10 different narratives written in the second person; each first described the scene, including the locations of five critical objects in front of you, in back of you, to your left or your right, beyond your head, and beyond your feet. Next, the narrative oriented you the reader toward one of the three horizontal objects and queried you about the objects located at the five possible locations. Then, the narrative oriented you toward another of the three objects and repeated the questions in random order, and so on. Reaction times to identify the objects located at head, feet, front, back, right, and left were the dependent variable of interest.[2]

The hotel scene will serve as an example. The critical objects, those whose locations will be queried, are here in italics, but they were not in the versions subjects read.

---

[2] These experiments used only five objects to keep memory load at a minimum; later experiments using six objects obtained the same results.

You are at the Jefferson Plaza Hotel, where you have just taken the escalator from the first to the second floor. You will be meeting someone for dinner in a few minutes. You now stand next to the top of the escalator, where you have a view of the first floor as well as the second floor. You first look directly to your left, where you see a shimmering indoor *fountain* about 10 yards beyond a carpeted walkway. Though you cannot see beyond the low stone wall that surrounds it, you suppose that its bottom is littered with nickels and pennies that hotel guests have tossed in. The view down onto the first floor allows you to see that directly below you is a darkened, candle-lit *tavern*. It looks very plush, and every table you see seems to be filled with well-dressed patrons. Looking directly behind you, you see through the window of the hotel's *barbershop*. You can see an older gentleman, whose chest is covered by a white sheet, being shaved by a much younger man. You next look straight ahead of you, where you see a quaint little *giftshop* just on the other side of the escalator. You're a sucker for little ceramic statues, and you squint your eyes to try to read the hours of operation posted on the store's entrance. Hanging from the high ceiling directly above you, you see a giant *banner* welcoming the Elks convention to the hotel. It is made from white lettering sewn onto a blue background, and it looks to you to be about 25 feet long.

Thus, you might first be oriented toward the barber shop, then the fountain, and then the gift shop (orders were counterbalanced), and at each point queried about what was to your head, feet, front, and so on (also counterbalanced).

B. EQUIAVAILABILITY AND MENTAL TRANSFORMATION MODELS

Three classes of models to account for the response times were considered. According to the *equiavailability* model, all locations are equally available to the observer, as they would be in a picture or viewed scene; that is, no direction has priority over any other (Levine, Jankovic, & Palij, 1982; Sholl, 1987). But the scene described is a three-dimensional one, with the observer embedded in it. The equiavailability model makes more sense for a situation where the observer is outside the scene, looking on. According to the *mental transformation* model, the reader imagines him- or herself facing the designated object, and then mentally turning to the cued direction to verify the object. The classical models of imagery (e.g.,

Finke & Shepard, 1986; Kosslyn, 1980) based on internalized perception and mental transformations suggest imposing a mental transformation on an internalized equiavailable scene. It is as if the reader were viewing the scene and turning to inspect the cued direction to see what object is there. In this case, reaction times should increase with the objects' angular disparity from straightahead. This "mental rotation" is similar to that studied by Shepard and Cooper (1982) in that the observer imagines her- or himself perceiving an environment, but different in that the observer imagines him- or herself turning rather than imagining an object rotating. In imagery tasks where subjects were asked to make left/right (or same/ mirror image) judgments on pictures of hands (Cooper & Shepard, 1975; Parsons, 1987b; Sekiyama, 1982) or bodies with outstretched arms (Parsons, 1987a), reaction times indicated that subjects mentally moved their own bodies or parts of their bodies in an analog fashion to the depicted orientation to make the judgment.

Forming and transforming mental images (to transform a phrase of Shepard's) are effortful processes and may not be used when a simpler method of verification is available. Franklin and I (1990b) suggested that what readers in this task do is construct what we termed a *spatial frame-work,* or mental scaffolding, for keeping track of objects located in the directions of the three axes defined from our bodies. Our conceptions of space, unlike our perceptions of space, may give precedence to certain directions over others, rendering them more accessible. This is suggested by several analyses of spatial language, which in turn are based on asymmetries of the way human observers typically interact with the world (e.g., Clark, 1973; Levelt, 1984; Shepard & Hurwitz, 1984). These analyses served as a basis for our own.

C. SPATIAL FRAMEWORK: UPRIGHT CASE

According to the spatial framework model, the canonical position of the observer is upright, and the canonical world of the observer can be described by one vertical and two horizontal dimensions. The vertical dimension is correlated with the long axis of the body, an asymmetric axis. It is also correlated with gravity, which renders shapes of objects and movement in the world asymmetric along that axis. Canonical movement is horizontal, under which vertical spatial relations generally remain constant with respect to the observer, but horizontal spatial relations change. Whereas there are environmental reference points for the vertical dimension—the sky and the ground, for example—the reference points for the two horizontal dimensions are more arbitrary and changing, often defined only by the prominent dimensions of the observer's body. Thus, for the upright observer, the vertical dimension is predominant. Of the two horizontal dimensions, the front/back dimension predominates over the left/right. The former is asymmetric perceptually and functionally: the observer can more readily see, attend to, and move toward the front than the back. The left/right dimension, in contrast, is derived from the front/back, and has no salient asymmetries. Thus, for the upright observer, this model predicts that the vertical dimension should be fastest, followed by front/back, followed by left/right. In addition, it predicts that front should be faster than back. Data consistent with this analysis were obtained by Hintzman, O'Dell, and Arndt (1981), who asked subjects to point to real or imagined objects arrayed in a horizontal circle around the subject. They found correlations between degree of rotation and reaction time for a real scene (akin to mental rotation), but not for an imagined scene, where response times were fastest to front, followed by back, and slowest but equal to left and right.

D. EXPERIMENTS 5–7

We ran three separate upright-only experiments. In the first, the direction terms were those most popular in pilot testing: above, below, ahead, behind, left, and right. In the second experiment, we switched to direction terms derived from body parts: head, feet, front, back, left, and right. This meant that the terms were homogeneous, i.e., all referred to surfaces of the body and would allow later comparison to cases where the observer is not upright. In the third experiment, subjects were given explicit instructions to imagine themselves in the scene and to imagine themselves mentally turning to inspect the cued direction for the object. Despite those differences, the pattern of data obtained was the same, corresponding to that predicted by the spatial framework model: fastest reaction times to the vertical dimension, head/feet, next fastest to front/back, with front faster than back, and slowest to left/right (see Table I). The equiavailability model was rejected by any systematic effects of direction on reaction time, and the mental transformation model was rejected both because reaction times to the smallest angular displacement (front) were not the fastest and because reaction times to the largest angular displacement (back) were faster than those to smaller angular displacements (left and right).

E. SPATIAL FRAMEWORK: RECLINING CASE

There is potentially a problem with the previous conclusions. Times were fastest to the vertical axis, but the objects located at those axes were constant; unlike the other directions, the objects did not change as the reader/observer was reoriented. Moreover, the fastest times were to vertical, which may have a privileged status independent of asymmetries of the

TABLE I

Mean Response Times (sec) for
Each Dimension for
All Experiments[a]

	Experiment				
Dimension	1	2	3	4	5
Upright					
Head/feet	1.57	1.36	1.59	—	1.50
Front/back	1.84	1.58	1.81	—	1.72
Left/right	2.21	2.02	2.26	—	2.07
Reclining					
Head/feet	—	—	—	2.42	2.14
Front/back	—	—	—	2.26	1.82
Left/right	—	—	—	3.25	2.59

[a] From Franklin and Tversky (1990b). Copyright © 1990
by the American Psychological Association. Reprinted by
permission of the publisher.

body. The solution to this problem is to use narratives in which the
observer is horizontal, and reorients by rolling from side to front to back at
random.

Although the predictions from the equiavailability and mental transformation models are the same for the reclining case, the predictions for the
spatial framework are not. When the observer is reclining, the vertical axis
of the world no longer corresponds to any axis of the body. For this
reason, for reclining, according to the spatial framework model, only the
relative salience of the body axes determines the speed of accessibility, not
the relations of the body to the world. Clearly, the left/right axis is least
salient, having no asymmetries and being dependent for definition on the
front/back axis. Both the front/back and the head/feet axes have asymmetries; however, the front/back axis seems to dominate the head/feet
axis, especially given that pedal locomotion is not possible reclining. The
front/back axis still separates the world that can be perceived and manipulated from the world that cannot be perceived and manipulated. Thus, the
spatial framework model predicts that for the reclining observer, accessing
objects along the front/back axis should be fastest, followed by the head/
feet, and the left/right last.

F. Experiments 8 and 9

Two experiments investigated the reclining case by adapting the previous
narratives and using the previous procedures. In the first of these, all

narratives used only the reclining position; in the second, all narratives used both reclining and upright positions, counterbalancing order. Within a narrative, all three reorientations for upright or reclining were blocked.

Adopting a reclining perspective and accessing information from it appear to be more difficult than adopting an upright posture. It took much longer to answer all questions when the observer was described as reclining, in both the pure and mixed experiments. As before, the pattern of responding conformed to the spatial framework predictions and not to the predictions of equiavailability or mental transformation (see the last two columns of Table I). For the reclining case, the objects located at head and feet were still constant but the head/feet axis was not the fastest, indicating that constancy was not responsible for the rapid reaction times for head/feet in the upright posture. To test whether there was a special advantage to verticality, we grouped the front, back, left, and right reaction times that were on the vertical axis. The responses to vertically oriented objects were slower than those to front and back, so there is no special status to vertical when it is not reliably aligned with a body axis. Finally, because of the interaction of posture and direction, the differences in reaction times cannot be attributed solely to the direction terms. Consistent with the spatial framework, then, when the observer is upright, times are fastest to access objects at head/feet, then front/back, and then left/right. When the observer is reclining, times are fastest for front/back, followed by head/feet, and then left/right.

G. EXTENSIONS

Thus, the spatial framework accounts for the pattern of responding for both upright and reclining observers. The narratives were written in the second person to induce the reader to put her- or himself inside the scene described by the narrative. Novelists and journalists induce readers to identify with their characters without using this device. In subsequent experiments, we (Bryant et al., in press) found that readers adopted the perspective of observers described in the third person, rather than taking an outsider's perspective, and could take the perspective of same-sex and opposite-sex observers with equal ease. We also found that readers spontaneously adopted the perspective of a central inanimate object. Inanimate objects necessitated some change of terminology, namely, "head" to "top" and "feet" to "bottom," and that change of terminology slowed the responses to those terms in the reclining case. This was probably due to the conflicting meanings of "top" and "bottom" both as certain sides of objects and as upward-pointing or downward-pointing sides (see Clark, 1973). In yet other extensions, we probed with objects for directions, rather than vice versa as in the previous studies, and obtained the same pattern of results.

H.   New Directions: Other Perspectives

1.   External vs. Internal Arrays

In the narratives we have studied so far, the central character was surrounded by an array of objects, and the questions put to subjects were
about the spatial relations of the objects to that character. Readers adopted
the perspective of the central character when the character was described
as *you*, when the character was described as a third person, and even when
the "character" was an inanimate object. Other perspectives and arrays
are possible. In one study, we (Bryant et al., in press) described a cubic array
of objects from the point of view of an upright outsider looking into the
array, and questions were from the same point of view. As in the original
experiments (Franklin & Tversky, 1990b), the use of spatial reference
terms was deictic (Fillmore, 1975; Levelt, 1984; Miller & Johnson-Laird,
1976), but here the point of view was external to the array. Thus, *the
pumpkin is left of the ghost* meant to the left from the observer's point of
view (not from the pumpkin's), and *the pumpkin is in front of the ghost*
meant that the pumpkin was closer to the observer along the same line of
sight as the ghost (rather than the pumpkin was in front of the ghost's
front).

Spatial framework reasoning can be adapted to this situation, where the
array is external to the observer. Because the array is in front of rather
than surrounding the observer, the reader can keep in mind a two-
dimensional projection of a three-dimensional scene, rather than a three-
dimensional scene surrounding the observer. The conceptual field of view
in this case is smaller and more compact. This should be easier to keep in
mind.

Again, because the array is in front of rather than surrounding the
observer, the spatial framework analysis depends more on the axes of the
world and the field of view of the observer than on the asymmetries of the
observer's body axes. Many of the same predictions of the spatial framework for upright posture with surrounding array hold, but for different
reasons. For the external array, above/below is determined in large part by
the vertical axis of the world because the objects are not directly above or
below the observer, but rather above or below each other. As before,
gravity is aligned with the vertical axis of the world, and confers asymmetry on it. Of course, the head/feet axis of the observer is also aligned
with the vertical. For an outsider, objects are directly in front of the body,
but not directly behind; rather, objects described as behind objects in front
are also in front, but farther from the observer than the objects described
as in front. This axis still has an asymmetry, i.e., front objects are closer,
and relatively larger in size than behind objects. This is a weaker asym-

metry than in the internal case, where objects were in front and in back of the observer. In that case, objects to the front could be seen and objects to the back could not; here both front and back objects can be seen, but front objects are closer. As before, there is no asymmetry along the left/right axis; objects are equally close. Thus, the overall ordering of dimensions is predicted to be the same for the upright external perspective case as for the upright internal case: above/below should be fastest, followed by front/back, and then left/right. The advantage of front over back, however, should diminish or disappear. These predictions were obtained, and replicated in an experiment describing an outside observer examining an array of objects surrounding another character.

2. Two-Person Situations

Franklin and I have begun studying more complex cases with two observers (Franklin & Tversky, 1990a). Thus far, we have investigated narratives that described a set of objects around each of the characters, and readers were queried about the locations of the objects around each character relative to that character. Thus, one way readers could perform the task is by taking the perspectives of each of the characters in turn. If so, the upright internal spatial framework pattern of responses should appear for each character. Another strategy readers could take is to adopt a single survey perspective on both characters at once. In the former case, in order to answer questions, readers construct two smaller spatial mental models, one for each character, and switch back and forth. In the latter, readers construct a single large spatial mental model and switch focus within.

It appeared that readers adopted both of these strategies, depending on the situation described. In a "neutral" situation, where both characters were described as near each other but surrounded by different sets of objects, readers seemed to adopt a single survey perspective. Thus, they appear to prefer to use a larger, integrative mental model and constant perspective to shifting perspective between two smaller mental models. In a second study, both characters were described as being in such different scenes that it was difficult to construct a single unifying perspective, e.g., one person in a lagoon and the other in a museum. Then readers adopted the perspective of each of the characters in turn, yielding an upright spatial framework pattern around each character. In a third experiment, we provided readers with explicit bird's eye perspectives (e.g., from a helicopter; from a museum with a glass roof) on these scenes, and readers again chose a single integrative survey perspective. In this case, the data fit the equi-availability pattern, i.e., all directions were equally quick. This makes sense under analysis. If the reader's point of view is above the scene, then the axes of the observer and of the observer's world are not aligned with the axes of the characters and the axes of their world, unlike the previous external perspective. Given that the observer's body axes and world are misaligned with the characters' body axes and world, and given that questions are from the point of view of the character, there is no reason for any particular axis to predominate any other. In other words, in this situation the axes are treated arbitrarily and equally.

These extensions, to new arrays and to new perspectives, have led to modifications of the spatial framework analysis. That analysis is based on considerations of the body axes and the perceptual world from different perspectives. Thus, the spatial framework is more properly regarded as a family of related variants, deriving from the same set of general principles (similar to Lakoff's, 1987, "image schemas").

I. SPATIAL FRAMEWORKS

In these experiments, readers read narratives describing arrays of objects around observers, other characters, or other objects, and were later probed for objects by directions (or vice versa). The pattern of reaction times to access information from the spatial mental models did not show the analog, perceptual characteristics typical of imagery tasks. The pattern did correspond to the spatial framework model, according to which readers construct a mental scaffolding to keep track of the directions of objects from their bodies and each other, which can be updated as the situation changes.

The spatial framework derived from an analysis of our canonical interaction with the perceptual world, the asymmetries of that world and our bodies, posture, and perspective. The world as we view it has one vertical and two horizontal axes. The vertical axis is correlated with gravity, which exerts a considerable asymmetric force on the world, constraining how the world looks and how we maneuver in it. Moreover, the vertical has natural anchors in the environment: the ground and the sky for outside environments, floors and ceilings for indoors. In contrast, the two horizontal dimensions are not correlated with environmental forces or anchored to features in the environment. In many situations, then, two natural axes of our own bodies—the front/back and left/right axes—serve as reference points for horizontal axes of the world. Although the left/right axis is essentially symmetric, the front/back axis is not; both perception of the environment and manipulation of it are natural frontward, but difficult, if at all possible, backward. The third axis of the body, the head/feet axis, not only has asymmetry but also correlates with the vertical axis of the world, and with gravity, i.e., when we are in canonical upright orientation. For the upright observer surrounded by an array of objects, then, both body and environmental factors contribute to the predominance of the vertical head/feet axis. Body factors lead to the predominance of front/back over left/right.

The environmental and body factors change as the perspective of the observer changes. For a reclining observer, there is no body axis correlated with the distinguished environmental axis, gravity, so the predictions derive only from consideration of the body. Because the head/feet axis is not correlated with vertical when the body reclines, the front/back asymmetry looms larger than the head/feet, and the left/right remains least distinguished. The spatial framework analysis was confirmed for these two cases, upright and reclining observers, surrounded by arrays of object. Preliminary work has begun extending the spatial framework to other perspectives and arrays, yielding a family of spatial frameworks, i.e., situation-specific variants based on the same general principles. Thus, systematic exploration of people's responses to imaginary environments has revealed some of the ways we conceive of the visual world.

IV. Summary

Readers of spatial descriptions spontaneously construct spatial mental models of the described scenes as a natural consequence of reading for comprehension and memory, with no special training, instructions, or prior visual displays. Of courses, readers do not necessarily construct spatial models from all text; the text must be spatial, coherent, well integrated, and more or less determinate, among other characteristics (e.g., Denis & Denhiere, 1990; Ehrlich & Johnson-Laird, 1982; Mani & Johnson-Laird, 1982; Perrig & Kintsch, 1985). The spatial mental models constructed reveal people's conceptions of space, which, though built on their perceptions of space, are more abstract and general.

In the first set of experiments (Taylor & Tversky, in press), subjects read route or survey descriptions of four environments, and verified verbatim and inference statements about those environments from both the same and the other perspective. Subjects were equally fast and accurate in verifying inference statements from the read perspective and the other perspective. This led us to the conclusion that subjects' mental models capture the categorical spatial relations described in the text, but not from any particular perspective. Like structural descriptions, spatial mental models contain information about the parts of a scene and the relations between the parts. Unlike images, which have been likened to internalized perceptions, spatial mental models are perspective-free and allow the taking of many perspectives, required in order to verify the test statements.

The second set of studies examined perspective taking and information retrieval in a particular (imaginary) environment, one that is simple and common, that of an observer surrounded by objects (Franklin & Tversky, 1990b). We found that times to report what objects lie at six canonical directions from the observer (at head or feet, to the left or right, in front or back) differed reliably and systematically depending on the direction of the object and the posture of the observer. The times could not be accounted for by a model that assumed that readers imagined themselves in the place of the observer, and imagined themselves rotating in place to ascertain what objects are at what directions. Rather, the reaction times were accounted for by an analysis of how space is conceived in relation to the body, yielding a family of what we termed spatial frameworks.

We opened with the problem of understanding directions, instructions, and narratives, and observed that constructing a mental model of the situation described in the directions, instructions, or narrative not only seemed useful but also seemed to be what readers and listeners do when the conditions are right. The experiments reported here have added to that body of research, uncovering many features of spatial mental models in the process. Consider the ladder in the following passage from F. Scott Fitzgerald (1922/1950). "Fifth and Sixth Avenues, it seemed to Anthony, were the uprights of a gigantic ladder stretching from Washington Square to Central Park. Coming up-town on top of a bus toward Fifty-second Street invariably gave him the sensation of hoisting himself hand by hand on a series of treacherous rungs, and when the bus jolted to a stop at his own rung, he found something akin to relief as he descended the reckless metal steps to the sidewalk" (p. 10). On the one hand, the ladder describes the appearance of that part of the city, two broad avenues, anchored in one park and reaching toward another, with many narrow cross-streets. Yet the ladder is also used to convey the effort and precariousness of coming uptown, fighting against gravity on an unwieldy apparatus. Spatial mental models do more than capture a physical setting; instilled by a gifted writer, they are replete with meaning.

ACKNOWLEDGMENTS

I have been fortunate to have Nancy Franklin, Holly Taylor, and David Bryant as collaborators, and I am grateful for their insightful comments on a previous draft of this manuscript. The research reported here was supported by the Air Force Office of Scientific Research, Air Force Systems Command, USAF under Grant #AFOSR 89-0076 to Stanford University.

References

Abelson R, (1975). Does a story understander need a point of view? In R. Schank & B. L. Nash-Webber (Eds.), *Theoretical issues in natural language processing.* Washington, DC: Association for Computational Linguistics.

Anderson, R. C., & Pichert, J. W. (1978). Recall of previously unrecallable information following a shift in perspective. *Journal of Verbal Learning and Verbal Behavior, 17,* 1–12.

Bly, B. (1989). *Perspective in mental models of text.* Unpublished manuscript, Stanford University, Stanford, CA.

Bower, G. H. (1978). Experiments on story comprehension and recall. *Discourse Processes, 1,* 211–231.

Bransford, J. D., Barclay, J. R., & Franks, J. J. (1972). Sentence memory: A constructive versus interpretive approach. *Cognitive Psychology, 3,* 193–209.

Bryant, D., Tversky, B., & Franklin, N. (in press). Internal and external spatial frameworks for representing described scenes. *Journal of Memory and Language.*

Byrne, R. M. J., & Johnson-Laird, P. N. (1989). Spatial reasoning. *Journal of Memory and Language, 28,* 564–575.

Byrne, R. W. (1979). Memory for urban geography. *Quarterly Journal of Experimental Psychology, 31,* 147–154.

Chase, W. G. (1983). Spatial representations of taxi drivers. In D. R. Rogers & J. A. Sloboda (Eds.), *Acquisition of symbolic skills.,* New York, Plenum.

Clark, H. H. (1973). Space, time, semantics and the child. In T. E. Moore (Ed.), *Cognitive development and the acquisition of language,* (pp. 27–63). New York: Academic Press.

Cooper, L., & Shepard, R. N. (1975). Mental transformations in the identification of left and right hands. *Journal of Experimental Psychology: Human Perception and Performance, 104,* 48–56.

Denis, M., & Cocude, M. (1989). Scanning visual images generated from verbal descriptions. *European Journal of Cognitive Psychology, 1,,* 293–307.

Denis, M., & Denhiere, G. (1990). Comprehension and recall of spatial description. *European Bulletin of Cognitive Psychology, 10,* 115–143.

Ehrlich, K., & Johnson-Laird, P. N. (1982). Spatial descriptions and referential continuity. *Journal of Verbal Learning and Verbal Behavior, 21,* 296–306.

Evans, G. W., & Pezdek, K. (1980). Cognitive mapping: Knowledge of real-world distance and location information. *Journal of Experimental Psychology: Human Learning and Memory, 6,* 13–24.

Fillmore, C. J. (1975). *Santa Cruz lectures on deixis.* Bloomington: Indiana University Linguistics Club.

Finke, R. A., & Shepard, R. N. (1986). Visual functions of mental imagery. In K. R. Boff, L. Kaufman, & J. P. Thomas (Eds.), *Handbook of perception and human performance.* New York, Wiley.

Fitzgerald, F. Scott, (1950). *The beautiful and the damned.* New York: Scribner's (Original work published 1922).

Foos, P. W. (1980). Constructing cognitive maps from sentences. *Journal of Experimental Psychology: Human Learning and Memory, 6,* 25–38.

Franklin, N. (1991). *Representation of spatial information in described routes: Distance, turns, and objects.* Manuscript, State University of New York-Stony Brook.

Franklin, N., & Tversky, B. (1990a). *Mental spatial frameworks for different perspectives.* Poster presented at the Psychonomic Society meetings, New Orleans, LA.

Franklin, N., & Tversky, B. (1990b). Searching imagined environments. *Journal of Experimental Psychology: General, 119,* 63–76.

Garnham, A. (1981). Mental models as representations of text. *Memory & Cognition, 9,* 560–565.

Glenberg, A. M., Meyer, M., & Lindem, K. (1987). Mental models contribute to foregrounding during text comprehension. *Journal of Memory and Language, 26,* 69–83.

Hintzman, D. L., O'Dell, C. S., & Arndt, D. R. (1981). Orientation in cognitive maps. *Cognitive Psychology, 13,* 149–206.

Hirtle, S. C., & Jonides, J. (1985). Evidence of hierarchies in cognitive maps. *Memory & Cognition, 13,* 208–217.

Johnson-Laird, P. N. (1983). *Mental models.* Cambridge, MA: Harvard University Press.

Kosslyn, S. M. (1976). Can imagery be distinguished from other forms of internal representation? Evidence from studies of information retrieval time. *Memory & Cognition, 4,* 291–297.

Kosslyn, S. M. (1980). *Image and mind.* Cambridge, MA: Harvard University Press.

Lakoff, G. (1987). *Women, fire, and dangerous things: What categories reveal about the mind.* Chicago, IL: University of Chicago Press.

Levelt, W. J. M. (1982). Linearization in describing spatial networks. In S. Peters & E. Saarinen (Eds.), *Processes, beliefs, and questions.* (pp. 199–220). Dordrecht, The Netherlands: Reidel.

Levelt, W. J. M. (1984). Some perceptual limitations on talking about space. In A. J. van Doorn, W. A. de Grind, & J. J. Koenderink (Eds.), *Limits in perception.* Utrecht, The Netherlands: VNU Science Press.

Levine, M., Jankovic, I., Palij, M. (1982). Principles of spatial problem solving. *Journal of Experimental Psychology: General, 111,* 157–175.

Linde, C., & Labov, W. (1975). Spatial structures as a site for the study of language and thought. *Language, 51,* 924–939.

Maki, R. H. (1981). Categorization and distance effects with spatial linear orders. *Journal of Experimental Psychology: Human Learning and Memory, 7,* 15–32.

Mani, K., & Johnson-Laird, P. N. (1982). The mental representation of spatial descriptions. *Memory & Cognition, 10,* 181–187.

Marr, D. (1982). *Vision: A computational investigation into the human representation and processing of visual information.* New York: Freeman.

Marr, D., & Nishihara, H. K. (1978). Representation and recognition of the spatial organization of three-dimensional shapes. *Proceedings of the Royal Society of London, Series B, 200,* 269–291.

McNamara, T. P. (1986). Mental representations of spatial relations. *Cognitive Psychology, 18,* 87–121.

Miller, G. A., & Johnson-Laird, P. N. (1976). *Language and perception.* Cambridge, MA: Harvard University Press.

Minsky, M. (1975). A framework for representing knowledge. In P. H. Winston (Ed.), *The psychology of computer vision.,* New York: McGraw-Hill.

Moar, I., & Bower, G. H. (1983). Inconsistency in spatial knowledge. *Memory & Cognition, 11,* 107–113.

Morrow, D. G., Bower, G. H., & Greenspan, S. (1989). Updating situation models during narrative comprehension. *Journal of Memory and Language, 28,* 292–312.

Morrow, D. G., Greenspan, S., & Bower, G. H. (1987). Accessibility and situation models in narrative comprehension. *Journal of Memory and Language, 26,* 165–187.

Noton, D., & Stark, L. (1971). Eye movements and visual perception. *Scientific American, 224,* 34–43.

Novick, L. R., & Tversky, B. (1987). Cognitive constraints on ordering operations: The case of geometric analogies. *Journal of Experimental Psychology: General, 116,* 50–67.

Palmer, S. E. (1977). Hierarchical structure in perceptual representation. *Cognitive Psychology, 9,* 441–474.

Parsons, L. (1987a). Imagined spatial transformation of one's body. *Journal of Experimental Psychology: General, 116,* 172–191.

Parsons, L. (1987b). Imagined spatial transformation of one's hands and feet. *Cognitive Psychology, 19,* 178–241.

Perrig, W., & Kintsch, W. (1985). Propositional and situational representations of text. *Journal of Memory and Language, 24,* 503–518.

Pinker, S. (1980). Mental imagery and the third dimension. *Journal of Experimental Psychology: General, 109,* 354–371.

Pinker, S. (1984). Visual cognition: An introduction. *Cognition, 18,* 1–63.

Sekiyama, K. (1982). Kinesthetic aspects of mental representations in the identification of left and right hands. *Perception & Psychophysics, 32,* 89–95.

Shepard, R. N., & Cooper, L. A. (1982). *Mental images and their transformations.* Cambridge, MA: MIT Press/Bradford Books.

Shepard, R. N., & Hurwitz, S. (1984). Upward direction, mental rotation, and discrimination of left and right turns in maps. *Cognition, 18,* 161–194.

Shepard R. N., & Podgomy, P. (1978). Cognitive processes that resemble perceptual processes. In W. K. Estes (Ed.), *Handbook of learning and cognitive processes.* Hillsdale, NJ: Erlbaum.

Sholl, M. J. (1987). Cognitive maps as orienting schemata. *Journal of Experimental Psychology: Learning, Memory, and Cognition, 13,* 615–628.

Stevens, A. L., & Coupe, P. (1978). Distortions in judged spatial relations. *Cognitive Psychology, 10,* 422–437.

Streeter, L. A., Vitello, D., & Wonsiewicz, S. A. (1985). How to tell people where to go: Comparing navigational aids. *International Journal of Man-Machine Studies, 22,* 549–562.

Taylor, H. A., & Tversky, B. (1990). *Spatial descriptions and depictions.* Paper presented at the Psychonomic Society meetings, New Orleans, LA.

Taylor, H. A., & Tversky, B. (in press). Spatial mental models derived from survey and route descriptions. *Journal of Memory and Language.*

Thorndyke, P. W. (1981). Spatial cognition and reasoning. In J. Harvey (Ed.), *Cognition, social behavior, and the environment.* Hillsdale, NJ: Erlbaum.

Thorndyke, P. W., & Hayes-Roth, B. (1982). Differences in spatial knowledge acquired from maps and navigation. *Cognitive Psychology, 14,,* 560–589.

Tulving, E. (1962). Subjective organization in free recall of "unrelated" words. *Psychological Review, 69,* 344–354.

Tversky, B. (1981). Distortions in cognitive maps. *Cognitive Psychology, 13,* 407–433.

Ullman, S. (1989). Aligning pictorial descriptions: An approach to object recognition. *Cognition, 32,* 193–254.

van Dijk, T. A., & Kintsch, W. (1983). *Strategies of discourse comprehension.* New York: Academic Press.

Wagener-Wender, M., & Wender, K. F. (1990). Expectations, mental representations, and spatial inferences. In A. C. Graesser & G. H. Bower (Eds.), *Inferences and text comprehension,* (pp. 137–157). San Diego, CA: Academic Press.

Wilton, R. N. (1979). Knowledge of spatial relations: The specification of information used in making inferences. *Quarterly Journal of Experimental Psychology, 31,* 133–146.

MEMORY'S VIEW OF SPACE

Timothy P. McNamara

I. Introduction

Estimate the distance in your home between the refrigerator and the stove. Describe a path from your office to the main entrance of the building. Point to the nearest airport from where you are sitting. People commonly report that they solve problems like these by constructing and using images of the scenes. These images often seem to have compelling spatial properties; in particular, relative distances and directions seem to be represented to a high degree of fidelity.

My goal in this article is to summarize and evaluate research that speaks to how interobject spatial relations are represented in long-term memory. Historically, models of spatial representation have taken one or the other of two opposing forms: One proposal is that spatial representations are map-like and preserve Euclidean properties of the world (e.g., Thorndyke, 1981). This view is certainly consistent with the experiences that I and many other people have when solving spatial problems. The other view, which seems at first to be much less compelling, is that spatial representations are abstract conceptual representations that may or may not preserve Euclidean properties of the world (e.g., Stevens & Coupe, 1978). My conclusion at the end of this article is that spatial representations are certainly not the former and they may be even more extreme than the latter; spatial representations may be purely nonmetric.

The article is organized in the following way: First, I discuss a number of methodological issues, in particular, some concerns that have recently arisen regarding the use of certain tasks to investigate spatial memories. Next, I review a number of studies that have looked at the structure of spatial memories. This section of the paper is organized around principles of spatial representation that have emerged in recent years. Finally, I conclude by discussing two possible models consistent with the available data and suggest ways to distinguish between the models.

II.   Methods and Measures

The primary goal of most of the research described below was to discover properties of spatial representations. As any cognitive psychologist knows, however, properties of mental representations must be inferred from performance in cognitive tasks, and performance is a function both of how things are represented and of how they are processed. Thus, when one finds that some variable, such as the presence or absence of physical boundaries, affects performance in a task, such as distance estimations, it is difficult to know whether the effects are due to the mental representation, the mental processes, or both (Anderson, 1978; Pylyshyn, 1979).

To my knowledge, there are two solutions to this problem. One strategy is to use converging operations (Garner, Hake, & Eriksen, 1956). The idea is that if performance in several tasks is affected by a variable in the same way, then the likelihood is low that these effects are caused by unique features of the tasks. If the only common feature of the tasks is the presumed mental representation that supports performance, then one can conclude with some confidence that the variable affects how information is mentally represented. A second strategy is to use tasks that are well understood or that are accomplished quickly, relatively effortlessly, and without much conscious activity on the part of the participants. I have tried to employ both strategies in my own research.

In particular, I have for some time been an advocate of using spatial priming to investigate mental representations of spatial relations. In a typical experiment, subjects learn locations of objects in a spatial layout and then participate in a recognition test. Object names are displayed one at a time on a computer terminal screen; the subjects' task is to decide whether or not the named object was in the layout. The variable of interest is priming between sequential items in the recognition test as a function of the spatial relations between corresponding objects in the layout. In one experiment (McNamara, 1986), for example, I showed that locations in the same region of a spatial layout primed each other more than locations in different regions, even when Euclidean distance was held constant.

Recognition priming is particularly useful for investigating spatial memory because it is not influenced by retrieval strategies. Ratcliff and Mc-Koon (1981) showed that priming in memory for text has a very fast onset and is insensitive to the frequency of related items in the test lists. McNamara, Hardy, and Hirtle (1989) demonstrated further that inhibition does not occur in spatial priming at brief stimulus onset asynchronies (SOA). These qualities indicate that recognition priming is an automatic process (as defined by Posner & Snyder, 1975a, 1975b).Consequently, priming in recognition should be informative about the structure and content of memory rather than about strategies and inferences employed at the time of testing (Tulving, 1976).

Recently, the use of priming in recognition to investigate spatial memory has been questioned. The first sign of trouble appeared in studies investigating naturally acquired spatial memories. McNamara, Altarriba, Bendele, Johnson, and Clayton (1989), for example, showed that spatial priming did not occur in a standard item recognition task when subjects were tested on their memory of a campus (also see, Clayton & Chattin, 1989; Merrill & Baird, 1987). Spatial priming does not seem to occur in naturally acquired spatial memories unless the task requires subjects to retrieve information about spatial location (Clayton & Chattin, 1989; McNamara, Altarriba et al., 1989).

McNamara, Altarriba et al., (1989) suggested that the difference between experimentally and naturally acquired spatial memories might be that the latter were "decontextualized" (cf. Clayton & Chattin, 1989). The hypothesis was that when people learn a spatial layout or a map in an experiment, the initial memory representation is a highly contextualized, unitary representation of object identities and locations. Consequently, subjects cannot retrieve the name of an object without also retrieving the location of that object. One result of these interdependencies is that objects close to each other in a spatial layout, and consequently "close" to each other in memory, prime each other in recognition, even though the recognition task does not require subjects to retrieve knowledge about these spatial interrelations. But when spatial environments are learned over long periods of time and objects in those environments are experienced in different contexts (Evans & Pezdek, 1980), the identities and the locations of objects become dissociated, possibly leading to multiple internal representations. One consequence of having multiple sources of familiarity or multiple internal representations is that names of buildings can be retrieved from memory without activating spatial knowledge.

Although this hypothesis has not been ruled out, there are reasons to believe that it is incorrect and that the correct explanation is much simpler. The hypothesis was tested indirectly in two experiments by attempting to transform a contextualized memory into a decontextualized memory (Bendele, 1990). In the first experiment, subjects in two groups first learned a map of a fictitious campus. Immediately after learning the map, subjects in both groups were given a recognition test in which spatial priming was the measure of interest. Subjects in the experimental group then learned facts about buildings on the fictitious campus, whereas subjects in the control group learned facts about buildings on the Vanderbilt campus (which had no relation to the fictitious map learned). All subjects were then given a second recognition test. The decontextualization hypothesis predicts that spatial priming should appear in both groups in the first recognition test (replicating the usual spatial priming effect), but that it should appear only in the control group in the second recognition test. In fact, there was not even a hint of an interaction: The priming effect was significant for both groups at both test points. In a second experiment, the manipulation was strengthened by having subjects learn the map and the facts simultaneously over several days. It was still the case, however, that spatial priming was unaffected. These results certainly do not bode well for the decontextualization hypothesis.

Recent experiments by Clayton and Habibi (in press) and by Sherman and Lim (1990) elucidate the problem more clearly. Clayton and Habibi set out to investigate the relative contributions of temporal and of spatial contiguity to priming in recognition. In most previous investigations (but see McNamara, Ratcliff, & McKoon, 1984, Experiment 2), temporal and spatial contiguity were confounded: When two items were close in space, they were also experienced together in time. Clayton and Habibi unconfounded these variables by having a computer present the names of map locations one item at a time. Although subjects saw the entire configuration of dots on the computer screen, they saw only one name at a time during the learning phase. For one group of subjects, names were presented in an order that confounded temporal and spatial contiguity, i.e., spatially close names followed each other in the learning sequence and spatially distant names were separated by several other names in the learning sequence. For a second group of subjects, critical items were always temporally distant, even though their spatial distance might be close or far. The results of this experiment in terms of recognition reaction times are summarized in Table I. The basic result was that although "spatial" priming was found in the confounded group (superscript "a"), it was not found in the unconfounded group (superscript "b").

Clayton and Habibi (in press) extended this result in two additional experiments. In Experiment 2, temporal contiguity was held at close for one group but at far for a second group (replicating the unconfounded group in Experiment 1). The spatial priming effect was very small (4 or

TABLE I

Summary of Results Obtained by Clayton and Habibi (in Press)[a]

	Temporal distance	
	Close	Far
Experiment 1		
Spatial distance		
Close	623[a]	600[b]
Far	—	646[a]/604[b]
Experiment 2		
Spatial distance		
Close	624[a]	601[b]
Far	628[a]	606[b]
Experiment 3		
Spatial distance		
Close	—	—
Far	574[a]	594[a]

[a] Within each experiment, conditions with a common superscript were varied within subjects; conditions with different superscripts were varied between subjects. Latencies are in milliseconds.

5 msec) and not significant. In Experiment 3, temporal contiguity was varied but spatial contiguity was held constant (at far). In this experiment, there was a 20-msec priming effect, which was significant. This series of experiments indicates that when temporal contiguity is controlled, spatial distance has no effect on priming in recognition.

In another investigation of similar issues, Sherman and Lim (1990) had subjects learn the locations of objects in a real environment. Subjects learned the locations so that temporal and spatial contiguity were confounded or so that these variables were "independent."[1] The major results were as follows: (1) spatial priming occurred in a recognition test only when temporal and spatial contiguity were confounded, and (2) spatial priming occurred in a location judgment test even when spatial and temporal contiguity were not confounded. Sherman and Lim used these results to explain why spatial priming does not occur in recognition but does occur in location judgments if subjects' memories of a campus are tested. The

[1] The meaning of "independent" is not clear from the paper. My reading is that subjects were taken to locations in a random order, which means that on the average, spatially contiguous locations were no closer than spatially distant locations in the exposure order.

authors suggested that when people learn a large-scale environment, like a campus, their paths through the environment may not force them to experience spatially contiguous objects, such as buildings, close together in time.

There are several ways to view these results, but before I even attempt an explanation, I want to describe some research that is underway in our lab. Subjects in two experiments learned the locations of object names in spatial arrays (see Fig. 1) using procedures very similar to those developed by Clayton and Habibi (in press). The entire configuration of dots was visible during learning, but the names of the locations were displayed one at a time on the computer screen in an order that controlled for temporal and spatial contiguity. Unlike Clayton and Habibi, we manipulated both of these variables within subjects.

After subjects learned an array, they were given two or three tasks: Subjects in Experiment 1a ($N = 16$) participated in item recognition and location judgment tasks, whereas subjects in Experiment 1b ($N = 16$) participated in these tasks plus distance estimations. In the location judgment task, object names appeared one at a time on a computer screen; subjects had to decide whether each name had been on the right or the left side of the boundary, and priming was the variable of interest. The data for all three tasks are summarized in Table II.

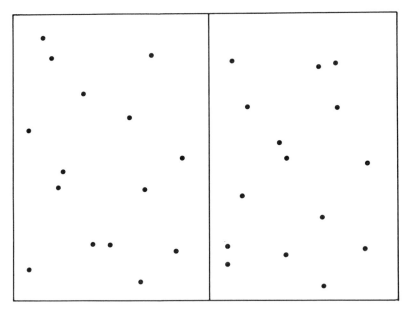

Fig. 1.   One of the spatial arrays used in the space–time experiments.

A number of important results appeared in these experiments: First, spatial and temporal distance had interactive effects in recognition priming ($F = 9.62$). Priming occurred only for names that had appeared near each other in space and in time. These results contrast with those obtained by Clayton and Habibi (in press): In their experiments, spatial priming did not occur in recognition when temporal contiguity was controlled, and in the case where spatial distance was held constant there was still a temporal priming effect.

Second, spatial and temporal contiguity had (statistically) additive effects in the location judgments ($F = 26.07$, 26.15, and 0.93, for space, time, and the interaction, respectively). This result is important because it shows that priming as a function of spatial contiguity can be obtained even when temporal contiguity is controlled. This finding replicates and extends the results of Sherman and Lim (1990), who found that spatial priming

TABLE II

Summary of Results of Space–Time Experiments[a]

	Temporal distance	
	Close	Far
Recognition (N = 32)		
Spatial distance		
Close	604	669
Far	647	655
Location judgments (N = 32)		
Spatial distance		
Close	702	893
Far	824	1092
Distance estimations (N = 16)		
Spatial distance		
Close	0.23	0.29
Far	2.30	2.33

[a] Latencies are in milliseconds; distance estimates are in inches.

occurred in location judgments even when items were not temporally contiguous. The sizes of the response latencies suggest that the priming effects might have been strategically mediated. Evidence against this possibility can be garnered from two sources. First, although mean latencies in Experiment 1a were much faster than mean latencies in Experiment 1b (733 vs. 1022 msec), the pattern of results was identical. Second, in other experiments (McNamara, Halpin, & Hardy, 1990, discussed below), we have shown that distance effects appear in location judgments even when the SOA is short and processing time on the target is held to 550 msec.

The last major result of the experiment was that there were no reliable effects of temporal contiguity in distance estimations ($F < 1$). This result replicates the findings reported by McNamara and LeSueur (1989), who found no effects of semantic or episodic associations in distance estimations.

These experiments and those reported by Clayton and Habibi (in press) and by Sherman and Lim (1990) converge on some results but diverge on others. The major point of convergence is this: When spatially contiguous names were not experienced together in time, spatial priming did not occur in a recognition test for those names. This result held up despite wide differences in materials and procedures. The divergent results are that (1) we obtained a spatial priming effect for temporally contiguous names but Clayton and Habibi did not, and (2) we did not obtain a temporal priming effect for spatially distant names but Clayton and Habibi did.

The methods used by Clayton and Habibi (in press) and by us differ enough to make the task of understanding the differences in results an arduous one. For example, we manipulated temporal and spatial contiguity within subjects, whereas Clayton and Habibi manipulated one or the other of these variables between subjects; the distance manipulation was much stronger and the close locations were much more salient in our experiments than in Clayton and Habibi's; our maps contained more locations than theirs (30 vs. 18); and finally, our maps were divided into two regions.

An examination of the maps used in the two studies yields one obvious difference, and that is that the distance manipulation was much stronger in our experiments than in Clayton and Habibi's (in press) (distance ratio of 8:1 vs. 4:1). The close pairs on our maps were perceptually quite close. This difference probably accounts for the fact that we obtained a spatial effect for temporally contiguous items but Clayton and Habibi did not.

The cause of the absence of a temporal effect for spatially distant items is not clear, but it almost certainly is not a weak manipulation of temporal distance. The temporal effect was quite large in location judgments at both levels of distance. In addition, nearly all of the subjects reported that they had learned the temporal order of the object names to facilitate acquisition of the map. Finally, data reported by McNamara et al. (1984) show that temporal priming may not occur in recognition even when a temporal manipulation is strong.

The recognition data in Table II actually replicate data reported by McNamara et al. (1984). In the second experiment of that study, subjects learned fictitious road maps in which critical pairs of cities were close in Euclidean and in route distance (CE–CR), close in Euclidean but not in route distance (CE–FR), and far in both (FE–FR). Although subjects saw the entire map when they studied it, they were forced by the experimenter to rehearse the cities and recall their locations in an order that guaranteed that names in the CE–CR condition and in the CE–FR condition were the same temporal distance apart. Names in the FE–FR condition were always far apart in the rehearsal protocols. Given that route distance was the primary determinant of priming in that experiment, one can reclassify the conditions as follows: CE–CR = close in space, close in time; CE–FR = far in space, close in time; and FE–FR = far in space, far in time. The data from this experiment are reproduced in Table III.

Note that for temporally contiguous items, there was still a spatial priming effect. This effect, again, was probably caused by the strong manipulation of spatial distance in that experiment: Items close in route distance were connected by a line, but items close in Euclidean distance were not. Importantly, the temporal effect for spatially distant items was quite small (10 msec), even though the temporal manipulation was very strong. Subjects in that experiment were required to recall all of the city names after learning a map. Seven of the 12 subjects recalled all 16 cities on each of three maps in exactly the same order as the cities had been learned,

TABLE III

RESULTS OF EXPERIMENT 2
OF MCNAMARA, RATCLIFF, AND
MCKOON (1984)[a]

Route distance	Temporal distance	
	Close	Far
Close	620	—
Far	658	668

[a] Latencies are in milliseconds.

and an eighth subject got the order right for all three maps but left out one city on one map. Across all 12 subjects and three maps learned, the mean distances between primes and targets in the recall protocols (where a value of 1 means the cities were next to each other) were 1.18 in the CE–CR condition (close in time, close in space), 1.34 in the CE–FR condition (close in time, far in space), and 6.46 in the FE–FR condition (far in time, far in space).

In summary, a consideration of the location judgments and subjects' informal reports in the present studies and of the data collected by McNamara et al. (1984) indicates that temporal priming may not occur in recognition even when temporal distance is varied. Of course, the same may be said of spatial priming in recognition. The causes of these results are not obvious, but they must have something to do with the kinds of information that can be used to make a recognition judgment and the relative availability of these sources of information in various learning situations.

Even though many questions remain unanswered, some useful conclusions can be drawn from this line of research. First, the mode of acquisition of a spatial array can affect priming in recognition in ways that, at this point, are not entirely predictable. Second, mode of acquisition also affects priming in location judgments, but in a much more predictable fashion. Finally, mode of acquisition has no discernible effect on distance estimations.

The latter two results suggest a powerful strategy for investigating spatial representations: If a variable affects distance estimations and location judgments in the same way, it is probably having its effects on the spatial representation and is probably not a product of retrieval strategies. An example would be the effects of boundaries (see below). If, however, a variable affects distance estimations but not priming, one would be inclined to argue that the effects are strategic. Finally, a variable that affects priming but not distance estimations may be influencing subjects' encoding in a nonspatial way.

Although priming in recognition has been sullied by the data reported above, a dismissal of this method would be premature. There are many unresolved questions about how mode of acquisition affects recognition performance in particular, and the types of mental representations that people construct in general. It is possible, for example, that the mental representations produced by the learning procedures outlined above are considerably different from those produced by normal spatial learning. Moreover, a number of experiments (reviewed below) have revealed striking similarities in results obtained from recognition and distance estimation tasks. It is difficult to attribute these results to happenstance.

III.   Structure and Content of Spatial Representations

In this section, I review studies that have examined memory for interobject spatial relations. This review is organized around principles of spatial representation that seem to hold in a variety of situations.

A.   SPATIAL REPRESENTATIONS HAVE A HIERARCHICAL COMPONENT

Attempts to capture the structure of spatial memories can be divided into two general classes. According to *hierarchical theories*, spatial memories contain nested levels of detail (e.g., Hirtle & Jonides, 1985; McNamara, 1986; Stevens & Coupe, 1978). The structure of these memories can be expressed in graph-theoretic trees, such that global and local properties of an environment are represented at different levels of a tree. Region membership is an important global property of many spatial environments, where regions can be defined by physical boundaries (e.g., walls between rooms), perceptual boundaries (e.g., lines on a map), or subjective distinctions (e.g., uptown vs. downtown). *Nonhierarchical theories* constitute the second class of theories. The prototypical example of a nonhierarchical theory is probably the mental image, in which spatial relations are represented holistically (e.g., Kosslyn, Ball, & Reiser, 1978; Levine, Jankovic, & Palij, 1982; Thorndyke, 1981). The important claim is that spatial representations do not contain nested levels of detail or separate codes for global and local properties; in short, they lack hierarchical structure.

Although the form of the representation (abstract-symbolic vs. analogical) has often been used to distinguish hierarchical and nonhierarchical theories, it is not the appropriate characteristic. The critical differences between these two classes of theories exist in the kinds of information represented in memory and the structure of the representations. Hierarchical representations encode information about entities of differing levels of ontological status (e.g., particular objects vs. sets of objects), and this information is organized, at least in part, under the relation of containment. For example, a hierarchical representation of an office might include memory traces corresponding to actual objects in the office (e.g., a telephone on a desk), to sets of objects in the office (e.g., all objects on the desk), and to the office itself. These traces must specify relative containment relations: that a particular object on the desk is in the set of objects on the desk, which in turn is in the office. Such a structure can be expressed in a tree in which terminal nodes correspond to objects and nonterminal nodes correspond to various clusters of objects, but alternative descriptions, such as overlaid images, are equally plausible. In contrast, nonhierarchical representations do not simultaneously encode information about entities of differing levels of ontological status. For example, no distinction is made between objects and collections of objects in either Thorndyke's (1981) theory, which is image-based, or Byrne's (1979) theory, which is propositional.

Stevens and Coupe (1978) were the first investigators to propose that spatial memories are hierarchical. Indeed, they took the extreme position that memories for interobject spatial relations were represented in a hierarchical, propositional network. Figure 2 contains a depiction of the proposed representation of the spatial relations among a few states and cities of the United States.

The support for this model came from the errors that people made when judging spatial relations. For example, subjects thought that Reno was northeast of San Diego, even though it is actually northwest, and that Seattle was southwest of Montreal, when in fact it is northwest. Presumably, judgments of spatial relations were based on or influenced by superordinate spatial relations: Nevada is east of California and the United States is south of Canada, so Reno must be east of San Diego and Seattle must be south of Montreal. Stevens and Coupe showed that these kinds of errors also occurred for artificial stimuli.

Additional evidence consistent with hierarchies in spatial memory includes the effects of barriers on distance estimations (e.g., Kosslyn, Pick, & Fariello, 1974; Newcombe & Liben, 1982) and the effects of region

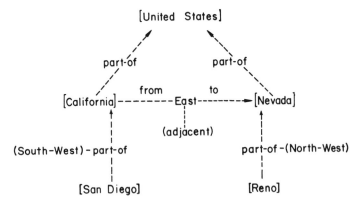

Fig. 2.   Schematic illustration of a hierarchical spatial representation based on the model proposed by Stevens and Coupe (1978).

membership on judgments of relative location (e.g., Maki, 1981; Wilton, 1979) and of spatial proximity (e.g., Allen, 1981).

This evidence has intuitive appeal, but it does not constitute strong evidence for hierarchical encoding of spatial relations. In many of these studies, it is possible that subjects simply misencoded the spatial relations between objects. For example, a person might judge (incorrectly) that Santiago, Chile was west of New York, New York because his or her memory of North and South America specified that Santiago was west of New York (see, e.g., B. Tversky, 1981). But more importantly, all of these experiments used tasks that are potentially greatly influenced by retrieval strategies.

More compelling evidence for hierarchical representations can be found in the experiment reported by McNamara (1986; see also Sherman, 1987). In this experiment, subjects learned the locations of real objects in spatial layouts or the locations of object names on maps of these layouts. These spaces were divided into four, equal-sized regions using boundaries that did not obstruct vision (see Fig. 3). Critical pairs of objects could be close together or far apart, in the same region or in different regions, and, when in different regions, aligned or misaligned with respect to the spatial relations between superordinate regions (cf. zipper–wrench and hammer–pencil).

After learning a layout or a map, subjects participated in three tasks. The first task was item recognition. The measure of interest was priming between sequential items in the recognition test as a function of the spatial relations between corresponding objects in the layout. Subsequent to the recognition test, subjects participated in a direction judgment test, in which they judged the direction of one object relative to another, and a distance estimation test, in which they estimated Euclidean distances between pairs of objects.

Results showed that subjects recognized an object name faster, on the average, when it was immediately preceded in the test list (i.e., "primed") by the name of an object from the same region than when it was primed by the name of an object from a different region. Subjects also recognized an object name faster when it was primed by the name of a close object than when it was primed by the name of a distant object. The first result indicated that locations in the same region were "closer" in subjects' memories than locations in different regions. In the direction judgment task, judgments were distorted to correspond to superordinate spatial relations between regions. This result replicates findings of Stevens and Coupe (1978) and is analogous to the Reno–San Diego and Seattle–Montreal examples mentioned above. Finally, subjects underestimated distances between objects in the same region relative to distances between

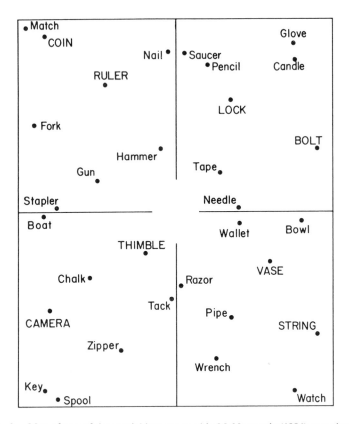

Fig. 3.   Map of one of the spatial layouts used in McNamara's (1986) experiment.

objects in different regions. This result also is consistent with the claim that objects in the same region of a spatial layout were closer in subjects' memories than objects in different regions. An examination of the relation between response latencies and distance estimations indicated that the within-region priming effect could not be explained by nonuniform "stretching" of a nonhierarchical representation. An explicit parameterization of a hierarchical theory provided a good account of the recognition latencies.[2]

[2] It may be worth noting that when I originally conducted this research, I believed that the boundary effects in distance estimations and orientation judgments were artifacts of the tasks used. Heavily influenced as I was by the work of Shepard, Kosslyn, and their respective colleagues (e.g., Kosslyn, 1980; Shepard & Cooper, 1982), I thought that spatial representations preserved most metric constraints in the real world. Hierarchical effects would be limited, I thought, to the relatively uninteresting cases of strong perceptual and navigational boundaries (e.g., walls between rooms).

B. SPATIAL REPRESENTATIONS HAVE A HIERARCHICAL
   COMPONENT, EVEN WHEN BOUNDARIES ARE ABSENT

The initial evidence for this principle came from an experiment conducted
by Hirtle and Jonides (1985), who examined subjects' memories of a
natural spatial environment (Ann Arbor, Michigan). Subjects memorized
the names of landmarks in Ann Arbor so that they would be able to recall
the names and to draw maps locating each landmark. Subjects then participated in several tasks, including multiple-trial recall, map drawing and
map construction, and distance estimation. Recall protocals from individual subjects were submitted to the ordered-tree algorithm developed by
Reitman and Rueter (1980). This algorithm constructs hierarchical trees
consistent with the internal organization of recall protocols. Items that are
recalled together are clustered together in the same subtree. Hirtle and
Jonides were able to isolate subjective regions of the campus by examining
which landmarks were clustered together in ordered trees.

Hirtle and Jonides found that data from map drawing, map construction,
relative distance judgments, and absolute distance judgments depended on
whether landmarks were clustered together in the trees obtained from
subjects' recall protocols. For example, subjects tended to judge two
landmarks as close together (relative to a standard), when the landmarks
were in fact far apart, if the landmarks were in the same subtree. Absolute
distance estimates also depended on whether or not landmarks were clustered together. Specifically, between-cluster distances tended to be overestimated relative to within-cluster distances.

These findings were extended in two experiments reported by McNamara, Hardy, and Hirtle (1989). In these experiments, subjects learned
either real spatial layouts or maps. These spatial arrays did not contain
physical or perceptual boundaries of any kind. Subjects then participated
in three tasks: recognition, free and cued recall, and Euclidean distance
estimation. Recall protocols were submitted to the ordered-tree algorithm
used by Hirtle and Jonides (1985); the program produced hierarchical trees
consistent with output order. Ordered trees were obtained for each subject
and each layout separately. The recognition and distance estimation data
were then conditionalized on whether pairs of objects appeared in the
same subtree or in different subtrees. Different subtrees presumably corresponded to different subjective regions of the psychological space.

The results provided strong support for hierarchical encoding of spatial
relations. Well-structured trees could be obtained for most subjects.
Moreover, priming was greater between objects in the same subtree than
between objects in different subtrees. Similarly, distance estimations were
smaller within subtrees than across subtrees. Importantly, none of these
effects was confounded with actual interobject distance.

Lest there be a misunderstanding here, I want to emphasize that the hierarchical trees were obtained from recall protocols, not from the recognition and distance estimation data. Hence, the dependency of the results in the latter two tasks on the structure of the trees is not trivial. Furthermore, the order in which tasks were administered—recognition, recall, distance estimation—guarantees that we were not simply modeling a retrieval structure that was created during recall. In summary, these results indicate that spatial memories contain a hierarchical component even when objective boundaries are not present.

C.   HIERARCHICAL EFFECTS ARE NOT PRODUCED BY NONSPATIAL ASSOCIATIONS

Evidence for this principle comes from the dissociation between hierarchical effects and associative effects in distance estimations. In a series of experiments reported by McNamara and LeSueur (1989), subjects learned maps in which pairs of object names were related semantically (e.g., cup–saucer), episodically (via a paired-associate learning task that preceded map learning), or both semantically and episodically. The critical result for current purposes was that distance estimations were not affected by these nonspatial, associative relations. A parallel result was found in the investigations of temporal and spatial factors in spatial priming (see above). Hierarchical effects, on the other hand, are at least as strong in distance estimations as they are in spatial priming (McNamara, 1986; McNamara, Hardy, & Hirtle, 1989).

D.   HIERARCHICAL EFFECTS ARE NOT PRODUCED BY VISUAL ILLUSIONS

It is natural to ask whether interobject spatial relations are misperceived when the objects are separated by boundaries. There is very little research on this issue, but I doubt that much is needed. The only experiment I know of that has tested this issue was reported informally by Stevens and Coupe (1978, p. 427). Subjects were asked to judge the direction of one object relative to another while looking at spatial displays. The displays were the same as those that had produced distortions in judgments from memory. According to Stevens and Coupe, subjects in this visual control condition were "perfect."

This result can be verified by the reader using Fig. 3. Place the tip of a pencil on a sheet of paper and imagine that it is resting on the location of the tack. While looking at Fig. 3, draw a line indicating the direction of the razor. Perform the same task for nail and saucer. These judgments should be equally accurate. In contrast, when these judgments are based on memory of the layout, the former is much less accurate than the latter (McNamara, 1986).

The fact that boundary effects cannot be attributed to visual illusions does not imply that perception plays no role in the formation of categories in spatial memory. Perceptual grouping almost certainly contributes to clustering in memory, i.e., locations that form clusters by virtue of good form or proximity are likely to be clustered in memory as well (e.g., Chattin, 1988).

E. SPATIAL REPRESENTATIONS MAY VIOLATE METRIC AXIOMS

The evidence reviewed above indicates that physical, perceptual, and subjective boundaries distort psychological distances between remembered objects. The formal properties of these distortions and the structure of the psychological space within the boundaries is less clear. Given that distances between points on maps and between objects in local environments form a metric scale, it is natural to begin investigations of these problems by asking whether or not psychological distances satisfy metric constraints and, if not, how and why they fail.

A metric is a scale that assigns to every pair of points, x and y, a distance, $d(x,y)$, such that three conditions are satisfied:

1. Positivity: $d(x,x) = 0$ and $d(x,y) > 0$ if $x \neq y$
2. Symmetry: $d(x,y) = d(y,x)$;
3. The triangle inequality: $d(x,z) \leq d(x,y) + d(y,z)$.

People are often surprised at how little structure the metric axioms impose. For example, the axioms are satisfied by the assignments $d(x,x) = 0$ and $d(x,y) = 1$, for all $x \neq y$. In Euclidean geometry, which is of interest here, it is further assumed that any two points are joined by a segment along which distances are additive:

4. Segmental additivity: Any two points x and z are joined by a segment such that for any point y on the path from x to z, $d(x,z) = d(x,y) + d(y,z)$.

A distance measure that satisfies axioms 1–4 is called a metric with additive segments. Segmental additivity imposes substantive and testable constraints on a metric.

1. Symmetry

Of all of the axioms underlying metric and dimensional representation, positivity and symmetry are probably the most fundamental. Tests of positivity are difficult to devise and to interpret (but see Podgorny &

Garner, 1979). It is hard to imagine, for example, that subjects would provide nonzero distance estimates between an object and itself. Although repetition priming could be assessed, its interpretation would be problematic because of the repetition of encoding operations and because the second recognition decision might be based on physical features of the stimulus or on memory of the first response. Test of symmetry, however, are relatively easy to devise and have been informative (e.g., A. Tversky, 1977). Surprisingly, however, there have been relatively few direct tests of symmetry in the spatial memory literature.

The earliest investigations of which I am aware were reported by Stea (1969, attributed to Buckman, 1966) and by Cadwallader (1979). These studies suggested that psychological distances might be asymmetric. However, the effects were not large and, moreover, they are difficult to evaluate given the informal nature of the reports. Sadalla, Burroughs, and Staplin (1980) provided the first systematic investigation of asymmetries in spatial memory.[3]

Sadalla et al. (1980) examined whether distances from a "reference" point to a "nonreference" point were conceived to be symmetric. Reference points were identified as locations on and around the Arizona State University campus that were visited often, well known, and historically and culturally important. In the experiment most relevant to current concerns (Experiment 1), subjects were given response sheets, each of which consisted of a semicircular grid with a location name printed at the origin.[4] Subjects were asked to place a second name on the grid at a point that best represented the distance between the two locations. Subjects estimated the distance when the reference point was fixed at the origin and when the appropriate nonreference point was fixed at the origin. The critical results were that distance estimates were significantly smaller, on the average, when the reference point was fixed at the origin ($M = 72.6$ mm) than when the nonreference point was fixed at the origin ($M = 78.6$ mm). Sadalla et al. concluded from these data that

> the cognitive distance between reference points and nonreference points is asymmetrical; nonreference points were judged nearer to reference points than were reference points to nonreference points. (p. 526)

[3] The research by Holyoak and Mah (1982) is sometimes cited as providing evidence for asymmetries in spatial memory. Actually, these experiments demonstrated that distances between objects near a point of reference were overestimated relative to distances between objects far from a point of reference (but see Birnbaum & Mellers, 1978). These findings may be related to asymmetries in spatial memory, but the relation is not essential or obvious.

[4] Sadalla et al. (1980) reported the results of five experiments, but only two of them examined the symmetry of interpoint distances. Experiment 1 is described in the text. In Experiment 2, subjects placed location names in the sentence frame _____ is close to _____. Reliable asymmetries were found, but the authors did not report whether or not previously identified reference points were members of asymmetric pairs.

These data are provocative but can be criticized on two grounds. First, because naturally-acquired spatial memories were investigated, the experimenters had no control over the materials or the learning experiences. Second, we know from previous research (McNamara & LeSueur, 1989; McNamara et al. 1984) that distance estimations are time consuming (average latencies range from 2 to 8 sec) and hence may be influenced by strategic processes. We hoped to remedy these problems in our own experiments.

In the first experiment, 40 subjects learned the locations of 24 object names on each of two maps. One of the maps is reproduced in Fig. 4. The locations were grouped in four sets of six locations. Near the center of each subset was a "landmark," which was capitalized. These landmarks were also names of objects, but they served a special role during map learning. In particular, subjects were instructed to treat these names as landmarks and to learn the locations of the other names in relation to the landmarks. Subjects were allowed to study a map for 2 min, at which point the map was taken away and subjects were given a sheet of paper that contained the four locations of the landmarks but no names of objects. Subjects were instructed to place the names of the landmarks at their correct locations and then to reproduce both the locations and the names of the remaining 20 objects. Subjects were allowed as many study-test trials as they needed to reproduce the map correctly. For the purposes of the experiment, eight of the names on each map composed four landmark–nonlandmark pairs. These names were separated by 1 in. and were mutual nearest neighbors (e.g., hat–radio, guitar–pillow, television–suitcase, brick–shoe).

After learning a map, subjects were given two tasks. First, they were given a recognition test in which they had to decide whether or not names of objects had been on the map just learned. The variable of interest was the relative level of priming when landmarks primed nonlandmarks and when nonlandmarks primed landmarks. Primes and targets appeared on sequential trials; the response–stimulus interval was 100 msec. In the second task, subjects estimated Euclidean distances between pairs of locations. Text appeared on the screen in the format below; subjects entered their estimate using the computer keyboard.

Estimate the distance from
guitar   to   pillow

Distance:

The variable of interest in this task was the average values of distance

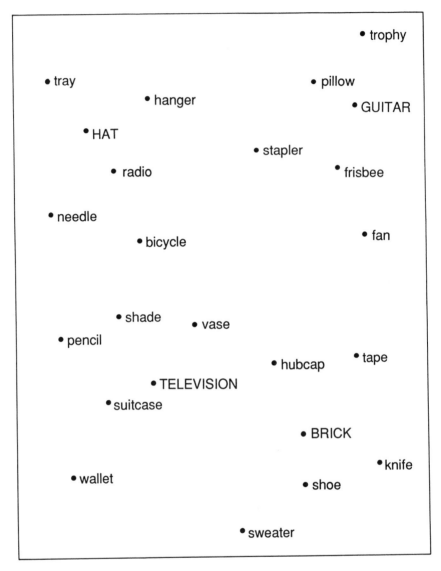

Fig. 4.   One of the maps used in the studies of symmetry.

estimates when subjects estimated distances from landmarks to non-landmarks and vice versa.

For reasons that will become clear later, I choose to discuss the distance estimation results first. These data can be found in Table IV. A given

TABLE IV

Asymmetries: Experiment 1[a]

	Distance estimations
First appearance	
Landmark → nonlandmark	0.978
Nonlandmark → landmark	1.209
Second appearance	
Landmark → nonlandmark	1.248
Nonlandmark → landmark	0.937

	Recognition latencies[b]	
	Prime	Target
Landmark	877	882
Nonlandmark	864	833

[a] Latencies are in milliseconds; distance estimates are in inches.
[b] Results for first appearance only.

landmark and its nonlandmark appeared twice in the distance estimation list; once in the order landmark–nonlandmark and once in the opposite order. For each subject, half of the pairs appeared first in the landmark–nonlandmark order and half appeared first in the nonlandmark–landmark order. It is obvious in Table IV that the serial order of appearance had a huge effect on distance estimations. When items appeared the first time, subjects gave smaller estimates from the landmark to the nonlandmark than vice versa; but when items appeared the second time, the pattern was reversed.

Although this result appears quite bizarre, it is easy to explain. A given pair of names switched conditions going from the first to the second appearance, i.e., if a pair of items appeared in the order landmark–nonlandmark the first time, it would appear in the order nonlandmark–landmark the second time. Thus, if subjects genuinely underestimated the former distance and remembered this estimate when the same items appeared again, the perfect interaction between condition and the appearance variable would occur. Importantly, the pattern of data for the first appearance is not confounded with subjects or materials, and hence should be taken as the "true" pattern.

It seems, then, that our results were different from those obtained by Sadalla et al. (1980). Recall that Sadalla and his colleagues reported that subjects underestimated distances from nonlandmarks to landmarks relative to the reverse. This conclusion, however, depends on how the task is interpreted. The finding was that when the reference point was fixed and subjects placed the nonreference point, distances were underestimated relative to the situation when the nonreference point was fixed and subjects placed the reference point. Sadalla et al. thought that the first situation (fixed reference point) corresponded to estimating the distance from the nonreference point to the reference point, and that the second situation (fixed nonreference point) corresponded to estimating the distance from the reference point to the nonreference point. This interpretation was based on Rosch's (1975) results on prototypes, which, as it turns out, have the same problem of interpretation (see below). In short, the results of Sadalla are the same as ours if placing y when x is fixed corresponds to estimating the distance from x to y.

The recognition priming data generally support the distance estimations, although the effects are not as strong or as reliable (see Table IV). The column labeled "prime" corresponds to the mean response latency when items served as primes (i.e., were not themselves primed); this is an ersatz neutral condition. The column labeled "target" corresponds to the mean response latency when the items served as targets (i.e., were primed by a nonlandmark, in the case of landmarks, or primed by a landmark, in the case of nonlandmarks). Although there is an indication that landmarks were better primes for nonlandmarks than vice versa, none of the differences in latencies in Table IV is significant.

In order to test our interpretation of Sadalla's data and to replicate the priming data, we conducted a second experiment. The maps and the learning procedures in this experiment were identical to those in the first experiment, but the recognition and distance estimation tasks were changed. A neutral priming condition was included in the recognition task. On each trial, a prime was displayed for 200 msec and then replaced by a target name; subjects were instructed to read both names but to decide whether the second name had been on the map. On some trials, landmarks and nonlandmarks were preceded by the neutral prime "ready." For the distance estimations, subjects were divided into two groups. One group of subjects provided numerical estimates of distances, as in Experiment 1. Subjects in a second group were given booklets, each page of which had an object name printed in the center of the page (next to a dot) and a second object name printed at the top of the page. The subjects' task was to place the second name at the appropriate distance from the first name. This response measure is very similar to the measure used by Sadalla et al. (1980).

The results of all three tasks can be found in Table V. The same pattern appeared in the numerical and the iconic distance estimations: For the first

TABLE V

Asymmetries: Experiment 2[a]

	Distance estimations	
	Numerical	Iconic
First appearance		
Landmark → nonlandmark	1.187	1.176
Nonlandmark → landmark	1.489	1.389
Second appearance		
Landmark → nonlandmark	1.596	1.226
Nonlandmark → landmark	1.239	1.075

	Recognition latencies[b]		
	Neutral prime	Landmark prime	Nonlandmark prime
Target			
Landmark	833	—	785
Nonlandmark	792	721	—

[a] Latencies are in milliseconds; distance estimates are in inches.
[b] Results for first appearance only.

appearance, subjects underestimated distances from the landmark to the nonlandmark relative to the reverse ordering; but for the second appearance, subjects overestimated distances from the landmark to the nonlandmark relative to the reverse ordering. Again, the simplest explanation of this interaction is that subjects remembered their initial estimate when producing the second one. Thus, the "true" pattern is best represented by the first appearance data.

The pattern in the recognition latencies is pretty clear, although the paucity of data (two or four data points per condition per subject) contributed to high variability. Responses were faster for both landmarks and nonlandmarks when they were primed by a neighboring object than when they were primed by the neutral prime ($F = 5.63$). Although the desired interaction between prime and target status was not significant, the 71-msec priming effect for nonlandmarks was reliable ($t = 2.31$) but the 48-msec priming effect for landmarks was not ($t = 1.56$). A tentative conclusion, then, is that landmarks were better primes for nonlandmarks than nonlandmarks were for landmarks. This finding is consistent with the hypothesis that the psychological distance from landmarks to nonlandmarks is less than the reverse, which is the apparent result of the distance estimations.

The priming data are not consistent with a fan effect (e.g., Anderson,

1976). To the extent that subjects followed instructions and learned the locations of nonlandmarks in relation to landmarks, the "fan" of the landmark would almost certainly be larger than the "fan" of the non-landmark. The landmark would therefore be a poor prime for the non-landmark because its activation would be distributed among several other locations. In contrast, all of the nonlandmark's activation would be sent to the landmark.

Let me summarize the data so far:

1. Subjects gave smaller numerical estimates when asked to estimate the distance from a landmark to a nonlandmark than when asked to estimate the distance from a nonlandmark to a landmark;
2. Subjects placed nonlandmarks closer to landmarks (fixed) than they placed landmarks to nonlandmarks (fixed);
3. Subjects recognized nonlandmarks faster when they were primed by landmarks than when they were primed by neutral names, and although a difference was also obtained for landmarks, it was not statistically reliable.

Taken together, these results suggest that the psychological distance from landmarks to nonlandmarks is less than the psychological distance from nonlandmarks to landmarks. Although this conclusion is exactly the opposite of the one reached by Sadalla et al. (1980), our data are exactly the same. Why did Sadalla et al. choose to interpret their results in the way that they did? Because Rosch (1975) had.

Subjects in Rosch's (1975) experiments judged the similarities between pairs of colors, pairs of lines of various orientations, and pairs of numbers. Rosch found in her first experiment that people were more likely to put a typical stimulus (e.g., a focal color) than an atypical stimulus in the reference slot of "linguistic hedge" sentence frames such as _____ is essentially _____, _____ is roughly _____, and the like (each subject contributed only one judgment to each category of stimuli). In the second experiment, Rosch had subjects place stimuli on a response grid that was similar to the one used by Sadalla et al. (1980). Each subject estimated the distance from a reference stimulus to a nonreference stimulus and vice versa. She found that the distance between stimuli was smaller when the reference stimulus was fixed at the center than when the nonreference stimulus was fixed at the center. This result, of course, is exactly what Sadalla et al. and we found. Rosch concluded, however, that reference points were farther from nonreference points than nonreference points were from reference points. This conclusion is perfectly reasonable given the data on linguistic hedges that Rosch had obtained in her first experiment.

There is one more piece to this puzzle. A. Tversky (1977) found that people preferred to put less prominent or less salient objects in the subject position and more prominent or more salient objects in the reference position of sentence frames such as _____ *is similar to* _____. Likewise, in direct judgments of similarity (and dissimilarity), less prominent or less salient objects were rated as being more similar to (and less different from) prominent or salient objects than the reverse. For example, subjects preferred the statement *North Korea is similar to Red China* to the statement *Red China is similar to North Korea*, and they gave higher similarity ratings when asked to rate the degree to which North Korea is similar to Red China than when asked to rate the degree to which Red China is similar to North Korea. This pattern held for countries, visual patterns, and auditory patterns. Most of these comparisons were performed between subjects, thus mitigating any concerns about misrepresentation due to averaging across repetitions of the same pair of stimuli.

It should be apparent by now that the data on asymmetries are not entirely consistent. The data collected by Rosch on linguistic hedges and the results reported by Tversky suggest that the psychological distance from less salient, nonreference stimuli to salient, reference stimuli is less than the psychological distance from salient, reference stimuli to less salient, nonreference stimuli. But the distance judgments reported by Rosch, by Sadalla et al., and now by us suggest that the reverse ordering holds. Although there are several ways to resolve this paradox, each of them leads to counterintuitive conclusions.

For example, one might argue that the original conclusion of Rosch and Sadalla et al. was correct, but that when subjects are asked to provide a numerical estimate of the distance from x to y (as they were in our experiments), they actually estimate the distance from y to x. This tack also forces one to accept the original interpretation of iconic distance estimations, namely, that the act of placing y when x is fixed corresponds to estimating the distance from y to x. This interpretation seems backward to me, and the comments that people have made to me when I have discussed this problem indicate that my opinion is the norm.

Of course, my interpretation of the results may be correct, but estimating perceptual, spatial, or semantic distance may be different in some way from rating similarity (or dissimilarity) and choosing appropriate sentence frames for statements of the same.

Still another possibility is that judging Euclidean distances from spatial memories is fundamentally different from rating perceptual or semantic similarity, which means that our data and those of Sadalla et al. are simply not comparable to those of Rosch and of Tversky.

Finally, one might question the results of the distance estimates obtained by Rosch (or by Sadalla et al.) because subjects estimated distances for both orders of the stimuli but only the average order was reported. A replication of Rosch's experiments may reveal that for the first appearance, distances from reference stimuli (fixed) to nonreference stimuli are larger than distances from nonreference stimuli (fixed) to reference stimuli. This outcome would be consistent with the data on linguistic hedges and the data reported by Tversky, but would drive a wedge between the nonspatial and the spatial findings.

In summary, evidence from a number of sources indicates that asymmetries exist in judgments of interpoint distances. Given that these asymmetries occur in estimates of distances, they probably are not caused by nonspatial associations, and given that they occur in priming, they probably are not produced by retrieval strategies or inferences. In other words, these asymmetries are produced by properties of the spatial representation.

This conclusion does not imply, however, that spatial representations are nonmetric. It is possible that distances in the spatial representation are symmetric but that judgments of interpoint distances are a function of (1) interpoint distances in the representation and (2) properties of the points themselves (e.g., Holman, 1979; Krumhansl, 1978; see Nosofsky, in press, for a discussion of these issues). Consider, as an illustration, a very simple model in which the estimated distance from object x to object y is given by the equation,

$$e(x,y) = d(x,y) + o(x)$$

where $d(x,y)$ is the symmetric distance between the points x and y, and o takes the value 1 if x is a nonlandmark, 0 otherwise. Thus, a landmark (l) and a nonlandmark (nl) c units apart in the spatial representation would produce the distance estimates,

$$e(l,nl) = d(l,nl) + o(l) = c + 0 <$$
$$e(nl,l) = d(nl,l) + o(nl) = c + 1.$$

This observation does not imply that the issue is indeterminable. Models in which asymmetries are attributed to properties of the stimuli can be falsified by examining, among other things, sets of proximity judgments. For example, if one found that estimated distances between a landmark and a nonlandmark were asymmetric, but that judgments between both of these objects and another object were symmetric, then a large class of symmetric distance models would be falsified (see Nosofsky, in press). We intend to investigate situations like this one in the near future.[5]

---

[5] Experiments conducted after proofs were received for this article indicate that our data on asymmetries should be interpreted cautiously. These experiments suggest that our original finding on the direction of the asymmetry might have been an artifact of the materials. Interested readers should write us for details.

2. The Triangle Inequality and Segmental Additivity

If one were willing to assume that psychological distances (and behavioral indices of them) were on a ratio scale, then the triangle inequality could be tested directly. To my knowledge, however, the scale properties of distances estimated from memory have not been investigated. In the absence of such investigations, it is imprudent to assume that these measures are on a ratio scale.

Unfortunately, testing the triangle inequality with interval-level data is not possible. The triangle inequality can always be satisfied in an interval-level measure by adding a suitably large constant to all interpoint distances. One solution to this problem is to test a stronger axiom, such as segmental additivity (e.g., Beals, Krantz, & Tversky, 1968). In general, segmental additivity will fail if a constant is added to interitem distances. A second strategy is to assume that the stimuli have a dimensional structure (e.g., Gati & Tversky, 1982; A. Tversky & Gati, 1982). It is possible in either approach to test the relevant axiom using only ordinal properties of the interitem proximities.

An informal test of segmental additivity can be made using the data reported by McNamara (1986, discussed in Section III,A). Recall that in this experiment subjects learned spatial layouts that were divided into four regions. Distance and region membership were factorially combined. The major results were these: In priming, the effect of a region boundary was 58 msec for close pairs, but only 22 msec for distant pairs; in distance estimations, a boundary increased estimates by 0.92 ft for close pairs, but only 0.375 ft for distant pairs. In short, for both priming and distance estimations, the effect of a boundary was about 60% less for distant pairs than for close pairs (it is noteworthy that this effect was so similar in the two tasks).

The nonadditive effect of boundaries on psychological distance implies that segmental additivity was violated across region boundaries. This can be demonstrated in several ways, but a particularly interesting one follows from work on the foundations of multidimensional scaling. Beals et al. (1968; see also A. Tversky & Krantz, 1970) analyzed the metric assumptions that underlie geometric representations of similarity. Beals et al. identified six ordinal axioms that must be satisfied by an observed similarity measure if it is generated by a metric with additive segments. Two of these axioms correspond directly to positivity and to symmetry. Three other axioms constitute regularity conditions that are imposed in order to guarantee that various equations can be solved. These axioms need not concern us here. The sixth axiom, however, is crucial and will be discussed in detail.

This condition rests on the notion of an *isodissimilarity contour*. An isodissimilarity contour is the set of all points at a fixed dissimilarity (called the radius) from a given point (called the center). In Euclidean space, isodissimilarity contours are circles in two dimensions and spheres in three dimensions. For an object x, the isodissimilarity contour of radius $\{xy\}$, where $\{xy\}$ designates the observed dissimilarity between x and y, is the set of all objects w, such that $\{xw\} = \{xy\}$. Contours are said to be concentric if they are defined about the same center. Isodissimilarity contours are determined by the data and do not depend on a dimensional characterization of the objects under study.

The critical axiom identified by Beals et al. (1968) states that concentric isodissimilarity contours must be parallel, in the sense that the psychological distance between concentric contours must be the same in all directions. Moreover, this relation must hold everywhere in the space; in other words, it must hold for all objects.

Isodissimilarity contours can be constructed using the data reported by McNamara (1986). Consider Fig. 5. Object x corresponds to the center of two isodissimilarity contours. Objects y_1 and y_2 are located such that the psychological distances between x and y_1 and between x and y_2 are the same; that is, the physical distance between these objects was chosen such that y_1 would prime x about the same amount as y_2 would prime x (see McNamara, 1986; contours also could be constructed using distance estimations). Similarly, z_1 and z_2 are located such that the psychological distances between x and z_1 and between x and z_2 are the same. In other

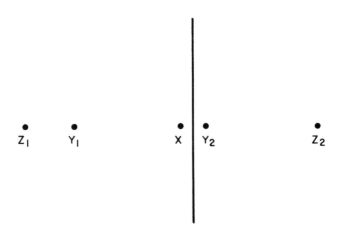

Fig. 5.   Four locations, z_1–z_2 and y_1–y_2, on two isodissimilarity contours centered at the point x.

words, y_1 and y_2 are on the same isodissimilarity contour, z_1 and z_2 are on the same isodissimilarity contour, and the two contours are concentric. The data relevant to segmental additivity are the psychological distances between y_1 and z_1 and between y_2 and z_2. These distances are not equal in the space and almost certainly would not be equal in the psychological space, i.e., z_1 would prime y_1 more than z_2 would prime y_2. In other words, the concentric isodissimilarity contours would not be parallel, and hence, segmental additivity would be violated. An appealing aspect of this analysis is that segmental additivity could be tested using only ordinal properties of the data.

In summary, available data suggest that segmental additivity may be violated in spatial memories. If this result holds up under systematic investigation, it would rule out a large class of models of spatial representation.

F.   SPATIAL AND NONSPATIAL INFORMATION CAN BE INTEGRATED IN MEMORY

When people learn the locations of objects in an environment, they typically acquire nonspatial information about the objects. For example, as students learn the locations of buildings on a campus, they also may learn which departments are housed in which buildings, the relative ages of the buildings, and whether or not a building's architectural style is pleasing. Indeed, as this example suggests, our spatial experiences with objects in an environment are often determined as much by nonspatial as by spatial properties of the objects. In a recent series of experiments (McNamara et al., 1990), we investigated whether people could integrate nonspatial information about an object with their knowledge of the object's location in space.[6]

Although the particular issue examined in this series of experiments had not been investigated previously, the general problem—whether or not visual-spatial and linguistic-nonspatial information can be integrated in memory—has a fairly long history. This problem first surfaced in the early investigations of the effects of misleading questions on eyewitness testimony (e.g., Loftus, 1975; Loftus, Miller, & Burns, 1978), and it was

---

[6] To account for the facts that people can talk about what they see and can construct images of scenes based on verbal instructions to do so, one must assume that there is some kind of connection between linguistic and nonlinguistic information. The level of connection, however, need not be representational; it is possible that linguistic codes and spatial codes can be intertranslated but that these translations are accomplished by rules or procedures that are not part of the memory representation itself. The fact that bilinguals, for example, can translate information from one language to another does not imply that the two languages are interconnected in memory.

examined systematically in a series of experiments on the effects of verbal statements on memory of pictures (Gentner & Loftus, 1979; Pezdek, 1977; Rosenberg & Simon, 1977). The results of these experiments indicated that spatial and nonspatial information could be integrated in memory.

Research by McCloskey and Zaragoza (1985) suggests that this conclusion is premature. They showed that the results of the early experiments on the effects of misinformation on memory could be accounted for even if the misinformation was impotent; more to the point, these results do not necessarily imply that spatial and nonspatial information were integrated in memory. In a recent examination of some of these issues, Belli (1989; see also B. Tversky & Tuchin, 1989) showed that misleading information interferes with the ability to retrieve the details of an event, but even his studies could not distinguish between explanations that require knowledge integration (e.g., memory impairment) and those that do not (e.g., source misattribution).

The approach we took to investigating this problem was much more direct than the approaches taken in previous research. Subjects first acquired a spatial layout. In Experiments 1 and 2, we had subjects learn a fictitious road map; whereas in Experiments 3–5, we recruited subjects who were already familiar with the locations of buildings on the Vanderbilt campus (see Fig. 6). Some of these cities or buildings were near one another, and others were far apart. On the campus, for example, Neely and Alumni Hall were close to each other but quite distant from Wesley Hall.

In the second phase of the experiment, subjects learned facts about the cities on the maps or the buildings on the campus. For example, subjects might have learned that Neely contains a dramatic theater, that Alumni Hall was named for alumni who died in World War I, and that Wesley Hall has a swimming pool in the basement. The question of interest was whether or not these nonspatial facts would be integrated in memory with the knowledge of the buildings' (or cities') locations.

After learning the facts, subjects were given either a recognition test or a location judgment test, depending on the experiment. Facts and either city or building names appeared sequentially on a computer terminal screen; the subjects' task was to make a recognition decision or a location judgment for each item. Knowledge integration was assessed by comparing performance in two experimental conditions: (1) when a city or a building name was primed by a fact about a neighboring city or building, and (2) when a city or a building name was primed by a fact about a distant city or building. We reasoned that if the spatial and the factual knowledge were integrated in memory, then a distance effect should be present in response latencies and accuracy: Responses to "Neely" should be faster and more accurate when primed by "World War I" (a fact about the neighboring

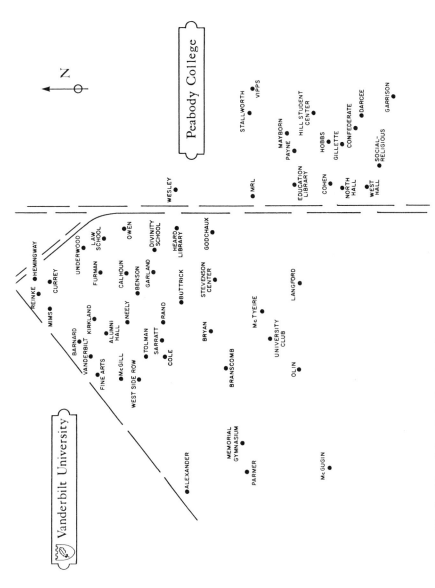

Fig. 6. Map of the relative locations of selected buildings on the Vanderbilt University campus.

building, Alumni Hall) than when primed by "Swimming Pool" (a fact about the distant building, Wesley Hall). In contrast, if the spatial and the factual knowledge were not integrated in memory, then a distance effect should not be present.

The results of these experiments were clear. Subjects' recognition decisions and location judgments were faster, more accurate, or both, when primed by a fact about a neighboring city or building than when primed by a fact about a distant city or building.

For example, in Experiment 5, we recruited subjects who were familiar with the Vanderbilt campus. Subjects learned facts about the buildings. After learning the facts, subjects participated in a task in which they had to decide whether buildings were on the main Vanderbilt campus or on the Peabody campus (see Fig. 6; Wesley Hall is actually part of the main campus). On each trial, a prime fact and a target building name were presented. The prime was displayed for 250 msec. The prime was then replaced by a building name. After 250 msec, a response signal (a row of asterisks) appeared below the target. The subjects were instructed (and trained in a preceding task) to respond exactly 300 msec after the appearance of the signal; no sooner, no later. Because response latencies were expected to be constant across conditions, error rates were the measure of interest. We examined the error rates when the building name was primed by (1) a fact about that building ("direct" condition, e.g., Dramatic Theater–Neely), (2) a fact about a neighboring building ("close" condition, e.g., World War I–Neely), and (3) a fact about a distant building ("far" condition, e.g., Swimming Pool–Neely). The results are reported in Table VI. The critical results were those for the close and the far conditions. Although response times in these conditions did not differ significantly (which shows that subjects complied with the instructions and that processing time was equivalent), error rates differed reliably: Subjects

TABLE VI

RESULTS OF EXPERIMENT 5
OF MCNAMARA, HALPIN, AND
HARDY (1990)[a]

Condition	RL (msec)	ER (%)
Direct	275	4.86
Close	331	9.37
Far	322	13.9

[a] RL = response latencies; ER = error rates.

had about 4.5% more information in the close condition than in the far condition at the same point in time.

These data, together with the converging support of four other experiments, indicate that the spatial and the nonspatial information were encoded in a common memory representation. On the one hand, it is easy to see how this kind of knowledge integration could occur if spatial relations were represented in an amodal conceptual code. It is not at all obvious, on the other hand, how linguistically conveyed nonspatial information could be integrated with an analogical spatial representation.

IV. Conclusions

Taken together, these results on hierarchical relations, apparent violations of metric axioms, and the integration of spatial and nonspatial information do not bode well for models of spatial representation in which interobject spatial relations are encoded solely in an analog format. It may come as no surprise that spatial representations of large-scale environments contain more information and structure than would be predicted by a pure analogical model. But when similar results are found for very simple spatial layouts, as many of the maps used in the studies reported here, the tenability of these models becomes doubly dubious. The problem, as I see it, is to reconcile this conclusion with the observations cited at the beginning of this article, namely, that people claim to use spatial images to solve numerous spatial problems. Although there may be many answers to this question, I want to close this article by discussing two that are of particular interest to me.

A. A RADICAL PROPOSAL

The radical proposal is that a small set of nonmetric relations, such as *contained in, next to*, and, perhaps, *above/below, left/right*, and so on, is used to represent interobject spatial relations. Long-term spatial memories may not contain metric information of any kind explicitly encoded.

The idea that spatial memories might be stored in a nonspatial format is not new. Kosslyn (1980) proposed that spatial relations were mentally represented in a propositional format. According to Kosslyn's model, images are generated from a propositional representation. The added claim here is that the propositional representation might not contain metric information (e.g., distances or spatial coordinates).

Consider, for example, the configuration in Fig. 7A. Imagine that this configuration is covered by a hierarchy of "tiles" of increasing size. All

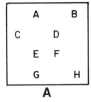

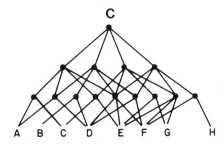

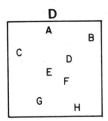

Fig. 7.   A, Configuration of eight objects. B, Grid used to explain how the space was encoded. C, Tree diagram of a nonmetric, hierarchical representation of A. D, Configuration produced by MDS based on the interpoint distances in the tree in C.

objects that fall within the areas delineated by tiles at the bottom of the hierarchy are grouped together and encoded as being within that subregion of space. All such tiles that fall within the areas delineated by tiles at the next level of the hierarchy are grouped together and encoded as being within that supersubregion, and so on. Eventually, this hierarchy converges on a single title that encodes that all subregions below it are in a common space. The structure of this representation can be captured, of course, in a tree. The distance between two objects can be defined as the number of links that must be traversed in order to move from one object to the other through their lowest common superordinate.

If the resulting hierarchy consists of nonoverlapping subregions, the tree will grossly misrepresent distance in the space. The problem is that in a nonoverlapping hierarchical tree, distances must satisfy the ultrametric inequality, which means that any three points must form an equilateral or isosceles triangle in which the unique side is the shortest.

One solution to this problem is to use overlapping subregions. To investigate the feasibility of this approach, I applied the method outlined above to the configuration in Fig. 7A. It is much easier to explain this encoding scheme if the space is divided into a 4 X 4 grid, as in Fig. 7B. At the lowest level of the hierarchy, tile T_1 covered cells 1, 2, 5, and 6, and encoded that A and C were in the same subregion; T_2 covered cells 2, 3, 6, and 7, and encoded that objects A and D were in the same subregion; T_3 covered cells 3, 4, 7, and 8; T_4 covered cells 5, 6, 9, and 10; T_5 covered cells 6, 7, 10, and 11; and so on, producing nine tiles in all. At the next level, tiles were clustered, producing the groups $\{T_1, T_2, T_4, T_5\}, \{T_2, T_3, T_5, T_6\}$, and so on, yielding four groups in all. Finally, at the uppermost level, there was a single cluster of the four clusters below. A tree diagram of the resulting structure can be found in Fig. 7C. I want to emphasize that the 4 X 4 grid plays no role in the encoding scheme; it simply provides a convenient way to talk about which areas of the configuration fall into which clusters.

I computed the distances between the eight objects in the tree using the number of links to a lowest common superordinate as the metric. This half-matrix of distances was then scaled in two dimensions using ordinal multidimensional scaling (MDS). The resulting configuration can be found in Fig. 7D (stress$_1$ < 0.001). This configuration is not perfect, but it would support reasonably accurate distance estimations and orientation judgments. The use of MDS to generate the display in Fig. 7D should not be taken too seriously; I am not arguing that people perform MDS in their heads. The claim is that in principle a reasonably accurate spatial display (i.e., an image) can be generated from a nonmetric representation of the original space.

A representation along these lines could easily handle many of the results cited above. Hierarchical effects would be obtained if boundaries in the space influenced how and where subregions overlapped; and the integration of spatial and nonspatial information would be expected given the amodal conceptual nature of the mental representation. It may be possible to incorporate asymmetric distances by transforming the tree into a hierarchical digraph. The model in its present form satisfies the triangle inequality, which may turn out to be a problem. Despite these problems, however, two points can be made. First, spatial memories need not contain a coordinate representation of location. Second, spatial memories need not even preserve metric information, as it is usually conceived.

B. A MODERATE PROPOSAL

This proposal follows from recent work on visual object recognition. Kosslyn (1987) has argued that two types of spatial relations are used in object recognition and image generation: *categorical* relations, which specify the nonmetric properties of containment and relative location (next to, above/below, etc.); and *coordinate* relations, which specify the positions of objects in a common coordinate space. According to Kosslyn, categorical spatial relations are useful for representing the relations between parts of flexible multipart objects (e.g., a human body), whereas coordinate spatial relations are useful for representing the metric relations between parts of relatively rigid objects (e.g., a chair). Kosslyn did not intend for this model to be applied to the representation of interobject spatial relations in long-term memory, but there is no obvious reason why it could not.

One of Kosslyn's (1987) more controversial claims is that categorical and coordinate spatial relations are computed by separate cognitive subsystems. In particular, the categorical subsystem is located in the left cerebral hemisphere and the coordinate subsystem is located in the right cerebral hemisphere. The tight connection between processing subsystems and memory (Squire, 1987) suggests that memories for these types of spatial relations also would be lateralized.

It may be the case that two mental representations are formed when people learn a spatial layout: a hierarchical structure, which is stored in categorical spatial memory, and a metric structure, which is stored in coordinate spatial memory. The hierarchical structure may represent the relative locations of objects and regions of the space in which objects reside. The metric structure, on the other hand, may represent absolute positions of objects in an abstract coordinate system. A dual representation like this could account for hierarchical effects, asymmetries, and the integration of spatial and nonspatial information. For example, when people learn facts about objects in a spatial layout, they may integrate the facts with the hierarchical structure.

A specific example of this kind of model has been proposed by Huttenlocher, Hedges, and Duncan (1990). Space does not permit a complete description of the model, but the fundamental claims are as follows: (1) Spatial location is represented at two levels, a fine-grained metric level that is inexact but unbiased and a coarse-grained categorical level; (2) reports of the location of an object are truncated at category boundaries, i.e., recollections that lie outside a category are reported as being within the category; and (3) reports of the location of an object are a weighted average of the actual location and the location of a "prototype" corresponding to the category.

This model correctly predicts boundary effects; it could in principle account for the integration of spatial and nonspatial information, but it has difficulty with asymmetric distance estimations. The model has been applied only to short-term memory for a single location, so it must be extended to apply to the estimation of distances based on long-term spatial memories. A natural and straightforward generalization is that people estimate the distance between two objects by first recalling the locations of the objects and then computing the distance between them. If the landmarks in our experiments function as prototypes, then the augmented model predicts that distances between landmarks and nonlandmarks will be underestimated (compared to the correct value) but symmetric. Both of these predictions were disconfirmed in our experiments.[7]

This analysis shows that specific versions of these two classes of models may be testable, even if general forms of them are not. If one could show, for example, that a spatial task requires metric information and that this task can be accomplished sufficiently quickly that direct retrieval is the most plausible explanation, then one would be inclined to reject a model, like the first, that proposed that metric information had to be computed. The first dual-representation model, on the other hand, makes strong predictions about laterality effects. Some of these predictions have already been verified in the visual domain (Hellige & Michimata, 1989; Kosslyn et al., 1989); it remains to be seen whether similar results can be found for spatial memories.

We are now beginning to see in the spatial memory literature an accumulation of findings, from a wide variety of methods, that illuminates the structure and the content of spatial memories. With additional work on some of the key problems identified above, such as symmetry and segmental additivity, we may in the near future begin to see formal models that can account for both the experimental and the experiential data.

---

[7] On the off-chance that the prototype might correspond to the "average" location within a cluster, I computed the centroids for each of the four regions on one of the maps. In all four cases, the centroid was between the landmark and the nonlandmark, in the sense that $d(c, l)$, $d(c, nl) \leq d(l, nl)$. This constraint also implies that distances between landmarks and non-landmarks would be underestimated and symmetric.

ACKNOWLEDGMENTS

Preparation of this chapter was supported in part by NSF Grant BNS 8820224 and a grant from the James S. McDonnell Foundation. I thank Keith Clayton for his comments on an earlier version of the manuscript.

REFERENCES

Allen, G. L. (1981). A developmental perspective on the effects of "subdividing" macrospatial experience. *Journal of Experimental Psychology: Human Learning and Memory, 7,* 120–132.

Anderson, J. R. (1976). *Language, memory, and thought.* Hillsdale, NJ: Erlbaum.

Anderson, J. R. (1978). Arguments concerning representations for mental imagery. *Psychological Review, 85,* 249–277.

Beals, R., Krantz, D. H., & Tversky, A. (1968). Foundations of multidimensional scaling. *Psychological Review, 75,* 127–142.

Belli, R. F. (1989). Influences of misleading postevent information; Misinformation interference and acceptance. *Journal of Experimental Psychology: General, 118,* 72–85.

Bendele, M. (1990). *Experimentally acquired knowledge: Can it be decontextualized?.*Unpublished master's thesis, Vanderbilt University, Nashville, TN.

Birnbaum, M. H., & Mellers, B. A. (1978). Measurement and the mental map. *Perception & Psychophysics, 23,* 403–408.

Buckman, I. (1966). *The metrics of psychological spaces: An experiment.* Unpublished manuscript.

Byrne, R. W. (1979). Memory for urban geography. *Quarterly Journal of Experimental Psychology, 31,* 147–154.

Cadwallader, M. (1979). Problems in cognitive distance: Implications for cognitive mapping. *Environment and Behavior, 11,* 559–576.

Chattin, D. B. (1988). *Organizational processes associated with memory for visual form.* Unpublished doctoral dissertation, Vanderbilt University, Nashville, TN.

Clayton, K. N., & Chattin, D. (1989). Spatial and semantic priming effects in tests of spatial knowledge. *Journal of Experimental Psychology: Learning, Memory, and Cognition, 15,* 495–506.

Clayton, K. N., & Habibi, A. (1991). Contribution of temporal contiguity to the spatial priming effect. *Journal of Experimental Psychology: Learning, Memory, and Cognition, 17,* 263–271.

Evans, G. W., & Pezdek, K. (1980). Cognitive mapping: Knowledge of real-world distance and location information. *Journal of Experimental Psychology: Human Learning and Memory, 6,* 13–24.

Garner, W. R., Hake, H. W., & Eriksen, C. W. (1956). Operationism and the concept of perception. *Psychological Review, 63,* 149–159.

Gati, I., & Tversky, A. (1982). Representations of qualitative and quantitative attributes. *Journal of Experimental Psychology: Human Perception and Performance, 8,* 325–340.

Gentner, D., & Loftus, E. F. (1979). Integration of verbal and visual information as evidenced by distortions in picture memory. *American Journal of Psychology, 92,*363–375.

Hellige, J. B., & Michimata, C. (1989). Categorization versus distance: Hemispheric differences for processing spatial information. *Memory & Cognition, 17,* 770–776.

Hirtle, S. C., & Jonides, J. (1985). Evidence of hierarchies in cognitive maps. *Memory & Cognition, 13,* 208–217.

Holman, E. W. (1979). Monotonic models for asymmetric proximities. *Journal of Mathematical Psychology, 20,* 1–15.

Holyoak, K. J., & Mah, W. A. (1982). Cognitive reference points in judgments of symbolic magnitude. *Cognitive Psychology, 14,* 328–352.

Huttenlocher, J., Hedges, L. V., & Duncan S. (1990). *Categories and particulars: Prototype effects in estimating spatial location.* Unpublished manuscript.

Kosslyn, S. M. (1980). *Image and mind.* Cambridge, MA: Harvard University Press.

Kosslyn, S. M. (1987). Seeing and imagining in the cerebral hemispheres: A computational approach. *Psychological Review, 94,* 148–175.

Kosslyn, S. M., Ball, T. M., & Reiser, B. J. (1978). Visual images preserve metric spatial information: Evidence from studies of image scanning. *Journal of Experimental Psychology: Human Perception and Performance, 4,* 47–60.

Kosslyn, S. M., Koenig, O., Barrett, A., Cave, C. B., Tang, J., & Gabrieli, J. D. E. (1989). Evidence for two types of spatial representations: Hemispheric specialization for categorical and coordinate relations. *Journal of Experimental Psychology: Human Perception and Performance, 15,*723–735.

Kosslyn, S. M., Pick, H. L., & Fariello, G. R. (1974). Cognitive maps in children and men. *Child Development, 45,* 707–716.

Krumhansl, C. L. (1978). Concerning the applicability of geometric models to similarity data: The interrelationship between similarity and spatial density. *Psychological Review, 85,* 445–463.

Levine, M., Jankovic, I., & Palij, M. (1982). Principles of spatial problem solving. *Journal of Experimental Psychology: General, 111,* 157–175.

Loftus, E. F. (1975). Leading questions and the eyewitness report. *Cognitive Psychology, 7,* 560–572.

Loftus, E. F., Miller, D. G., & Burns, H. J. (1978). Semantic integration of verbal information into a visual memory. *Journal of Experimental Psychology: Human Learning and Memory, 4,* 19–31.

Maki, R. H. (1981). Categorization and distance effects with spatial linear orders. *Journal of Experimental Psychology: Human Learning and Memory, 7,* 15–32.

McCloskey, M., & Zaragoza, M. (1985). Misleading postevent information and memory for events: Arguments and evidence against memory impairment hypotheses. *Journal of Experimental Psychology: General, 114,* 1–16.

McNamara, T. P. (1986). Mental representations of spatial relations. *Cognitive Psychology, 18,* 87–121.

McNamara, T. P., Altarriba, J., Bendele, M., Johnson, S. C., & Clayton, K. N. (1989). Constraints on priming in spatial memory: Naturally learned versus experimentally learned environments. *Memory & Cognition, 17,* 444–453.

McNamara, T. P., Halpin, J. A., & Hardy, J. K. (1990). *The representation and integration in memory of spatial and nonspatial information.* Unpublished manuscript.

McNamara, T. P., Hardy, J. K., & Hirtle, S. C. (1989). Subjective hierarchies in spatial memory. *Journal of Experimental Psychology: Learning, Memory, and Cognition, 15,* 211–227.

McNamara, T. P., & LeSueur, L. L. (1989). Mental representations of spatial and nonspatial relations. *Quarterly Journal of Experimental Psychology, 41A,* 215–233.

McNamara, T. P., Ratcliff, R., & McKoon, G. (1984). The mental representation of knowledge acquired from maps. *Journal of Experimental Psychology: Learning, Memory, and Cognition, 10,* 723–732.

Merrill, A. A., & Baird, J. C. (1987). Semantic and spatial factors in environmental memory. *Memory & Cognition, 15,* 101–108.

Newcombe, N., & Liben, L. S. (1982). Barrier effects in the cognitive maps of children and adults. *Journal of Experimental Child Psychology, 34,* 46–58.

Nosofsky, R. M. (1991). Stimulus bias, asymmetric similarity, and classification. *Cognitive Psychology, 23,* 94–140.

Pezdek, K. (1977). Cross-modality semantic integration of sentence and picture memory. *Journal of Experimental Psychology: Human Learning and Memory, 3,* 515–524.

Podgorny, P., & Garner, W. R. (1979). Reaction time as a measure of inter- and intraobject visual similarity: Letters of the alphabet. *Perception & Psychophysics, 26,* 37–52.

Posner, M. I., & Snyder, C. R. (1975a). Attention and cognitive control. In R. L. Solso (Ed.), *Information processing and cognition* (pp. 55–85). Hillsdale, NJ: Erlbaum.

Posner, M. I., & Snyder, C. R. (1975b). Facilitation and inhibition in the processing of signals. In P. M. A. Rabbitt (Ed.), *Attention and performance V* (pp. 669–682). London: Academic Press.

Pylyshyn, Z. W. (1979). Validating computational models: A critique of Anderson's indeterminacy of representation claim. *Psychological Review, 86,* 383–394.

Ratcliff, R., & McKoon, G. (1981). Automatic and strategic priming in recognition. *Journal of Verbal Learning and Verbal Behavior, 20,* 204–215.

Reitman, J. S., & Rueter, H. H. (1980). Organization revealed by recall orders and confirmed by pauses. *Cognitive Psychology, 12,* 554–581.

Rosch, E. (1975). Cognitive reference points. *Cognitive Psychology, 7,* 532–547.

Rosenberg, S., & Simon, H. A. (1977). Modelling semantic memory: Effects of presenting semantic information in different modalities. *Cognitive Psychology, 9,* 293–325.

Sadalla, E. K., Burroughs, W. J., & Staplin, L. J. (1980). Reference points in spatial cognition. *Journal of Experimental Psychology: Human Learning and Memory, 6,* 516–528.

Shepard, R. N., & Cooper, L. A. (1982). *Mental images and their transformations.* Cambridge, MA: MIT Press.

Sherman, R. C. (1987). *Regional structure in cognitive maps.* Unpublished manuscript.

Sherman, R. C., & Lim, K. M. (1990). *Determinants of spatial priming in environmental memory.* Unpublished manuscript.

Squire, L. R. (1987). *Memory and brain.* New York: Oxford University Press.

Stea, D. (1969). The measurement of mental maps: An experimental model for studying conceptual spaces. In K. R. Cox & R. G. Golledge (Eds.), *Behavioral problems in geography: A symposium.* Evanston, IL: Northwestern University Press.

Stevens, A., & Coupe, P. (1978). Distortions in judged spatial relations. *Cognitive Psychology, 10,* 422–437.

Thorndyke, P. W. (1981). Distance estimation from cognitive maps. *Cognitive Psychology, 13,* 526–550.

Tulving, E. (1976). Ecphoric processes in recall and recognition. In J. Brown (Ed.), *Recall and recognition.* London: Wiley.

Tversky, A. (1977). Features of similarity. *Psychological Review, 84,* 327–352.

Tversky, A., & Gati, I. (1982). Similarity, separability, and the triangle inequality. *Psychological Review, 89,* 123–154.

Tversky, A., & Krantz, D. H. (1970). The dimensional representation and the metric structure of similarity data. *Journal of Mathematical Psychology, 7,* 572–596.

Tversky, B. (1981). Distortions in memory for maps. *Cognitive Psychology, 13,* 407–433.

Tversky, B., & Tuchin, M. (1989). A reconciliation of the evidence on eyewitness testimony: Comments on McCloskey and Zaragoza. *Journal of Experimental Psychology: General, 118,* 86–91.

Wilton, R. N. (1979). Knowledge of spatial relations: The specification of the information used in making inferences. *Quarterly Journal of Experimental Psychology, 31,* 133–146.

MADE IN MEMORY: DISTORTIONS IN RECOLLECTION AFTER MISLEADING INFORMATION

Elizabeth F. Loftus

I. The Misinformation Effect

The recollections of people who have initially seen an important event such as an accident or crime can be altered by the introduction of new information that occurs after the important event. When the new information is misleading it can produce errors in what a person reports. A large degree of distorted reporting has been found in scores of studies involving a wide variety of materials. People have recalled nonexistent broken glass and tape recorders, a clean-shaven man as having a mustache, straight hair as curly, stop signs as yield signs, hammers as screwdrivers, and even something as large and conspicuous as a barn in a bucolic scene that contained no buildings at all.

We refer to the change in report arising from postevent misinformation as the misinformation effect (Loftus & Hoffman, 1989). In numerous laboratories, the misinformation effect has been obtained, and there seems to be little doubt that erroneous reporting is easy to induce. False reports of memories stimulated by misleading postevent event exposures have surfaced not only in the United States, but also in Canada, United Kingdom, Germany, Australia, and the Netherlands (e.g., Belli, 1988, 1989; Bonto & Payne, in press; Bowman & Zaragoza, 1989; Ceci, Ross, & Toglia, 1987a, 1987b; Ceci, Toglia, & Ross, 1988; Chandler, 1989, 1991;

THE PSYCHOLOGY OF LEARNING
AND MOTIVATION, VOL. 27

Gibling & Davies, 1988, Hammersley & Read, 1986; Kohnken & Brockmann, 1987; Kroll & Ogawa, 1988; Lindsay, 1990; Lindsay & Johnson,
1989; Loftus, Donders, Hoffman, & Schooler, 1989; Morton, Hammersley, & Berkerian, 1985; Pirolli & Mitterer, 1984; Register & Kihlstrom,
1988; Schooler, Gerhard, & Loftus, 1986; Sheehan, 1988; Sheehan &
Tilden, 1986; Smith & Ellsworth, 1987; Tversky & Tuchin, 1989; Wagenaar & Boer, 1987; Zaragoza, McCloskey & Jamis, 1987).

Research on the misinformation effect typically involves a three-stage
procedure in which subjects first experience an event, then receive new
information about the event, and finally take a test of memory for the
event. In misinformation studies people report that they have seen objects
as part of an event when in fact those objects came from other sources. The
findings support the notion that the process of remembering involves a
highly constructive activity that gathers bits and pieces from different
sources and "constructs" a memory.

Misinformation typically becomes available when people who experience the same event talk to one another, overhear each other talk, or gain
access to new information from the media, interrogators, or other sources.
After more than a decade investigating the power of misinformation,
researchers now know quite a bit about the conditions that make people
particularly susceptible to its damaging influence. For example, people are
particularly prone to having their recollections modified when the passage
of time allows the original memory to fade. In its weakened condition,
recollection—like the disease-ridden body—becomes especially vulnera-
ble to repeated assaults on its essence. Other factors associated with
distorted recollection include (1) the nature of the event itself; (2) the
intervals of time between the event, postevent information, and test;
(3) the presence of warnings; (4) the mode of presenting the postevent
information; (5) the age of the subject. The research relates to the important topic of how people combine information from various sources to
report on past experiences.

Although the misinformation effect, as a psychological phenomenon, is
now well established and many of its boundary conditions have been
identified, the interpretation of the phenomenon is not clear (Loftus, Korf,
& Schooler, 1989; Wells & Turtle, 1987). A major issue that has been
debated is whether misinformation actually impairs a person's ability to
remember event details. Put another way, are memory traces actually
altered by postevent misinformation? There are several ways in which
misinformation could impair the ability to remember event details. First,
misinformation could cause "trace impairment," i.e., it could update or
alter the previously formed memory. New information could combine
with earlier traces to actually change the representation. A second way

in which misinformation could impair event memory is through "retrieval impairment," i.e., misinformation may not alter the original memory trace but may simply make it less accessible (Bekerian & Bowers, 1983; Chandler, 1989; Morton et al., 1985). Impairment of some sort is implied by either the trace impairment or retrieval impairment mechanisms.

The notion of trace impairment can be found in recent theoretical discussions of memory. Leading theoretical psychologists such as Tulving (1983, 1984) have suggested that underlying memories can actually be modified by postevent information. In his landmark book, *Elements of Episodic Memory* (1983), he noted that one of the most pervasive facts about episodic memory has to do with changes over time in recollective experience and memory performance pertaining to a given event. Some changes in memory performance, he argued, can be attributed to changes in retrieval factors, while other come about because of changes in "engrams" (p. 164). He gave the name recoding to the class of processes that take place after an event is encoded that cause changes in the engram associated with that event. A variation of the idea of recoding appears in many modern day connectionist models. In the distributed, superpositional conceptualization of McClelland and Rumelhart (1985, 1986), for example, there is the explicit suggestion that we do not keep separate memories in separate places, but rather we superimpose them so that what the memory contains is a composite from various inputs. In its formulation, the memory system superimposes past instances, while allowing retrieval of the precise pattern of only certain instances (such as the most recent instance). An important aspect of this formulation is that it allows the potential integration of episodic memory for particular items, even though there may be initial identification of those items (Bruce, 1988). Predictions from one specific distributed model (CHARM, see Metcalfe, 1990) that incorporates the idea of composite memory traces are well matched to the bulk of recent data on the misinformation effect.

Some theorists have rejected the notion that misinformation impairs the ability to remember event details (McCloskey & Zaragoza, 1985; Zaragoza et al., 1987). McCloskey and Zaragoza disagreed with the idea that the misinformation effect was due to recoding processes or updating of previously sorted memories or that the misinformation effect arose because the older memory was rendered less accessible through a mechanism of inhibition or suppression (Morton et al.,1985). McCloskey and Zaragoza argued instead that the misinformation does not affect memory at all. Rather, misinformation may only influence subjects' memory reports first, if subjects never encoded (or do not recall) the original event, then instead of guessing at the time of test, these subjects might be lured into "guessing'' the misinformation item. Second, misinformation effects could also be obtained if subjects remember both sources of information but select the misleading information because they believe it could be correct.

To test their hypothesis that misinformation does not impair earlier memories, McCloskey and Zaragoza used a test procedure that differs from previous procedures. The standard procedure permits a subject to respond to a multiple-choice test question with the misinformation. If the subject originally saw a hammer as part of a crime scene, and later received misinformation about a screwdriver, the standard test offers a choice between *hammer* and *screwdriver*. The McCloskey and Zaragoza modified test, on the other hand, does not permit the subject to give the misinformation response *screwdriver*. If the subject originally saw a hammer and later received misinformation about a screwdriver, the modified test options might be *hammer* and *wrench*. The rationale for using the modified test is as follows: If misleading information somehow impairs memory for event details, then misled subjects (who presumably have impaired memories) would have to guess on the modified test, while control subjects (who presumably have unimpaired memories) would not. On the other hand, if there is no impairment due to misinformation, then misled subjects should be as accurate as control subjects. Misled subjects who remember the postevent item and assume it had to have been part of the event will not be able to show any favoritism toward the postevent item. Any decrements in performance cannot be due to processes such as these.

McCloskey and Zaragoza's data could not have been clearer. Using the modified test, they observed no effect of misinformation on performance. Consequently, they concluded that the original memory trace was not affected by exposure to misinformation.

II. Criticisms of the Modified Test

Researchers have criticized the modified test on a number of grounds. For example, Belli (1989) claimed that it is insensitive to detecting memory impairment. There are some forms of memory impairment that require that the postevent item be an alternative on the test. More specifically, if the postevent item had not been excluded, perhaps there would have been preferential access to it, rendering the original event less accessible. The modified test does not allow us to see whether this is the case. Moreover, the modified test does not permit us to see whether subjects, when left to their own devices, would make a source misattribution error (Lindsay & Johnson, 1987). Would subjects remember the postevent item and mistakenly think it came from the event itself? The modified test does not allow us to see source misattribution at work. Other claims that the modified test is insensitive are based on the high probability (50%) of responding correctly on the test by chance alone (Chandler, 1989; Loftus, Schooler, & Wagenaar, 1985). The argument is that if, say, 20% of the memories of people who got misinformation were impaired, the resulting decrement in performance on the modified test would be only 10%.

Although the modified test does not permit a subject who has a "memory" for the misinformation option to select that option, an important question remains: Why are subjects so good at choosing the correct answer (say, *hammer*) on the modified test? Several possible reasons come to mind. Perhaps the modified test communicates to the subject that the postevent item (say, *screwdriver*) is wrong. The test options act like new information, "educating" the subject about the right answer, or instructing the subject rather clearly that *screwdriver* cannot be the right answer.

Another perspective on the modified test focuses on the novel option (*wrench*). Tversky and Tuchin (1989) made the point that subjects can succeed in the modified test because they know they have not seen the novel item (*wrench*) even if they are not sure about the event item (*hammer*). Another possibility is that misinformation weakens the original memory, but all that is needed for successful performance on the modified test is for some tiny aspect of event memory to be preserved. As long as that bare thread remains, misled subjects can accurately discriminate event items from novel items.

Zaragoza and McCloskey (1989) have acknowledged that the modified test might not be sensitive to some types of memory impairment (those that involve choosing the postevent item on the test). Nonetheless, they still claim that the test is sensitive to a weakening in the event memory due to misinformation. Whatever the criticisms of the modified test, let us consider for a moment what would have happened had the test shown deficits in performance. We would have taken these deficits as indicative of memory impairment. Thus, we can now ask whether there are any conditions under which the modified test does in fact consistently reveal deficits in performance. It turns out there are several published demonstrations of deficits in performance with the modified test. One study (Ceci, et al., 1987b) presented preschool children with stories followed by misinformation, and found impairment on the modified test. Another study (Chandler, 1989) presented adult subjects with visual scenes (e.g., nature scenes including ponds, flowers, mountains), and then provided similar visual scenes as postevent information. Subjects who received misinformation were less able to discriminate the original scene from a novel distractor. Belli and Winfrey (1990) noted the difficulty in generalizing from the results with nature scenes to the typical postevent misinformation study due to the differences in experimental materials. But they unhesitatingly acknowledged that the study "clearly indicates that the modified test is sensitive to memory impairment under the right conditions." Belli and Winfrey, armed with some new data of their own, suggested that one boundary condition for detecting memory impairment with the modified test is that there be a substantial amount of forgetting of event details, leading the memories to become increasingly susceptible to postevent suggestion.

Assume for the moment that decrements in performance on the modified test do reflect genuine impairment in memory. What conditions are reliably associated with such deficits?. Some new data from our laboratory suggest that one condition might be "commitment." Subjects first commit themselves to the misinformation and then take the modified test. The next section of this chapter describes the commitment studies; the pattern of results suggests that after commitment subsequent performance on the modified test is still above chance, yet reduced.

III. Commitment to Misinformation

How shall we induce subjects to commit themselves to misinformation? In past research, the standard test reliably produced misinformation effects, i.e., subjects select or commit to the misinformation option. When faced with the choice between *hammer* and *screwdriver*, many subjects willingly adopt the latter choice. Perhaps this postencoding phase is essential for the misinformation to become "consolidated" in memory. Any subsequent exposure to a modified test might reveal the deleterious effects of earlier exposure to misinformation. One can point to numerous examples in past literature where the act of recollecting erroneous information had negative effects on memory performance later on (M. J. A. Howe, 1970; Kay, 1955; Schooler, Foster, & Loftus, 1988). Thus, imagine a "misled" subject who was faced with a standard test—the choice between *hammer* and *screwdriver*—and thus had the opportunity to actually recollect the misinformation. When later given the modified test—*hammer* vs. *wrench*—would performance now be impaired? These considerations motivated an experiment by Whaley (1988).

In this experiment, subjects saw a slide sequence depicting a complex event. Following the slides they read a narrative containing some items of misinformation. Finally, some subjects took a standard test, followed by a modified test. That is, they chose between *hammer* and *screwdriver*, and then on a later test chose between *hammer* and *wrench*. Our prediction was that subjects who received misinformation and then chose that option on the standard test would exhibit reduced memory performance on the subsequent modified test. We describe the experiment in some detail to give the flavor of how these experiments are conducted. Follow-up experiments are described briefly.

A. METHOD

1. Subjects and Materials

The subjects were 288 University of Washington students who received class credit for participation. They were randomly assigned to one of 24 groups with the restriction that each group contain an equal number of subjects.

Subjects watched a series of 39 slides depicting a maintenance man entering an office, speaking with a woman, repairing a chair, discovering desk keys, opening a desk drawer, removing a calculator, placing the calculator in his toolbox, and leaving the office. The sequence was an abbreviated version of that used by McCloskey and Zaragoza (1985). A Kodak Carousel 800H projector displayed the slides on a white wall from a distance of 15 ft. Subjects sat in individual students' desks arranged in three rows of four desks each.

The slide sequence contained four critical slides, occupying positions 4, 15, 23, and 33 in the series. Each critical slide showed one of four critical items: a coffee jar, a magazine, a soda can, and a hand tool. There were three possible versions of each critical item: The coffee label was Folgers, Maxwell House, or Nescafe; the magazine was *Glamour*, *Vogue*, or *Mademoiselle*; the soda can was Coca-Cola, 7-Up, or Sunkist Orange; and the hand tool was a hammer, a screwdriver, or a wrench. Counterbalancing resulted in one-third of the subjects viewing each version of each critical item.

A 250-word typed narrative described the theft depicted in the slides. The narrative was a condensed version of that used by McCloskey and Zaragoza (1985). The narrative was accurate except for details about the four critical items. It presented misleading information about two of the items (misled items) and neutral information about the other two (control items). Misled and control items were counterbalanced across subjects such that each version of each critical item was a misled item for half the subjects and a control item for the others. Thus for half the subjects who saw a hammer, the narrative referred to it as a *tool* (control) and for the other half as a *screwdriver* or a *wrench* (misled). The two misinformation possibilities were used equally often. Thus for subjects who saw a hammer and were misled, half read about a *screwdriver* and half about a *wrench*.

Subjects took two memory tests, a standard test and a modified test. Both tests were 21-item, two-alternative forced choice, recognition tests. Test items were in random order relative to the chronology of events depicted in the sequence and related by the narrative. Items were in the same order for all subjects on all tests. Four test items were critical and the remainder were simply fillers. Critical items occupied positions 4, 10, 16, and 20 on the test. For the standard test, subjects chose between the event item and the postevent item. Thus subjects who saw a hammer and were misled with *screwdriver* chose between *hammer* and *screwdriver*. For the modified test, the postevent item was not an option. Here, subjects who saw a hammer and were misled with *screwdriver* chose between *hammer* and *wrench*. The position of the event (first or second) item was counterbalanced. For each item subjects indicated their confidence on a scale from 1 to 5, where 1 denoted guessing and 5 denoted high confidence.

2. Procedure

Subjects were first told they would see a slide sequence depicting a theft, then would read a narrative describing the event, and finally would answer questions about the event. Subjects viewed the slides at a 5-sec presentation rate. This was followed by a 10-min filler activity involving the performance of simple arithmetic. They were told that the narrative was written by a highly paid trained professional observer who had viewed the slides carefully. They read the narrative, spent another 10 min doing arithmetic, and then took the first memory test. Subjects were told explicitly to select the alternative that represented what they had seen and to indicate how confident they were that the alternative they chose was seen in the slides. They performed another 10 min of arithmetic and then took the second memory test.

3. Design

Technically, this is a within-between, split-plot design. There were two within-subjects factors, each having two levels. The first within-subjects factor was "type of test" (standard vs. modified). The second within-subjects factor was "type of item" (misled vs. neutral). The single between-subjects factor was test sequence; half the subjects took the standard test first, and half took it second. Twelve unique combinations of stimuli were required to counterbalance three versions of four critical items as either event, postevent, or novel information, and to do this for each of the two test sequences. Each unique combination served as a stimulus for two groups of subjects; one group for each test sequence. Each group contained 12 subjects. There were 24 groups total, representing 12 combinations by two test sequences. It should be evident that each unique combination of stimuli occurred once in each test sequence. Overall the test sequences used identical stimulus materials; they differed only in the order in which the tests were given.

B. RESULTS

1. Replication of Past Results

The data demonstrate that past results obtained with these materials were replicated here, which means examining performance on the first test only. The results for the standard test showed that mean test performance was 57% correct for misled items and 77% correct for control items. Thus, a large misinformation effect (misled–control difference) was obtained. The results for the modified test revealed no misinformation effect (75% correct for both misled and control items). Statistical analyses confirmed that when the standard test was given first, a large misinformation effect occurred. When the modified test was given first, no misinformation effect was obtained.

2. Response Accuracy on the Second Test

Of primary concern was performance on the modified test when it occurred in the second position. Our hypothesis was that misinformation would impair performance in this instance. However, only a small reduction in performance occurred. Mean second-test performance was 83% correct for misled items, slightly less than the 89% correct score for control items.

By contrast, the results for the standard test showed that mean second-test performance was 68% correct for misled items and 87% correct for control items. Thus a large misinformation effect was obtained despite the fact that the subjects had earlier taken the modified test.

Figure 1 shows more clearly performance as a function of type of information, type of test, and test position. Notice first that subjects were significantly more accurate on the second test. Thus there is a "practice effect" observed in that subjects appear to be learning something from the first test. Another aspect of the data worth noting is that misinformation had a large effect on memory performance when assessed by the standard test, no matter whether that test came first or second. However, misinformation had little effect when assessed by the modified test. When the modified test was first, the misled–control difference was zero; when the modified test was second, the misled–control difference was a mere 6%. Thus, we see a modest reduction in performance on the modified test when it is second.

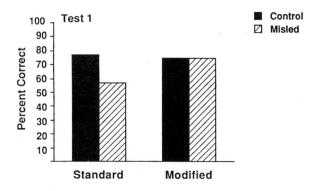

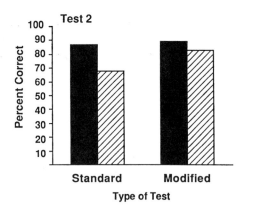

Fig. 1.   Percentage correct on the standard and the modified test.

3. Accuracy on Second Test Depends on Accuracy on
First Test

The data depicted in Fig 1. are collapsed over the subject's response on the
first test. Yet the conditionalized responses could potentially provide
valuable information about performance. In Table I, we present the percentage of subjects who correctly chose the event item on the second test
as a function of how they chose earlier. Several apsects of the data deserve
mention. Consider those subjects who took the standard test first and
incorrectly chose the postevent option. When they subsequently were
given the modified test, they correctly chose the event item 74% of the
time. Thus it is safe to say that those who were lured into initially choosing
the postevent option on the first test did not simply guess when they were
given the modified test later. They preferred the original event item over
the novel item.

TABLE I

Choice Proportions on Test 2 as a Function of Choice on Test 1

Test condition and event item	Postevent	Test 1	Test 2 (%)[a]		
			H	W	S
Standard test first					
Hammer	Screwdriver	Hammer	91	9	—
		Screwdriver	74	26	—
Hammer	—	Hammer	92	8	—
		Screwdriver	69	31	—
Modified test first					
Hammer	Screwdriver	Hammer	H=81, S=19		
		Wrench	H=31, S=69		
Hammer	—	Hammer	H=96, S=4		
		Wrench	H=62, S=38		

[a] H, hammer; S, screwdriver; W, wrench.

But another perspective on the performance score of 74% is that it is not particularly good. It is clearly worse than the performance of individuals who had earlier selected the correct option on the standard test; they chose the correct item over 90% of the time. It is noticeably below the overall performance on the modified test when given second; collapsing over first-test selection, subjects who took the modified test second scored an average of about 85% correct.

There is a small group of subjects who scored even lower on the modified test when it was second. These are control subjects who initially selected the wrong item on the first test. They preferred a totally novel item to the event item and then, when later on the modified test that same event item was paired with a new novel item, they correctly chose the event item only 69% of the time.

C. Discussion

Several results emerged from this study. Performance consistently improved on the second test. But more to the point of the study, misinformation impaired performance when tested via the standard test in which the misinformation option was a possible choice. However, misinformation did not impair performance when tested via the modified test in the first position, and had only a small (6%) effect when the modified test came second.

We expected that subjects who incorrectly embraced the misinformation option on the first test would subsequently show impaired performance on the modified test. Although their second-test performance was somewhat lower, they still preferred the correct event item nearly three-quarters of the time. How shall we think about these results? Some might argue that even the small reduction of 6% is important in showing impairment in memory in some subjects (Wagenaar, 1990). But there is another reason why the impairment may not have been as large as we expected: By the time subjects had gotten to the modified test when it was second, they had already had two previous exposures to the event item. They saw it in the slides, and they saw it during the standard test. They see it now on the modified test. Perhaps subjects select the event item on the modified test when second because they have been exposed to it so many times, and they have never seen the novel item with which it is paired. They essentially "figure out" that the event item must be the correct answer.

The idea that a test, in this case the first test, can affect the representation of information in memory is not new. In other settings, subjects have been able, purely as a byproduct of taking memory tests, to restore new items that might have otherwise been "forgotten" (M. L. Howe & Brainerd, 1989). Did the standard test, which exposed subjects to the event item once again, operate in this fashion and thereby facilitate subsequent performance on the modified test? If we could only gain a commitment to the misinformation item without reexposure to the event item, would performance on the subsequent modified test now be more strongly influenced?

D. A FOLLOW-UP EXPERIMENT

To empirically address this issue, a follow-up experiment was conducted with 216 subjects (N. Korf, unpublished data, 1989). This experiment was procedurally identical to that of Whaley (1988) in every respect until the first test. Subjects saw the same slide sequence and then read a narrative containing some misleading information. However, their first test was simply a "yes–no" test on the postevent item, and the second test was the modified test. Consider subjects who get misinformation, and then claim "yes" they saw it on the first test. How would they perform on the modified test? Given that they constitute an isolated a group of subjects who have embraced the misinformation without further exposure to the event item, would their performance on the modified test be impaired?

Performance on the modified test for control items was 66%, which was only one percentage point higher than overall performance on the modified test for misled items (65%). However, when we look specifically at the subjects who got misinformation, and then embraced it on the first test, we see lower performance on the second modified test (60% correct). The figure is slightly above chance, indicating that even when subjects embrace the misinformation, they still have some knowledge of the event item to help them on the next test. The 60% figure is far below that of subjects who got misinformation but then rejected it on the first test; their performance rate on the second modified test was the highest of any group: 76%.

In both the Whaley (1988) experiment and the N. Korf (unpublished data, 1989) follow-up, commitment to an incorrect misinformation response was associated with lower performance on a subsequent modified test. The effects were small. In both cases, performance on the modified test was above chance, indicating that subjects still possessed some event information.

Why might commitment to an incorrect misinformation response reduce subsequent recovery of the event information? One explanation is in terms of changes in relative strength of the event vs. postevent information. When postevent competitors are strong relative to older event items, interference occurs. Commitment to a postevent item quite naturally strengthens that item, and this could be expected to enhance the likelihood of suppression of the event detail. Gaining commitment by including the competitor in a test, it has been argued, should especially increase the chance of accessing the competitor and "blocking" the event detail (Chandler, 1991).

IV.   After the Modified Test, What?

McCloskey and Zaragoza concluded that misinformation does not change people's memories. Performance on the modified test is equivalent for control and misled items. Yet simply because performance on the modified test is the same does not mean that subjects are not changed in some way. In several experiments these subjects subsequently take a new test, and the impact of misinformation emerges.

First, consider portions of the Whaley experiment that pertain to this issue. Consider subjects who first took the modified test. Their performance was unaffected by misinformation; approximately three-quarters of the items were correct. But when these subjects went on to take the standard test second, evidence of a misinformation effect emerged. To see this, assume that subjects saw *hammer*, were misled with *screwdriver*, and then chose *hammer* on the first modified test. When given a standard test second, 19% of these individuals switched to *screwdriver* even though *hammer* was still an option (see Table I). On the other hand, control subjects who had chosen *hammer* on the first (modified) test rarely switched. In this case, only 4% switched to *screwdriver* on the second (standard) test.

Evidence of a misinformation effect also can be seen when one considers those subjects who were wrong on the first (modified) test. In our example, these individuals initially incorrectly chose *wrench*. Presumably these subjects were merely guessing; after all, they chose an option that was never seen or read. Yet when subsequently given the standard test, misled subjects' performance vastly differed from that of control subjects. The majority of misled subjects preferred *screwdriver* over *hammer* (69 to 31%), while the majority of control subjects preferred *hammer* over *screwdriver* (62 to 38%).

We have conducted other studies to explore ways in which control and misled subjects who perform equivalently on an initial modified test might not really be equivalent. Consider a follow-up experiment conducted with 80 subjects. The experiment used the same basic initial design. Subjects saw the slide sequence and then read a narrative containing misleading or neutral information. Their first test was the modified test. Again, control and misled subjects had a statistically close performance: 73% correct for control items; 71% correct for misled items.

Two to three days after their participation in the study, subjects were telephoned at home by the experimenter. They were told that through a computer error, some of their data had been lost. They were asked if they would answer just a few questions about the incident they had seen in order to save the "experimenter" from deep trouble. A total of 48 students were reached by phone and agreed to answer questions. Subjects could respond with the event item (*hammer*), the postevent item (*screwdriver*), the novel item from the modified test (*wrench*), some other item, or claim they could not remember. One result is of particular interest to the present discussion: for control items, subjects responded with the "postevent option" (one they had not seen or read) only 2% of the time. However, for misled items, subjects responded with the postevent item 23% of the time. In short, many misled subjects who had initially been quite correct on the modified test subsequently reported the postevent item when given the freedom to do so.

V.   Implicit Tests and Misinformation

The commonly used tests that explore the misinformation effect are all explicit tests of memory. When taking an explicit test of memory, subjects are instructed to remember recent events and to base their responses on those memories. Implicit measures, on the other hand, are those in which subjects are not told to remember particular events, but rather are asked to perform some other task, such as solving an anagram or completing a word fragment. Performance on this task, then, is measured by transfer from prior experience. If the prior experience influences the implicit measure relative to some baseline, we say that "priming" has occurred (Graf & Schacter, 1985, 1987; Roediger, Weldon, & Challis, 1989; Schacter, Cooper, & Delaney, 1990; Tulving & Schacter, 1990).

Implicit measures have been known to reveal evidence of memory where explicit measures fail to do so. In the now classic work with amnesic patients, for example, brain-damaged individuals were impaired relative to normals at learning a short list of words presented to them even a brief time earlier. However, when asked to complete word fragments in which they could use the recently presented words (an implicit test), they performed at normal levels (Warrington & Weiskrantz, 1970). Similar dissociations between explicit and implicit memory tests have been shown in normal subjects as well (Roediger, 1990).

Explicit tests have routinely shown impairment in memory for event items when subjects receive postevent misinformation. There are scores of examples of explicit memory deficits. One, for example, is that Belli's (1989) subjects were less likely on a yes–no recognition test to acknowledge having seen critical items during a slide series when they got misinformation about those items. Would implicit tests also show memory impairment for event items when subjects subsequently received misinformation? Put another way, assuming that an event item memory can prime performance on an implicit test, would the priming be less if subjects had subsequently been exposed to misinformation?

In exploring whether prior experience with an event detail transfers to a subsequent implicit test, the question arises as to what type of implicit test to use. Most of the implicit tests used in the past require a perceptual or data-driven type of processing. In order to exhibit priming, such tests rely heavily on a match between perceptual operations during the prior experience and the perceptual operations during the implicit testing. The tests are highly sensitive to manipulations that change the surface form of information, e.g., from auditory to visual input (Jacoby & Dallas, 1981). Thus, a standard implicit test that reflects a perceptual form of memory, such as word fragment completion, might not show priming from a prior experience of viewing slides. In other words, seeing a screwdriver in the slide series might not prime subsequent completion of the fragment *sc__wd__v__*. To circumvent this problem, Dodson and Reisberg (1989) gave a verbal accuracy test after the slides followed by an implicit lexical decision-making task. They found no evidence for impairment due to misinformation on the implicit lexical task, but the presence of the accuracy test makes this result hard to interpret.

A more promising type of implicit test is one that employs meaningful or conceptually driven processing (Blaxton, 1989). For this reason we used category member generation (e.g., "Name the first five tools that come to mind"). To see the rationale for the implicit memory test, assume that subjects saw a screwdriver in the slides, and subsequently had to name members of the *tool* category. Priming would be exhibited if, relative to baseline, more subjects produced the event item *screwdriver* among their top five tools. (Notice that we deliberately assumed that subjects originally saw a screwdriver in this example, rather than seeing a hammer, which is the event memory used as an example throughout the chapter. This is because *hammer* is already the most commonly produced tool and thus is near ceiling in associative norms.) Assume further that we mislead subjects into thinking that they saw a wrench. The question of interest then was whether misinformation about *wrench* would lower the subsequent production of *screwdriver* on the instance generation test. T. Kilmer (unpublished data, 1990) conducted a study to explore this issue.

It is reasonable to hypothesize that misinformation might reduce the likelihood that the event item would be produced on the implicit test. One mechanism by which this could occur is the following. Assume that the misleading postevent item is brought to mind during the implicit test and, after being generated itself, the item stimulates the generation of related items. Necessarily fewer opportunities would then be available for the event item to be produced. An example will help to illustrate this mechanism. Suppose a subject sees a physics textbook and is then misled with the information that it is an economics text. On the implicit test, economics comes to mind and stimulates thoughts of other social sciences. The subject then generates these members as the first five to come to mind. Necessarily, physics has less of a chance to be generated. The experiment tests this possibility.

A. METHOD

1. Subjects and Materials

The subjects were 338 students from the University of Washington. They participated in exchange for partial course credit. Subjects were tested in group sizes ranging from 3 to 10 persons. Of the 338 subjects, 103 provided baseline data for the implicit memory test and 235 participated in a four-stage experiment described below.

The slide sequence shown in the first stage depicted a male college student ("Jim") visiting the local book store. In the slides, Jim shoplifts several items, including a candy bar and a package of batteries. He watches a handyman fix various items around the bookstore, he talks to a classmate, and he eventually leaves the store. The series contained 54 slides, presented at a rate of 2.5 sec/slide.

The slides were the same for all subjects except for eight critical slides displayed in one of two versions. The critical items in the slides included a shoplifted candy bar (Butterfinger/Snickers), a tool (screwdriver/wrench), a package of batteries (Energizer/Eveready), a textbook (economics/physics), a can of soda (7-Up/Sunkist), a cartoon character printed on a sweatshirt (Mickey Mouse/ Daffy Duck), a jar of instant coffee (Maxwell House/Nescafe), and a magazine (GQ/Esquire). Counterbalancing ensured that each version of the eight critical slides was shown roughly equally often.

2. Procedure

The majority of the subjects participated in a four-stage procedure. They were first shown a series of slides of a complex event, then they read a narrative about the event, then they took an inplicit memory test under the belief that it was a different experiment. Finally, they took an explicit recognition test concerning items they had seen in the event. The subjects in the baseline condition did not see any slides, read any narrative, or take the explicit test. They only took the implicit memory test to provide baseline data.

Immediately after viewing the slides, subjects performed a 5-min filler activity that consisted of drawing geometric objects. Following the filler, subjects read a postevent narrative at their own pace. The narrative was two pages, singe-spaced, and written in a rather literary and absorbing style. It ends with Jim, the shoplifter, getting caught by the police. The subjects were instructed to rate the narrative on grammar, writing style, moral of the story, etc. The narrative presented to each subject misleading information concerning four of the critical items. In other words, the narrative contained four details that contradicted four items that were seen in the event. For example, if the subjects saw Jim shoplift a Butterfinger candy bar, the narrative misled them by suggesting that it was Snickers (e.g., *Jim coolly stuffed a Snickers into his pack and walked away*). For the other four critical items, no misinformation was presented. In these cases the critical item was referred to by its generic category (e.g., *Jim coolly stuffed a candy bar into his pack and walked away*). Counterbalancing ensured that each version of a critical item (e.g., Butterfinger) acted roughly equally often as a control item, as an event item that would be a target of misinformation, and as postevent information. After rating the narrative, subjects participated in the implicit memory portion of the experiment.

For purposes of disguising the implicit test, subjects were asked to participate in a "second, unrelated experiment." They were told that another graduate student was conducting a short study on category norms and that their help was needed. They filled out a new "informed consent" form for this second study and participated in a separate room. The implicit test consisted of a list of 44 categories, with five lines below each category name. Embedded in the categories were the critical category names encompassing the eight critical items from the slides (e.g., *Name five types of candy/candy bars; name five tools; name five magazines*; and so on).

The explicit test was a two-alternative forced-choice test. Each test item consisted of a sentence with a blank that could be filled in with one of two options, (e.g., *The handyman was using a (screwdriver/wrench) to fix something when Jim first saw him; Jim stole a (Butterfinger/Snickers) bar*). Subjects were instructed to circle the one answer that they remembered seeing in the slides. For each item, one of the choices was always correct, and the other was an item that was used as postevent information for some subjects. Eight of the questions dealt with critical items and the other nine were filler items. With respect to the critical items, four tested memory for control items and four tested memory for misinformation target items. The order of presentation in the test question was varied.

B. RESULTS

1. Explicit Memory

Memory for control items was substantially better than memory for misinformation items (67.4% vs. 43.1% correct). Differential performance was obtained whether the data were analyzed by treating subjects as a random effect or by treating items as a random effect. Thus we present only the item analyses. Table II shows the control and misled performance for each of the 16 critical items. As can be seen, every one of the 16 critical items showed a misinformation effect. Thus, the misleading postevent information strongly reduced performance on the explicit memory test.

Since there were two critical items per category, one member was necessarily more dominant in the category than the other. The more dominant item in a category is the one that is more likely to be produced when people are asked for the first-category members to come to mind. For example, in the category of carpenters' tools, *screwdriver* is more dominant than *wrench*. In a widely used set of category norms (Battig & Montague, 1969), screwdriver was the fourth most commonly produced tool, whereas wrench was the ninth. It remains more dominant today. Poolnig across categories, Fig. 2 shows explicit memory performance as a function of whether the event item was the higher or lower dominant category member. Memory for control items was better than memory for

TABLE II

PERCENTAGE CORRECT FOR EACH CRITICAL ITEM

	Explicit test condition	
Critical item	Control	Misled
Butterfinger	89.8	80.8
Snickers	90.3	80.6
Screwdriver	82.7	71.4
Wrench	46.9	28.1
Eveready	51.9	26.5
Energizer	92.5	53.1
Physics	60.4	34.6
Economics	59.4	16.9
7-Up	75.5	26.9
Sunkist	34.4	22.4
Mickey Mouse	92.3	53.1
Daffy Duck	40.6	17.2
Nescafe	24.0	10.2
Maxwell House	86.6	33.9
Esquire	75.0	67.3
GQ	76.6	66.2
Mean %	67.4	43.1

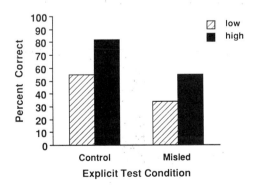

Fig. 2. Percentage correct on the standard explicit test for both high and low dominant items.

misinformation items, and this held true whether the event item was high or low in dominance.

2. Implicit Memory

Analyses of implicit memory begin by asking whether items seen in the slides in the control condition are produced more often than those that are produced in the baseline condition. In other words, is there priming in the control condition? A look at the first two vertical bars in Fig. 3 reveals priming. Subjects produced the critical item in the control condition 43.2% of the time, whereas they produced it significantly less often in the baseline condition (35.9% of the time). For 14 of 16 items, control performance was higher than baseline performance (see Table III).

We then come to the question of utmost interest: Did misinformation reduce priming? The answer, overall, is *no*. Misleading postevent information did not reduce the likelihood that the critical event item would be produced on the implicit test. Despite misinformation, the original event item was produced 45.5% of the time, which was significantly higher than baseline production but not significantly different from control production. Put another way, despite the increase in generation of the misled item, the event item was produced just as often by "misled" subjects—at least when we considered all subjects responding to all items in the misled condition.

We had expected misinformation to reduce the likelihood that the event item would be produced on the implicit test. This might have occurred had the misleading postevent item been brought to mind during the implicit test and, after being generated itself, stimulated the generation of related items. Necessarily fewer opportunities would have been available for the event item to be produced. However, this did not happen; overall, the

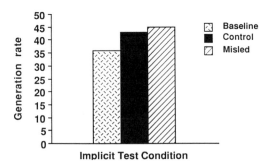

Fig. 3. Percentage generating critical category members in the baseline, control, and misled conditions.

TABLE III

PERCENTAGE GENERATING EACH CRITICAL ITEM

Critical item	Baseline	Implicit test condition		
		Event item control	Event item misled	Postevent item misled
Butterfinger	17.5	42.3	60.8	54.3
Snickers	65.1	78.7	87.9	88.6
Screwdriver	79.6	84.8	85.1	91.4
Wrench	67.0	74.2	72.1	68.8
Eveready	71.8	76.5	65.2	62.5
Energizer	61.2	70.3	72.3	68.8
Physics	2.9	6.1	5.8	0.0
Economics	8.7	14.1	12.5	15.2
7-Up	66.0	59.1	71.4	78.1
Sunkist	10.7	22.8	6.2	5.9
Mickey Mouse	34.9	26.9	35.4	42.9
Daffy Duck	22.3	23.8	32.8	32.4
Nescafe	4.8	5.9	8.2	8.8
Maxwell House	35.0	37.9	32.8	20.0
Esquire	4.8	20.9	26.5	30.3
GQ	21.4	46.8	53.3	43.8
Mean %	35.9	43.2	45.5	44.5

event item was generated just as often in the face of misinformation as in its absence. One might wonder whether the postevent item was too subtle to be noticed, but this could not be since the misinformation effect on the explicit test was large. One can still wonder if the postevent item was being generated on the implicit test. The results show that indeed it was being generated about as often as the event item, 44.5% of the time, a figure significantly above the baseline. Thus, misleading information did increase the chances that the postevent item would be produced on the implicit test, but not at the expense of the event item being produced.

But our analysis of the impact of misinformation on the rate of generating the event detail did not stop here. Upon further analysis, it became apparent that occasionally the postevent item led to a revival of memory for the event item. This seemed to happen when the postevent item was rather blatantly contradictory. In these cases the subjects appeared to notice a discrepancy between it (the postevent detail) and what they had initially viewed. In these instances, one might expect an even greater priming of the event item in the misled condition than in the control condition.

To assess the plausibility of this line of thought, we divided the items into *blatant* and *nonblatant* items, according to how control subjects performed. For example, the candy bar items were particularly blatant. When subjects saw a Snickers candy bar, they correctly selected it over 90% of the time in the control condition. Presentation of misinformation about the candy bar (suggesting to Snickers viewers that they had seen a Butterfinger candy bar) was readily noticed. Reading about Butterfinger thus appeared to remind about Snickers, and could have enhanced its subsequent priming. In fact, this happened for the candy bar items. In the face of misinformation, priming for the event item was even greater than in its absence. For example, the baseline production of Butterfinger was 18%. When it was a control item, it was produced 42% of the time; however, when misinformation was given, the item was produced 61% of the time, more than three times its baseline performance.

To explore the role of an item's blatancy on implicit test performance, we divided the critical items into two categories. Those for which control performance on the explicit test was high (over 75%) were arbitrarily called blatant. Implicit test performance was then examined separately for the blatant and nonblatant items. The data are shown in Fig. 4. For the blatant items, there is priming in the control condition relative to baseline (52.0% vs. 42.8%). Misinformation was associated with even more productions of the event item (58.4%). For the nonblatant items, a different pattern emerged. There was priming in the control condition relative to baseline (31.9% vs. 26.9%). But misinformation was now associated with an intermediate level of priming (28.9%), a figure that was not significantly different from either control or baseline.

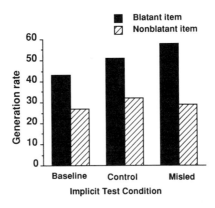

Fig. 4.   Percentage generating critical category members for blatant vs. nonblatant items.

One last analysis of the data proved crucial. The question motivating the analysis was, What happens if we look only at the generation of event items for those subjects who ultimately "bought" the misinformation? When we calculated the generation rate of misled subjects who went on to correctly select the event detail on the explicit test, the generation rate was 59%—far higher than the baseline of approximately 36%. However, the generation rate of misled subjects who went on to select the postevent option on the explicit test was lower, 32%. Put another way, the generation of event details for those subjects who bought the misinformation was back near baseline levels. This breakdown of the implicit test performance for misled subjects who ultimately were correct vs. incorrect on the explicit test can be seen in Fig. 5.

C. Discussion

When people are given explicit memory tests, interference is a common finding. However when given implicit memory tests, interference is not a common finding (e.g., Graf & Schacter, 1987). Kilmer's (unpublished data, 1990) findings are provocative in this regard. When she examined the implicit test performance of misled subjects, collapsing across all subjects and items, no reduction below control performance was observed. However, when she examined implicit test performance for misled subjects who ultimately embraced the misinformation option on the explicit test, a clear reduction in performance was observed.

Previous attempts to find changes in implicit test performance in the misinformation arena have met with mixed results. Dodson and Reisberg

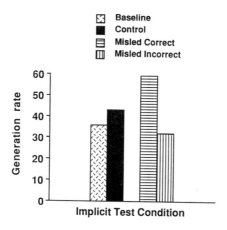

Fig. 5.   Percentage generating critical category members.

(1989) found no evidence for impairment of event memory, as indicated above, using lexical decision making as a measure of implicit memory. But they had subjects rehearse the event items before attempting to mislead them. This procedure could have seriously influenced the misinformation effect. Such an influence might be explained as follows: Assume that subjects produce the misinformation response for one of several reasons. Some subjects simply guess. Some subjects never encode the event item, and the misinformation is just accepted into memory. Some subjects remember both the event and postevent items, and deliberate about them when making their test response. By requiring that subjects rehearse the event item before misleading them, Dodson and Reisberg may have succeeded in ensuring that most of the misinformation responses are a result of deliberation.

There is another empirical demonstration involving implicit testing in an arena somewhat akin to the misinformation arena (Birch & Brewer, 1990). In this research subjects first read sentences known to produce a high degree of lexical substitution during recall. For example, when subjects hear the sentence *The saw was concealed in the cake* they often recall *The saw was hidden in the cake* (a synonym substitution). When they make the mental substitutions, they are in effect supplying themselves with misinformation. Later, subjects had to recognize items they previously read (explicit test) or they completed word fragments on the original lexical items (implicit test).

Birch and Brewer asked an important question about the consequences of substitution: Is memory for the original event item (e.g., concealed) affected by the lexical substitution or does the original representation remain intact? The implicit test data provided evidence for impairment of event memory. Of course, the materials and the method of "misleading" subjects used in the Birch and Brewer experiment are quite different from those used in the present research; nontheless, the results do suggest that it is possible to detect impairment in event memory with implicit measures of memory.

We must acknowledge that Kilmer may have found what she did because of the particular implicit test that she used, namely, category generation. This test permitted subjects to make five responses, thus they could have produced both the event detail and the postevent detail. In that sense, it resembles the "modified-modified-free recall test (MMFR)" (cf. Barnes & Underwood, 1959) used in earlier interference studies to distinguish among various theories of forgetting. Earlier the MMFR approach was capable of providing evidence for extinction of previously learned responses (Adams, 1967). It may be that this modern-day variation showed an analogous result for analogous reasons. But Kilmer's result could have occurred for another reason. It is possible that that the post-event information, when it was processed led to the production of the postevent item on the implicit test, which in turn led to other items being produced that were related to the postevent item. This would have then left fewer opportunities for producing the event item on the implicit test. Reduced generation of the event item would then occur, but would not necessarily mean that the event item had been "impaired" in memory. Some form of the response competition could have been responsible for the changes in implicit test performance.

One last possible interpretation of the results does not assume impairment of event memories. It is possible that the misled subjects ultimately chose the misled option because they never encoded the event detail in the first place. Since they had no initial memory for the event detail at all, they would not be expected to show any priming due to prior exposure of the event detail.

VI. General Discussion

Does misinformation impair a subject's ability to remember original details? The study involving an implicit test of memory produced results that are consistent with the notion of memory impairment. However, there are other possible explanations for the results, given the particular implicit test (category generation) that was used. Further experimentation is needed to show that impairment can be observed when other implicit tests are employed or when other details of the experiment are changed. We fully expect that whether changes in performance on the implicit test are observed in future studies will depend on the specific parameters of the study, especially the salience of the misleading postevent information. Chandler (1991), among others, has argued that interference with event memory is more likely to occur when the competition from postevent misinformation is "overwhelmingly strong."

The studies of commitment suggest that when a person commits to a postevent item, then performance on a subsequent modified test can be reduced, at least to a small degree. Taken together with several other demonstrations of reduced performance on the modified test (e.g., Ceci et al., 1987b; Chandler, 1989), our results suggest that memory impairment does play some role in the misinformation effect. It may be that the role is minor compared to that played by the mere acceptance of misinformation by subjects who would otherwise be guessing, or compared to the role played by misremembering the source of the misleading items.

The identification of different mechanisms by which a subject could produce the misinformation item (e.g., misinformation acceptance, source misattribution, guessing) raises an important issue for this line of research that has largely been ignored. Namely, when different people use different strategies (or when a single person uses different strategies on different trials), averaging data generated by those strategies may distort conclusions about performance. This point has been nicely illustrated in the domain of addition and subtraction (Siegler, 1987, 1989). In the subtraction study, for example, when the data were averaged from all trials and over all strategies, the conclusion reached was that children solved subtraction problems mostly by counting down from the larger number or counting up from the smaller one. However, when the data were analyzed separately according to the particular strategy that a child claimed to use, a different picture was suggested.

A similar research strategy would yield useful data in the misinformation domain. If data were analyzed separately, according to some retrospective indication of the specific strategy subjects claimed to use on the trial, more informed conclusions about the impact of misinformation might be reached.

Apart from the issue of whether postevent misinformation impairs event memory, the other heavily debated issue is whether subjects genuinely believe in their misinformation memories. If a memory for a screwdriver that came about through the process of suggestion was subjectively very real to the subject, this would be important from both a theoretical and applied perspective. Even if these misinformation memories were a small subset of all misinformation responses, they would be interesting in their own right, for they tell us something about the creation of new memories. We already know that such memories can be held with great conviction and are acted on as though they were genuine experiences. When a memory is created via postevent suggestion, the precise process may be somewhat different from the creation of memory in the usual way, from perceptual experience. Nonetheless such creations appear to be part of the human experience and every bit as worthy of our sustained interest.

Acknowledgments

The research described here was supported by a grant from the National Institute of Mental Health. Thanks to H. L. Roediger for his helpful comments on portions of this article.

References

Adams, J. A. (1967). *Human memory*. New York: McGraw-Hill.
Barnes, J. M., & Underwood, B. J. (1959). The "fate" of first-list associations in transfer theory. *Journal of Experimental Psychology, 58*, 97–105.

Battig, W. F., & Montague, W. E. (1969). Category norms for verbal items in 56 categories: A replication and extension of the Connecticut Category norms. *Journal of Experimental Psychology: Monograph, 80,* 1–46.

Bekerian, D., & Bowers, J. (1983). Eyewitness testimony: Were we misled? *Journal of Experimental Psychology: Learning, Memory, & Cognition, 9,* 139–145.

Belli, R. F. (1988). Color blend retrievals: Compromise memories or deliberate compromise responses. *Memory & Cognition, 16,* 314–326.

Belli, R. F. (1989). Influences of misleading postevent information: Misinformation interference and acceptance. *Journal of Experimental Psychology: General, 118,* 72–85.

Belli, R. F., & Winfrey, S. E. (1990). *Detecting memory impairment with a modified test procedure.* Unpublished manuscript, Creighton University, Omaha, NE.

Birch, S. L., & Brewer, W. F. (1990). *Memory permanence versus memory replacement in sentence recall.* Unpublished manuscript, University of Illinois at Urbana-Champaign.

Blaxton, T. A. (1989). Investigating dissociations among memory measures: Support for a transfer appropriate processing framework. *Journal of Experimental Psychology: Learning, Memory, and Cognition, 15,* 657–668.

Bonto, M. A., & Payne, D. G. (in press). On the role of environmental context in eyewitness memory. *American Journal of Psychology.*

Bowman, L., & Zaragoza, M. (1989). Similarity of encoding context does not influence resistance to memory impairment following misinformation. *American Journal of Psychology, 102,* 249–264.

Bruce, V. (1988). *Recognising faces.* Hillsdale, NJ: Erlbaum.

Ceci, S. J., Ross, D. F., & Toglia, M. P. (1987a). Age differences in suggestibility: Narrowing the uncertainties. In S. J. Ceci et al. (Eds.), *Children's eyewitness testimony* (pp. 79–91). New York: Springer.

Ceci, S. J., Ross, D. F., & Toglia, M. P. (1987b). Suggestibility of children's memory: Pscholegal implications. *Journal of Experimental Psychology: General, 116,* 38–49.

Ceci, S. J., Toglia, M. P., & Ross, D. F. (1988). On remembering . . . more or less: A trace strength interpretation of developmental differences in suggestibility. *Journal of Experimental Psychology: General, 117,* 201–203.

Chandler, C. C. (1989). Specific retroactive interference in modified recognition tests: Evidence for an unknown cause of interference. *Journal of Experimental Psychology: Learning, Memory and Cognition, 15,* 256–265.

Chandler, C. C. (1991). How memory for an event is influenced by related events: Interference in modified recognition tests. *Journal of Experimental Psychology: Learning, Memory and Cognition, 17,* 115–125.

Dodson, C., & Reisberg, D. (1989). *Indirect tests of eyewitness memory: The absence of a misinformation effect.* Unpublished manuscript, Reed College, Portland, OR.

Gibling, F., & Davies, G. (1988). Reinstatement of context following exposure to post-event information. *British Journal of Psychology, 79,* 129–141.

Graf, P., & Schacter, D. L. (1985). Implicit and explicit memory for new associations in normal and amnesic subjects. *Journal of Experimental Psychology: Learning, Memory, and Cognition, 11,* 501–518.

Graf, P., & Schacter, D. L. (1987). Selective effects of interference on implicit and explicit memory for new associations. *Journal of Experimental Psychology: Learning, Memory, and Cognition, 13,* 45–53.

Hammersley, R., & Read, J. D. (1986). What is integration? Remembering a story and remembering false implications about the story. *British Journal of Psychology, 77,* 329–341.

Howe, M. J. A. (1970). Repeated presentation and recall of meaningful prose. *Journal of Educational Psychology, 61,* 214–219.

Howe, M. L., & Brainerd, C. J. (1989). Development of children's long-term retention. *Developmental Review, 9*, 301–340.

Jacoby, L. L., & Dallas, M. (1981). On the relationship between autobiographical memory and perceptual learning. *Journal of Experimental Psychology: General, 110*, 306–340.

Kay, H. (1955). Learning and retaining verbal material. *British Journal of Psychology, 46*, 81–100.

Kohnken, G., & Brockmann, C. (1987). Unspecific postevent information, attribution of responsibility, and eyewitness performance. *Applied Cognitive Psychology, 1*, 197–207.

Kroll, N. E. A., & Ogawa, K. H. (1988). Retrieval of the irretrievable: The effect of sequential information on response bias. In M. M. Gruneberg, P. E. Morris, & R. N. Sykes (Eds.), *Practical aspects of memory: Current research and issues: Vol 1*. New York: Wiley.

Lindsay, D. S. (1990). Misleading suggestions can impair eyewitness' ability to remember event details. *Journal of Experimental Psychology: Learning, Memory, and Cognition, 16*, 1077–1083.

Lindsay, D. S., & Johnson, M. K. (1987). Reality monitoring and suggestibility: Children's ability to discriminate among memories from different sources. In S. J. Ceci, M. P. Toglia, & D. F. Ross (Eds.), *Children's eyewitness memory*. New York: Springer-Verlag.

Lindsay, D. S., & Johnson, M. K. (1989). The eyewitness suggestibility effect and memory for source. *Memory & Cognition, 17*, 340–358.

Loftus, E. F., Donders, K., Hoffman, H. G., & Schooler, J. W. (1989). Creating new memories that are quickly accessed and confidently held. *Memory & Cognition, 17*, 607–616.

Loftus, E. F., & Hoffman, H. G. (1989). Misinformation and memory: The creation of new memories. *Journal of Experimental Psychology: General, 118*, 100–104.

Loftus, E. F., Korf, N., & Schooler, J. W. (1989). Misinformation and memory. In J. Yuille (Ed.), *Credibility assessment: A theoretical and research perspective* (pp. 155–174). Kluwer: Dordrecht.

Loftus, E. F., Schooler, J. W., & Wagenaar, W. A. (1985). The fate of memory: Comment on McCloskey & Zaragoza. *Journal of Experimental Psychology: General, 114*, 375–380.

McClelland, J. L., & Rumelhart, D. E. (1985). Distributed memory and the representation of general and specific information. *Journal of Experimental Psychology: General, 114*, 159–188.

McClelland, J. L., & Rumelhart, D. E. (1986). *Parallel distributed processing* (Vol. 1). Cambridge, MA: MIT Press.

McCloskey, M., & Zaragoza, M. (1985). Misleading postevent information and memory for events: Arguments and evidence against memory impairment hypotheses. *Journal of Experimental Psychology: General, 114*, 1–16.

Metcalfe, J. (1990). Composite holographic associative recall model (CHARM) and blended memories in eyewitness testimony. *Journal of Experimental Psychology: General, 119*, 145–160.

Morton, J., Hammersley, R. H., & Bekerian, D. A. (1985). Headed records: A model for memory and its failures. *Cognition, 20*, 1–23.

Pirolli, P. L., & Mitterer, J. O. (1984). The effect of leading questions on prior memory: Evidence for the coexistence of inconsistent memory traces. *Canadian Journal of Psychology, 38*, 135–141.

Register, P. A., & Kihlstrom, J. F. (1988). Hypnosis and interrogative suggestibility. *Personality and Individual Differences, 9*, 549–558.

Roediger, H. L. (1990). Implicit memory: Retention without remembering. *American Psychologist, 45*, 1043–1056.

Roediger, H. L., Weldon, M. S., & Challis, B. H. (1989). Explaining dissociations between implicit and explicit measures of retention: A processing account. In H. L. Roediger & F. I. M. Craik (Eds.), *Varieties of memory and consciousness*. Hillsdale, NJ: Erlbaum.

Schacter, D. L., Cooper, L. A., & Delaney, S. M. (1990). Implicit memory for unfamiliar objects depends on access to structural descriptions. *Journal of Experimental Psychology: General, 119*, 5–24.

Schooler, J. W., Foster, R. A. & Loftus, E. F. (1988). Some deleterious consequences of the act of recollection. *Memory & Cognition, 16*, 243–251.

Schooler, J. W., Gerhard, D., & Loftus, E. F. (1986). Qualities of the unreal. *Journal of Experimental Psychology: Learning, Memory and Cognition, 12*, 171–181.

Sheehan, P. W. (1988). Confidence, memory, and hypnosis. In H. M. Pettinati (Ed.), *Hypnosis and memory* (pp. 95–127). New York: Guilford Press.

Sheehan, P. W., & Tilden, J. (1986). The consistency of occurrences of memory distortion following hypnotic induction. *International Journal of Clinical and Experimental Hypnosis, 34*, 122–137.

Siegler, R. S. (1987). The perils of averaging data over strategies: An example from children's addition. *Journal of Experimental Psychology: General, 116*, 250–264.

Siegler, R. S. (1989). Hazards of mental chronometry: An example from children's subtraction. *Journal of Educational Psychology, 81*, 497–506.

Smith, V. L., & Ellsworth, P. C. (1987). The social psychology of eyewitness accuracy: Misleading questions and communicator expertise. *Journal of Applied Psychology, 72*, 294–300.

Tulving, E. (1983). *Elements of episodic memory*. New York: Oxford University Press.

Tulving, E. (1984). Precise of elements of episodic memory. *Behavioral & Brain Sciences, 7*, 223–238.

Tulving, E., & Schacter, D. L. (1990). Priming and human memory systems. *Science, 247*, 301–306.

Tversky, B., & Tuchin, M. (1989). A reconciliation of the evidence on eyewitness testimony: Comments on McCloskey & Zaragoza. *Journal of Experimental Psychology: General, 118*, 86–91.

Wagenaar, W. A. (1990). *The misinformation feud: Parameterized models and undeterminate differences*. Unpublished manuscript, Leiden University, Leiden, The Netherlands.

Wagenaar, W. A., & Boer, H. P. A. (1987). Misleading postevent information: Testing parameterized models of integration in memory. *Acta Psychologica, 66*, 291–306.

Warrington, E. K., & Weiskrantz, L. (1970). Amnesic syndrome: Consolidation or retrieval? *Nature (London), 228*, 629–630.

Wells, G. L., & Turtle, J. W. (1987). Eyewitness testimony research: Current knowledge and emergent controversies. *Canadian Journal of Behavioral Science, 19*, 363–388.

Whaley, R. (1988). *Tests, testing, and the misinformation effect*. Unpublished doctoral dissertation, University of Washington, Seattle.

Zaragoza, M. S., & McCloskey, M. (1989). Misleading postevent information and the memory impairment hypothesis: Comment on Belli and reply to Tversky and Tuchin. *Journal of Experimental Psychology: General, 118*, 92–99.

Zaragoza, M. S., McCloskey, M., & Jamis, M. (1987). Misleading postevent information and recall of the original event: Further evidence against the memory impairment hypothesis. *Journal of Experimental Psychology: Learning, Memory, and Cognition, 13*, 36–44.

COGNITIVE PROCESSES AND MECHANISMS IN LANGUAGE COMPREHENSION: THE STRUCTURE BUILDING FRAMEWORK

Morton Ann Gernsbacher

I. The Structure Building Framework

Language can be viewed as a specialized skill involving language-specific processes and language-specific mechanisms. Another position views the processing of language—be it comprehension or production—as drawing on many general cognitive processes and mechanisms. Such processes and mechanisms might also underlie nonlinguistic tasks as well. This commonality might arise because, as Bates (1979), Lieberman (1984), and others have suggested, language comprehension evolved from other nonlinguistic cognitive skills. Or the commonality might arise simply because the mind is best understood by reference to a common architecture, e.g., a connectionist architecture.

In recent work, I have adopted the view that many of the processes and mechanisms involved in language comprehension are general cognitive processes and mechanisms. This article describes a few of those cognitive processes and mechanisms, using a simple framework, the structure building framework, as a guide. According to the structure building framework, the goal of comprehension is to build a coherent, mental representation, or *structure*, of the information being comprehended. Several component processes are involved. First, comprehenders lay foundations for their mental structures. Next, comprehenders develop their mental structure by mapping on information when that incoming information is coherent or related to previous information. However, if the incoming information is less coherent or related, comprehenders employ a different process: They shift and initiate a new substructure. Thus, most representations comprise several branching substructures.

The building blocks of these mental structures are memory nodes. Memory nodes are activated by incoming stimuli. Initial activation forms the foundation of mental structures. Once a foundation is laid, subsequent information is often mapped onto a developing structure because the more coherent the incoming information is with the previous information, the more likely it is to activate the same or connected memory nodes. In contrast, the less coherent the incoming information is, the less likely it is to activate the same or connected memory nodes. In this case, the incoming information might activate a different set of nodes, and the activation of this other set of nodes might form the foundation for a new substructure.

In addition, once memory nodes are activated, they transmit processing signals to either enhance other nodes' activation (they boost or increase those nodes' activation) or suppress (dampen or decrease) other nodes' activation. In other words, once memory nodes are activated, two mechanisms control their level of activation: suppression and enhancement. Presumably memory nodes are enhanced because the information they represent is necessary for further structure building. They are suppressed when the information they represent is no longer as necessary.

This article discusses the three subprocesses involved in the structure building process: laying a foundation, mapping coherent or relevant information onto that foundation, and shifting to initiate a new substructure. This article also discusses the two mechanisms that control the structure building processes: enhancement, which increases activation, and suppression, which dampens it.

When discussing these processes and mechanisms I begin by describing the empirical evidence to support them. Then, I describe some exemplary phenomena for which these processes and mechanisms account. Let me stress that I assume that these processes and mechanisms are general, i.e., the same processes and mechanisms should be involved in nonlinguistic phenomena.

This orientation suggests that some of the reasons that individuals differ in comprehension skill might not be specific to language. Toward the end of this article, I describe research investigating this suggestion. But first, I describe the processes and mechanisms involved in structure building, beginning with the process I refer to as *laying a foundation*.

II. The Process of Laying a Foundation

According to the structure building framework, the initial stage of comprehension involves laying a foundation for the mental representation or structure. Laying this foundation should require additional processing. What manifestations might we see of this additional processing? One possibility is increased comprehension time, and indeed, a large body of converging data suggest that comprehension slows down when comprehenders are laying their mental foundations for these mental structures.

For instance, experiments measuring the reading time for each sentence in a paragraph show that initial sentences take longer to read than subsequent sentences (see citations in Gernsbacher, 1990). In fact, this is the case regardless of where the paragraph's topic sentence occurs (Greeno & Noreen, 1974; Kieras, 1978, 1981). In addition, the first sentence of each miniepisode in a story takes longer to read than other sentences in that miniepisode (Haberlandt, 1980, 1984; Haberlandt, Berian, & Sandson, 1980; Mandler & Goodman, 1982).[1]

Similarly, experiments measuring the reading time for each word within a sentence show that initial words take longer to read than subsequent words (Aaronson & Ferres, 1983; Chang, 1980). In fact, the same word is read more slowly when it occurs at the beginning of a sentence or phrase than when it occurs later (Aaronson & Scarborough, 1976).[2] The same comprehension time effects are observed when comprehenders self-pace their viewing of nonverbal picture stories. Comprehenders spend more time viewing the initial picture of each story and the initial picture of each subepisode (Gernsbacher, 1983).

When comprehending spoken language, subjects are slower to identify a target phoneme or a target word when that target occurs during the beginning of its sentence or phrase than when it occurs later (see citations in Gernsbacher, 1990). So both the comprehension time and the target identi-

---

[1] Some regression analyses of sentence-by-sentence reading times do not show a simple "serial position" effect (e.g., Graesser, Hoffman, & Clark, 1980). Perhaps this is because the stimulus sentences vary in length, and length is also a substantial predictor of reading time. Indeed, when the same sentences are read word by word, and the regression analyzes average word-by-word reading times per sentence (and therefore equates sentence length), these analyses also show that initial sentences take longer to read (Haberlandt & Graesser, 1985).

[2] This effect is not manifested when subjects are required to memorize (as opposed to comprehend) the stimulus sentences. Neither is the effect manifested when subjects are required to perform a second task (e.g., answer a question or press a key to signal an anomaly) immediately after they finish reading each sentence. In preparation of this second task, subjects often delay their reading of the last words of the sentences.

fication data display the pattern one expects if comprehenders use initial words and sentences to lay foundations for their mental representations of larger units, such as phrases, sentences, story episodes, and paragraphs. But, rather importantly, this pattern is not displayed when stimuli do not lend themselves to coherent mental representations, e.g., when the sentences or paragraphs are self-embedded or extensively right branching, as in (1), which is a self-embedded version of (2) (Foss & Lynch, 1969; Greeno & Noreen, 1974; Hakes & Foss, 1970; Kieras, 1978, 1981).

(1) *Grants, manuscripts, graduate students, committees, articles, data, experiments, classes, the professor taught, conducted, collected, published, served on, trained, reviewed, and submitted.*

(2) *The professor taught classes, conducted experiments, collected data, published articles, served on committees, trained graduate students, reviewed manuscripts, and submitted grants.*

Memory data also support the proposal that a general cognitive process involved in comprehension is first laying a foundation. For instance, sentences are recalled better when they are cued by their first content words or by pictures of those first content words than when they are cued by later occurring words (Bock & Irwin, 1980; Prentice, 1967; Turner & Rommetveit, 1968). Similarly, story episodes are recalled better when they are cued by their first sentences than when they are cued by later occurring sentences (Mandler & Goodman, 1982). These data suggest that initial stimuli serve as a foundation onto which subsequent information is added.

Indeed, initial information plays such a fundamtneal role in organizing mental structures that when comprehenders are asked to recall the main idea of a paragraph, they are most likely to select the initial sentence—even when the actual theme is captured by a later occurring sentence (Kieras, 1980). This phenomenon also suggests that the initial process of comprehension involves laying a foundation.

A. THE ADVANTAGE OF FIRST MENTION

Another phenomenon that could be the result of the process of laying a foundation is what I refer to as the *advantage of first mention*. The advantage is this: After comprehending a sentence involving two participants, it is easier to remember the participant mentioned first than the participant mentioned second. For example, after reading the sentence,

(3) *Tina beat Lisa in the state tennis match.*

if subjects are asked whether the name *Tina* occurred in the sentence, they respond considerably faster if *Tina* was the first person mentioned in the sentence, as she was in (3), than if *Tina* was the second person mentioned in the sentence, as she is in,

(4)   *Lisa beat Tina in the state tennis match.*

The first-mentioned participant is more accessible from comprehenders' mental representations, which is what I mean by the advantage of first mention.

The advantage of first mention has been observed numerous times by several researchers (Chang, 1980; Corbett & Chang, 1983; Gernsbacher, 1989; Stevenson, 1986; von Eckardt & Potter, 1985). As a point of interest, when Corbett and Chang (1983) observed this advantage, they included filler trials in which they measured the accessibility of concepts that were words other than participants' names; so the advantage does not depend on some strategy that subjects might employ when they think that they only have to remember the names of sentence participants.

One explanation of the advantage of first mention draws on the proposal that comprehension involves laying a foundation. For this reason, first-mentioned participants are more accessible—both because they form the foundations for their sentence level representations and because it is through them that subsequent information is mapped onto the developing representation. However, there are other explanations of the advantage of first mention, and these other explanations draw on the linguistic structure of English.

For example, first-mentioned participants might be more accessible because in English declarative sentences they are virtually always the syntactic relation known as *subject*, and they typically also fill the semantic role known as *agent*. In a series of experiments (Gernsbacher & Hargreaves, 1988), we tried to untangle these linguistic factors from the advantage of first mention. In our first experiment, we discovered that the advantage of first mention was not attributable to semantic agency. That is, the participant *Tina* was just as accessible when she was the agent of the action, as in (5), as when *Tina* was the recipient of the action or the semantic patient, as she is in (6).

(5)   *Tina beat Lisa in the state tennis match.*

(6)   *Tina was beaten by Lisa in the state tennis match.*

The crucial factor affecting accessibility was whether the participants were mentioned first, as *Tina* is in (5) and (6). Participants were less accessible when they were mentioned second, as *Tina* is in (7) and (8).

(7)   *Lisa beat Tina in the state tennis match.*

(8)   *Lisa was beaten by Tina in the state tennis match.*

These results are presented in the leftmost panel of Fig. 1. Before prematurely accepting the null hypothesis, we conducted a replication experiment with an increased subject sample size of 120. The results of the replication experiment were identical to those of the first experiment.

In our third experiment and its replication we investigated whether the advantage of first mention depended on the first-mentioned participants being literally the initial words of our stimulus sentences. If so, our laboratory task might be somewhat to blame as the first word of each sentence was preceded by an attention-getting warning signal, which was itself preceded by a brief blank period. To investigate this, we manipulated whether an adverbial phrase like *two weeks ago* was preposed at the beginning of the sentence, as in

(9)   *Two weeks ago Tina mailed Lisa a box full of clothes.*

Or it was postposed at the end of the sentence, as in

(10)   *Tina mailed Lisa a box full of clothes two weeks ago.*

Or it did not occur at all, as in

(11)   *Tina mailed Lisa a box full of clothes.*

We discovered that the advantage of first mention remained regardless of whether the first-mentioned participants were literally the initial words of their stimulus sentences (see the center panel of Fig. 1). Thus, the advantage must depend on each participant's position relative to the other participants.

In our fifth, sixth, and seventh experiments, we investigated whether the advantage of first mention was due to the first-mentioned participants being syntactic subjects. This, of course, is the typical sequence of events in a language like English that is considered an SVO (subject–verb–object) language (Greenberg, 1963). However, in our fifth experiment, the advantage of first mention was not attenuated when the two participants were both subjects, e.g., when both *Tina* and *Lisa* were the syntactic subjects, as in (12), as opposed to *Tina* being the sole subject, as in (13).

(12)   *Tina and Lisa argued during the meeting.*

(13)   *Tina argued with Lisa during the meeting.*

(See the rightmost panel of Fig. 1.) In fact, in our sixth and seventh experiments, the advantage of first mention was not attenuated even when the first-mentioned participant was no longer its sentence's syntactic subject, as *Tina* is in

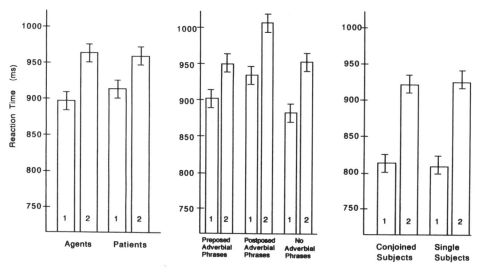

Fig. 1. Results from Gernsbacher and Hargreaves (1988; Experiments 1, 3, and 5). The data displayed are the subjects' mean verification latencies to first- vs. second-mentioned sentence participants when the sentence participants were agents vs. patients (leftmost panel), when the sentences had preposed adverbial phrases, postposed adverbial phrases, or no adverbial phrases (center panel), and when the sentence participants were conjoined subjects vs. single subjects (rightmost panel).

(14)   *Because of Tina, Lisa was evicted from the apartment.*

We concluded that the advantage of first mention does not arise from any of the linguistic factors that we investigated. Instead we suggested that it is a result of general cognitive processes that occur naturally during comprehension. These involve laying a foundation and mapping subsequent information onto that foundation.

B.   THE ADVANTAGE OF FIRST MENTION VS. THE ADVANTAGE OF CLAUSE RECENCY

The advantage of first mention seems to contradict another well-known advantage—what I shall call the advantage of clause recency. The advantage of clause recency occurs immediately after subjects hear or read a two-clause sentence; words from the most recently read or heard clause are often more accessible than words from an earlier clause. For instance, the word *oil* is more accessible immediately after subjects hear (15) than it is immediately after they hear (16) (Caplan, 1972).

(15)   *Now that artists are working fewer hours, oil prints are rare.*

(16)   *Now that artists are working in oil, prints are rare.*

Presumably this advantage arises because the word *oil* was in the most recent clause in (15). So the advantage of clause recency is also an advantage for the order of mentioning concepts, but the advantage is for the most recently or second-mentioned concept (see also Chang, 1980; Kornfeld, 1973; von Eckardt & Potter, 1985).

In a series of experiments (Gernsbacher, Hargreaves, & Beeman, 1989), we resolved this discrepancy and discovered something about how comprehenders build mental representations of clauses. In these experiments, we measured the accessibility of sentence participants in two-clause sentences, e.g.,

(17)   *Tina gathered the kindling, and Lisa set up the tent.*

The first-mentioned participants were the syntactic subjects of the first clauses, and the second-mentioned participants were the syntactic subjects of the second clauses.

We began with the proposal that comprehenders represent each clause of a multiclause sentence in its own substructure. So comprehending (17) would require first building a substructure to represent the clause *Tina gathered the kindling,* and then building a substructure to represent the clause *Lisa set up the tent.* We also predicted that comprehenders have greatest access to the information represented in the substructure that they are currently developing. We tested this prediction in our first experiment. Our goal was to measure accessibility of the sentence participants at the point where comprehenders were just finishing building their representation of the second clause. We thought that if we could capture that point, we would find an advantage of clause recency; in other words, we expected to observe an advantage of the second-mentioned participant.

To capture that point, we presented the test names coincident with the last words in the sentences, but we presented those test names at a different place on the computer screen than where we presented the sentences. We assumed that by the time our subjects shifted their eyes and their attention (Posner, 1980) to the test names, our coincident presentation was comparable to an extremely short delay. And indeed, at this point we observed a second- as opposed to first-mentioned participant's advantage; in other words, we observed an advantage of clause recency, similar in magnitude to those advantages observed by Caplan (1972) and others. Our data are displayed in the two leftmost bars of Fig. 2. These data suggest that comprehenders do have greatest access to information represented in the substructure that they are currently developing.

After comprehenders represent each clause, we assume that they must

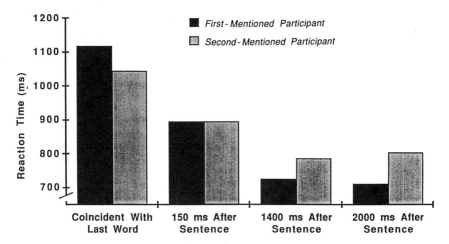

Fig. 2. Results from Gernsbacher, Hargreaves, and Beeman (1989; Experiments 1, 2, 3, and 5). The data displayed are the subjects' mean verification latencies to first- vs. second-mentioned sentence participants when the first-mentioned participants were the subjects of the first clauses of two-clause sentences, and the second-mentioned participants were the subjects of the second clauses.

map their second-clause representation onto their first-clause representation. In other words, to fully represent a two-clause sentence, comprehenders must incorporate the two substructures into one. Our goal in our second experiment was to catch comprehenders after they had built their representations of each clause, but before they had mapped their representation of the second clause onto their representation of the first clause. We predicted that at that point information would be equally accessible from each clause. And indeed, the first-mentioned and second-mentioned participants were equally accessible (see Fig. 2). We observed the same effect in a replication experiment.

In our fourth experiment, we predicted that if we measured accessibility a little bit later—say, a second later—we would find that by this point the first-mentioned participants would be more accessible. This would suggest that comprehenders had successfully mapped the two clauses together and that the first clause was serving as a foundation for the second. And indeed, by this time, the first-mentioned participants were more accessible (see Fig. 2). In fact, the advantage of first mention was identical in magnitude to the advantage we observed with simple sentences.

To review our results: At our earliest test point, we observed that the second-mentioned participants were more accessible or, in other words, we observed an advantage of clause recency. I suggest that at this point comprehenders were still developing their representations of the second clauses. When we meassured accessibility 150 msec later, the two participants were equally accessible. I suggest that at this point comprehenders had built their representations of both clauses but had not begun mapping those representations together. When we measured accessibility after 1400 msec, we observed an advantage of first mention. I suggest that at this point comprehenders had finished mapping the second clause onto the first, and the information from the first clause was more accessible because it served as the foundation for the whole sentence level representation. Each of these results is displayed in Fig. 2.

An alternative explanation is that the change in accessibility that we observed over time was due to catching subjects at different stages while they were cyclically rehearsing the two participants' names (e.g., *Tina . . . Lisa . . . Tina . . . Lisa*). To rule out this explanation, we conducted one final experiment in which we delayed the test point even longer, for a total of 2000 msec. At that point the first-mentioned participants were still more accessible; in fact, at that point the first-mentioned participants were even more accessible than they had been at the 1400 msec test point (see two rightmost bars in Fig. 2). This finding suggests that the advantage of first mention is a relatively long-lived characteristic of the representation of a sentence. I suggest that this advantage arises because first-mentioned participants form the foundations for their sentence level representations, and it is through them that subsequent information is mapped onto the developing representation.

In contrast, the advantage of clause recency appears to be relatively short-lived. I suggest that the advantage of clause recency arises because comprehenders build a substructure to represent each clause of a multiclause sentence, and they have greatest access to information represented in the substructure that they are currently developing. Thus, two seemingly contradictory phenomena are not mutually exclusive when comprehension is viewed as structure building. In fact, according to the structure building framework, we should be able to observe both phenomena simultaneously. That was the goal in our sixth experiment.

In this sixth experiment, we measured the accessibility of each of four participants, e.g., the four participants mentioned in (18).

(18)   *Dave and Rick gathered the kindling, and John and Bill set up the tent.*

As in (18), two participants (e.g., *Dave* and *Rick*) were the conjoined subjects of the first clause, and two participants (e.g., *John* and *Bill*) were the conjoined subjects of the second clause. In other words, two participants were the first- and second-mentioned participants of the first clause, and two participants were the first- and second-mentioned participants of the second clause.

We predicted that in both clauses we would observe an advantage of first mention: Within each clause, first-mentioned participants would be more accessible than second-mentioned participants. In addition, we predicted that if we could catch comprehenders at the point where they were completing their representations of the second clause, we would observe an advantage of clause recency: Both participants from the second clause would be more accessible than both participants from the first clause. And, indeed, that is what we found.

As shown in Fig. 3, in both clauses the first-mentioned participants were significantly more accessible than the second-mentioned participants; in other words, we observed an advantage of first mention. As also illustrated in Fig. 3, participants from the second clause were significantly more accessible than participants from the first clause; in other words, when we tested accessibility 150 msec after the end of each sentence, we also observed an advantage of clause recency. In a final experiment, when we delayed the test point to 2000 msec after each sentence, we no longer observed an advantage of clause recency—only an advantage of first mention.

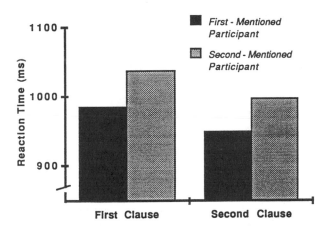

Fig. 3.   Results from Gernsbacher, Hargreaves, and Beeman (1989; Experiment 6). The data displayed are the subjects' mean verification latencies to first- vs. second-mentioned sentence participants in the first clause of two-clause sentences, and first- vs. second-mentioned sentence participants in the second clause of two-clause sentences.

C. Functional Role of First Mention

Given the privileged role that initial information plays in comprehenders' mental representations, speakers and writers should seriously confront what Levelt (1981) dubbed the linearization problem: "what to say first, what to say next, and so on" (p. 305).

Indeed, functional grammarians argue that different orders of mention code different pragmatic dimensions; therefore, speakers' and writers' selection of a specific order serves a communicative function (Chafe, 1976; Firbas, 1974; Givón, 1979; Halliday, 1967). However, opinions differ over which dimension initial mention codes and which function speakers and writers intend to accomplish when they select among the grammatical forms that involve different orders of mention. According to one perspective, initial mention codes importance and functions to attract attention (Givón, 1986). According to another perspective, first mention codes givenness and functions to create a context for subsequent comprehension (Clark & Clark, 1977).

Both perspectives are supported by experiments employing a range of laboratory tasks designed to simulate sentence production. These tasks include elicited sentence formulation, oral sentence recall, sentence acceptability, sentence ratings, and sentence verification (of pictures, for example).

Experiments that have manipulated importance via perceptual salience, animacy, definiteness, or other markers have shown that important concepts are mentioned first. Similarly, experiments that have manipulated givenness via explicit prior mention, verbatim or pictorial cueing, or implicit presupposition have shown that given concepts are mentioned first (see citations in Gernsbacher, 1990). However, one cannot adopt the two perspectives simultaneously without entering into a paradox. That is, initial mention can only code importance and givenness simultaneously if one assumes that new information is always less important or that important information is always old. Both assumptions seem unintuitive. Thus, the two perspectives conflict.

Bock (1982) discusses a few resolutions to this conflict from the perspective of sentence production. In Gernsbacher and Hargreaves (in press), we did not attempt to resolve this conflict for sentence comprehension, but we did point out how the structure building account accomodates both functions. If first mention is selected in order to signal importance, then the function is accomplished because—by virtue of being first mentioned— initial information gets represented at the core or foundation of the structure. As mentioned above, this privileged position leads to greater accessibility, and presumably the goal of marking information as important is to gain this greater accessibility.

On the other hand, if first mention is selected in order to signal givenness, then the function is also accomplished because—by virtue of being first mentioned—initial information organizes the representation of subsequent information. That is, subsequent information gets mapped onto the developing structure vis-à-vis the initial information. Presumably, the mapping process proceeds more smoothly when new (subsequent) information is mapped onto given (initial) information rather than the other way around.

Thus, functional linguists suggest that speakers and writers exploit different grammatical forms, such as passivization or left dislocation, to accomplish certain communicative functions, such as attracting attention or signaling givenness. I suggest that the cognitive processes involved in laying a foundation for mental structures accomplish these functions.

III. Processes of Mapping and Shifting

According to the structure building framework, once a foundation is laid, incoming information that is coherent with the previous information is mapped onto the developing structure or substructure. Presumably the more coherent (relevant, related, or similar) the incoming information is, the easier the mapping process should be. How would ease in mapping be manifested? Again, one candidate is comprehension time, and again, data from reading time experiments support this assumption.

Sentences that literally or conceptually repeat a previous word or a phrase—and thereby signal coherence overtly—are read faster than comparable sentences that are not literally or conceptually repetitive (see citations in Gernsbacher, 1990). For example, comprehenders more rapidly read the sentence *The beer was warm* after they read (19a) than after they read (19b).

(19) a. *We got some beer out of the trunk. The beer was warm.*

b. *We checked the picnic supplies. The beer was warm.*

The benefit does not derive solely from literally repeating the word *beer*, as a sentence that simply mentions *beer*, such as (20), does not facilitate mapping too much more than the picnic supplies sentence (Haviland & Clark, 1974; see also Johnson-Laird, 1983, p. 379).

(20) *Andrew was especially fond of beer. The beer was warm.*

In addition, the assumption that coherent information is represented in the same mental substructure is supported by memory data. Sentences and phrases that are coreferenced by repetition are more likely to be remembered when one phrase cues or primes the recall or recognition of the other; such phrases are also more likely to be "clustered" in comprehenders' recall protocols (Hayes-Roth & Thorndyke, 1979; Kintsch, Kozminsky, Streby, McKoon, & Keenan, 1975; McKoon & Ratcliff, 1980b).

On the other hand, according to the structure building framework, when incoming information is less coherent, comprehenders employ the process of shifting: They shift from actively building one substructure and initiate another. Laying the foundation for this new substructure requires additional processing. Again, this additional processing should be manifested in increased comprehension time. And again, numerous reading time experiments support this assumption: Sentences and words that change the ongoing topic, point of view, or setting take substantially longer to comprehend than those that continue it (see citations in Gernsbacher, 1990).

Consider the following example. This example draws on the narrative point of view, which is the narrator's location in relation to the action (Black, Turner, & Bower, 1979). For instance, (22) locates the narrator inside the lunchroom.

(22)   *The door to Henry's lunchroom opened and two men came in.*

In contrast, (23) locates the narrator outside the lunchroom.

(23)   *The door to Henry's lunchroom opened and two men went in.*

After reading (24), comprehenders presumably adopt the narrator's point of view, inside the living room.

(24)   *Bill was sitting in the living room reading the evening paper.*

Then, they have difficulty reading a sentence that switches this point of view, as does (25), compared with a sentence that maintains the point of view, as does (26).

(25)   *Before Bill had finished the paper, John went into the room.*

(26)   *Before Bill had finished the paper, John came into the room.*

Comprehenders also have more difficulty retrieving information presented before a change in topic, point of view, or setting than they do retrieving information presented after such a change (A. Anderson, Garrod, & Sanford, 1983; Clements, 1979; Mandler & Goodman, 1982). Presumably, this is because comprehenders shift when they encounter a change in topic, point of view, or setting. If so, then the information that occurred before the change in topic, point of view, or setting will be represented in one substructure, while the information that occurred after the change in topic, point of view, or setting will be represented in another substructure.

A. Shifting as the Cause of Comprehenders' Rapid Inaccessibility to Information

The process of shifting from building one structure or substructure to initiating another also accounts for a well-known language comprehension phenomenon. Shortly after hearing or reading a passage, comprehenders quickly lose access to recently comprehended information (Gernsbacher, 1985). In particular, information typically considered "surface" information becomes less accessible (but see von Eckardt & Potter, 1985).

This phenomenon is well known partly because we experience it everyday and partly because it has been repeatedly demonstrated in the laboratory (see citations in Gernsbacher, 1990). In Gernsbacher (1985), I too demonstrated this phenomenon, but my demonstration was made with passages composed of professionally drawn pictures; these stories were "told" completely without words. An example sequence is shown in Fig. 4A. While subjects comprehended these nonverbal stories I measured how well they could remember each picture's original left-vs.-right orientation, as illustrated in Fig. 4B.

Two goals directed this research. First, I wanted to demonstrate that this phenomenon was not unique to language-based comprehension. This goal was met by my first four experiments. The first experiment demonstrated that comprehenders had more difficulty accessing recently comprehended information after they comprehended all four picture stories than after they comprehended each of the four picture stories. The second experiment demonstrated that comprehenders had more difficulty accessing recently comprehended information after they comprehended an entire picture story than after they comprehended each half of that story. So these first two experiments replicated the phenomenon in which comprehenders rapidly lose access to previously comprehended information, but in these experiments the phenomenon was observed during the comprehension of nonverbal stimuli. The data from these two experiments are summarized in Table I.

The third and fourth experiments replicated a more intriguing aspect of the phenomenon. Several language experiments have demonstrated that apart from the passage of time or the comprehension of more information, the structure of the passage greatly affects the time course of accessibility. More specifically, information becomes markedly less accessible just after comprehension crosses a constituent boundary; e.g., just after comprehenders finish a clause, a phrase, a sentence, a paragraph, or a miniepisode (see citations in Gernsbacher, 1990).

The third experiment demonstrated that comprehenders could segment the picture stories into their constituents or subepisodes. The fourth ex-

Fig. 4. A picture story used in Gernsbacher (1985). A, example sequence. B, example picture displayed in one orientation (top) and its reverse (bottom).

periment demonstrated that recently comprehended information was less accessible after crossing these constituents' boundaries than before, even though the test interval—in terms of the number of stimuli and the amount of time—was the same in the after-boundary vs. the before-boundary conditions (see Table I).

The second goal of my research was to investigate why this phenomenon occurs. Four explanations were considered. The first was the linguistics hypothesis: Information becomes less accessible because sentence comprehension requires syntatic detransformation. Though detransformation provides syntactic tags that can be used to reconstruct the original sentence, the tags are often lost (Mehler, 1963; Miller, 1962; Sachs, 1967).

One major problem with this explanation is that it requires a set of syntactic rules specifying the necessary transformations used during comprehension. In other words, it requires a psychologically "real" transformational grammar. Specifying such a grammar for English sentences has proved to be no easy task (Bresnan & Kaplan, 1982; Garnham, 1983). And though there have been novel attempts to specify grammars for nonverbal media—for example, Carroll (1980) attempted a grammar for cinematic films, and Bernstein (1976) attempted one for musical symphonies—the possibility of specifying a grammar to describe my picture stories seemed remote.

Another problem with the linguistic hypothesis was that over two decades of experiments using verbal stimuli alone, this explanation has steadily lost support (Fodor, Bever, & Garrett, 1974; Garnham, 1983; Gough & Diehl, 1978). So I abandoned the linguistics hypothesis and

TABLE I

Subjects' Mean Percentage Correct and Discrimination (A') Scores in Gernsbacher (1985)

Experiment	Manipulation	% Correct	A'
1	After comprehending ONE vs.	66	.752
	SEVERAL picture stories	57	.634
2	After comprehending HALF vs. an	74	.835
	ENTIRE picture story	62	.705
4	BEFORE a constituent boundary vs.	79	.872
	AFTER a constituent boundary	70	.795
5	After comprehending a NORMAL vs. a	68	.782
	SCRAMBLED picture story	62	.700
6	After comprehending a NORMAL vs. a	70	.787
	SCRAMBLED written story	72	.700

searched for an explanation outside the language domain. This approach is not unusual; when other phenomena originally believed to be unique to language processing were demonstrated outside that domain (e.g., categorical perception and selective adaptation), amodal explanations were sought for them too (Diehl, 1981).

The second explanation I considered was the memory limitations hypothesis, whereby recently comprehended information becomes less accessible because the limitations of a short-term memory are exceeded. These limitations might be quantitative; short-term memory can hold only a limited number of items. Or they might be temporal; short-term memory can hold information for only a limited period of time (Miller, 1956).

However, my fourth experiment and other constituent boundary experiments illustrate an aspect of the phenomenon that memory limitations cannot explain. These experiments demonstrate that apart from the amount of information or the passage of time, the structure of the information affects its accessibility. That is, accessing recently comprehended information does not depend completely on how much information has been held or how long that information has been held in a hypothetical short-term memory.

To account for such findings, a corollary assumption is often made: Recently comprehended information is held in short-term memory until a meaningful unit has been comprehended; then it is lost (Jarvella, 1979; Sanford & Garrod, 1981). However, this assumption undermines the original explanation. All constituents are not the same size, so they would not consume the same amount of space or be held for the same period of time. If while waiting for a constituent to end, short-term memory can hold a variable amount of information for a variable period of time, then why is the information ever lost? Perhaps the system is so "smart" that when anticipating a time or space limitation it chooses to expunge at a structurally appropriate interval. But this leaves us without an a priori specification of how long or how much information can be held, and no causal link. Therefore, I also considered the memory limitations hypothesis insufficient.

The third explanation was the recoding hypothesis, whereby recently comprehended information becomes less accessible because during comprehension it is recoded into a more meaningful representation, usually referred to as gist. So even though initially all verbatim information is vital for successful comprehension, the more successful the comprehension, the more likely it is that verbatim information becomes recoded into gist (Bransford & Franks, 1971, 1972).

Consider the analogy of baking a cake. As the cake bakes, several raw ingredients (salt, flour, butter, sugar) become increasingly "recoded." In fact, if the baking process is successful, it is difficult to extract any of the ingredients in their original raw forms. Now consider Bransford and Franks's (1971) seminal experiment. Subjects comprehended a series of thematically cohesive sentences and on a later recognition test they were poor at remembering structural information about sentence boundaries.

Less well known is a later experiment by Peterson and McIntyre (1973). In one condition, they perfectly replicated Bransford and Franks (1971). In a second condition, their input sentences were not thematically cohesive and, for these sentences, comprehenders were considerably better at remembering sentence boundaries. One explanation is that in Bransford and Franks's paradigm, the input sentences could easily be recoded into gist, but in Peterson and McIntyre's unrelated (second) condition, they could not—so they had to remain in their relatively raw form.

Other data converge on this explanation. For instance, comprehenders' memory for the original (active vs. passive) voice of a sentence is significantly worse when the input sentences form a cohesive story than when the sentences are semantically unrelated (J. R. Anderson & Bower, 1973, p. 224). Comprehenders make more synonym substitutions when recalling sentences originally processed as a thematic story than when the sentences seem unrelated (de Villiers, 1974; Luftig, 1981; Pompi & Lachman, 1967). Similarly, bilinguals' memory for the language in which different words were originally spoken is worse when the words compose a unified sentence rather than an unrelated list (Saegert, Hamayan, & Ahmar, 1975; see also Rose, Rose, King, & Perez, 1975).

In each of these situations, recoding the input into a more meaningful representation apparently caused some of its information to become less accessible. However, the situations that best support the recoding hypothesis least represent typical comprehension. In these situations the to-be-comprehended stimuli were semantically unrelated and void of thematic integrity (or at least it appeared that way to subjects). It is difficult to draw conclusions about comprehension from situations where comprehension—in the usual sense—cannot actually occur (for comparable arguments, see Moeser, 1976; Perfetti & Goldman, 1974).

A more valid test of the recoding hypothesis would involve two experimental conditions; in both, comprehension could occur, but recoding would be less likely in one than the other. That was one purpose of the fifth experiment (in Gernsbacher, 1985). A second purpose was to test another explanation, the shifting hypothesis. This fourth explanation was derived from the structure building framework.

According to the shifting hypothesis, recently comprehended information becomes less accessible because comprehenders shift from developing one substructure to develop another. Presumably, information represented in one substructure is most available during the active processing of that substructure. Once a processing shift has occurred, information represented in the previous substructure becomes less available.

In my fifth experiment (Gernsbacher, 1985), half the stories were presented with their pictures in their normal, chronological order and half were presented with their pictures in a scrambled order. This scrambling manipulation served three purposes. First, it provided a more valid test of the recoding hypothesis because unlike lists of isolated or seemingly unrelated sentences, stories composed of scrambled stimuli possess a theme. With appropriate instructions, subjects attempt to obtain the gist of scrambled stories and meet with some success, though much less than with normal ones (see citations in Gernsbacher, 1990).

Second, the scrambling manipulation provided an empirical test of the shifting hypothesis because stimuli presented in a scrambled order are by definition relatively less coherent. Therefore, building a mental structure of a scrambled story should induce more shifting. Third, the scrambling manipulation pit the two hypotheses against one another because the predictions derived from each were in opposition. According to the recoding hypothesis, recently comprehended information becomes less available because it gets recoded into gist. Therefore, the lower the probability of recoding, the more accessible the information should be. Because comprehending scrambled stories leads to a lower probability of recoding, the prediction derived from the recoding hypothesis was that recently comprehended information would be *more* accessible in the scrambled than the normal condition.

But according to the shifting hypothesis, recently comprehended information becomes less accessible because of shifting from building one substructure to developing another; the higher the probability of shifting, the less accessible the information should be. Because comprehending scrambled stories leads to a higher probability of shifting, the prediction derived from the shifting hypothesis was that recently comprehended information would be *less* accessible in the scrambled than the normal condition.

The results of this fifth experiment using picture stories were clearly those predicted by the shifting hypothesis, i.e., information was less accessible in the scrambled than the normal condition (see Table I). These results were replicated in a sixth experiment using the more traditional stimuli, namely, written stories (see Table I). Thus, the cognitive process of shifting appears to be an adequate amodal explanation of why comprehenders rapidly lose access to recently comprehended information.

B. Linguistic Cues for Shifting

How do comprehenders know when to shift and initiate a new substructure? Presumably speakers and writers—and even picture story authors—signal their readers and listeners via various devices. For instance, when producing sentences, speakers and writers use certain devices to signal that they are beginning a new clause or phrase (Bever, 1970; Clark & Clark, 1977; Fodor et al., 1974; Frazier & Fodor, 1978; Kaplan, 1975; Kimball, 1973; Wanner & Maratsos, 1978). Indeed, one of Kimball's (1973) seven parsing principles was that "the construction of a new node is signalled by the occurrence of a grammatical function word" (p. 29). Thus, comprehenders might, as Clark and Clark (1977) suggested, use signals such as determiners (*a, an, the*) and quantifiers (*some, all, six,* etc.) to initiate a new substructure representing a new noun phrase. Similarly, they might use signals such as subordinating conjunctions (*because, when, since,* etc.) to initiate a new substructure representing a new clause (Clark & Clark, 1977, p. 62).

At the level of passages, speakers and writers use other devices to signal an upcoming change, e.g., a change in topic, point of view, or setting (Carpenter & Just, 1977; Halliday, 1967). One relatively subtle linguistic device is what I have referred to as an adverbial lead (Gernsbacher, 1984). This involves simply placing an adverb like *Then* or *Next* at the beginning of a sentence. In several experiments, we have found that adverbial leads stimulated behavioral responses indicative of processing shifts.

In many of these experiments, subjects read seven-sentence passages that began like

(27)　*The lifeguard was watching the children swim. He noticed one child was struggling. He thought the child might be drowning.*

Then, either the fourth or fifth sentence began with an adverb like *then* or *next*, as in (28) or (29):

(28)　*Next, he jumped into the water. He began to administer CPR.*

(29)　*He jumped quickly into the water. Next, he administered CPR.*

In one experiment I measured sentence reading times and found that adverbial leads slowed comprehension (Gernsbacher, 1984, Experiment 1). This suggests that adverbial leads trigger comprehenders to begin laying a foundation for a new substructure. In a second experiment, I measured question-answering latencies and found that comprehenders had more difficulty accessing information presented before an adverbial lead than information presented afterward (Gernsbacher, 1984, Experiment 2). This suggests that the information occurring after an adverbial lead is represented in a different mental substructure.

In another experiment, Wisegarver (1986) used the priming-in-item-recognition task pioneered by McKoon & Ratcliff (1980a, 1980b). In this task, subjects first read a passage and then attempt to recognize whether each of a short list of words occurred in that passage. Wisegarver (1986) found that a word from one sentence of a passage was a worse prime for a word from another sentence when an adverbial lead intervened between the two.

Finally, using different passages from the one illustrated above, Beeman and I (1991) found that comprehenders' ability to draw inferences between two facts was severely disrupted when one of those facts was presented prior to an adverbial lead and the other was presented after the adverbial lead. In sum, adverbial leads appear to stimulate behavior indicative of processing shifts; perhaps speakers and writers use them to signal their readers or listeners of an upcoming change.

IV. Mechanisms of Suppression and Enhancement

According to the structure building framework, the building blocks of mental structures are memory nodes. Presumably, memory nodes are activated by incoming stimuli. Once activated, they transmit processing signals that either suppress (decrease or dampen) or enhance (increase or boost) the activation of other memory nodes. In other words, the activation of memory nodes is controlled by the mechanisms of suppression and enhancement. Suppression and enhancement might be responsible for many linguistic as well as nonlinguistic phenomena.

A.   ROLE OF SUPPRESSION IN FINE-TUNING THE MEANINGS OF WORDS

The mechanism of suppression appears to control a phenomenon I refer to as "fine-tuning" the activation of lexical concepts, e.g., fine-tuning the appropriate meaning of an ambiguous word. The reason why such a fine-tuning process is needed is that—contrary to intuition—immediately after comprehenders hear or read an ambiguous word such as *bug*, multiple meanings are activated. In fact, multiple meanings are activated—even when a particular meaning is specified by the preceding semantic context, as in "spiders, roaches, and other *bugs*," or the preceding syntactic context, as in "I like *the* watch" vs. "I like *to* watch" (see citations in Gernsbacher, 1990).

Cognitive psychologists usually attribute this multiple activation to some form of automatic (or semiautomatic) activation (Burgess & Simpson, 1988; Simpson, 1984; Simpson & Lorsbach, 1983). Computer models usually simulate the pattern by allowing all meanings of an ambiguous word to receive facilitation prior to getting any input from a semantic or syntactic processor (Charniak, 1983). However, behaviorally the phenomenon becomes more complex very shortly after the multiple meanings are simultaneously activated. As intuition suggests, only one meaning is available to consciousness after a period as brief as 200 msec. So the question arises, what happens to the inappropriate meanings?

Some have suggested that inappropriate meanings become less accessible through a mechanism that I have dubbed *mutual inhibition*. Their suggestion is that the appropriate meanings' growth in activation causes the inappropriate meanings' decline in activation, as in a seesaw effect (McClelland & Kawamoto, 1986; Waltz & Pollack, 1985). Unfortunately, the behavioral data do not demonstrate this compensatory pattern.

Another explanation is that the inappropriate meanings simply decay (J. R. Anderson, 1983). However, we tested this decay explanation and found that in its purest sense it cannot explain all the data (Gernsbacher & Faust, 1990).[3] This experiment examined the activation of multiple meanings of an ambiguous word like *quack*. In one condition, the ambiguous words were biased by a previous semantic context. For example, subjects read either (30) or (31).

(30)   *Pam was diagnosed by a quack.*

(31)   *Pam heard a sound like a quack.*

In this condition the typical, multiple activation phenomenon was observed: Immediately after the subjects read the ambiguous words, both meanings were activated, but within about 350 msec the inappropriate meanings were no longer activated. In a second condition, the ambiguous words were left ambiguous, as in (32).

(32)   *Pam was annoyed by the quack.*

In this condition, both meanings remained activated at 350 msec; in fact, they were both activated at 750 msec (see also Hudson & Tanenhaus, 1984). If the decreased activation of an inappropriate meaning is due to decay, then surely one or both of the meanings should have decayed in this

---

[3] A third explanation is that this phenomenon is attributable to backward priming (Glucksberg, Kreuz, & Rho, 1986; van Petten & Kutas, 1987; but see Burgess, Tanenhaus, & Seidenberg, 1989).

neutral condition. Instead, I suggest that both meanings remained activated because neither was suppressed by the semantic context. More
recent pilot work suggests that the strength of the context affects the time
course of the suppression mechanism.

I also suggest that the mechanism of suppression operates to finely tune
the multiple associations of unambiguous words. That is, all concepts have
multiple associations, e.g., *apple* is associated with both *pie* and *tree*
(Marshall & Cofer, 1970). However, in some contexts the association
between *apple* and *pie* is more relevant, as in (33); in other contexts, the
association between *apple* and *tree* is more relevant, as in (34).

(33) *James baked the apples.*

(34) *James picked the apples.*

At some point during comprehension associations must be finely tuned.
Indeed, a wealth of data demonstrate that more relevant associations
provide better memory cues. For instance, *pie* would cue (33) better,
whereas *tree* would cue (34) better (see citations in Gernsbacher, 1990).

Just like the multiple meanings of ambiguous words, the multiple associations of unambiguous words are immediately activated (Gernsbacher &
Faust, 1990). However, after a brief period, only the more relevant association remains activated (see also Kintsch, 1988). Again, I suggest that less
relevant associations—like the inappropriate meanings of ambiguous
words—are suppressed. Moreover, a less efficient suppression mechanism while fine-tuning the activation of lexical concepts appears to characterize less skilled comprehenders (Gernsbacher, Varner, & Faust, 1990;
see also Merrill, Sperber, & McCauley, 1981).

B. ROLE OF SUPPRESSION AND ENHANCEMENT IN IMPROVING
    REFERENTIAL ACCESS

Another phenomenon that the mechanisms of suppression and enhancement appear to control is referential access via anaphora (Gernsbacher,
1989). All languages have devices called *anaphors* that are used to refer to
previously mentioned concepts called *antecedents*. For example, to refer
to the antecedent *John* in (35), one could use a variety of anaphors.

(35) *John went to the store.*

One could use a repeated name, such as *John*, a synonymous noun phrase,
such as *the guy*, a pronoun, such as *he*, or even a zero anaphor, as in

(36) *John went to the store and ∅ bought a quart of milk.*

In the past few years, understanding how language users negotiate anaphora has been the focus of considerable psycholinguistic research (see Gernsbacher, 1989, for a review). Why has anaphora captured so much attention? For one reason, anaphors are very common linguistic devices. Consider only pronoun anaphors; in English, they are some of the most frequently occurring lexical units. For instance, in Kucera and Francis's (1967) samples of literary text, pronouns accounted for nearly a third of the 50 most common lexical types and over 40% of their corpus of one million tokens. One would assume that pronouns occur even more frequently in informal, oral discourse.

But perhaps more important, the process of understanding anaphors presents an extremely interesting case of lexical access. Maybe more than any other lexical unit, the meaning of an anaphor greatly depends on the context in which it occurs. So how do comprehenders understand these ubiquitous but chameleon-like lexical units?

In Gernsbacher (1989), I suggested that the mechanisms of enhancement and suppression control referential access via anaphora. Recall that enhancement involves increasing or boosting activation, and suppression involves dampening activation. If anaphors enhanced or increased their antecedents' activation, that would surely improve those antecedents' accessibility. Similarly, if anaphors suppressed or dampened the activation *of other concepts*, that would surely improve those antecedents' accessibility. By suppressing the activation of other concepts, a rementioned concept would gain a privileged position in the queue of potential referents.

Six experiments demonstrated that anaphors such as pronouns and repeated proper names do improve their antecedents' accessibility by the mechanisms of suppression and enhancement (Gernsbacher, 1989). In each of these experiments, subjects read sentences that introduced two participants in their first clauses and referred to one of those two participants in their second clauses, e.g.,

(37)   *Ann predicted that Pam would lose the track race, but **she/Pam** came in first very easily.*

As in (37), the second-clause anaphor was either a pronoun, like *she*, or a proper name, like *Pam*. At different points while subjects were reading each sentence, one participant's name was presented (e.g., *Ann* or *Pam*), and the subjects' task was to verify whether that participant had occurred in the sentence they were reading. Subjects' verification latencies provided an index of how the anaphors affected both the antecedents, like *Pam*, and what I shall refer to as the nonantecedents, like *Ann*.

The first experiment measured activation immediately before and imme-

diately after the pronoun vs. name anaphors, i.e., the participants' names
were tested at the two points marked with asterisks in (38).

(38)   *Ann predicted that Pam would lose the track race, but * **she/Pam** *
       came in first very easily.*

This experiment demonstrated that proper name anaphors immediately
use both suppression and enhancement to improve their antecedents'
referential access. The data from this experiment are displayed in Fig 5.
What is displayed is the mean time it took subjects to verify that either the
antecedents (e.g., *Pam*) or the nonantecedents (e.g., *Ann*) occurred in the
experimental sentences as a function of whether the anaphors were names
vs. pronouns.

As shown in Fig. 5, when the anaphors were names, responses to the
antecedents were substantially faster after the anaphors than before. This
effect supports the hypothesis that name anaphors immediately enhance
their antecedents such that antecedents are more accessible after anaphors
than before. Also when the anaphors were names, responses to the nonantecedents were substantially *slower* after the anaphors than before. So, in
addition to enhancing the activation of their antecedents, the name
anaphors also appeared to suppress the activation of the nonantecedents.
It was as if rementioning one participant made the other participant less
accessible. However, in this first experiment, the evidence of enhancement and suppression emerged with the name anaphors only. As shown in
Fig. 5, there was no immediate change in activation as a result of subjects
having read the pronouns.

All of these results were replicated in a second experiment, with the
slight change that when activation was measured before the anaphors, it
was measured at the end of the first clause instead of after the beginning of
the second. In other words, the participants' names were tested at the two
points marked with asterisks in (39).

(39)   *Ann predicted that Pam would lose the track race, * but **she/Pam** *
       came in first very easily.*

Again, the name anaphors both immediately enhanced the activation of
their antecedents and immediately suppressed the activation of other nonantecedents. And again there was no immediate change in activation
before vs. after the pronouns. This pattern for the pronouns also replicated
a study by Tyler and Marslen-Wilson (1982). They too found that pronouns
did not immediately affect the activation of their antecedents.

However, the third experiment of Gernsbacher (1989) demonstrated
that pronouns do suppress other nonantecedents; they simply take more
time to do so. In this experiment activation was measured at two new test

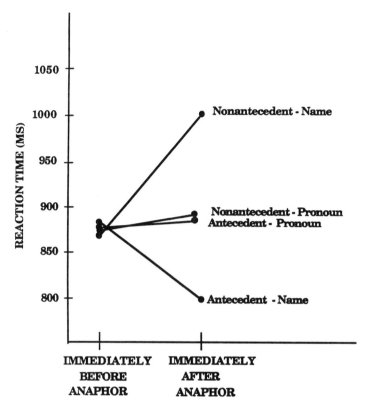

Fig. 5. Results of Gernsbacher (1989; Experiment 1). The data displayed are the subjects' mean verification latencies to antecedents vs. nonantecedents in sentences containing name vs. pronoun anaphors.

points, immediately after the pronoun or name anaphors and at the ends of the sentences, as in

(40)   *Ann predicted that Pam would lose the track race, but* **she/Pam** *∗ came in first very easily.* ∗

And indeed, by the ends of the sentences, the pronouns' nonantecedents had become considerably less activated. Thus, sometime over the course of the second clauses, the pronouns suppressed their nonantecedents. One reason that these pronouns might have taken longer to suppress their nonantecedents is that it was not until the second clause that the pronouns were semantically disambiguated; that is, prior to the second clause, the pronouns could have referred to either sentence participant. However, a fourth experiment demonstrated very similar results, even though the pronouns were disambiguated by a prior semantic context, as in

(41)   *Bill lost a tennis match to John.*

(42)   *Accepting the defeat, **he** walked quickly toward the showers.*

Or

(43)   *Enjoying the victory, **he** walked quickly toward the showers.*

A fifth experiment demonstrated that pronouns still do not employ suppression immediately even when they match the gender of only one participant, as in

(44)   *Tim predicted that Pam would lose the track race, but **she** came in
       first very easily.*

But once they do employ suppression, it is more powerful than when the
pronouns are not gender-disambiguated.

   The sixth and final experiment demonstrated that rementioned participants are not the only ones who improve their referential access by suppressing other participants; newly introduced participants do so as well.
That is, introducing a new participant, as in (45), has the same effect as
rementioning an old participant, as in (46).

(45)   *Ann predicted that Pam would lose the track race, but Sue*

(46)   *Ann predicted that Pam would lose the track race, but Pam*

Both suppress the activation of other participants. Thus, suppression
seems to be a powerful mechanism controlling referential access.

C.   ROLE OF ENHANCEMENT AND SUPPRESSION IN
        CATAPHORIC ACCESS

Just as there are anaphoric devices that enable access to previously mentioned concepts, I propose that there are also cataphoric devices that
improve access to subsequently mentioned concepts. Recently, we
(Gernsbacher & Shroyer, 1989) explored one device that might serve this
cataphoric function. The device we studied was the unstressed, indefinite
article *this*.

   Most of us are familiar with the indefinite *this*; we use it to introduce
concepts in jokes, as in "So *this* man walks into a bar" or "So a man walks
into a bar with *this* parrot on his shoulder." We also use it to introduce
concepts in narratives or conversations, as illustrated by one of Larson's
(1982) cartoon characters, a cocktail waitress recounting the events of a
bar room brawl.

(47) *So then* **this** *little sailor dude whips out a can of spinach,* **this** *crazy music starts playin', and well, just look at this place.* [emphasis mine]

Actually, only the first two occurrences of *this* in (47) are examples of the indefinite *this*; the third *this* as in "well, just look at *this* place" is an example of the stressed *this*. The indefinite *this* differs from both the stressed *this* and the deictic *this* as in "*This* is a mess" or "Look at *this*" because both the stressed and deictic *this* are definite (Perlman, 1969). According to linguists, a classic test of indefiniteness is occurrence in the existential-*there* construction. As demonstrated in (48)–(50), the indefinite article *this* and the indefinite article *a* pass this test, but the definite article *the* fails, making (50) agrammatical as indicated by the asterisk.

(48) *There was* **this** *guy in my class who*

(49) *There was* **a** *guy in my class who*

(50) **There was* **the** *guy in my class who*

The indefinite *this* is interesting for a couple of reasons. First, it is a relative newcomer to English; Wald (1983) suggests that its use dates back only to the late 1930s. Second, the indefinite *this* occurs considerably more often in informal, spoken dialects than formal or written ones—although some prescriptive grammarians dictate that it is unacceptable in any dialect.

Because it is an indefinite article, the indefinite *this*—like the indefinite *a* or *an*—is used to introduce new concepts into a discourse. In fact, of the 243 occurrences of the indefinite *this* that Prince (1981) observed in Terkel's (1974) book *Working*, 242 introduced a distinctly new concept; the only exception was arguably introducing the same lexical form but with a different referent. But more interestingly, in 209 of those 242 occurrences, the noun introduced with the indefinite *this* was referred to again and, as Prince said, "within the next few clauses."

This observation was quantified more explicitly by Wright and Givón (1987). They recorded 8- and 10-year olds telling one another jokes and informal stories. When the children introduced nouns with the indefinite *this*, they referred to those nouns an average of 5.32 times in the subsequent 10 clauses that they produced; in contrast, when they introduced nouns with the indefinite *a*, they referred to those nouns an average of only 0.68 times in their next 10 clauses. These data suggest that speakers use the indefinite *this* to introduce concepts that are going to play a pivotal role in the subsequent narrative. Thus, the indefinite *this* is a likely candidate for what I call a cataphoric device.

In Gernsbacher and Shroyer (1989), we asked the following question: Does introducing a concept with the indefinite *this*, as opposed to the more typical *a*, make that concept more accessible? To answer this question, we auditorily presented 20 informal narratives to subjects, telling them that at some point in each narrative the narrator would stop talking; when that happened, it was their job to continue telling the narrative. We constructed our narratives so that the last clause introduced a new noun. We manipulated whether this critical noun was marked by the indefinite *this* or the more typical indefinite *a*, e.g.,

(51)   *I went to the coast last weekend with Sally. We'd checked the tide schedule 'n we'd planned to arrive at low-tide—cus I just love beachcombin'. Right off, I found three whole sanddollars. So then I started lookin' for agates, but I couldn't find any. Sally was pretty busy too. She found **this**/**an** egg*

From the transcriptions of our 45 subjects' continuations, we measured three manifestations of accessibility: frequency of mention, immediacy of mention, and anaphoric explicitness. We found reliable effects of all three measures: When the nouns were marked by *this*, subjects mentioned the nouns more frequently, often within the first clauses that they produced, and typically via less explicit anaphors such as pronouns. In contrast, when the nouns were marked by *a*, subjects mentioned the nouns less frequently, and typically via more explicit anaphors such as full noun phrases.

These results suggest that concepts initially marked with the indefinite *this* are subsequently more accessible. Therefore, the indefinite *this* operates as a cataphoric device. Indeed, Prince (1981) has suggested that the indefinite *this* parallels a device in American Sign Language in which a signer establishes an absent third person on his or her right so that the signer might later refer to that individual; an absent person who is not intended to be later referred to is not established this way. Clearly, this American Sign Language device is also operating cataphorically.

How do cataphoric devices improve the accessibility of their concepts? In Gernsbacher and Jescheniak (1990), we demonstrated that cataphoric devices—like anaphoric devices—improve referential access via the mechanisms of suppression and enhancement. Cataphoric devices improve their concepts' accessibility by suppressing the activation of other concepts and by making their concepts more resistant to suppression by other concepts.

D. ROLE OF SUPPRESSION AND ENHANCEMENT IN THE LOSS
    OF ACCESS TO SURFACE INFORMATION

The mechanisms of suppression and enhancement might also explain why "surface" information, as opposed to thematic information, becomes less accessible more rapidly during comprehension (Sachs, 1967, 1974). To understand how these mechanisms can account for this, one must consider what surface information is. Typically, surface information is defined as information about a stimulus that does not contribute to its meaning, e.g., the syntactic form of a sentence. But another definition is that the surface properties of any stimulus are those that change the most rapidly. For example, consider a passage of text. If the passage is well composed, then each sentence conveys the same thematic idea. But each sentence does not present the same syntactic form. Because the passage's syntactic form changes more rapidly than its thematic contact, its syntactic form is considered surface information while its thematic content is not.

Based on this definition, the mechanisms of suppression and enhancement explain why surface information becomes less accessible more rapidly than thematic information. Because surface information is constantly changing, the newer surface information is constantly suppressing the old. In contrast, because thematic information is constantly being reintroduced, it is repeatedly enhanced. The net result is that thematic information is more activated than surface information; therefore, thematic information is more accessible.

This definition, accompanied by the mechanisms of suppression and enhancement, can also explain why surface information is less accessible after comprehension of thematically organized than seemingly unrelated materials (A. Anderson et al., 1983; de Villiers, 1974; Peterson & McIntyre, 1973). With unrelated sentences, surface information is no longer more rapidly changing than thematic information; therefore, it would be less likely to be suppressed or more likely to be enhanced.

For instance, in J. R. Anderson and Bower's (1973) experiment, they presented sentences either grouped together as a related story or randomly arranged as an unrelated list. In both conditions, half the sentences were presented in the active voice and half in the passive voice. Because the sentences in the unrelated condition had no thematic continuity, their greatest common denominator was their syntactic form. On the other hand, the greatest common denominator of the sentences in the related condition was their thematic content.

This definition of surface information and the mechanisms of suppression and enhancement can also explain another pattern of results: Surface information (tested by synonym substitution) is more accessible after comprehending abstract than concrete sentences. In contrast, thematic information (tested by subject–object reversal) is more accessible after comprehension of concrete than abstract sentences (Begg & Paivo, 1969; Johnson, Bransford, Nyberg, & Cleary, 1972; Moeser, 1974; Pezdek & Royer, 1974). However, in studies demonstrating this pattern, the abstract sentences differed fundamentally from the concrete sentences; the abstract sentences were less "comprehensible" according to several criteria (Holmes & Langford, 1976; Holyoak, 1974; Klee & Eysenck, 1973; Moeser, 1974; Schwanenflugel & Shoben, 1983).

In other words, the abstract sentences had less thematic content than the concrete ones. So comprehending the words of abstract sentences might have been like comprehending the sentences of unrelated groups (not thematically cohesive). On the other hand, comprehending the words of concrete sentences might have been like comprehending the sentences of related groups (thematically cohesive). Thus, performance with the abstract sentences could have resulted from less enhancement of their thematic information or less suppression of their surface information. On the other hand, performance with the concrete sentences could have resulted from greater enhancement of their thematic information or greater suppression of their surface information. Evidence already exists to support this explanation: When the abstract sentences were each embedded in their own contextual paragraph, i.e., a thematic idea was supplied, the pattern disappeared (Pezdek & Royer, 1974). With the added thematic continuity, comprehending abstract sentences mimicked comprehending concrete ones.

In sum, the mechanisms of suppression and enhancement during structure building appear to play a fundamental role in many comprehension phenomena: the fine tuning of lexical concepts, the accessibility of concepts via anaphoric and cataphoric reference, and rapid inaccessibility of surface as opposed to thematic information.

V.   Individual Differences in General Comprehension Skill

According to the structure building framework, many of the processes and mechanisms involved in language comprehension are general cognitive processes and mechanisms. This orientation suggests that some of the reasons that individuals differ in comprehension skill might not be specific to language. In this last section, I describe how the structure building framework has provided a guide for understanding which cognitive processes and mechanisms underlie differential comprehension skill.

Experience informs us that individuals differ in comprehension skill. Laboratory research documents this as well (see reviews by Carr, 1981; Gibson & Levin, 1975; Perfetti, 1985; Smith & Spoehr, 1974). Unfortunately, the focus of much of this research has been on comprehension of one modality (i.e., the printed word) and on individuals who differ at one stage of skill development, i.e., beginning readers. So it's not too surprising that the processes and mechanisms previously suggested to underlie differences in comprehension skill are processes and mechanisms specific to reading. But when studying adult comprehension skill, one can go beyond those sources.

This is because at an adult level of proficiency, skill at comprehending written language is highly correlated with skill at comprehending spoken language (Daneman & Carpenter, 1980; Jackson & McClelland, 1979; Palmer, MacLeod, Hunt & Davidson, 1985; Perfetti & Lesgold, 1977; Sticht, 1972). Furthermore, the high correlations between comprehending written and spoken language and the strong parallels between comprehending language and nonlinguistic media (Baggett, 1975, 1979; Gernsbacher, 1983, 1985; Jenkins, Wald, & Pittenger, 1978) suggest the hypothesis that differences in adult comprehension skill might not depend completely on facility with language.

In Gernsbacher et al. (1990), we tested this hypothesis by creating a "multimedia" comprehension battery (Gernsbacher & Varner, 1988). The battery comprises six stimulus stories: two are presented via written sentences, two via auditory sentences, and two via pictures. The battery was administered to 270 college-aged subjects; the correlation between reading and listening was .92, between reading and picture viewing .82, and between listening and picture viewing .72. In addition, a factor analysis revealed only one possible factor, most likely a "general" comprehension skill. To explain differences in this general comprehension skill, one must look for general cognitive processes.

A starting point for investigation comes from a finding observed by Perfetti and Goldman (1976) and Perfetti and Lesgold (1977). They pinpointed a characteristic of less skilled comprehenders that appears during both reading and listening: Less skilled comprehenders have worse access to recently comprehended information. That is, although all comprehenders have difficulty remembering the wording of a recently comprehended sentence, less skilled comprehenders have even more difficulty. Because I previously demonstrated that this phenomenon was not unique to language comprehension, I hypothesized that poorer access to recently comprehended information might be a good "marker" of less skilled comprehenders regardless of the modality they were comprehending.

We tested this hypothesis by selecting a set of less and a set of more

skilled comprehenders from the extreme thirds of the distribution of subjects who had been tested on the multimedia battery (Gernsbacher et al.,
1990, Experiment 2). These subjects comprehended six new stimulus
stories: two in each of the three modalities. At two points during each
story, the comprehenders' access to recently comprehended information
was tested. The two points were after the subjects had comprehended half
of a story and after they had comprehended an entire story.

The results of this experiment, expressed in average percent correct, are
displayed in Fig. 6. The more skilled comprehenders are indicated by the
hashed lines and the less skilled by the unfilled bars. As illustrated in the
figure, the less skilled comprehenders did indeed have poorer access to
recently comprehended information. And this was the case in all three
modalities. Thus, less skilled comprehenders' poorer access to recently
comprehended information is not limited to language-based comprehension.

On the face of it, these findings might suggest that less skilled comprehenders are plagued by smaller memory capacities. But within the
normal range of comprehension skill, which is the range of interest to us

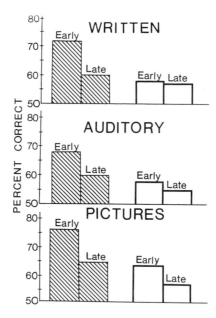

Fig. 6.   Results of Gernsbacher, Varner, and Faust (1990; Experiment 2). The data
displayed are averages of subjects' percentage correct recognition of a recently comprehended sentence or picture. The more skilled comprehenders are indicated by the hashed
bars and the less skilled comprehenders by the unfilled bars.

here, less skilled comprehenders cannot be distinguished from more skilled comprehenders by traditional immediate or short-term memory measures (see citations in Gernsbacher, 1990).

In the spirit of Perfetti and his colleagues, I suggest that poorer access to recently comprehended information is not the *cause* of poorer comprehension skill; it is only a symptom. To understand the underlying cause or causes, one must understand why any comprehender loses access to recently comprehended information. According to the structure building framework, this results from shifting from actively building one structure or substructure to initiating another. Because information represented in one substructure is most available during the active processing of that substructure, once the comprehender has shifted to a new substructure, the information represented in the previous substructure becomes less available.

But meshing this explanation with the trademark of less skilled comprehenders—namely, poorer access to recently comprehended information—yields the rather unusual hypothesis that less skilled comprehenders suffer from shifting too often. That is, instead of continuing to map incoming information onto the structure that they are developing, less skilled comprehenders have a tendency to shift and initiate a new substructure.

We tested this hypothesis by selecting two more sets of more and less skilled comprehenders from the subjects tested with the comprehension battery (Gernsbacher et al., 1990, Experiment 3). These subjects also comprehended six new stimulus stories, two in each modality. And information accessibility was again tested at two test points: after half a story, and after an entire story. However, unlike our second experiment, our third experiment included a manipulation that was specifically designed to induce shifting. The manipulation was scrambling the sentences or pictures within a story. That is, of the six stories that the subjects comprehended, half were presented scrambled and half were presented in normal order, one in each modality.

By presenting half of the stories scrambled and half in their normal order, we could compare a situation in which we know that all comprehenders have to shift more frequently (during the scrambled stories) with a situation in which we hypothesize that less skilled comprehenders might also be shifting too frequently (during the normal stories).

The results of this experiment, again expressed in average percent correct, are shown in Fig. 7. Again, the more skilled comprehenders are indicated by hashed lines and the less skilled by unfilled bars. As illustrated in the top panel, this third experiment replicated the second experiment by demonstrating that less skilled comprehenders have poorer access to re-

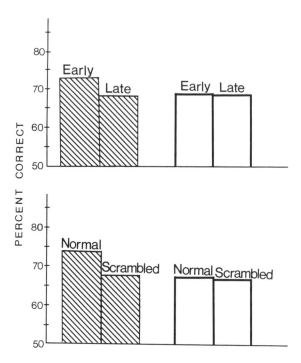

Fig. 7. Results of Gernsbacher, Varner, and Faust (1990; Experiment 3). The data displayed are subjects' average latencies to reject an inappropriate meaning of an ambiguous hended sentence or picture (all three modalities averaged). Top panel displays the difference between the two test points; bottom panel displays the effect of the scrambling manipulation. The more skilled comprehenders are indicated by the hashed bars and the less skilled comprehenders by the unfilled bars.

cently comprehended information. Again this difference was observed for all three modalities.

The novel finding of this experiment is illustrated in the bottom panel. For the more skilled comprehenders, scrambling the stories significantly reduced their access to recently comprehended information. However, for the less skilled comprehenders, there was virtually no difference between the normal vs. scrambled stories. One interpretation of these data is that for less skilled comprehenders, comprehending normal stories is like comprehending scrambled ones, i.e., it involves almost as many processing shifts. Thus, these data support the hypothesis that less skilled comprehenders shift too often during ordinary comprehension.

Why might less skilled comprehenders shift too often? Consider the consequences of a less efficient suppression mechanism. Information that is less relevant or even inappropriate to the structure being developed would remain activated. Because this irrelevant information could not be mapped onto the developing structure, its activation might lay the foundation for a new substructure. Thus, one consequence of an inefficient suppression mechanism would be the development of too many substructures—in other words, a greater tendency toward shifting.

In our fourth experiment, we tested the hypothesis that less skilled comprehenders are less able to selectively suppress irrelevant information. We did this with a task that measures how well comprehenders can suppress irrelevant information. We called this task *context verification* and the procedure was as follows: Subjects read a sentence and were then presented with a probe word. Their task was to verify whether the probe word matched the context of the sentence just read. In half the trials, the probe word did indeed match the context, but we were more interested in trials in which the probe word did not match the context.

In half of those trials, the last word of the sentence was an ambiguous word, e.g.,

(52)   *The man dug with the* **spade**.

The probe word was the meaning of the ambiguous word that was inappropriate to the context, e.g., ACE. We compared how rapidly subjects verified that a word like ACE was not related to the sentence with how rapidly they verified that ACE was not related to the same sentence but with the last word replaced by an unambiguous word, e.g.,

(53)   *The man dug with the* **shovel**.

This comparison gave us a measure of how activated the inappropriate meaning of the ambiguous word was. The slower subjects were to reject ACE after the "spade" sentence, the more activated the inappropriate meaning must have been (i.e., the less they were able to suppress the inappropriate meaning). We referred to this measure as the amount of interference the comprehenders experienced.

We measured interference at two test points: immediately after subjects finished reading each sentence and three-fourths of a second later. We predicted that at the immediate test point both the less and more skilled comprehenders would show interference. This prediction was based on the vast literature demonstrating that immediately after an ambiguous word is read, multiple meanings are activated regardless of context. Our novel predictions concerned what would happen at the delayed test point. If the decreased activation of the inappropriate meanings is due to suppression, and if this suppression mechanism is less efficient in less skilled comprehenders, then the less skilled comprehenders should still be experiencing a reliable amount of interference. And, indeed, that is what we found.

The results of this experiment, expressed in msec of interference, are shown in Fig. 8. Immediately after the more skilled comprehenders read the ambiguous word, they experienced a significant amount of interference, suggesting that the inappropriate meaning was highly activated. However, three-fourths of a second later, they were no longer experiencing a reliable amount of interference, suggesting that the inappropriate meaning had become considerably less activated—perhaps via the mechanism of suppression.

In contrast, for our less skilled comprehenders, even as late as three-fourths of a second after they read the ambiguous word, the inappropriate meaning was still strongly activated. That is, the less skilled comprehenders were still experiencing a significant amount of interference; in fact, they were experiencing the same level of interference as they had experienced immediately after the ambiguous word. This finding suggests that less skilled comprehenders are plagued with a less rapid (and therefore less efficient) suppression mechanism. This, in turn, could lead to their greater tendency toward shifting and their poorer access to recently comprehended information.

VI. Summary and Conclusions

In this chapter, I have identified and described three general cognitive processes involved in language comprehension, i.e., laying a foundation for a mental structure, mapping coherent or relevant information onto that

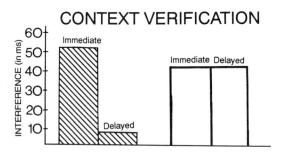

Fig. 8. Results of Gernsbacher, Varner, and Faust (1990; Experiment 4). The data displayed are subjects' average latencies to reject an inappropriate meaning of an ambiguous word minus their average latencies to reject the same words preceded by an unambiguous word (see text for a fuller description). The more skilled comprehenders are indicated by the hashed bars and the less skilled comprehenders by the unfilled bars.

structure, and shifting to develop a new structure when the incoming information is less coherent or relevant. I also suggested that two general cognitive mechanisms underlie the processes of structure building. They are suppression and enhancement.

These general cognitive processes and mechanisms account for many linguistic and nonlinguistic comprehension phenomena. For example, the process of laying a foundation accounts for the advantage of first mention: After comprehending a sentence involving two participants, it is easier to access the first-mentioned participant than the second-mentioned participant. This advantage is not due to linguistic or structural factors such as the first-mentioned participant's greater tendency to be semantic agents or syntactic subjects. Rather I suggest that the advantage arises because comprehension involves laying a foundation. And for this reason, first-mentioned participants are more accessible both because they form the foundations for their sentence level representations and because it is through them that subsequent information is mapped onto the developing representation.

The process of laying a foundation also accounts for the change in accessibility of concepts from multiclause sentences. When comprehenders are still developing their representations of a final clause, concepts in that final clause are more accessible than concepts from an initial clause. After comprehenders have built their representations of both clauses, but before they begin mapping those representations together, concepts from both clauses are equally accessible. A little bit later, concepts from the first clause become more accessible. I suggest that at that point, comprehenders have finished mapping the second clause onto the first, and the first clause serves as the foundation for the whole sentence level representation. The greater accessibility of concepts from the first clause strengthens over time, demonstrating that order of mention is a relatively long-lived characteristic of the mental representation of a sentence.

The process of laying a foundation also accomplishes what linguists suggest are the functional roles of order of mention. According to some linguists, initial mention codes importance and functions to attract attention; according to others, first mention codes givenness and functions to create a context for subsequent comprehension. If first mention is selected in order to signal importance, then the function is accomplished because— by virtue of being first mentioned—initial information gets represented at the core or foundation of the structure. This causes the information to be more accessible, which is most likely the goal of marking information as important. If first mention is selected in order to signal givenness, then the function is also accomplished because—by virtue of being first mentioned—initial information organizes the representation of subsequent information. That is, subsequent information gets mapped onto the developing structure vis-à-vis the initial information.

Other processes involved in structure building account for other comprehension phenomena. For example, the process of shifting accounts for why comprehenders rapidly lose access to recently comprehended information. According to this explanation, information becomes less accessible because comprehenders shift from developing one substructure in order to develop another. Presumably, information represented in one substructure is most available during the active development of that substructure. Once a comprehender has shifted to initiate a new substructure, information represented in the previous substructure becomes less available. In Gernsbacher (1985), I demonstrated that comprehenders' rapid loss of access to recently comprehended information was not specific to language-based comprehension, and I tested the shifting explanation against a recoding explanation (information becomes less accessible because it is recoded into gist). The explanation based on the cognitive process of shifting clearly accounted for the phenomenon during both language and nonlanguage comprehension.

The process of shifting also predicts comprehenders' responses to speakers' and writers' cues for a new phrase, clause, topic, setting, or point of view. Comprehenders slow their comprehension when they encounter these cues. This suggests that these cues trigger comprehenders to begin laying a foundation for a new substructure. Comprehenders also have more difficulty accessing information presented before these cues than information presented after. This suggests that the information presented after these cues is represented in a different mental substructure than that of information presented before.

The mechanisms of suppression and enhancement also account for many comprehension phenomena. For example, suppression helps fine-tune the meanings of ambiguous words and the associations of unambiguous words by suppressing the activation of ambiguous words' inappropriate meanings and unambiguous words' less relevant associations.

Both suppression and enhancement play a role in referential access via anaphora, in other words, the act of referring to previously mentioned concepts (antecedents) via anaphors such as pronouns and repeated names. Some anaphors, such as repeated names, improve their antecedents' accessibility by enhancing or increasing those antecedents' activation. Other anaphors, such as pronouns as well as repeated names, improve their antecedents' accessibility by suppressing or dampening the activation of other concepts.

Suppression and enhancement also control referential access via cataphoric devices. That is, just as there are anaphoric devices that enable access to previously mentioned concepts, cataphoric devices improve access to subsequently mentioned concepts. The unstressed indefinite *this* appears to operate in such a way. Cataphoric devices improve their concepts' accessibility by enhancing the activation of those concepts, by suppressing the activation of other concepts, and by making their concepts more resistant to suppression.

Suppression and enhancement also explain why surface information often becomes less accessible more rapidly than thematic information. In a cohesive passage, the surface information is the most rapidly changing characteristic, whereas the thematic information is constantly being conveyed. Because surface information is constantly changing, the newer surface information is constantly suppressing the old. In contrast, because thematic information is constantly being reintroduced, it gets repeatedly enhanced. The net result is that thematic information is more activated than surface information and thus more accessible.

Finally, the structure building framework provides a blueprint for investigating individual differences in "general" comprehension skill. For example, beginning with the finding that less skilled comprehenders have poorer access to recently comprehended information, we have found that this phenomenon occurs during the comprehension of nonlinguistic stories as well. We have also traced it to less skilled comprehenders' tendency to shift too often. And we have suggested that this tendency results from a less efficient suppression mechanism.

Thus, the structure building framework and its component processes and mechanisms account for many comprehension phenomena. This framework should also be useful for understanding the comprehension of other media, e.g., music (Lerdahl & Jackendoff, 1983; Sloboda, 1985). This is because in many domains the goal of comprehension is to build a coherent representation of the entire stimulus.

ACKNOWLEDGMENTS

This research was supported by National Science Foundation Grant BNS 85-10096, NIH Research Career Development Award KO4 NS-01376, and Air Force Office of Sponsored Research Grants 89-0258 and 89-0305.

REFERENCES

Aaronson, D., & Ferres, S. (1983). Lexical categories and reading tasks. *Journal of Experimental Psychology: Human Perception and Performance, 9,* 675–699.
Aaronson, D., & Scarborough, H. S. (1976). Performance theories for sentence coding: Some

quantitative evidence. *Journal of Experimental Psychology: Human Perception and Performance, 2*, 56–70.

Anderson, A., Garrod, S. C., & Sanford, A. J. (1983). The accessibility of pronominal antecedents as a function of episode shifts in narrative text. *Quarterly Journal of Experimental Psychology, 35A*, 427–440.

Anderson, J. R. (1983). *The architecture of cognition*. Cambridge, MA: Harvard University Press.

Anderson, J. R., & Bower, G. H. (1973). *Human associative memory*. Washington, DC: Winston.

Baggett, P. (1975). Memory for explicit and implicit information in picture stories. *Journal of Verbal Learning and Verbal Behavior, 14*, 538–548.

Baggett, P. (1979). Structurally equivalent stories in movie and text and the effect of the medium on recall. *Journal of Verbal Learning and Verbal Behavior, 18*, 333–356.

Bates, E. (1979). *The emergence of symbols*. New York: Academic Press.

Beeman, M., & Gernsbacher, M. A. (1991). *Structure building and coherence inferencing during comprehension*. Manuscript submitted for publication.

Begg, I., & Paivio, A. (1969). Concreteness and imagery in sentence meaning. *Journal of Verbal Learning and Verbal Behavior, 8*, 821–827.

Bernstein, L. (1976). *The unanswered question. Six talks at Harvard*. Cambridge, MA: Harvard University Press.

Bever, T. G. (1970). The cognitive basis for linguistic structures. In J. R. Hayes (Ed.), *Cognition and the development of language* (pp. 279–362). New York: Wiley.

Black, J. B., Turner, T. J., & Bower, G. H. (1979). Point of view in narrative comprehension, memory, and production. *Journal of Verbal Learning and Verbal Behavior, 18*, 187–198.

Bock, J. K. (1982). Toward a cognitive psychology of syntax: Information processing contributions to sentence formulation. *Psychological Review, 89*, 1–47.

Bock, J. K., & Irwin, D. E. (1980). Syntactic effects of information availability in sentence production. *Journal of Verbal Learning and Verbal Behavior, 19*, 467–484.

Bransford, J. D., & Franks, J. J. (1971). The abstraction of linguistic ideas. *Cognitive Psychology, 2*, 331–350.

Bransford, J. D., & Franks, J. J. (1972). The abstraction of linguistic ideas: A review. *Cognition, 1*, 211–249.

Bresnan, J., & Kaplan, R. M. (1982). Grammars as mental representations of language. In J. Bresnam (Ed.), *The mental representation of grammatical relations* (pp. xvii–lii). Cambridge, MA: MIT Press.

Burgess, C., & Simpson, G. B. (1988). Cerebral hemispheric mechanisms in the retrieval of ambiguous word meanings. *Brain and Language, 33*, 86–103.

Burgess, C., Tanenhaus, M. K., & Seidenberg, M. S. (1989). Context and lexical access: Implications of nonword interference for lexical ambiguity resolution. *Journal of Experimental Psychology: Learning, Memory, and Cognition, 15*, 620–632.

Caplan, D. (1972). Clause boundaries and recognition latencies for words in sentences. *Perception & Psychophysics, 12*, 73–76.

Carpenter, P. A., & Just, M. A. (1977). Integrative process in comprehension. In D. LaBerge & S. J. Samuels (Eds.), *Basic processes in reading: Perception and comprehension* (pp. 217–241). Hillsdale, NJ: Erlbaum.

Carr, T. H. (1981). Building theories of reading ability. *Cognition, 9*, 73–114.

Carroll, J. M. (1980). *Toward a structural psychology of cinema*. New York: Mouton.

Chafe, W. L. (1976). Givenness, contrastiveness, definiteness, subjects, topics, and points of view. In C. N. Li (Ed.), *Subject and topic* (pp. 25–56). New York: Academic Press.

Chang, F. R. (1980). Active memory processes in visual sentence comprehension: Clause effects and pronominal reference. *Memory & Cognition, 8,* 58–64.

Charniak, E. (1983). Passing markers: A theory of contextual influence in language comprehension. *Cognitive Science, 7,* 171–190.

Clark, H. H., & Clark, E. V. (1977). *Psychology and language: An introduction to psycholinguistics.* New York: Harcourt Brace Jovanovich.

Clements, P. (1979). The effects of staging on recall from prose. In R. O. Freedle (Ed.), *New directions in discourse processing* (pp. 287–330). Norwood, NJ: Ablex.

Corbett, A. T., & Chang, F. R. (1983). Pronoun disambiguation: Accessing potential antecedents. *Memory & Cognition, 11,* 283–294.

Daneman, M., & Carpenter, P. A. (1980). Individual differences in working memory and reading. *Journal of Verbal Learning and Verbal Behavior, 19,* 450–466.

de Villiers, P. A. (1974). Imagery and theme in recall of connected discourse. *Journal of Experimental Psychology, 103,* 263–268.

Diehl, R. L. (1981). Feature detectors for speech: A critical reappraisal. *Psychological Bulletin, 89,* 1–18.

Firbas, J. (1974). Some aspects of the Czechoslovakian approach to problems of functional sentence perspective. In F. Danes (Ed.), *Papers on functional sentence perspective* (pp. 11–37). The Hague: Mouton.

Fodor, J. A., Bever, T. G., & Garrett, M. F. (1974). *The psychology of language: An introduction to psycholinguistics and generative grammar.* New York: McGraw-Hill.

Foss, D. J., & Lynch, R. H., Jr. (1969). Decision processes during sentence comprehension: Effects of surface structure on decision times. *Perception & Psychophysics, 5,* 145–148.

Frazier, L., & Fodor, J. D. (1978). The sausage machine: A new two-stage parsing model. *Cognition, 6,* 291–325.

Garnham, A. (1983). Why psycholinguists don't care about DTC: A reply to Berwick and Weinberg. *Cognition, 15,* 263–269.

Gernsbacher, M. A. (1983). *Memory for the orientation of pictures in nonverbal stories: Parallels and insights into language processing.* Unpublished doctoral dissertation, University of Texas at Austin.

Gernsbacher, M. A. (1984). Cognitive responses to (linguistic) topic changes. *In Proceedings of the Sixth Annual Conference of the Cognitive Science Society* (pp. 82–88). Hillsdale, NJ: Erlbaum.

Gernsbacher, M. A. (1985). Surface information loss in comprehension. *Cognitive Psychology, 17,* 324–363.

Gernsbacher, M. A. (1989). Mechanisms that improve referential access. *Cognition, 32,* 99–156.

Gernsbacher, M. A. (1990). *Language comprehension as structure building.* Hillsdale, NJ: Erlbaum.

Gernsbacher, M. A., & Faust, M. (1990). The role of suppression in sentence comprehension. In G. B. Simpson (Ed.), *Understanding word and sentence* (pp. 97–128). Amsterdam: North-Holland.

Gernsbacher, M. A., & Hargreaves, D. (1988). Accessing sentence participants: The advantage of first mention. *Journal of Memory and Language, 27,* 699–717.

Gernsbacher, M. A., & Hargreaves, D. (in press). The advantage of first mention: Experimental data and cognitive explanations. *Typological studies in language.*

Gernsbacher, M. A., Hargreaves, D., & Beeman, M. (1989). Building and accessing clausal representations: The advantage of first mention versus the advantage of clause recency. *Journal of Memory and Language, 28,* 735–755.

Gernsbacher, M. A., & Jescheniak, J. D. (in press). *Cataphoric devices in spoken discourse. Cognitive Psychology.*

Gernsbacher, M. A., & Shroyer, S. (1989). The cataphoric use of the indefinite *this* in spoken narratives. *Memory & Cognition, 17,* 536–540.

Gernsbacher, M. A., & Varner, K. R. (1988). *The multi-media comprehension battery* (Tech. Rep. No. 88-03). Eugene: University of Oregon, Institute of Cognitive and Decision Sciences.

Gernsbacher, M. A., Varner, K. R., & Faust, M. (1990). Investigating differences in general comprehension skill. *Journal of Experimental Psychology: Learning, Memory, and Cognition, 16,* 430–445.

Gibson, E. J., & Levin, H. (1975). *The psychology of reading.* Cambridge, MA: MIT Press.

Givón, T. (1979). *On understanding grammar.* New York: Academic Press.

Givón, T. (1986). *The pragmatics of word order: Predictability, importance, and attention.* Amsterdam: Benjamins.

Glucksberg, S., Kreuz, R. J., & Rho, S. H. (1986). Context can constrain lexical access: Implications for models of language comprehension. *Journal of Experimental Psychology: Learning, Memory, and Cognition, 12,* 323–335.

Gough, P. B., & Diehl, R. L. (1978). Experimental psycholinguistics. In W. O. Dingwall (Ed.), *A survey of linguistic science* (pp. 247–266). Stamford, CT: Greylock Publishers.

Graesser, A. C., Hoffman, N. L., & Clark, L. F. (1980). Structural components of reading time. *Journal of Verbal Learning and Verbal Behavior, 19,* 135–151.

Greenberg, J. H. (1963). *Some universals of grammar with particular reference to the order of meaningful elements.* Cambridge, MA: MIT Press.

Greeno, J. G., & Noreen, D. L. (1974). Time to read semantically related sentences. *Memory & Cognition, 2,* 117–120.

Haberlandt, K. (1980). Story grammar and reading time of story constituent. *Poetics, 9,* 99–118.

Haberlandt, K. (1984). Components of sentence and word reading times. In D. E. Kieras & M. A. Just (Eds.), *New methods in reading comprehension research* (pp. 219–252). Hillsdale, NJ: Erlbaum.

Haberlandt, K., Berian, C., & Sandson, J. (1980). The episode schema in story processing. *Journal of Verbal Learning and Verbal Behavior, 19,* 635–650.

Haberlandt, K. F., & Graesser, A. C. (1985). Component processes in text comprehension and some of their interactions. *Journal of Experimental Psychology: General, 114,* 357–374.

Hakes, D. T., & Foss, D. J. (1970). Decision processes during sentence comprehension: Effects of surface structure reconsidered. *Perception & Psychophysics, 8,* 413–416.

Halliday, M. A. K. (1967). Notes on transitivity and theme in English: II. *Journal of Linguistics, 3,*199–244.

Haviland, S. E., & Clark, H. H. (1974). What's new? Acquiring new information as a process in comprehension. *Journal of Verbal Learning and Verbal Behavior, 13,* 512–521.

Hayes-Roth, B., & Thorndyke, P. W. (1979). Integration of knowledge from text. *Journal of Verbal Learning and Verbal Behavior, 18,* 91–108.

Holmes, V. M., & Langford, J. (1976). Comprehension and recall of abstract and concrete sentences. *Journal of Verbal Learning and Verbal Behavior, 15,* 559–566.

Holyoak, K. J. (1974). The role of imagery in the evaluation of sentences: Imagery or semantic factors? *Journal of Verbal Learning and Verbal Behavior, 13,* 163–166.

Hudson, S. B., & Tanenhaus, M. K. (1984). Ambiguity resolution in the absence of contextual bias. *In Proceedings of the Sixth Annual Conference of the Cognitive Science Society* (pp. 188–192). Hillsdale, NJ: Erlbaum.

Jackson, M. D., & McClelland, J. L. (1979). Processing determinants of reading speed. *Journal of Experimental Psychology: General, 108,* 151–181.

Jarvella, R. J. (1979). Immediate memory and discourse processing. In G. H. Bower (Ed.), *The psychology of learning and motivation* (Vol. 13, pp. 379–421). New York: Academic Press.

Jenkins, J. J., Wald, J., & Pittenger, J. B. (1978). Apprehending pictorial events: An instance of psychological cohesion. In C. W. Savage (Ed.), *Minnesota studies in the philosophy of science: Vol. IX. Perception and cognition issues in the foundations of psychology* (pp. 129–163) Minneapolis: University of Minnesota Press.

Johnson, M. K., Bransford, J. D., Nyberg, S. E., & Cleary, J. J. (1972). Comprehension factors in interpreting memory for abstract and concrete sentences. *Journal of Verbal Learning and Verbal Behavior, 11,* 451–454.

Johnson-Laird, P. N. (1983). *Mental models.* Cambridge, MA: Harvard University Press.

Kaplan, R. (1975). On process models for sentence analysis. In D. Norman & D. Rumelhart (Eds.), *Explorations in cognition* (pp. 117–135). San Francisco, CA: Freeman.

Kieras, D. E. (1978). Good and bad structure in simple paragraphs: Effects on apparent theme, reading time, and recall. *Journal of Verbal Learning and Verbal Behavior, 17,* 13–28.

Kieras, D. E. (1980). Initial mention as a signal to thematic content in technical passages. *Memory & Cognition, 8,* 345–353.

Kieras, D. E. (1981). Component processes in the comprehension of simple prose. *Journal of Verbal Learning and Verbal Behavior, 20,* 1–23.

Kimball, J. P. (1973). Seven principles of surface structure parsing in natural language. *Cognition, 2,* 15–47.

Kintsch, W. (1988). The role of knowledge in discourse comprehension. A construction-integration model. *Psychological Review, 95,* 163–182.

Kintsch, W., Kozminsky, E., Streby, W. J., McKoon, G., & Keenan, J. M. (1975). Comprehension and recall of text as a function of content variables. *Journal of Verbal Learning and Verbal Behavior, 14,* 196–214.

Klee, H., & Eysenck, M. W. (1973). Comprehension of abstract and concrete sentences. *Journal of Verbal Learning and Verbal Behavior, 12,* 522–529.

Kornfeld, J. R. (1973). Syntactic structures and the perception of sentences: Some evidence for dominance effects. In C. Clorum, P. F. Smith, & A. Weiser (Eds.), *You take the high node and I'll take the low node: Papers from the parasession on subordination* (pp. 372–386). Chicago, IL: Chicago Linguistics Society.

Kucera, H., & Francis, W. N. (1967). *A computational analysis of present day American English.* Providence, RI: Brown University Press.

Larson, G. (1982). *The far side.* New York: Andrews, McMeel, & Parker.

Lerdahl, F., & Jackendoff, R. S. (1983). *A generative theory of tonal music.* Cambridge, MA: MIT Press.

Levelt, W. J. M. (1981). The speaker's linearization problem. *Philosophical Transactions of the Royal Society of London, Series B, 295,* 305–315.

Lieberman, P. (1984). *The biology and evolution of language.* Cambridge, MA: Harvard University Press.

Luftig, R. C. (1981, August). *Normalization in paraphrase and recall.* Paper presented at the annual meeting of the American Psychological Association, Los Angeles, CA.

Mandler, J. M., & Goodman, M. S. (1982). On the psychological validity of story structure. *Journal of Verbal Learning and Verbal Behavior, 21,* 507–523.

Marshall, G., & Cofer, C. N. (1970). Single-word free-association norms for 328 responses from the Connecticut cultural norms for verbal items in categories. In L. Postman &

G. Keppel (Eds.), *Norms of word association* (pp. 321–361). New York: Academic Press.

McClelland, J. L., & Kawamoto, A. H. (1986). Mechanisms of sentence processing: Assigning roles to constituents of sentences. In J. L. McClelland & D. E. Rumelhart (Eds.), *Parallel distributed processing: Explorations in the microstructure of cognition: Vol. 1. Foundations* (pp. 272-325) Cambridge, MA: MIT Press.

McKoon, G., & Ratcliff, R. (1980a). Priming in item recognition. The organization of propositions in memory for text. *Journal of Verbal Learning and Verbal Behavior, 19*, 369–386.

McKoon, G., & Ratcliff, R. (1980b). The comprehension processes and memory structures involved in anaphoric reference. *Journal of Verbal Learning and Verbal Behavior, 19*, 668–682.

Mehler, J. (1963). Some effects of grammatical transformations on the recall of English sentences. *Journal of Verbal Learning and Verbal Behavior, 2*, 250–262.

Merrill, E. C., Sperber, R. D., & McCauley, C. (1981). Differences in semantic encoding as a function of reading comprehension skill. *Memory & Cognition, 9*, 618–624.

Miller, G. A. (1956). The magical number seven plus or minus two. *Psychological Review, 63*, 81–97.

Miller, G. A. (1962). Some psychological studies of grammar. *American Psychologist, 17*, 748–762.

Moeser, S. D. (1974). Memory for meaning and wording in concrete and abstract sentences. *Journal of Verbal Learning and Verbal Behavior, 13*, 682–697.

Moeser, S. D. (1976). Inferential reasoning in episodic memory. *Journal of Verbal Learning and Verbal Behavior, 15*, 193–212.

Palmer, J., MacLeod, C. M., Hunt, E., & Davidson, J. E. (1985). Information processing correlates of reading. *Journal of Memory and Language, 24*, 59–88.

Perfetti, C. A. (1985). *Reading ability*. New York: Oxford University Press.

Perfetti, C. A., & Goldman, S. R. (1974). Thematization and sentence retrieval. *Journal of Verbal Learning and Verbal Behavior, 13*, 70–79.

Perfetti, C. A., & Goldman, S. R. (1976). Discourse memory and reading comprehension skill. *Journal of Verbal Learning and Verbal Behavior, 14*, 33–42.

Perfetti, C. A., & Lesgold, A. L. (1977). Discourse comprehension and sources of individual differences. In M. A. Just & P. A. Carpenter (Eds.), *Cognitive processes in comprehension* (pp. 141–183). Hillsdale, NJ: Erlbaum.

Perlman, A. (1969). 'This' as a third article in American English. *American Speech, 44*, 76–80.

Peterson, R. G., & McIntyre, C. W. (1973). The influence of semantic ''relatedness'' on linguistic information and retention. *American Journal of Psychology, 86*, 697–706.

Pezdek, K., & Royer, J. M. (1974). The role of comprehension in learning concrete and abstract sentences. *Journal of Verbal Learning and Verbal Behavior, 13*, 551–558.

Pompi, K. F., & Lachman, R. (1967). Surrogate processes in the short-term retention of connected discourse. *Journal of Experimental Psychology, 75*, 143–150.

Posner, M. I. (1980). Orienting of attention. *Quarterly Journal of Experimental Psychology, 32*, 3–25.

Prentice, J. L. (1967). Effects of cueing actor vs cueing object on word order in sentence production. *Psychonomic Science, 8*, 163–164.

Prince, E. F. (1981). On inferencing of the indefinite-this NPs. In A. Joshi, B. Webber, & I. Sag (Eds.), *Elements of discourse understanding* (pp. 231–250). Cambridge, UK: Cambridge University Press.

Rose, R. G., Rose, P. R., King, N., & Perez, A. (1975). Bilingual memory for related and unrelated sentences. *Journal of Experimental Psychology: Human Learning and Memory, 1,* 599–606.

Sachs, J. S. (1967). Recognition memory for syntactic and semantic aspects of connected discourse. *Perception & Psychophysics, 2,* 437–442.

Sachs, J. S. (1974). Memory in reading and listening to discourse. *Memory & Cognition, 2,* 95–100.

Saegert, J., Hamayan, E., & Ahmar, H. (1975). Memory for language of input in polyglots. *Journal of Experimental Psychology: Human Learning and Memory, 1,* 607–613.

Sanford, A. J., & Garrod, S. C. (1981). *Understanding written language: Explorations in comprehension beyond the sentence.* New York: Wiley.

Schwanenflugel, P. J., & Shoben, E. J. (1983). Differential context effects in the comprehension of abstract and concrete materials. *Journal of Experimental Psychology: Learning, Memory, and Cognition, 9,* 82–102.

Simpson, G. B. (1984). Lexical ambiguity and its role in models of word recognition. *Psychological Bulletin, 96,* 316–340.

Simpson, G. B., & Lorsbach, T. G. (1983). The development of automatic and conscious components of contextual facilitation. *Child Development, 54,* 760–772.

Sloboda, J. A. (1985). *The musical mind: The cognitive psychology of music.* Oxford, UK: Oxford Press.

Smith, E. E., & Spoehr, K. T. (1974). The perception of printed English: A theoretical perspective. In B. H. Kantowitz (Ed.), *Human information processing: Tutorials in performance and cognition* (pp. 231–275). Hillsdale, NJ: Erlbaum.

Stevenson, R. J. (1986). The time course of pronoun comprehension. In C. Clifton (Ed.), *Proceedings from the Eighth Annual Conference of the Cognitive Science Society* (pp. 102–109). Hillsdale, NJ: Erlbaum.

Sticht, T. G. (1972). Learning by listening. In R. O. Freedle & J. B. Carroll (Eds.), *Language comprehension and the acquisition of knowledge* (pp. 285–314). Washington, DC: Winston.

Terkel, S. (1974). *Working.* New York: Avon.

Turner, E. A., & Rommetveit, R. (1968). Focus of attention in recall of active and passive sentences. *Journal of Verbal Learning and Verbal Behavior, 7,* 543–548.

Tyler, L. K., & Marslen-Wilson, W. (1982). The resolution of discourse anaphors: Some on-line studies. *Text, 2,* 263–291.

van Petten, C., & Kutas, M. (1987). Ambiguous words in context: An event-related potential analysis of the time course of meaning activation. *Journal of Memory and Language, 26,* 188–208.

von Eckardt, B., & Potter, M. C. (1985). Clauses and the semantic representation of words. *Memory & Cognition, 13,* 371–376.

Wald, B. (1983). Referents and topics within and across discourse units: Observations from current vernacular English. In S. Klen-Andrew (Ed.), *Discourse perspectives on syntax* (pp. 91–116). New York: Academic Press.

Waltz, D. L., & Pollack, J. B. (1985). Massively parallel parsing: A strongly interactive model of natural language interpretation. *Cognitive Science, 9,* 51–74.

Wanner, E., & Maratsos, M. (1978). An ATN approach to comprehension. In M. Halle, J. Bresnan, & G. A. Miller (Eds.), *Linguistic theory and psychological reality* (pp. 119–161). Cambridge, MA: MIT Press.

Wisegarver, K. (1986). *The effects of adverbial leads on the mental representations of narratives.* Unpublished honors thesis, University of Oregon, Eugene.

Wright, S., & Givón, T. (1987). The pragmatics of indefinite reference: Quantified text-based studies. *Studies in Language, 11,* 1–33.

TEMPORAL LEARNING

John E. R. Staddon
Jennifer J. Higa

If it is to justify itself as a separate form of publication, a book article must present something different from a journal article. In a book the process of discovery, rather than just its outcome, can be described. If we're lucky, the description will be entertaining; but at least it should be accurate, and it can provide a factual counterpoint to the bowdlerized historical account— inexorable in its logic, unerring in its course—dictated by journal conventions. We are not yet able to present in this article a finished account of the dynamics of timing. Instead we try to summarize the history of the problem and work in progress on it in a way that is intended to do three things: (1) describe a set of rather elegant experimental data that are probably novel to most psychologists and cognitive scientists even though many of the papers are now quite old; (2) show how dynamic modeling can help us appreciate the remarkable complexity of what has often been presented either as a "given" needing no further analysis or as an essentially static problem suitable mainly for psychophysical treatment; (3) describe (with suitable diffidence) a particular real-time model for temporal learning, the diffusion-generalization model.

I. Introduction

People will probably bicker for many years about B. F. Skinner's most enduring contribution to psychology, but his discovery of *schedules of reinforcement* will always rank high. Schedules have fallen somewhat out of favor these days, which is unfortunate. The order and apparent simplicity of the response patterns pigeons and other animals produce as they adapt to schedules certainly played a key role in attracting us to psychology, a field not much noted for these qualities. Schedule performances have still not been satisfactorily explained, even though they constitute perhaps the closest thing that psychologists have to a *natural history*, i.e., a body of phenomena "given" by nature. The history of biology shows that theoretical advances very often grow out of the inductive study of natural phenomena. We psychologists ignore the few available to us at our peril.

There are historical reasons why theoretical understanding of performance on reinforcement schedules has lagged so far behind experimental elaboration. The chief reason is, of course, the radical, antitheoretical, behavioristic ethos with which early students approached schedule performance. Nevertheless, sympathetic study of that untidy "bible," *Schedules of Reinforcement* (Ferster & Skinner, 1957), reveals numerous provocative theoretical fragments. Stimuli are discussed as "elicitors" and as "context setters," as well as "controllers"; behavior is referred to as a "stimulus" for other behavior; reinforcers both strengthen and maintain behavior; many patterns of dynamic interaction between behavior and its consequences are verbally sketched.[1] And paradoxical phenomena such as the pause in responding after the completion of a fixed-ratio schedule are discussed in terms of "temporal control," which is then compared indirectly to some kind of internal clock.

For reasons that will remain obscure until the psychology of creative thought has reached a much higher pitch than today, most of these intriguing ideas were never made explicit. Theory, in the book and in papers by the school that followed it, was scrupulously held to a Procrustean verbal form that all followed. Quantitative "laws" were admitted with reluctance perhaps because of the precedent set by psychophysics, the most respectable of the "hard" psychologies. But mathematical or physiological "speculations" were firmly prohibited. Internal states were explicitly eschewed, their place taken by covert "stimuli" and "responses." Upon

---

[1] A particularly enigmatic example is the following, at the end of the lengthy chapter on fixed-interval (FI) schedules: "To the extent that the bird's *behavior* is an event varying in time and correlated consistently with the FI schedule, it can be thought of as a clock by which the bird may modify its *behavior* with respect to reinforcement" (Ferster & Skinner, 1957, p. 266, our italics). The book is full of similar bootstrap conjectures in which behavior is both the controlled and the controlling variable. These ideas could be given real meaning with the aid of modern dynamic analysis (and there are some theories that can plausibly be traced to these ideas: Killeen & Fetterman, 1988). But in their day they were the behaviorist equivalent of the Trinity: something that the faithful were supposed to believe but could not be expected to explain to infidels.

what did these internal stimuli act? What agent made the responses? Agent and object alike were unspecified. No matter: the experiments—often fascinating, frequently unfocused—went on. The fact that their results could be described in a behavioristic language that effectively concealed the complexity of the underlying processes only added to their appeal.

Ferster and Skinner were quick to leave the reader in no doubt as to the ultimate importance of any theory that might emerge from the work: "Such a 'theoretical' analysis is only one result, however, and possibly the least important" (1957, p. 3). The really important things were "control" and "high levels of activity" (to be generated in subject and experimenter alike). In this way, by hustle and bustle, proscription of speculation, well-trained habits of expository hygiene, and Skinner's rhetorical art, the fiction that *Schedules of Reinforcement* is entirely about "behavior" could plausibly be maintained .

Nevertheless, there is a theoretical theme that runs through the book, and that theme is the overwhelming influence of *time* relations on behavior, i.e., time between the response and the reinforcer that is dependent on it, time between reinforcers, and time between "neutral" events and reinforcers. Time is involved even when it is not a programmed part of the schedule. Not that the book contains anything so crass as an explicit statement about the role of time. But its importance can be inferred from statements like: "A response cannot be reinforced [on fixed-ratio schedules] within a shorter period of time than that required to count out the ratio at the highest possible rate. . . . time since reinforcement and the number of responses since reinforcement vary together when the rate is constant. . . . Hence, some allowance must be made for such a factor" (p. 40). Much might be read into the cryptic phrase: "allowance must be made." We cannot guess what Ferster and Skinner meant, but we do here accept the implicit challenge to understand the role of time in schedule performance—which is to say, in learning in general.

Our central thesis is that regular time relations between a time marker (and food delivery is itself a particularly good time marker) and the next food delivery act through timing processes to produce the main features— perhaps all the features—of performance on reinforcement schedules. These timing processes are much more complex than the deceptively simply verbal accounts that are usually offered for them. We believe that this complexity can only be unraveled through research in which both experiment and real-time modeling cooperate closely. Without an attempt to model temporal learning its complexities go unnoticed; without experiment the multitude of possible models cannot be evaluated. This article recounts work in progress on the problem of timing processes. The work is still at a very preliminary stage. We have identified a set of experimental results that seem to hang together and demand a unified explanation. And we believe we can discern the outlines of the kind of process that might be responsible. By laying out the problem and sketching a theoretical approach to it we hope to increase our own understanding—and to attract others to a fascinating area that seems to be ripe for new advances.

II. Experimental Background: Performance on Patterned Interval Schedules of Reinforcement

Pavlov was probably the first in recent times to study the learned sensitivity of animals to periodic events. Procedures closely related to delay, trace, and temporal conditioning are still basic to the study of ways in which animals adapt to temporal regularity. Nevertheless, the automated methods pioneered by Skinner, and the longevity of the laboratory pigeon, have combined to make operant procedures the methods of choice for studying temporal learning in animals.

The simplest operant procedure for the study of time discrimination is the *fixed-interval* (FI) schedule: A reinforcer (almost invariably food delivery) becomes available after a fixed time I has elapsed following the preceding food delivery. The first operant response after I sec gets the food. Figure 1 shows the prototypical pattern of cumulative key pecking by a pigeon with much experience on a relatively long FI schedule. The main features of these records are (1) the pause or waiting time after each food delivery (the horizontal part of the record after each food), and (2) the accelerated, "scalloped" pattern of pecks after the first. Pigeons, rats, and numerous other animals, including humans under certain conditions, show both these features after sufficient experience with the procedure (see the review in Richelle & Lejeune, 1980). The waiting time varies under different conditions but is usually between $0.2I$ and $0.5I$. The rest of this article deals with the causation of waiting times.

What happens when the animal is trained with more than one time interval? The simplest such procedure is a schedule in which long and short interfood intervals (IFIs) alternate. An early example of the performance is shown in Fig. 2. The figure shows lever pressing by a rat on alternating FI schedules of 2 and 8 min. The jagged record and very short waiting times suggest that these data were taken after relatively little experience with the procedure. Nevertheless, there is a striking contrast between performance here and on simple FI schedules. A glance at the record shows that the average response rate is clearly higher when food deliveries are further apart. Waiting time is very short and clearly not proportional to IFI, as it is on simple FI schedules. Evidently animals

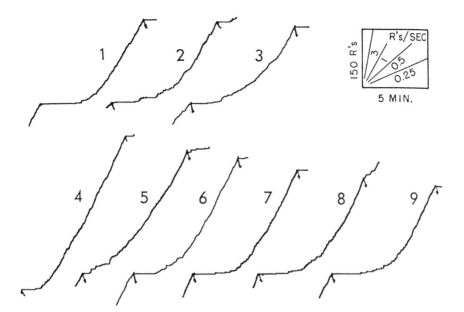

Fig. 1. Cumulative record segments from a pigeon long-trained on a fixed-interval 8-min schedule. Hash marks indicate food deliveries. Scales are shown in the upper right corner. The "scalloped" form of the record is generally assumed to be typical of performance on long FIs like this. (From Ferster & Skinner, 1957, Fig. 156.)

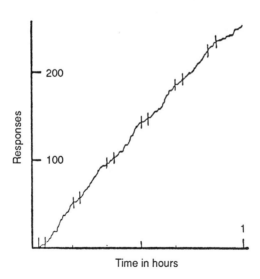

Fig. 2. Cumulative record segments from a rat trained on an interval schedule in which 2-min and 8-min IFIs alternated. Hash marks indicate food deliveries. (From Skinner, 1938, p. 272.)

adapt poorly to a schedule in which the IFI changes frequently, even if the pattern is completely predictable.

Other studies have found pigeons also unable to adapt to simple alternating patterns of intervals. For example, Fig. 3 shows the average waiting time after each food delivery in another two-valued interval schedule (Staddon, 1967). In this "square-wave" schedule 12 "short" IFIs (60 sec) regularly alternate with 4 "long" (180 sec). Even after 40 or more experimental sessions (more than 160 of these 12-short, 4-long cycles) the pigeons waited in all intervals a time appropriate to the shorter of the two with only small pertubations (points labeled "b" in Fig. 3) to show any effect of the long–short transition—and no discernible effect of the short–long transition.

Other experiments with square-wave schedules varied the number of long intervals and their value, with results that are similar or show even less adaptation to the long intervals. Figure 4 (replotted from Innis & Staddon, 1970) shows the waiting time in an average cycle on a square-wave schedule with twelve 60-sec intervals followed by six 120-sec intervals (dashed lines) or two 360-sec intervals (solid lines). Waiting time in the short (60 sec) part of the cycle is similar in both cases, but waiting time increases slightly across the six 120-sec intervals, and actually *decreases* across the two 360-sec intervals. A later experiment (Kello & Staddon, 1974) extended the long-interval part of the cycle in the 12(60 sec), 2(360 sec) schedule to six intervals [i.e., 12(60 sec),6(360 sec)], which eliminated

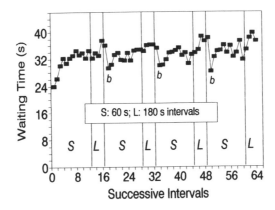

Fig. 3.   Postfood waiting time after each food delivery in an average session (13 sessions, four pigeons) on a "square-wave" interval schedule with a cycle of twelve 60-sec intervals followed by four 180-sec intervals, four cycles per session. Points labeled "b" show reliable decreases in waiting time after the first short interfood interval in each cycle. (Redrawn from Staddon, 1967, Fig. 3. Copyright © 1967 by the Society for the Experimental Analysis of Behavior, Inc.)

the decrease in waiting time seen in Fig. 4: waiting time was approximately constant across all long intervals and equal to waiting time in the short-interval part of the cycle.

It would be easy to conclude from these results that pigeons are absolutely unable to track (in terms of postfood waiting time) rapidly varying sequences of interfood intervals. The well-known absence of pausing in multivalued interval schedules (such as variable-interval) seems only to confirm this conclusion. Temporal learning is evidently slow work; pigeons seem to need many hundreds of exposures to a given interfood interval if they are to adapt adequately to it.

Nevertheless, this conclusion would be absolutely wrong, as Fig. 5 shows. The figure shows average waiting time after each food delivery in an average session under five different "triangular" cyclic-interval schedules. Successive interfood intervals in each schedule followed the series $2t,3t,4t,5t,6t,7t,8t,7t,6t,5t,4t,3t,2t$, etc. (where t varied from 2 to 40 sec in different conditions), repeated four times within each experimental session. The figure shows that the waiting-time series follows (tracks) the series of interfood intervals with a lag of one or zero intervals for all t values. In an extensive series of experiments soon after the Innis and Staddon paper, Keller (1973) confirmed that pigeons can track sinusoidally varying sequences of interfood intervals.

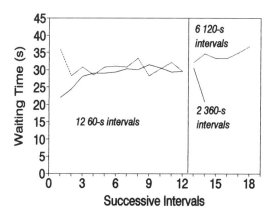

Fig. 4. Postfood waiting times in an average cycle (four pigeons, five sessions, four cycles/session) long trained on two square-wave interval schedules: 12(60 sec),6(120 sec), dashed lines; or 12(60 sec),2(360 sec), solid lines. (Redrawn from Innis & Staddon, 1970.)

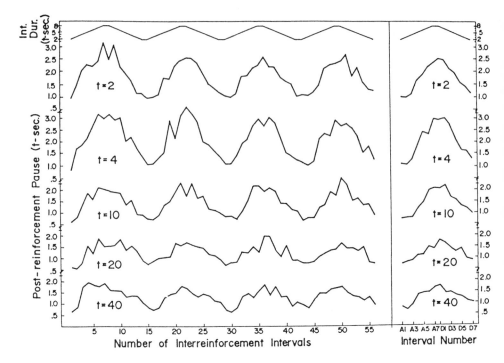

Fig. 5.   Average postfood waiting time (four pigeons, five sessions) under steady-state conditions in five "triangular" cyclic-interval schedules. The input cycle appears at the top of the figure. Left panel: average waiting time across an entire session. Right panel: an average output cycle. (From Innis & Staddon, 1971, Fig. 1. Copyright © 1971 by the Society for the Experimental Analysis of Behavior, Inc.)

III.   A Markovian Dynamic Hypothesis

What are we to make of this apparent contradiction? Pigeons are evidently unable to track even two-or three-valued cyclic-interval schedules (Innis, 1981, Figs. 11-4, 11-6; Skinner, 1938).[2] Yet they track adequately on cyclic schedules that vary in a more progressive way, with more than three intervals in the ascending and descending halves of the cycle. The form of progression seems to be less important than the number of intervals. Good tracking has been observed with sinusoidal, triangular, and logarithmic (negatively accelerated) functions. Tracking of a geometric (positively accelerated) progression is not quite as good (Innis & Staddon, 1971), suggesting that large percentage changes in interval value from one interval to the next are damaging to the process. But small deviations from

---

[2] We discuss an apparent exception to this later.

"progressivity" have little ill effect. Innis (1981), for example, reports good tracking of a triangular schedule in which five arithmetically progressing intervals were presented in ascending and then descending order, but each interval was repeated five times in the cycle: $2t,2t,2t,2t,2t,3t,3t,3t,3t,3t$, etc., for one overall cycle per session; t was either 5 or 20 sec. "Flat-top" tests in which the longest and shortest intervals in the simple triangular cycle were repeated several times also produced good tracking (Innis & Staddon, 1971).

How are we to account for pigeons' ability to track progressive schedules and their evident inability to track schedules in which interfood intervals vary abruptly or unpredictably? One possibility, which Innis and Staddon (1971) favored, is that when pigeons track progressive, cyclic schedules the animals have in some sense learned the cycle. They had no direct evidence in favor of this rather ill-defined hypothesis; there just seemed to be no alternative.

All then knew that stable schedule performance requires many tens of experimental sessions. An obvious implication, that pigeons learn almost nothing from one interfood interval to the next, was also tacitly accepted. Thus, the idea that interfood interval N could directly affect waiting time in the succeeding interval $N + 1$ seemed highly implausible. Moreover, Innis and Staddon had evidence that seemed to rule out a "one-back" tracking hypothesis of this sort. They rejected the idea that waiting time in interfood interval $N + 1$ is determined by the duration of interfood interval N because in test sessions waiting times after a single very long IFI were not excessively long. However, with the clarity of hindsight we can now see that this was a weak test—because it was based on a single test interval and because the interval was *longer* (rather than shorter) than all others. A small but cumulative effect of earlier short intervals, $N - 1, N - 2$, etc., might well swamp the effect of a single long interval N on waiting time in interval $N + 1$ because any tendency to respond at a short postfood waiting time can *preempt* even a strong tendency to respond after a longer time. A relatively weak tendency to begin responding at a short postfood time can preempt a stronger tendency to respond at a later time just because the short time comes up first (cf. Staddon, Wynne, & Higa, in press).

The implications of the tautology that short times must precede long are not self-evident so we need to elaborate. Consider an animal that has been exposed to 10 short IFIs—20 sec, say— and as a result has a strong tendency to begin responding 5 sec (a quarter of the IFI) after food. Suppose the 11th IFI is 40 sec long. The animal waits 5 sec in IFI 11 (based on the preceding ten 20-sec IFIs), but what will he do in the *next* IFI (IFI 12)? He still has a relatively strong, though weakening, tendency to respond at a postfood time of 5 sec (based on IFIs 1–10), as well as a strong tendency to respond at a postfood time of 10 sec (based on IFI 11, which is 40 sec long). But it is pretty obvious that what we will see in IFI 12 is a waiting time of 5 sec, not 10—not because the animal has learned nothing about the 40-sec IFI and has no tendency to respond at the 10-sec point, but because a weaker tendency to respond at the 5-sec point will neverthe-less preempt the longer waiting time. Because waiting time is defined by the *first* postfood response, there is an unavoidable asymmetry in the waiting-time business: short waiting times have an advantage over long. This asymmetry is well known. Nevertheless, history shows that its impli-cations are easy to miss. The implications for the Innis and Staddon experiment is that failure to wait longer after a single long IFI is not conclusive evidence that the long IFI had no effect.

Recent data have begun to shed new light on these questions and the one-back idea has become more plausible. For example, Wynne and Stad-don (1988) presented results showing that under some conditions waiting time seems to be largely determined by the preceding interfood interval. They used a response-initiated delay (RID) schedule. In RID schedules a single key peck (after a waiting time t) initiates a delay T after which food is delivered. Using an RID schedule in which food delay T depended on the preceding waiting time t, Wynne and Staddon devised an indirect test of the idea that the just-preceding IFI plays a determining role in current waiting time. The test was as follows: Suppose that waiting time in IFI $N + 1$, t_{N+1}, is proportional to the immediately preceding IFI I_N: $t_{N+1} = AI_N$ (i.e., the one-back tracking hypothesis). Suppose that the schedule now arranges that food delay in interfood interval N is propor-tional to waiting time in that cycle: $T_N = \alpha t_N$, where α is a constant set by the experimenter. Given that interfood interval, $I = T + t$, it is easy to see that there are only two stable outcomes of this autocatalytic schedule: either $t \to 0$ [if $A(1 + \alpha) < 1$] or $t \to \infty$ [if $A(1 + \alpha) > 1$]. Wynne and Staddon found results of this general sort: when α was small (1 or 2), waiting times rapidly became very short, but when α was large (4 or 7), waiting times tended to increase explosively across a few cycles. Although these results do not prove that IFI N determines waiting time in IFI $N + 1$, they are consistent with it. These results imply that waiting time adjusts rapidly to the prevailing interfood interval, at least when typical interfood intervals are less than about 20 sec.

Higa, Wynne, and Staddon (in press) present data[3] showing that Innis

---

[3] Higa et al. used a "response-initiated delay" (RID) schedule, in which food was delivered at the end of a fixed time providing a single peck (which produced a stimulus change) occurred at any time in the interfood interval. The differences between this procedure and the fixed-interval schedule are not important for the present argument, however.

and Staddon's hypothesis that pigeons "learn the cycle" on cyclic-interval schedules is almost certainly false. Higa et al. used an RID schedule in which the interfood interval varied according to a sinusoidal cycle, 16 IFIs/cycle. Each day the number of cycles of the schedule, and the point in the cycle at which the session began, varied as shown in Fig. 6. There were two groups of subjects. For one group, the interfood intervals varied between 5 and 15 sec (short), for the other between 30 and 90 sec (long). Each session ended with at least 16 IFIs at the longest value (15 or 90 sec). The constant period allowed Higa et al. to see whether the pigeons showed any residual cyclicity after their cyclic experience each day. The variable number and phase of the cycles meant that no cues other than IFI (such as time-in-session) were available to aid tracking each day.

Figure 7 shows the average waiting time for one pigeon during the 16 IFIs of the last cycle and the ensuing 16 constant IFIs, averaged across all 22 sessions of the short condition. The data are typical of both conditions and show good tracking, with a phase lag of about one interval. Moreover, the pattern during the constant-IFI period shows no evidence of cyclicity—by this measure, the birds had not "learned the cycle." The lag of one is consistent with a one-back tracking process.

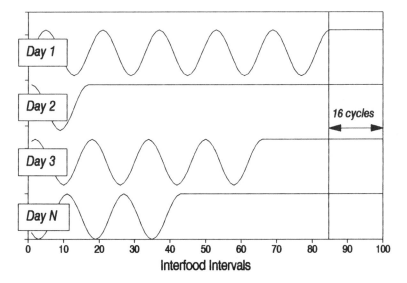

Fig. 6.   Experimental procedure in the tracking experiment of Higa et al. (in press). The figure shows examples of the daily variation in phase and number of cycles presented each day. (Redrawn from Higa et al., Fig. 3.)

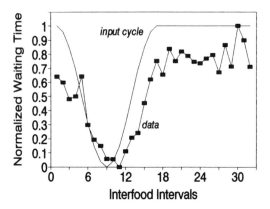

Fig. 7. Normalized average waiting time for a single pigeon (bird 174) during the last cycle of a sinusoidal response-initiated delay schedule with interfood intervals varying between 5 and 15 sec. (Redrawn from Higa et al., in press, Fig. 5.)

Examination of tracking performance session by session across the experiment showed no sign of improvement: the pigeons did about as well during their first experimental session as during the last. The fact that tracking was as good during the first session as during the last also argues strongly against the hypothesis that the animals' tracking performance reflects any learning about the cycle itself.

The data from these two experiments, Wynne and Staddon (1988) and Higa et al. (in press), therefore point to a very simple, Markovian tracking process of the form:

$$t(N + 1) = AI(N), \qquad (1)$$

where $t(N + 1)$ is the waiting time in interfood interval $N + 1$, $I(N)$ is the value of interfood interval N, and A is a constant of proportionality on the order of 0.25. We have termed this dynamic process *linear waiting* (Staddon et al., in press; Wynne & Staddon, 1988).

The one-back idea got its most direct support in a third experiment in the Higa et al. study. In this experiment the pigeons were exposed to 100 IFIs each day, ninety-nine 15 sec long, one 5 sec long. The 5-sec "impulse" interval occurred unpredictably between IFIs 15 and 85 each day. An obligatory one-back tracking process should clearly lead to a reliable decrease in waiting time just in the next interval after the short interval. Figure 8 shows the average waiting time in the 15 IFIs preceding the short IFI, in the short IFI, and in the 16 following IFIs. This pigeon was typical in showing a reliable decrease in postfood waiting time restricted to the IFI

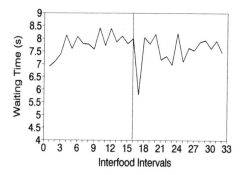

Fig. 8. Average waiting time in the fifteen 15-sec interfood intervals preceding the 5-sec interfood interval , in the 5-sec IFI, and in the 16 following 15-sec IFIs for bird 174. (Redrawn from Higa et al., in press, Fig. 11.)

following the short IFI. Moreover, this effect usually appeared immediately and did not change progressively across sessions.

IV. A Diffusion-Generalization Model

These recent data all point strongly to a very simple one-back process. Yet some properties even of the recent results show that this cannot be the whole story. For example, tracking on cyclic schedules often has a phase lag of one interval, which is consistent with a one-back process; but phase lags of zero are not infrequent. A zero phase lag is inconsistent with (1). The two-back process of (2),

$$t(N + 1) = AI(N) + B[I(N) - I(N - 1)], \tag{2}$$

can produce a zero phase lag if positive constants A and B are properly chosen, but this model is inconsistent with the "impulse" data of Higa et al., which showed that for three of four pigeons the effects of the isolated short IFI were restricted to the next IFI.

The old data discussed earlier also argue against (1) and (2). When long and short IFIs instead of being in the proportion 99:1 are in the proportion 4:12 as in the "square-wave" experiment of Staddon (1967; see Fig. 3), waiting time is essentially the same in all IFIs. The long IFIs have essentially no effect: waiting time is completely determined by the short IFIs.

We are left with the conclusion that either the Markovian approach is just an approximation that works under a limited set of conditions, or the animal can in effect change parameter values, and perhaps also the order (one-back, two-back, N-back, and so on) of the process, from one situation to the next. The remainder of the article sketches one alternative to the Markovian approach.

The data in Fig. 9 (taken from Catania & Reynolds, 1968) suggest a couple of things that are missing from the Markovian account. The figure shows average, steady-state performance of a pigeon on three interval schedules. The heavy line is the pattern of key pecking throughout a 240-sec fixed interval. The points are average key peck rates in a series of twenty-four 10-sec bins throughout the interfood interval. After an initial period of low responding, response rate accelerates to a maximum, terminal, rate in the usual way. The light solid line shows the effect of adding an occasional second, short IFI to the fixed-interval schedule. Even though only one IFI in 20 is at the 30-sec value, the pattern of responding within the 240-sec IFI is completely altered. The initial pause is abolished and response rate early in the IFI is much elevated. The dashed line shows a further elevation, and a small peak near the 30-sec postfood point, when the probability p of the short IFI is increased from .05 to .5.

The data in Fig. 9 are ambiguous in one sense because they are an average across all interfood intervals. We cannot tell from these data whether the average pattern was characteristic of all IFIs or reflects a strong effect of the infrequent 30-sec IFI that was restricted to the following one or two IFIs. Nevertheless, the data suggest that short IFIs have a special effect: apparently, even a relatively infrequent short IFI can com-

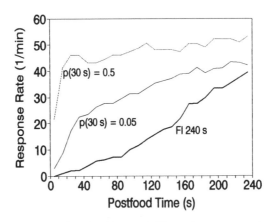

Fig. 9. Effect of a short interfood interval. Heavy line: average key peck rate as a function of postfood time of a pigeon long trained on a fixed-interval 240-sec schedule. Light solid line: effect of occasionally (1 IFI in 20) reinforcing the pigeon at the 30-sec postfood point. Dashed line: Effect of 50% short and long IFIs. (Redrawn from Catania & Reynolds, 1968, Fig. 20. Copyright © 1968 by the Society for the Experimental Analysis of Behavior, Inc.)

pletely disrupt waiting time attuned to a longer IFI. We discussed this earlier as "preemption" of long waiting times by short. Also, the difference between the low- ($p = .05$) and high-probability ($p = .5$) conditions shows that the relative frequency of long and short IFIs is important. The more frequent the short IFI, the greater its disruptive effect.

These two factors, the preemption effect of short IFIs and their relative frequency, taken together can account for the different results of the Higa et al. impulse experiment and the earlier Staddon (1967) square-wave experiment. Higa et al. found that if the short IFI is sufficiently infrequent, 1 in 100, then its effect can be confined to the next one or two intervals. Conversely, Staddon found that when the short (60 sec) IFI makes up a half or more of all IFIs, its effect is extended over all intervals, and long (180 sec or more) IFIs have no effect on waiting time. The relevant difference may just be the relative frequency of short IFIs, something that finds no place in an account that looks only at the one or two preceding IFIs as determiners of waiting time in the current IFI.

This conclusion has been confirmed in a study by Wynne and Staddon (in preparation), who have shown that when long and short IFIs are presented in repeating blocks of four, LSSSLSSS, etc., average waiting time changes smoothly from the value appropriate to the long IFI, when the frequency of the short IFI is 0 or 1 in 4 (i.e., LLLL or LLLS), to the value appropriate to the short, when the frequency of the short is 2, 3, or 4 in each block of 4 (i.e., LLSS, LSSS, or SSSS): The more frequent the shorter IFI, the shorter the average waiting time (see also Innis, 1981, Fig. 11-4, for similar data).

Is there any way to reconcile the Markovian view, which accounts so well for tracking data and the Higa et al. impulse effect, with the data from Catania and Reynolds and many subsequent experiments showing that the frequency of IFIs of different lengths, averaged over some rather long time period (on the order of tens or even hundreds of IFIs), affects waiting time? Can the failures to track square-wave and three-valued schedules also be accomodated? Our method has been to look for a real-time model, i.e., a model in which the memory representation of past events is a dynamic process that changes with the passage of time. Although the model we will discuss is far from the last word, it does allow us to link together in a natural way the various empirical factors that have been shown to affect waiting time.

We sought a dynamic model in which the tendency to respond at each postfood time is linked to the past postfood times at which food occurred, each weighted in some way by both the frequency and the age of those events. For example, suppose that the typical IFI is 30 sec, but occasionally there is a short, 10-sec IFI. We will naturally expect less of an effect on the current waiting time if the last 10-sec IFI was yesterday than if it was the most recent IFI (cf. the Higa et al. impulse data). Moreover, even if the last 10-sec IFI was a while ago, we will expect more of an effect if in the past it occurred frequently. The appropriate real-time model should take account of frequency and recency. The model should also account in a natural way for the *scalar property* of temporal discrimination (Gibbon, 1977), i.e., that the standard deviation of waiting-time distributions is proportional to the mean and that the mean waiting time is proportional to the typical interfood interval.

Our first stab at such a model is a dynamic version of the old idea of stimulus generalization—in this case, generalization along the continuum of postfood time. It seems reasonable to include in any model the idea that food delivery at postfood time I not only strengthens the tendency to respond at that postfood time but also increases the likelihood of responding at neighboring times. The dynamic property of our model is also reminiscent of Pavlov's (1927) idea that as time passes the effects of a stimulus "irradiate" across the cortex. However, unlike Pavlov, we make no neurophysiological claims.

It may help if we first give a very informal account of the essential features of the *diffusion-generalization* model before getting to the formal details. The basic idea is extremely simple and can be illustrated with the aid of the following simile. Imagine that time is represented in memory by something with the properties of blotting paper. When each time marker (usually food delivery, in these experiments) occurs, a strip of blotting paper is reeled out at a constant rate. When the next food delivery occurs, a blob of red ink is dropped onto the blotting paper, which is instantly reeled in and at once begins reeling out again. A photocell adjacent to the ink dispenser is looking at the strip of paper. It records the density of ink at each postfood time and drives responding: the tendency to respond at any instant of postfood time is directly related to the ink density on the bit of paper strip passing beneath the photocell at that time. Because the ink diffuses in real time, the ink density at any point on the strip is not constant. Points that represent (i.e., appear under the photocell at) postfood times close to the time when the ink was deposited will initially be clear, but as time elapses they will pick up some ink as "activation" spreads in time. It should be pretty obvious that if, for example, food delivery is periodic, a declining gradient of activation, centered on the postfood time at which food occurs, will soon develop, yielding a pattern of postfood responding quantitatively similar to the typical FI "scallop."

More formally stated, the ingredients of the diffusion-generalization model are as follows:

1. Postfood time is represented internally (i.e., in "memory") like any other stimulus dimension. We assume initially a discrete, linear representation: an internal integer[4] variable—the number of a formal "element" or "unit"—is proportional to real time t. A linear series of units is thus the internal representation of the dimension.

2. At any given represented postfood time i there will be a certain internal *activation strength* x_i associated with each unit i (x_i is the density of ink along the tape in our mechanical simile). x_i changes with real time, so that the pattern of activation strength across all represented times can be denoted by $x_i(t)$; function $x_i(t)$ is fixed at any value of t but changes as t increases.

3. The actual response strength at real time t, $V_i(t)$ is just the value of x_i for $i \rightarrow t$ which is to be read as the i value that represents the current value of real time t [In our simile, $V_i(t)$ is the density of ink in that bit of the tape passing beneath the photocell at postfood time t.] That is, as real postfood time elapses, the model "reads out" from the pattern of activation as a function of represented time $x_i(t)$ the response strength appropriate for the actual time t. Thus, at any instant, the state of the model will be a vector $x(t)$, which is the activation strength at all the represented times x_i. But the tendency to respond will be determined by only one of the elements in this vector, namely, that element for which $i \rightarrow t$.

The basic idea is that when food delivery occurs it adds to the activation strength at that postfood time (i.e., adds another blob of ink, in the mechanical simile). For example, if food is delivered I sec after the previous food, an increment S_I is added to activation strength at represented postfood time $i \rightarrow I$. Initially the increment in activation is assumed to accrue just to x_i ($i \rightarrow I$). But as real time elapses, this activation strength spreads to adjacent represented times $i + 1$ and $i - 1$, $i + 2$ and $i - 2$, etc., according to a simple diffusion process. This diffusion process generates a dynamic generalization gradient around the given postfood time.

The size of each increment (i.e., size of the ink blob) S is presumably related to the magnitude of food and the animal's deprivation state.

These ideas can be made more concrete as follows. Imagine a row of formal "units," 0, 1, 2, . . . , i, . . . representing postfood time and connected as shown in Fig. 10 (inset). Unit 0 represents a postfood time of 0, unit 1 represents a postfood time of 1, and so on. Thus, the unit number corresponds to represented time i. With each unit is associated an activation strength x_i. x_i changes as a function of three things: real time,

---

[4] We choose an integer for convenience because the present version of the process is discrete. This assumption is obviously not essential.

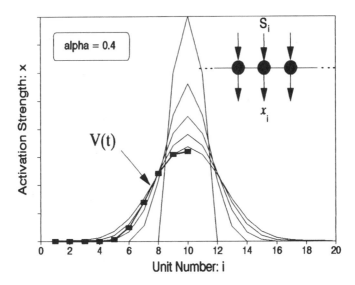

Fig. 10.   Activation strength x_i, as a function of real time (iterations) after a single food delivery at postfood time (iterations) $t = 10$. The activation gradient is clamped at zero at the origin ($i = 0$) and $i = 20$, and diffusion is at the rate of one unit per iteration. Light lines show $x_i(t)$ for $t = 1, 3, 5, 7,$ and 9. Heavy line is the resulting response strength function $V(t)$. Inset: formal network showing x_i and S_i, the time marker input.

activation levels of the two adjacent units, and occurrence of food deliveries. All three effects can be captured by a single difference equation (Staddon & Reid, 1990):

$$x_i(t + 1) = \alpha x_i(t) + \frac{(1 - \alpha)[x_{i-1}(t) + x_{i+1}(t)]}{2} + S_i(t + 1) \qquad (3)$$

where $x_i(t + 1)$ is the activation strength of the ith unit at real postfood time $t + 1$, $x_{i-1}(t)$ and $x_{i+1}(t)$ are the activation strengths of the two adjacent units at time t, α is the diffusion rate parameter, and $S_i(t + 1)$ is the value of the food stimulus at time $t + 1 \rightarrow i$ ($S_i > 0$ when food is delivered at time $t + 1 \rightarrow i$; 0 otherwise).

The form of the equation is straightforward. In the absence of any food delivery at the appropriate postfood time ($S_i = 0$), x_i approaches the average of its neighbors' activation levels ($[x_{i-1}(t) + x_{i+1}(t)]/2$) at a rate determined by parameter α: the smaller the value of α, the faster x_i approaches the average of x_{i-1} and x_{i+1}; α must be between 1/3 and 1 if x_i is not to lose more with each iteration than is gained by the two adjacent units. Food delivery at postfood time $t \rightarrow i$ simply adds an amount S_i to the activation strength of the ith unit. As time elapses, this added activation spreads to neighboring units according to Eq. (3).

This model is not overweighted with free parameters. There are two: the diffusion rate parameter α, and the scaling of iterations ("time units") to real time (i.e., the mapping of i onto t). These are not totally independent; to some extent the effect of scale change can be mimicked by changing α. But because α is bounded, larger changes can be effected by changing the number of iterations corresponding to a given lapsed time.

This process is illustrated in Fig. 10, which shows activation strengths in each unit during a period of extinction after a single food delivery at a postfood time of 10 time units (i.e., at a time represented by $i = 10$). The light lines show how the activation profile spreads and decays as a function of postfood time. Curves at postfood times of $t = 1$ (highest curve), 3, 5, 7, and 9 time units are shown. The curves all peak at unit 10 because the single food delivery occurred at that postfood time.[5] The heavy line with symbols shows the response strength $V(t)$ at each instant of postfood time. The $V(t)$ curve connects points in the series of activation curves: $V(t)$ at $t = 5$, for example, equals $x_5(5)$, the activation in unit 5 at time 5, and so on. The relation of $V(t)$ to $x_i(t)$ is easier to see in Fig. 11, which is a magnification of Fig. 10 between $i = 5$ and $i = 9$. Figure 11 shows how $V(5)$ and $x_5(5)$ coincide, how $V(7)$ and $x_7(7)$ coincide, and so on.

The process incorporates most of the factors the data show to be important: The occurrence of food at a particular postfood time is represented by the peak of the gradient. The fact that this experience is less influential the longer ago it occurred is represented by the collapse of the gradient as time elapses. Gradient decay also allows for generalization: Food at one postfood time also enhances the tendency to respond at neighboring times. Moreover, this generalization is presumed to increase with time; the base of the gradient expands by one unit at each iteration. This covariation between gradient spread and elapsed time is theoretically convenient—but has not been demonstrated experimentally.

Figure 10 shows that even after a single food delivery, response strength $V(t)$ has already taken on the increasing form characteristic of responding on fixed-interval schedules. Repeated food deliveries at the same IFI will increase the tendency to respond at that IFI. Thus, the frequency with which a particular IFI has occurred is represented by the height of the gradient. The gradient does not increase without limit, however, as we show in a moment.

The predictions of this model are based on function $V(t)$, response

---

[5] For simplicity, in all discussions of the model we assume that one real-time unit is equal to one represented-time unit.

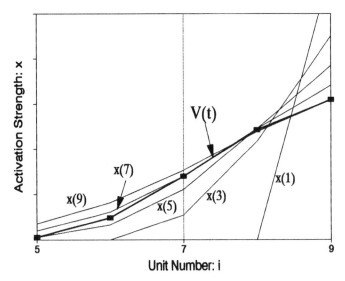

Fig. 11. Portion of Fig. 10 magnified to show the relation between activation strength $x_i(t)$ and response strength $V(t)$. The curves labeled x(9), x(7) etc., show the activation function x_i at $t = 7$, $t = 9$, etc.

strength as a function of postfood time. How stable is $V(t)$ and how does it change with experience? Figure 12 shows the form of $V(t)$ for a simple 24-time-unit fixed-interval schedule after varying numbers of training intervals. $V(t)$ approaches a straight line, and after about 200 food deliveries (with this time scale and this value for α) is essentially at asymptote—the curves for 200 and 2000 IFIs lie on top of one another.

A.   Response Rule

The model lacks an explicit *response rule*, i.e., a rule that relates the output of the model to the time at which operant responses should occur. The output of the model is function $V(t)$, response strength as a function of postfood time (see Figs. 11 and 12). Response strength presumably has something to do with the rate of response and, as we will see, there is a simple mapping between $V(t)$ and empirical postfood response rate functions on FI schedules. But we are less sure of the best way to translate $V(t)$ into postfood waiting time. We consider some possibilities in a moment.

How well does this model do in explaining some of the data we have discussed? Let's look at some examples.

B.   Scalar Timing

Scalar timing is a name for two properties of waiting time on fixed-interval schedules: the proportionality between waiting time and IFI, and a fixed

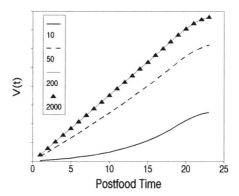

Fig. 12. Response strength $V(t)$ as a function of postfood time on a fixed-interval schedule after 10, 50, 200, and 2000 training intervals. Note that no further changes take place after 200 IFIs. The maximum of the activation strength function x_i was clamped (held at zero) at $i = 48$ (clamping the function at higher i values has negligible effect); $\alpha = 0.4$.

ratio of the mean and standard deviation of the waiting-time distribution (constant coefficient of variation: Gibbon, 1977). For example, Dews (1970; see also Gibbon, 1977, Figure 1) many years ago plotted steady-state response rate as a function of the maximum rate in successive fifths of fixed-interval schedules ranging from 30 to 3000 sec in length. The functions are linear and identical for all the FI values. The diffusion-generalization model easily reproduces both results. After many iterations, the steady-state form for the activation gradient $x_i(t)$, and thus the response strength gradient $V(t)$, is a straight line. Figure 13 shows steady-state $V(t)$ functions for six fixed-interval values: 4, 8, 16, 24, 32, and 36 time units. Clearly, if response rate is proportional to response strength, then these simulations correspond to Dews's result.[6]

How should waiting time be derived from these response strength functions? The experimental data are clear: Waiting time is an approximately fixed fraction of interfood interval. The line of negative slope in Fig. 13 connects points in the various $V(t)$ functions for which $t =$ one-quarter of the prevailing IFI, which is approximately the empirical value of the

---

[6] It is probably not correct to explain the whole pattern of postfood responding solely by reference to post*food* time. In an earlier theoretical paper (Staddon, Wynne, & Higa, 1991), we argued that the entire fixed-interval "scallop" is to be explained, at least partially, by a recursive property of temporal learning, i.e., as each postfood response occurs it provides a time marker for later responses. However, empirical data show that this essentially Markovian process (each response determines the next) cannot be the whole story. For example, the later a pigeon begins to peck in a given fixed interval, the more closely the next peck follows (Staddon & Frank, 1975), which implies some effect of postfood time in addition to (or instead of) postresponse time. The identity of the effective time marker(s) at different places in the postfood behavior sequence is still not known with precision.

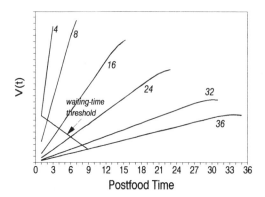

Fig. 13. Response strength $V(t)$ as a function of postfood time on six different fixed-interval schedules. Line of negative slope connects $V(t)$ values for which t equals one-quarter the interfood interval. $\alpha = 0.4$.

waiting "fraction." Thus, this line can be thought of as a sort of response threshold. Its most interesting property is that it is not constant. Evidently this kind of model requires us to assume either that the response threshold decreases as the prevailing IFI increases, or that there is a fixed threshold but the response function $V(t)$ is normalized.

The diffusion-generalization model is deterministic, hence cannot speak directly to the second property of scalar timing, the constancy of the coefficient of variation. We are not sure how to incorporate variability into the model.

C. TWO-VALUED INTERVAL SCHEDULES

Figure 14 shows the steady-state form for the response strength function $V(t)$ on a two-valued schedule in which IFIs of 3 and 24 time units occur in alternation. This procedure is analogous to the Catania and Reynolds experiment illustrated in Fig. 9 (top curve). The heavy solid line shows $V(t)$ in the 24-unit IFI (i.e., following the short IFI); the light solid line shows $V(t)$ in the 3-unit IFI (i.e., following the long IFI). The dashed line shows $V(t)$ under a 24-unit fixed-interval schedule for comparison. These functions show two effects:[7] (1) a sequential, "tracking" effect (response strength just after food is clearly increased after the short IFI; compare the heavy line, after-3, with the light line, after-24); and (2) a general elevation

---

[7] These effects depend to some extent on the value of parameter α. In general, sequential effects (i.e., tracking) are greater if α is small because the system then has a short "memory," hence is most sensitive to recent events. However, aggregate effects such as those shown in Fig. 14 are not very sensitive to the value of α.

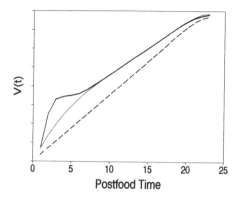

Fig. 14. Steady-state (2000 IFIs) response strength functions $V(t)$ on a two-valued schedule. Light solid line: $V(t)$ after 24-unit IFI; heavy solid line: $V(t)$ after 3-unit IFI. For comparison purposes, both functions are computed out to 24 time units, even though during "training" the post-24 function is always terminated after 3 units by the arrival of food. Dashed line is the $V(t)$ function for FI 24. $\alpha = 0.4$.

of the IFI 24 function at shorter postfood times (compare the light line, after-24, and the dashed line, FI-24, functions). We have also looked at the case where the short IFI is infrequent ($p = .05$) and find slightly larger sequential effects, i.e., the difference between the response strength $V(t)$ function after the short IFI and after the penultimate long IFI is greater when there are 19 long IFIs for every short IFI. The effect on the average $V(t)$ function is of course less when the short IFI is infrequent.

Catania and Reynolds did not present sequential data, so we do not know if their data, like our simulations, showed different response rate profiles after long vs. short IFIs. But the second effect in the simulations, a general elevation of response strength at short postfood times even when the short IFI is infrequent, clearly corresponds to their results.

Figure 15 shows a simulation of the Higa et al. impulse experiment. In this experiment, out of every 100 IFIs, 99 were 15 sec and one was 5 sec. The heavy solid line in each panel shows $V(t)$ after the 15-unit IFIs. The light line shows $V(t)$ after the short, five-unit IFI. The elevation in the curve after the short IFI is clear in all three panels, and larger the smaller the value of α, the diffusion parameter. The dotted lines show that there is a small effect of the short IFI even after two succeeding food deliveries. Only one of the four pigeons in the Higa et al. study showed an effect of the short IFI extending beyond the next interval. Thus, the simulation slightly exaggerates the persistence of the short-IFI effect.

Figure 16 shows $V(t)$ functions generated by a schedule similar to the 12(60 sec),4(180 sec) square-wave schedule studied by Staddon (1967).

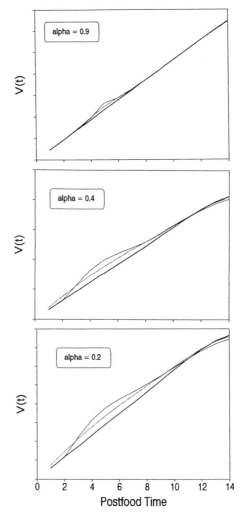

Fig. 15.   Steady-state $V(t)$ functions for an "impulse" schedule: in each cycle 99 inter-food intervals were 15 units, one IFI was 5 units. In all panels, heavy solid line: after the 15-unit IFIs; light line: first 15-sec IFI after the 5-unit IFI (5-1); dotted line: second 15-sec IFI after the 5-unit IFI (5-2).

The figure shows simulations of a 12(6),4(18) schedule. Each curve shows the postfood response strength profile $V(t)$ at a particular place in the 16-IFI cycle. The highest curve, for example, is after the 12th six-unit IFI and the four curves below it are after the first through fourth 18-unit IFIs. The general pattern is as one would expect: response strength decreases across the four long (18-unit) IFIs, but the difference between 6- and

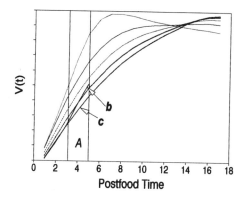

Fig. 16. Steady-state $V(t)$ functions for a square-wave schedule. In each cycle there are twelve 6-unit IFIs, followed by four 18-unit IFIs. The highest curve is after the twelfth 6-unit IFI (i.e., during the first 18-unit IFI). The four curves below are after the first, second, through fourth 18-unit IFI. The short curve (b-arrow) is after the first 6-unit IFI. A, b, and c are discussed in the text. $\alpha = 0.4$.

18-unit gradients is much less than it would be under steady-state conditions (cf. Fig. 13). The short curve labeled "b" is the profile after the first short IFI in each cycle. Notice that in the region labeled "A" it signifies a higher response strength, hence shorter waiting time, than during the preceding IFI, i.e., it is above the curve for fourth 18-unit IFI ("c"). This perhaps corresponds to the "blips" (labeled "b") in the waiting-time record in Fig. 3. But too much should not be made of this correspondence because it obviously depends critically on where the threshold function is made to cross these curves. If the threshold were set to intersect the curves to the left of region A, for example, there would be no special effect of the first short IFI. And no matter where the threshold is set, the simulation shows a systematic increase in response strength (reduction in waiting time) across the 12 six-unit IFIs, which (with the exception of the single point b) is also not found in the data in Fig. 3. The curves in Fig. 16 also signify a decrease, albeit relatively small, in response strength across the four long IFIs. A small effect of this sort is apparent in Fig. 3, especially during the last two cycles, but Fig. 4 (right panel) shows the opposite effect: a decrease in waiting time across two long IFIs. The present scheme cannot account for the latter effect.

D. Cyclic Schedules

The fact that the activation gradient decays with time means that the form of the $V(t)$ function is most strongly affected by the most recent IFI. The model is therefore potentially able to track in a one-back, Markovian fashion. Figure 17 shows the results of some preliminary simulations. The figure shows the $V(t)$ function following each IFI during the second cycle of exposure to a triangular cyclic schedule: 6, 8, 10, 12, 14, 16, 14, 12, and so on. The left panel shows $V(t)$ after IFIs in the ascending part of the cycle; the right panel shows the descending part. It is just possible to draw a threshold line through these curves in such a way that waiting times track IFI—the left panel shows an example—but the region over which this is possible is quite limited, especially in the descending half of the cycle. The model in this form does a rather poor job of tracking.

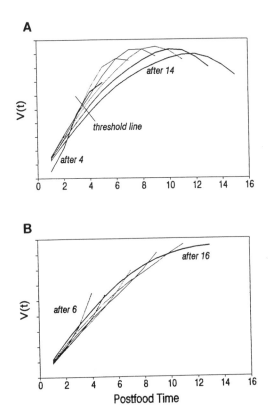

Fig. 17.   Tracking a triangular cyclic schedule. Steady-state $V(t)$ as a function of post-food time t following each IFI in an arithmetic, triangular schedule: IFIs 4,6,8,10,12,14,16,14,12,10,8,6,4, etc. A, ascending half cycle. B, descending half cycle. $\alpha = 0.4$.

E. WHERE DOES IT FAIL, AND WHAT IS MISSING?

What is missing? There are several possibilities. First, we have by no means explored the full range of parameter values. More iterations per second of real time allows for greater decay and a reduced effect of earlier IFIs on the $V(t)$ function in the current IFI. However, the effects shown in the simulations do not seem to be very sensitive to the value of the diffusion rate parameter α. We have not explored nonlinear mappings of real time onto the unit number i, yet a little thought strongly suggests that a linear mapping is unlikely, if only because linear representation stores temporal information in a very inefficient way. With a linear representation, very long delays, which are much less important to the animal than short ("In the long run, we are all dead," said Maynard Keynes), take up the most room. An alternative approach to this problem is to allow diffusion rate to depend on absolute time: high at short postfood times, slower at longer times, e.g., with an appropriate mapping assumption to preserve the scalar timing property.

A major omission is any assumption about inhibition. It is easy to show that tracking of progressive IFI sequences is greatly facilitated by inhibition (i.e., a negative gradient) associated with omission of a previously presented reinforcer. A long IFI following a short in this view is assumed to cause inhibition around the postfood time equal to the shorter IFI. This assumption amounts to a dynamic version of Spence's (1937) interacting-gradients model, in which transposition—extrapolation of a two-member sequence—is accounted for by the interaction between excitatory and inhibitory generalization gradients. As successive IFIs increase in length, for example, a gradient of inhibition around the previously reinforced, but subsequently unreinforced, IFIs shifts the net gradient and allows waiting time to extrapolate the sequence in a dynamic version of the peak shift effect (cf. Staddon, 1977; and in preparation). In the interests of parsimony, we wanted to see how much could be explained by a strictly excitatory system. Nevertheless, the rather poor prediction of tracking in Fig. 17 strongly suggests that some assumption about inhibition is necessary for a full account of how pigeons adapt to patterns of interfood intervals.

Finally there are one or two findings that seem beyond the reach even of a version of the diffusion-generalization model expanded to include inhibitory effects. Keller (1973) systematically varied the number of reinforcers per cycle in a sinusoidal schedule. As one might expect, the fewer the number of reinforcers, the poorer the tracking—until the number was reduced to two. In contrast to the old Skinner data in Fig. 2, Keller's pigeons tracked an extreme (20- and 180-sec) two-valued schedule with zero phase lag and better than schedules with three and more IFIs per cycle. The results suggest some kind of gestalt "grouping" principle—the two closely spaced food deliveries spanning the short IFI were in some sense treated as one, and provided the cue for the long IFI—but the potential mechanism is obscure.

V. Conclusion

We are not yet able to present in this article a finished account of the timing processes that underlie animals' adaptation to patterned interval schedules of food reinforcement. Instead, we have presented a summary of the history of the problem and work in progress on it with three objects in view: (1) to bring together the scattered experimental data that describe the striking and orderly adaptations of pigeons to cyclic schedules of reinforcement; (2) to advocate dynamic modeling as an aid to understanding the complexity of temporal learning, a process that has in the past been presented either as a commonplace that requires no analysis or else as a static problem suitable mainly for psychophysical treatment; and (3) to illustrate the point with the aid of a tentative real-time model for temporal learning, the diffusion-generalization model.

The phenomena we describe, pigeons' adaptation to different kinds of cyclic schedules of reinforcement, were originally studied 20 or more years ago with the aid of primitive technology that made anything but aggregate measurements (session-average response rates and waiting times) difficult and error-prone. Nevertheless, some sequential data were obtained and they were remarkably orderly, although very hard to explain. Theorizing, which is never easy, was also harder then than now, because computers, those lifesavers for the mathematically impaired, were slow and difficult to use—and the behavioristic temper of the times was implacably hostile to modeling of any sort. Our first objective in this chapter is to reintroduce the psychological audience to these fascinating problems, which are still unsolved but which now seem much more soluble.

Our second objective has been to show by example how one can begin to unravel the complexities of temporal learning through dynamic modeling. Temporal control has traditionally been described in a simple way that utterly conceals numerous difficult questions. These questions are laid bare merely by the attempt to make a dynamic model. For example, how does the animal recognize that one occurrence of a time marker is like another? That is, how does it recognize recurrence? All models assume that the animal's "internal clock" is in some way "reset" by the time marker. There are also data showing that if food delivery (for example) is the relevant time marker, events that resemble food delivery cause a "partial reset" (Kello, 1972). What is the mechanism that allows the organism to make this identification? More generally, is it always a single event that acts as a time marker, or can groups of events, distributed in time, also serve this function? The problem of recognizing recurrence has traditionally been concealed by the term *generalization*; the problems of reset and time measurement by the term *temporal control*. We have taken a first step towards answering the latter question; the first question is still beyond us.

Our third objective has been to play around a bit with a particular model for temporal learning, the diffusion-generalization model. We hold no special brief for this model. Indeed, it begs at least one vital question about temporal learning by assuming that time is represented in some way. And the form of representation we have chosen, a spatial array of formal "units," though convenient is not even particularly likely from a neural point of view. Ideally, the form of the representation should both be biologically plausible and emerge as a natural consequence of the timing process. We have some ideas about how this might work, but they are too ill formed for a book article. Nevertheless, the diffusion-generalization idea is sufficiently simple, and seems to embody enough of the factors that are known to be important to time discrimination on schedules (such as temporal generalization, the scalar property, and the effects of frequency and recency), to be worth exploring, if only to reveal its defects and highlight our areas of ignorance. We continue to pursue variants on this approach, and alternative approaches, that may after not too many years allow us to bring together all the varied patterns of adaptation to interval reinforcement schedules that we have described.

ACKNOWLEDGMENTS

We are grateful to Nancy K. Innis for comments on earlier versions. The research reported here was supported by grants from the NSF and NIMH.

REFERENCES

Catania, A. C., & Reynolds, G. S. (1968). A quantitative analysis of the responding maintained by interval schedules of reinforcement. *Journal of the Experimental Analysis of Behavior, 11,* 327–383.

Dews, P. B. (1970). The theory of fixed-interval responding. In W. N. Schoenfeld (Ed.), *The Theory of Reinforcement Schedules* (pp. 43–61). New York: Appleton-Century-Crofts.

Ferster, C. B., & Skinner, B. F. (1957). *Schedules of reinforcement.* New York: Appleton-Century-Crofts.

Gibbon, J. (1977). Scalar expectancy and Weber's law in animal timing. *Psychological Review, 84,* 279–325.

Higa, J. J., Wynne, C. D. L., & Staddon, J. E. R. (in press). Dynamics of time discrimination. *Journal of Experimental Psychology: Animal Behavior Processes.*

Innis, N. K. (1981). Reinforcement as input: Temporal tracking on cyclic interval schedules. In M. Commons & J. A. Nevin (Eds.), *Quantitative analysis of behavior: Discriminative properties of reinforcement schedules.* New York: Pergamon.

Innis, N. K., & Staddon, J. E. R. (1970). Sequential effects in cyclic- interval schedules. *Psychonomic Science, 19,* 313–315.

Innis, N. K., & Staddon, J. E. R. (1971). Temporal tracking on cyclic- interval reinforcement schedules. *Journal of the Experimental Analysis of Behavior, 16,* 411–423.

Keller, J. (1973). *Responding maintained by sinusoidal cyclic-interval schedules of reinforcement: A control-systems approach to operant behavior.* Unpublished doctoral thesis, University of Maryland, College Park. (University Microfilms, Ann Arbor, MI.)

Kello, J. E. (1972). The reinforcement-omission effect on fixed-interval schedules: Frustration or inhibition? *Learning and Motivation, 3,* 138–147.

Kello, J. E., & Staddon, J. E. R. (1974). Control of long-interval performance on mixed cyclic-interval schedules. *Bulletin of the Psychonomic Society, 4,* 1–4.

Killeen, P. R., & Fetterman, J. G. (1988). A behavioral theory of timing. *Psychological Review, 95,* 274–295.

Pavlov, I. P. (1927). *Conditioned reflexes* (G. V. Anrep, Trans.). Oxford: Oxford University Press.

Richelle, M., & Lejeune, H. (1980). *Time in animal behaviour.* New York: Pergamon.

Skinner, B. F. (1938). *The behavior of organisms.* New York: Appleton-Century.

Spence, K. W. (1937). The differential response in animals to stimuli varying in a single dimension. *Psychological Review, 44,* 435–444.

Staddon, J. E. R. (1967). Attention and temporal discrimination: Factors controlling responding under a cyclic-interval schedule. *Journal of the Experimental Analysis of Behavior, 10,* 349–359.

Staddon, J. E. R. (1977). Behavioral competition in conditioning situations: Notes toward a theory of generalization and inhibition. In H. Davis & H. M. B. Hurwitz (Eds.), *Operant-Pavlovian interactions.* Hillsdale, NJ: Erlbaum.

Staddon, J. E. R., & Frank, J. A. (1975). Temporal control on periodic schedules: Fine structure. *Bulletin of the Psychonomic Society, 6,* 536–538.

Staddon, J. E. R., & Reid, A. K. (1990). On the dynamics of generalization. *Psychological Review, 97,* 576–578.

Staddon, J. E. R., Wynne, C. D. L., & Higa, J. J. (1991). The role of timing in reinforcement schedule performance. *Learning and Motivation, 22,* 200–225.

Wynne, C. D. L., & Staddon, J. E. R. (1988). Typical delay determines waiting time on periodic-food schedules: Static and dynamic tests. *Journal of the Experimental Analysis of Behavior, 50,* 197–210.

Wynne, C. D. L., & Staddon, J. E. R. (in preparation). *The Dynamics of Waiting in Pigeons.*

BEHAVIOR'S TIME

Peter R. Killeen

I. Introduction

Time is the dimension along which structure expands into function, attitude into action, stance into behavior. We understand changes in time only through changes in events that evolve through time. It has been our habit to identify events that seem to evolve or recur regularly—in early days the return of the sun or the progress of its shadow, in later days the vibrations of atoms—and to use these as our criteria for the passage of time. Changes in such criterion events serve as the denominator in differential equations to which changes in all other events are referenced. Newton's assumption that time flowed uniformly was not a conclusion about nature, but rather a postulate that permitted the simplest system of mechanics. It was a procrustean postulate, but one for which we were prepared by the quotidian demands of sun and season. In organisms less sophisticated than physicists we are likely to find a casual indifference to the existence and properties of such things as Universal Time, and an opportunism concerning the events that serve as criteria for time's passage. Time is relative, not only to sidereal velocities, but to more important if homely things, such as the recurrence of prey, predators, and mates.

Because behavior is stance evolving through time, our analysis of it will be simplified if we can identify behavior's time—the events with respect to which our observations of actions may be organized into the simplest system of behavior—presumably those events to which the organism itself references its activities. Newton's time remains our lingua franca, easily communicated yet remote from the insights provided by a vernacular. To learn behavior's language, we begin, like any ethnologist, by drawing the organism's attention to an object and recording the response it makes. We replicate the experiment to sift out the generalities, and then elaborate nuances by asking for distinctions between similar objects. We may ensure that we and our informants are referring to the same objects by finding or establishing events of central importance to them. In experimental psychology, this has meant pay or credit for impoverished or indentured students, and food or water for deprived rats and pigeons.

In this article, I shall review some of the effects of giving food to hungry animals according to different temporal regimens. The dependent variable will be some change in the stance of the organism—around the chamber, toward a switch, between two switches. It will be either a direct (contemporaneous) "effect" of the passage of time, measured by analysis of what animals do while waiting for food or after receiving it, or an indirect effect, measured by their accuracy in discriminating intervals of time. In the latter case, the animal might be rewarded only if it can correctly indicate whether the shorter or the longer of two intervals had just elapsed (*retrospective timing*); or it might receive food after a short delay if it responds to one switch, after a longer delay if it responds to another switch (*prospective timing*). It is the thesis of the present analysis that the discrimination of temporal intervals is based on the discrimination of behaviors that are elicited by the direct (contemporaneous) effects of reinforcement, and that the latter comprise behavior's time.

II. Contemporaneous Effects

Let us present 15 sec to an animal, demarking it with presentations of food, and watch what it does. Figure 1 (from Haight & Killeen, in press) gives one picture; Staddon and Simmelhag (1971), Roper (1978), and Staddon and Ayres (1975) give others. The various activities inspired by the periodic presentation of reinforcers have been called *adjunctive* because they arise even when they are not instrumentally required for reinforcement, and persist despite contingencies that should discourage their emission. It is possible to shape the topographies of these behaviors, so that some such as "Neck Extension" may be transformed into the traditional operant response of key pecking. But while the details of the behavior may be amenable to shaping, attempting to move behaviors characteristic of the end of the interval (*terminal behaviors*) to earlier parts of it is a Sisyphean enterprise (Shull, 1970); requiring a pigeon to peck a key during the early

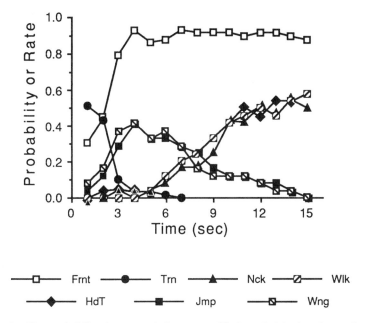

Fig. 1. The probability (open symbol) or rate (filled symbols) of various adjunctive behaviors as a function of the time through a 15-sec interval for one pigeon. The behaviors are: facing the front wall (Frnt), turning, (Trn), extending the neck (Nck), walking (Wlk), turning the head (HdT), jumping (Jmp), and flapping the wings (Wng). From Haight and Killeen (*Animal Learning and Behavior,* in press), reprinted by permission of Psychonomic Society, Inc.

parts of the interval generates only aversion to the schedule (Moore & Fantino, 1975). *Interim* behaviors, characteristic of the earlier parts of the interval, may be discouraged by contingencies but can rarely be eliminated by them. Different types of activities mark different parts of the interval. Falk (1972) and Staddon (1977) discuss in more detail the nature of such *schedule-induced* activities.

One of the activities characteristic of pigeons during the early part of the interval is pacing across the front wall of the chamber. Timberlake and Lucas (1985) relate this to food-begging behavior of squab. It is easily recorded by replacing the standard floor with hinged panels resting on microswitches. Figure 2 shows the rates of microswitch activation, averaged over four pigeons, when they were presented intervals of 25–400 sec, punctuated by the delivery of food. Note the orderly and syncopated way in which these data rise from the floor to their maximum about 25% of the way into each of the intervals, and then fall to asymptote. Food was delivered at the times corresponding to the normalized abcissae of 0.0 and

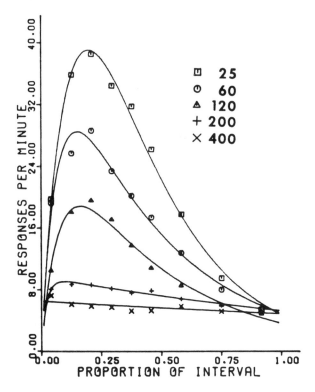

Fig. 2. The rate of activation of floor panels as a function of the time through various intervals, as denoted by the parameters. The data represent averages over four pigeons. The curves through the data are generated by Eq. (1). From Killeen (*Psychological Review, 82,* 89–115). Copyright © 1975 by the American Psychological Association. Reprinted by permission of the publisher.

1.0, but never within 5 sec of the last activity response. The smooth curves through the data are derived from Eq. (1):

$$R = A(e^{-t/C} - e^{-t/I}).\tag{1}$$

This equation may be understood in several ways. Figure 3 shows a literal interpretation. In it, the rising dashed line depicts the cumulative probability of the animal having left the initial state ($N = 0$) and entered an interim response state ($N > 0$). If entry into that state occurs with constant probability, then:

$$p(N > 0) = 1 - e^{-t/I},\tag{2}$$

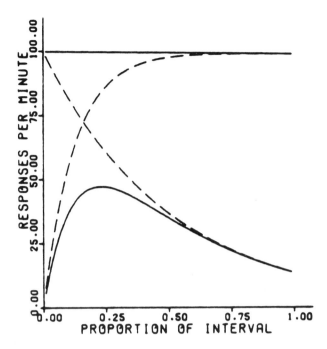

Fig. 3. Top solid line: Hypothetical level of arousal, decreasing minutely through the interval. Dashed lines: Probability of leaving the initial state [ascending curve; Eq. (2)] and probability of leaving the measured response state [descending curve; the complement of Eq. (3)]. Bottom solid line: The probability of being in the measured response state, as given by Eq. (1). From Killeen (*Psychological Review, 82,* 89–115). Copyright © 1975 by the American Psychological Association. Reprinted by permission of the publisher.

where I is the time constant of the process, $I > 0$. The falling dashed curve depicts the probability of not yet having entered into a subsequent state that competes with the measured interim activity. The probability of having entered that competing state is:

$$p(N > 1) = 1 - e^{-t/C}, \tag{3}$$

where C is the time constant for the expression of these competing activities, $C > 0$. The probability of being in the interim state is proportional to the difference of Eq. (2) and (3), i.e., Eq. (1).

This literal interpretation may be derived from control theory or, of more relevance to this system, from a series latency mechanism (McGill, 1963). If in the interval Δt the animal enters the measured response state with constant probabililty $\Delta t/I$, and then in another interval Δt leaves it with constant probability $\Delta t/C$, the probability that the animal will be in that state emitting measurable responses at any time t is the conditional evaluation (*convolution*) of those probabilities; in this case, the convolution results in Eq. (1) with $A = 1/(C - I)$, $C > I > 0$.

Figure 1 shows that in the interval between reinforcers, pigeons (and other organisms) will engage in perhaps a half-dozen recurrent behaviors. We may generalize Eq. (1) to describe the time course of any one of these behaviors; but the generalization is awkward, consisting of the sum of n exponentials, each weighted by a combination of the n time constants characteristic of each of the behaviors (McGill & Gibbon, 1965). Although such a generalized series latency mechanism may underlie the performance, it is a less than ideal description of it because the equation is too complex to be enlightening, and the resulting curves are too flexible, given the large number of parameters, to vindicate the model. This is a spendid example of what Niels Bohr called the "complementarity between truth and clarity" (French & Kennedy, 1985); as our descriptions of nature become more precise, they also become more obscure. We may operationalize Bohr's insight by measuring "truth" as the correspondence (the goodness of fit) between data and model, and obscurity as the number of free parameters in the model. We may then attempt to strike a reasonable balance between truth and clarity by appropriately curbing the flexibility of the generalized stochastic process.

The most obvious simplification is to assert that each of the adjunctive behaviors have the same time constant, $C = I = \tau$. The probability of having left the initial state and entered the first interim state is still given by Eq. (2), with $I = \tau$. Let us name the states $N = 0, 1, 2$, etc., corresponding to the initial state and each of the subsequent states. Then the probability of entering any particular state n is given by the *Erlang* distribution $F(n, \tau)$ (if n is an integer or, more generally, by the *gamma* distribution). The probability that the state at time t, $N(t)$, equals some particular value n (e.g., $n = 1$ for the continuous curve in Fig. 2) is found by calculating the probability that the animal has entered state n but has not yet entered state $n + 1$. This may be calculated as the distribution for n, $F(n, \tau)$, minus the distribution for $n + 1$, $F(n + 1, \tau)$ (Cox & Miller, 1965; Fetterman & Killeen, 1991). For the Erlang, it is:

$$p(N(t) = n) = \left(\frac{t}{\tau}\right)^n e^{-t/\tau}/n! \tag{4}$$

Equation (4) is the difference of two Erlang distributions and may be used to calcualte the probability that the animal is in the Nth state at any particular time t, presuming that it progresses from one state to the next with a constant probability $1/\tau$. These underlying assumptions constitute a *Poisson process*, with densities ranging from the exponential decay for the zeroth state ($n = 0$), highly skewed distributions (similar to the continuous curve in Fig. 2) for the first state, to increasingly symmetrical curves for higher states. As n gets large, the function described by Eq. (5) approaches the normal density:

$$p(N(t) = n) = \left(\frac{1}{\sqrt{2\pi}\sigma}\right)e^{-[(t - \mu)/\sqrt{2}\sigma]^2}, \tag{5}$$

and the probability of entering a state may be described by the corresponding distribution.

Figure 4 shows that Eqs. (1) and (4) provide comparably good descriptions of interim behaviors, while Eqs. (4) and (5) provide comparably good descriptions of terminal behaviors such as key pecking. Equations (4) and (5) may be used to predict the probability of the animal being in a particular response state, presuming it stays there for only one pulse. If it stays longer, we must compute the difference of the two relevant cumulative

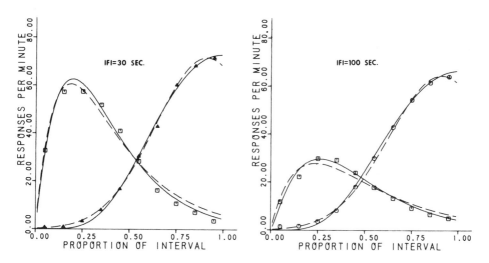

Fig. 4. Distributions of general activity (concave functions) and key pecking (ascending functions). The dashed lines through the former are from Eq. (1), and through the latter are from Eq. (5). The continuous lines are from Eq. (4). The data are averaged over three pigeons, for two intervals given by the parameters. From Killeen, Hanson, and Osborne (*Psychological Review, 85,* 571–581). Copyright © 1978 by the American Psychological Association. Reprinted by permission of the publisher.

distributions. In general, the difference of two normal distributions [Eq. (6)] will provide the standard model for temporal discriminations. If the means of these two distributions are very close together, the resulting curve approaches one whose rule is Eq. (5). As the means are moved farther apart (relative to their standard deviations), the curve rises closer to 1.0 according to a cumulative normal distribution and eventually decreases in the same manner toward 0.0. In many experiments only the ascending or descending limb is measured; this is referred to as a *psychometric function*.

A. PACEMAKER–COUNTER SYSTEMS

Imagine a Geiger counter near a milligram of radium that is emitting particles randomly at an average rate of $1/\tau$. Clear the counter at time t_1, and read the counter at time $t_2 = t_1 + t$. The probability of seeing the number n on the counter at that time is given by Eq. (4). It is thus a short step from the agnostic description offered by a model such as Eq. (4) to a physical realization in a system such as radium near a Geiger counter, or in general to any "clock" in which a pacemaker generates events and a counter records them. When the behavior of animals is modeled by Eq. (4), it is convenient to speak of a pacemaker that emits pulses and drives activity from one state to the next, but all we really know is that a Poisson model with random transition between states, i.e., Eq. (4), captures the behavior both of animals and some clocks.

In most conceptualizations of clocks the counter is presumed to be perfectly accurate, and the pacemaker may be highly accurate (vibrations of a crystal), moderately accurate (oscillations of a pendulum), marginally accurate (taps of a foot) or extremely inaccurate (radioactive decay). In the last case, the pacemaker is as bad as it can be because the receipt of a pulse gives us absolutely no clue as to how long it has been since the last pulse. Strangely enough, as long as the transition probability does not change, this can still constitute part of an accurate clock: If we count enough pulses, the randomness will average out. Let us measure relative accuracy as the coefficient of variation—the standard deviation of the time at which the nth pulse is recorded divided by the mean of that time. For a Poisson process, the time of entry into the nth state has a mean of $\mu = (n + 1)\tau$, and a standard deviation of $\sigma = \sqrt{n + 1}\,\tau$ giving it a coefficient of variation of $1/\sqrt{n + 1}$. In timing an interval t, we can thus arbitrarily increase accuracy by increasing n (while decreasing τ to keep the mean constant).

The above analyses assumes that the counter is perfect. But what about a Poisson process in which the counter misses a proportion p of the counts? Or a clock in which the pacemaker is moderately accurate? Or an organism that emits the same measured response in two or more consecutive states? These scenarios are treated in Killeen and Fetterman (1988) and Killeen and Weiss (1987). When more than a few pulses are involved, the central limit theorem tells us that the normal distribution will provide a good approximation to the time at which the nth pulse is counted. If the animal enters the jth state upon receipt of the nth pulse, and does not exit until m additional pulses are registered, then the difference of two normal distributions will provide a good approximation to the probability of being in the jth state at any time t:

$$p(N(t) = j) \cong \Phi\{\mu_1, \sigma_1\} - \Phi\{\mu_2, \sigma_2\}, \qquad (6)$$

where Φ is the cumulative normal distribution. If these transitions are strictly Poisson, then $\mu_1 = n\tau$, $\mu_2 = (n + m)\tau$, $\sigma_1 = \sqrt{n}\tau$, and $\sigma_2 = \sqrt{n + m}\,\tau$ (Fetterman & Killeen, 1991).

Gibbon and Church (1990) recently reported correlations between the time at which responding starts and the time it stops, and between the time it starts and the duration of responding. The former are positive, consistent with any renewal system such as the Poisson process. The latter are negative, which is inconsistent with models based on simple renewal processes. But the measured periods of responding are not perfect indicators of presence in the state. If there is some random lag between receipt of a pulse and the onset of the state-appropriate responding, and some lag between the receipt of the next pulse and the end of responding, we could obtain just the pattern that was observed (Wing & Kristofferson, 1973), with the size of the correlations depending on the relative contributions from pacemaker variance and lag variance. Once again, the difference of two normal distributions would give the psychometric functions, although the parameters would be interpreted differently.

B. SCALAR TIMING

The judgment of time, like most judgments, is relative: Absolute accuracy decreases with the magnitude of the thing judged, but relative accuracy (measured, for example by the coefficient of variation) is often approximately constant over considerable ranges. This observation is known as *Weber's law*; applied to temporal judgments it is called *scalar timing* (Gibbon, 1977). A linear relation between variance (σ^2) and the square of the stimulus magnitude (t) is called a *generalized Weber's law*:

$$\sigma_\tau^2 = (\gamma_2 t)^2 + \gamma_0, \qquad (7)$$

with the coefficient γ_2 being called the *Weber fraction*. If γ_0 is 0.0, then γ_2 is also the coefficient of variation.

Given the many species of clocks that might underlie time perception in animals, uniformities such as scalar timing are welcome because they constrain the relevant models to a subset of the possibilities. These constraints were explored in different manners by Gibbon and Church (1981b, 1984; 1990) and Killeen and Weiss (1987). For Gibbon, scalar timing ruled out a Poisson process because, as we have seen, its coefficient of variation decreases with n, whereas the hallmark of scalar timing is a constant coefficient of variation. Gibbon (1977, 1986) formulated a seminal model of timing called *scalar expectancy theory* (SET) to explain both scalar timing and other regularities in behavior, such as the time course of adjunctive behaviors pictured in the above figures. The heart of his model was an accurate pacemaker, but one whose period (τ) varies from one interval to the next (Gibbon, Church, & Meck, 1984). If τ is normally distributed with variance σ_τ^2, then the estimates of an interval t will be normally distributed with a standard deviation of $t\sigma_\tau/\tau$ and thus have a constant coefficient of variation of σ_τ/τ. There are also other sources of variance in the model, such as encoding and retrieval of a comparison interval from memory, which are often (but not necessarily) scalar in nature.

Unlike Gibbon, Killeen and Weiss (1987) presumed that the speed of the pacemaker might be varied (or, equivalently, the subject could select among pacemakers of different characteristic periods). But the counter was allowed to be fallible, and to optimize accuracy subjects should choose a clock speed that would balance pacemaker error against counter error. Although the precise general solution is somewhat opaque, many special cases and approximate solutions were derived. For instance, under most conditions the asymptotic error in pacemaker-counter systems becomes independent of the characteristics of the pacemaker; at large values of t, the overall Weber fraction for time will be the Weber fraction for the counter component, with the contribution of the pacemaker becoming negligible.

If the speed of the pacemaker may vary, the Poisson process is no longer ruled out as a model of animal's behavior in time. This is reassuring because, as Fig. 4 shows, it [i.e., Eq. (4)] seems to describe the data very well. In particular, if the period of the pacemaker is proportional to the interval between reinforcements, $\tau = kt_R$, then the coefficient of variation, $1/\sqrt{n+1}$, will remain constant despite changes in interval length. Figure 5 shows that the values of τ required to fit Eq. (4) to various data were indeed proportional to t_R, with $k = 0.28$. Thus we have a Poisson model of

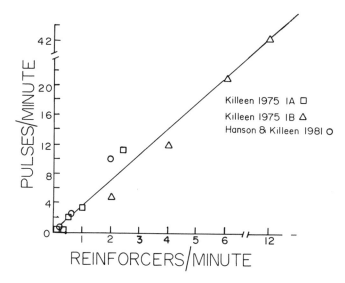

Fig. 5. Inferred rate of the pacemaker as a function of the rate of reinforcement. The regression has a slope of 3.6 pulses per reinforcer. From Killeen and Fetterman (*Psychological Review, 95,* 274–295). Copyright © 1988 by the American Psychological Association. Reprinted by permission of the publisher.

adjunctive behavior (and also of "operant" behavior such as key pecking) that generates scalar timing.

If the normal distributions fit to terminal behaviors such as key pecking and lever pressing do in fact derive from a Poisson process, it is straightforward to estimate the number of pulses from the coefficient of variation. Published Weber fractions (Lejeune & Wearden, 1991) suggest that 3 or 4 is typical for pigeons, 8 or 10 for rats. We expect—and find—fewer inferred interim states for cold-blooded animals and more for animals such as cats, monkeys, and humans.

III. Retrospective Timing

A. Temporal Discriminations

So far, we have analyzed behavior as it evolved over time and characterized the nature of that evolution. Next we ask animals to tell us about temporal intervals. Clearly, what animals can describe may be more or less than what they are affected by. This is the case, for instance, when they describe whether or not they caused the delivery of a reinforcer; increasing the amount of reinforcement simultaneously increases the likelihood that they will work to get it and decreases their ability to say that their behavior brought it about (Killeen & Smith, 1984). We may ask animals to tell us how much time has elapsed since the onset of a stimulus by turning the stimulus off and asking them to respond "long" or "short" by closing one of two switches. We may train them by habitually rewarding them for a "short" response when the stimulus was extinguished at t_1, and rewarding them for a "long" response when the stimulus was extinguished at t_2. We then reinforce them probabilistically, and on unrewarded trials probe their accuracy at other values of t. Numerous studies have found that the resulting psychometric functions resemble cumulative normal distributions (Church & Gibbon, 1982; Dreyfus, Fetterman, Smith, & Stubbs, 1988). Another ubiquitous feature of such discriminations is that the point of subjective equality (PSE)—the point at which the probability of both responses is equal—often falls near the geometric mean of the training stimuli.

How do animals make these discriminations? SET suggests that they consult an internal clock at time t, and take the difference of its reading from the value of t_1, and the difference from t_2, and respond short whenever the former is less than the latter (Gibbon, 1981a). Killeen and Fetterman's (1988) behavioral theory of timing (BeT) suggests that the animal learns that if the question is posed when one adjunctive behavior is under way, say, looking in the corner, a response to the left switch brings food; if the question is posed when another adjunctive behavior is under way, say, it is pacing the front wall, a response to the right switch brings food. This is a rather unsophisticated mechanism, one that we posited because of its transparent parsimony; it should be easily tested and cleared out of the way if inadequate.

How could we test this hypothesis? We could develop the model to see if it would account for known regularities in behavior. It did so successfully, predicting indifference at the geometric mean and several other effects. We could disrupt the adjunctive behaviors or confine animals in small enclosures where their execution would be cramped. Such restrictions should disrupt behaviorally mediated timing, but not cognitively mediated timing. However, it is already known that such restrictions do undermine timing accuracy (e.g., Frank & Staddon, 1974). Other restriction experiments have not always shown the disruption (McIntire, Lundervold, Calmes, Jones, & Allard, 1983; Richelle & Lejeune, 1980), but they used relatively unsalient or unmemorable events, such as a previous response, to mark the start of the interval. Such weak cues may not zero the counter (see, e.g., Staddon, 1974), thus accounting for the historically poor performance of animals on such tasks and the lack of restriction effects.

We could see if the presence or speed of stereotyped responses were correlated with accuracy; again, there were published reports suggesting this to be the case ("The rhythmic, stereotyped behavior of the two subjects with better [temporal] discrimination was more rapid that that of the subject with poor discrimination"; Church, Getty, & Lerner, 1976, p. 310). We could see if systematic observation of subjects in retrospective timing experiments would reveal a pattern of adjunctive behaviors that might subserve the discriminations. Figure 6 shows that this is the case.

B. PACEMAKER SPEED

Another line of attack on the assumptions underlying BeT concerns the speed of the pacemaker; if that could be manipulated independently of the interval to be timed, we would expect to see systematic shifts in the psychometric functions. But how can the pacemaker speed be manipulated? Drugs will do it (e.g., Meck, 1983), but they do not get at the issues that might distinguish SET from BeT. The same is true for circadian rhythmicity (Shurtleff, Raslear, & Simmons, 1990) and stimulus intensity (Wilkie, 1987). Figure 5 suggests another answer. If the speed of the pacemaker is related to the rate of reinforcement, we might attempt to manipulate that independently of the interval to be timed. Of course, we do not know beforehand whether the context that affects the clock speed is confined to the intervals being timed or if it extends to a larger context, such as the intertrial interval. Killeen and Fetterman (1988) reviewed several experiments where differences in interval length, rate of reinforcement, and intertrial interval were correlated with the predicted differences in accuracy and bias. Fetterman and Killeen (1991) explored a variety of ways to manipulate the speed of the pacemaker. They found little or no lasting effect on the PSEs, and manipulation of the intertrial interval gave mixed results. Over all of the experiments, however, they did find the predicted effect on the slope of the psychometric functions: Manipulations that increased the density of reinforcement steepened the gradients, and manipulations that decreased the density of reinforcement flattened the gradients. The regression relating clock speed to density of reinforcement had the same slope as that shown in Fig. 5, namely, 3.6 pulses per reinforcer.

One nice picture of such effects comes from an unpublished study by Fetterman, in which food was probabilistically available for pecks to a left key at 8 sec after the start of the trial, to a center key at 16 sec and to a right

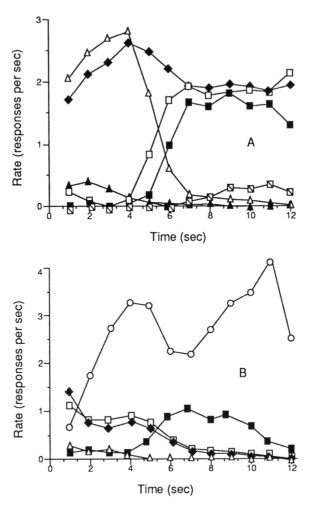

Fig. 6.   Rate of various adjunctive behaviors as a function of the time through the longer of two intervals (4 sec and 12 sec) that four pigeons were trained to discriminate. The behaviors were: neck extension (9), general pecking (10), crouching (11), walking (12), turning the head (13), raising the claw (14), wing flaps (15), and preening (16). From Fetterman and Killeen (1991); reprinted by permission of Academic Press.

key at 32 sec. He obtained smooth gradients of responding on the keys (see Fig. 7, filled symbols). The continuous curves through the baseline data come from Eq. (6) with $\tau = 0.50$ sec, and $n = m = 22$. Note that the coefficients of variation of these distributions (0.21 and 0.15) decrease with t. SET predicts a constant coefficient of variation, whereas BeT predicts

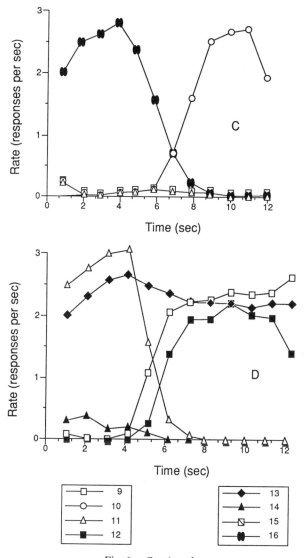

Fig. 6. *Continued.*

the obtained decrease because the value of τ is fixed by the density of reinforcement in the context, and different intervals can be discriminated only by differences in the correlated number of counts.

Next, Fetterman switched the pigeons to a partial reinforcement schedule, so that only 75% of the trials, rather than 100%, contained reinforce-

Peter R. Killeen

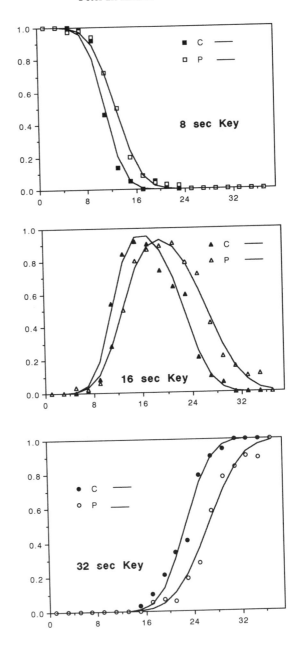

ment. If clock speed is driven by rate of reinforcement, we should see a slowing of the clock and a shift of the distributions to the right, along with an increase in their variance. The unfilled symbols in Fig. 7 show that this happened. Clearly, when the density of reinforcement is decreased, the speed of the pacemaker also decreases. When he returned the animals to 100%, the curves shifted back to their original positions. Because the average time between reinforcers was increased by one-third in the experimental condition, we expect a proportional increase in τ, and find it: The obtained value increased from .5 to .68. In the partial reinforcement condition the coefficients of variation again decreased with t as predicted (.22 and .16).

This experiment, along with the others cited above, reinforces the following predictions of BeT: Scalar timing between experimental conditions where the interval to be timed strongly determines the density of reinforcement (and thus τ); Poisson-type timing of intervals within the same experimental context; and covariation of the pacemaker speed with density of reinforcement. Some effects, such as shifts in the PSE, are transient; we believe that the behavior that serves as the most accurate cue for choosing "short" or "long" is quickly reconditioned (e.g., if the pacemaker is speeded, the animal will come to rely on the $N + 1$st or $N + 2$nd adjunctive state, rather than the Nth, as the critical cue).

The difference of two normal distributions provides an excellent fit to many of the timing data. But because the normal distribution is the limit to all renewal processes (of which pacemaker-counter systems are one instantiation, and the Poisson process a subset of that), this fact alone tells us little about the underlying mechanisms. But data such as Fetterman's suggest that the mechanism cannot always be a simple Poisson process. For one thing, to fit those data required very large values for n (22 and 44) and correspondingly small values for τ. For another, the animals spent much of this time engaged in pecking the keys, so it is unlikely that they were moving between adjunctive states in the same manner as the animals shown in Fig. 1. These data may tell us that the animals were merely

---

Fig. 7. Probability of pecking the left, center, or right key as a function of time through the interval. The pigeon was reinforced one-third of the time for the first peck on the left key after 8 sec, one-third of the time for the first peck on the center key after 16 sec, and one-third of the time for the first peck on the right key after 32 sec (filled symbols). In another condition, the overall probability of reinforcement on any trial was reduced to 75% (unfilled symbols). As predicted, the functions shift to the right under the partial reinforcement condition, presumably because of the slowing of the pacemaker. The functions shifted back to their original locations upon return to continual reinforcement. The curves through the data are given by Eq. (6). These data, and others showing the same effect, were collected by J. G. Fetterman, and are used with his permission.

counting (with less than perfect accuracy) key pecks whose emission occurred with more than Poisson regularity. Experimental analysis of such a possibility is provided by Fetterman, Stubbs, and MacEwen (in press). In general, large count numbers are an indication that some other renewal process, one whose variance does not depend so strongly on τ as does the Poisson (where $\sigma = \tau$), is operative in that situation.

C. Factors Affecting the Selection of a Pacemaker

We have assumed that animals are opportunistic about the cues they use to time an interval; when gross adjunctive behaviors loom as the most salient events, they will be chosen; but if the rate or scheduling of reinforcement locks the animal into one adjunctive state during the intervals to be discriminated, it must rely on topographies of behaviors occurring within that state. Some of these behaviors, such as pacing the front wall, or pecking the keys, may be much more regular than the Poisson pacemaker that governs transitions between adjunctive states. Killeen and Fetterman posited one such mechanism, a random oscillation across the front of the cage, to account for the accurate pair-comparison temporal discriminations published by Fetterman and Dreyfus (1986). This model is essentially a clock with a perfect pacemaker and Bernoulli variability in the counter. It is not unlikely that such pacemakers will also change their speed as incentive variables are manipulated. Whether they will generally vary with arousal in the same manner as adjunctive behaviors is not yet known.

We may then envisage a host of behaviors, ranging from the gross regularities of transitions between adjunctive states, the finer regularities of behaviors within states (e.g., pacing or pecking the front wall), to the precise progression of a single movement. As the scale gets finer, potential accuracy increases, but at the same time the number of events that must be counted increases, decreasing the likelihood that any one count will be regularly paired with reinforcement. If compound discriminations are possible (e.g., the third movement of the second state), accuracy will be enhanced, although Poisson progression between states puts a limit on accuracy for all but the first state. Taking a similar approach, Church and Broadbent (1990) have designed a neural model wherein the progression between states is strictly periodic and the complex of activated neurons at the end of the interval becomes conditioned to the correct response. Similarly, Grossberg and Schmajuk (1989) have constructed a neural model in which a spectrum of neurons, each with different time constants, are activated and selected among by the act of reinforcement.

When humans time intervals, they will often employ as the pacemaker regular movements of the foot, finger, or tongue (counting "one thousand one, one thousand two,'' and so on). When such movements are denied them, accuracy plummets and the task becomes aversive. The variance of such pacemakers may be less dependent on their period than is the case for a Poisson system but, even so, there are other factors that encourage fast pacemakers. The timing of events whose duration is on the same order as the period is inaccurate because of the difficulty of locating the precise point within the period at which an event times out. If no discrimination is possible in the period between the counts, even with a perfectly regular pacemaker accuracy is limited to the variance of a rectangular distribution with a width equal to the period $\tau^2/12$. As a case in point, Kristofferson's (1984) model for well-practiced subjects is equivalent to a pacemaker-counter system with no error in either the pacemaker or counter, but with a synchronization error at the start of the interval and a truncation error at the end, both contributing $\tau^2/12$ to the variance. Thus, there is pressure to select a fast pacemaker, especially when discriminating short intervals. Against this is the increasing error introduced by the counter, especially for fast pacemakers and long intervals (Fetterman & Killeen, 1990); observers balance these factors, by intuition or by conditioning, to choose some more or less optimal period for the pacemaker. The utility of conventionalized units such as seconds and minutes will tend to drive the compromise to be a submultiple of some standard unit. Thus we learn to tune our articulations during ''one-thousand-one'' so that each syllable requires as close to 0.25 sec as we can manage.

The uses to which temporal estimates will be put also determine the units. Very large numbers are intuitively useless, so we seldom count the number of seconds before Christmas. Counting the number of days before Christmas is common, but even more useful for some is the number of shopping days before Christmas. In general, it is not uncommon to disconnect the counter from the pacemaker over weekends and promise deliveries only within a certain number of working days of submission. Rats are no less flexible in their treatment of time (S. Roberts & Church, 1978). In all of these cases, we find a pragmatic opportunism about time; that beneath the flux of events around which we organize our behaviors there may flow some inexorable Newtonian time is as relevant to our everyday lives as the curvature of space and the twelve dimensions that compose it.

IV. Prospective Timing

I have argued that the judgment of time past is mediated by discrimination of recurrent events that are correlated with reinforcement. These events may be chimes of a grandfather clock or regularities in the subject's own

behavior. How do organisms discriminate between forthcoming time intervals? The easiest way to ask the question is to mark the end of the intervals
with rewards, presume that the organism will be more strongly reinforced
for choosing the sooner, and thus choose the sooner more often. When we
can detect a just-noticeable difference in an organism's preference, we can
infer a just-noticeable difference in the organism's perception of the time
intervals associated with each choice.

A. STATE REINFORCEMENT MODEL

The law of effect holds that when a response is followed by reinforcement,
it will increase in frequency. Not *that* particular response, of course,
because *it* is history; it is the predisposition to emit responses of the same
class that is increased. What places them in the same class is their surgence
as a terminal behavior along with their ability to be fine-tuned by their
contingent relation to reinforcement. Interim and terminal behavioral
"states" are periods of time during which a particular class of behavior is
predominant. The animal may be predisposed to such behaviors even if
they are not physically possible at the time. For instance, periodic feeding
of a rat will, over the course of a dozen sessions, lead to the consumption
of large amounts of water. It is reasonable to suspect a predisposition to
drink on intervals when water is not made available. It is our hypothesis
that when a pigeon has emitted a response such as pecking a red key, it
may remain in the relevant state for some time, whether or not the red key
is still available for pecking. If these particular terminal states of pecking
one key color or another act like other adjunctive states, there is a constant
probability of exiting from them; the probability of being in the peck-the-
red-key state after a delay of t sec (given that the animal was in the state at
$t = 0$, when it last pecked) is simply:

$$p[(N(t) = n)|(N(t_0) = n)] = e^{-t/\tau} \equiv S_P(t). \tag{8}$$

If reinforcement occurs at a time when the animal is still in that state,
that class of responses will be strengthened, but not otherwise. Equation
(8) is a "delay of reinforcement gradient." Historically it has been interpreted as the continuous decrease in the strengthening of a class of responses as a reward is delayed from an instance of that class. That
strengthening by primary reinforcement $S_P(t)$ was presumed to be operative with each (delayed) pairing. Here, however, it is interpreted as a
probabilistic reinforcement of a predisposition to repond. Contingencies
that force the animal out of this "retrospective"state undermine the
strengthening and bias the organism away from that schedule (Moore &

Fantino, 1975). Operations that forestall its decay enhance the effectiveness of a delayed reinforcer (Lett, 1975; Liberman, Davidson, & Thomas, 1985).

All of these effects will be buffered by the presence of conditioned reinforcers. Usually a response initiates not only a delay, but also a correlated stimulus change; if the situation is repeated, the stimulus inevitably becomes a conditioned reinforcer. Although the stimulus change always catches the animal in the "correct" response state, it is less potent than a primary reinforcer, and its potency decreases as the characteristic delay increases. For simplicity, I have assumed that conditioned reinforcement strength is proportional to the rate of reinforcement that is signals ($1/t$) (Killeen, 1982a). The ability of a delayed reinforcer to strengthen behavior will further depend on the frequency (r) with which it is paired with the behavior. If we denote the average interval between reinforcers as T, then $r = 1/T$, and:

$$S(t) = r(e^{-t/\tau} + 1/t). \qquad (9)$$

This equation constituted the key part of a model for choice between delayed reinforcers (Killeen, 1982b) in which the primary reinforcement gradient, Eq. (8), was derived, not as the transition out of a state, but rather as the blocking of the effects of the reinforcer on the choice response by intervening responses. The model provided an accurate summary of the existing data (see Fig. 8), with a value of $\tau = 8$ sec adequate for many of the studies analyzed.

But whichever way Eq. (8) is modeled with words (blocking, or exit from a response state), we should not expect its time constant to remain invariant over various experimental manipulations. In particular, if the animal's transition out of terminal states is akin to its progress through other adjunctive states, τ should be proportional to T (Fig. 3). If we force this relation to hold, employing the slope of the line in Fig. 3 as the constant of proportionality ($\tau = 0.28T$), the fit of the model to the data improves slightly.

A more important advantage of this modification of the model is that it clarifies its relation to another model of the same phenomena, Fantino's delay reduction theory (1981). A power series expansion of the exponential term in Eq. (9) reduces it to Fantino's model (Killeen & Fantino, 1990), without the conditioned reinforcement term. The conditioned reinforcement (reciprocal) and primary reinforcement (exponential) decay terms are sufficiently similar that the presence or absence of the former has little effect on predictions for the traditional paradigms. However, when conditioned reinforcers are differentially introduced or removed for one of the

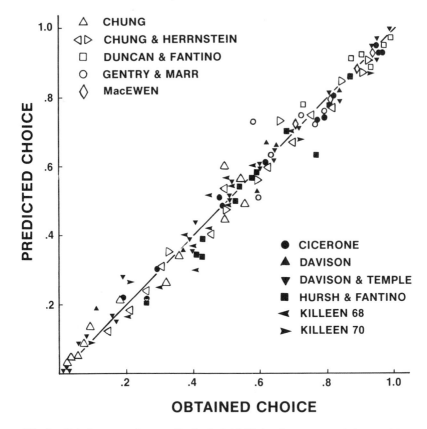

Fig. 8.   Relative rates of responding in the initial links of concurrent chain schedules as a function of the relative rates predicted by the relative values of Eq. (9). For the filled symbols, $\tau = 8$ sec and there was no bias. For the open symbols, either τ took a different value or a multiplicative bias parameter was set different from 1.0. From Killeen (1982c); reprinted by permission of Elsevier Science Publishers.

alternatives, there can be substantial effects on choice, indicating the importance of including that term in the general model.

A different power series expansion of the exponential term generates a model equivalent to Mazur's (1984) equivalence rule for indifference, except that Mazur's rule does not have a separate term for conditioned reinforcement, nor does it multiply the sum of primary and secondary reinforcement strength by overall rates of reinforcement (r). Mazur's is a model of discrete-trial choice experiments, where overall rates of reinforcement are apparently not so important in controlling indifference points. It may be that the parenthetical term of Eq. (9) measures the strength of reinforcement in both cases, but that the mechanism of rein-forcement in concurrent chain schedules is to strengthen switching be-tween the schedules. If this is the case, the factor r in Eq. (9) may represent the probability of reinforcement for switching.

Equation (9) was developed to map various manipulations, such as delaying the onset of the terminal link cues, delivering multiple reinforcers during the terminal links, and varying the magnitude of the reinforcer (Killeen, 1982b). It is closely tied to other models of choice behavior (e.g., McDowell & Kessel, 1979; Myerson, 1990), with the affinity based on their concern with directed arousal. In the avatar of delay reduction theory, it encompasses numerous other phenomena. It provides a generally accurate picture of prospective timing, failing only when one of the initial links of a concurrent chain schedule is very short, and in the "time-left" paradigm of Gibbon and Church (1981). Although Eq. (9) was developed in the context of relative strength models of timing, I look forward to its eventual integra-tion with dynamic models of choice, such as Myerson's kinetic model (Luco, 1990; Myerson & Hale, 1988).

B. CAUSAL ATTRIBUTIONS

The state reinforcement model is conceptually very different from the more traditional strength model: In the first, the response receives full strengthening if the animal is in the appropriate state, and not otherwise; in the latter, the response is always fractionally strengthened. How do we know if an animal is in one state or another? One way is to ask him. Consider an experiment in which a pigeon pecks a white key causing it to go off, and t sec later we present reinforcement. If the above analysis is correct, the probability that the delayed reinforcer will strengthen the key peck will be given by Eq. (8). But now, instead of reinforcing the pigeon at time t, let us ask it whether it thinks its key peck turned off the key light. If the state analysis is correct, we expect the same function to govern the probability of saying yes. However, unless we give the animal a reason for saying no, we should not be too surprised to find that instead it always said yes, or perhaps responded randomly. So now consider an experiment in which we turn off the key at equal rates after key pecks and at random times (i.e., independently of any measured behavior), and we ask the animal whether the peck caused the light to go out. We reinforce it when it is correct and measure accuracy with a nonparametric signal detection index such a A' (Grier, 1971). Figure 9 shows the answers we get. The open squares show the decrease in accuracy as a function of the time since the offset of the keylight. The dashed line is an exponential decay function with an intercept of $A'_{t=0} = .89$, corrected for guessing (i.e., with an

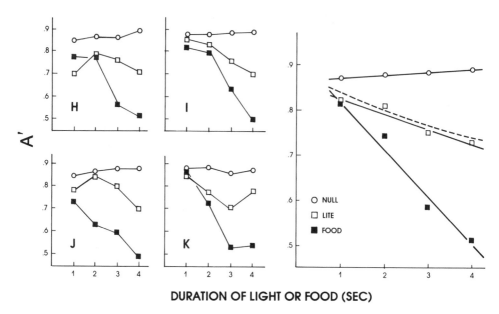

Fig. 9. Accuracy of four pigeons in reporting the agent of different events: illumination of the hopper light (*lite*), delivery of food (*food*), or direct transition to the choice keys (*null*). The panels on the left show individual performances, that on the right average performance. Continuous lines are regressions; dashed line is Eq. (8), with an intercept of $A' = 0.89$, an asymptote at chance ($A' = 0.50$), and a time constant of $\tau = 8$ sec. From Killeen and Smith (*Journal of Experimental Psychology, 10*, 333–345). Copyright © 1984 by the American Psychological Association. Reprinted by permission of the publisher.

asymptote of .50). Its time constant is the familiar $\tau = 8$ sec, thus affirming our hypothesis that memory for an event decays at the same rate as the primary reinforcement gradient, and that the latter might merely be a different name for the former.

What if the interval after key offset is filled with other events? For the data shown, the hopper aperture was lit during the interval. The purpose of this was to pull the pigeon away from the key and disrupt simple postural mediation. In another condition we reinforced the pigeon with food for turning the key off, and then asked the pigeon whether it caused the reinforcement or whether reinforcement was independent of its peck. The filled squares show the accuracy of those discriminations. The animals are clearly able to discriminate whether they caused the delivery of food, but their accuracy falls off at a very fast rate, reaching chance after 4 or 5 sec. [Part of the reason for the rapidly decreasing marginal utility of longer durations of reinforcers may be this inability to allocate credit for the last moments of them to the appropriate behavior (Killeen, 1985)].

Figure 9 shows how accuracy of causal attribution decays as a function of time and provides some support for our hypothesis that reinforcement acts by catching animals in the state they were in when they made the targeted response. How do animals attain such accuracy to start with? There are several possibilities, but perhaps the simplest is, once again, a temporal discrimination—in this case, between the response and the darkening of the keylight. Figure 10 shows pigeons' performance in experiments that varied bias by manipulating the delay (left panel) and the amount (right panel) of reinforcement, plotted in traditional signal detection coordinates. Figure 11 shows the probability of saying "*I caused it*" recorded as a function of the time between the key peck and the offset of the keylight. The data from the delay experiment, fall along four parallel curves whose parameter gives the ratio of delays for the two responses. The filled symbols are correct hits, the remaining symbols incorrect false alarms. Clearly, the propensity to attribute an event to a previous response depends on both the delay since the response and the relative expected value for each attribution. The curves in Fig. 10 come from a parameter-free model based on the delays between responses and the stimulus changes when they are caused by the pigeon, vs. those delays when they are not contingent on the pigeons' behavior. The curves are traced out by varying a motivational parameter over the range 0–∞. The curves in Fig. 11 derive the values of the motivational parameter from Eq. (9).

These experiments show us that the time between a response and subsequent event strongly predicts whether animals will attribute the event to their own behavior. The attributions become less accurate as time passes after the event, especially if that time is filled with a highly arousing activity such as eating. The initial temporal discrimination is quite accurate—when the delay between a peck and a stimulus is reduced to 20 msec, pigeons can reliably discriminate that from a 60-msec delay (Killeen & Smith, 1984). This means that they can move from one response state to another quickly when that is required by the contingencies of reinforcement. In the current experiment that might entail a transition as simple as *Peck the key and move your head fast; if you're still in front of the key when it goes off, presume you caused it.*

The above discussion should not be interpreted as suggesting that learning is *mediated by* a causal ascription. The argument is simpler than that: It takes learning to be *tantamount* to a causal ascription, one that might be construed by an experimenter who suitably questions the organism. The course of learning is affected by all of the factors that philosophers hold relevant to causal inference—temporal and spatial contiguity, precedence, correlation, diffusion of control in earlier links of a chain,

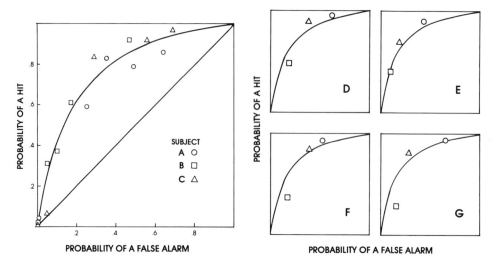

Fig. 10.   Probability of pigeons' correctly attributing a change in the keylights to their own agency (*Hit*) as a function of attributing a computer-initiated event to their own agency (*False Alarm*). The bias in reporting was manipulated by varying the delay between an attribution and food over the range 1.0–2.5 sec (left panel), and by manipulating the amount of food received for a correct response over the range 1.0–4.0 sec (right panel). From Killeen and Smith (*Journal of Experimental Psychology, 10*, 333–345). Copyright © 1984 by the American Psychological Association. Reprinted by permission of the publisher.

ascriptions when events are surprising, blocking in the presence of correlated antecedents, and "interventionist" manipulations (Killeen, 1981b).
Contingencies of reinforcement constitute signals embedded in a background of noise; it is the animals' task to discriminate which response will
hasten the reinforcement—to accurately allocate credit for the reward to
the appropriate part of its repertoire. Optimal values of the above factors,
including appropriate values for τ, speed the discrimination and, *pari
passu*, constitute the optimal conditions for learning.

V.   Time Horizons

When an organism is presented with intervals of several minutes and then
asked whether a short or a long time has elapsed, the units of the response
may be on the order of dozens of seconds; when much finer discriminations of briefer intervals are called for, as in the allocation-of-credit problem described above, the units are on the order of dozens of milliseconds.

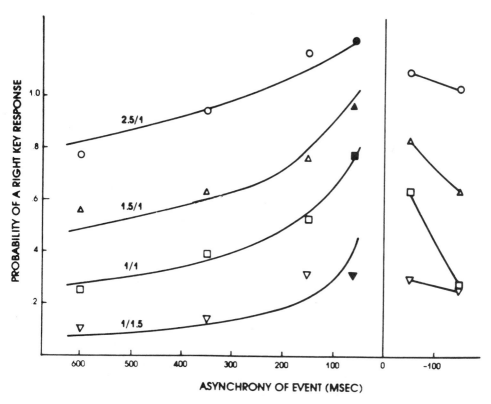

Fig. 11.   Probability of pigeons' responding on the right ("*I caused it*") key as a function of the asynchrony between a center key peck and the onset of the side key lights. Filled symbols represent *Hits*, unfilled symbols *False Alarms*. The paramteres signify the delay of reinforcement for correct responses. For clarity, each curve and its associated data are elevated 10 points above the one below it. Negative asynchronies indicate that a center key peck occurred after the side key lights had been turned on. Data are averaged over the three subjects shown in the left panel of Fig. 10. From Killeen and Smith (*Journal of Experimental Psychology, 10,* 333–345). Copyright © 1984 by the American Psychological Association. Reprinted by permission of the publisher.

Optimal values for the clock speed (or choices of clocks with optimal speed) have presumably been shaped by evolutionary pressure. Accurate causal ascriptions require very fast clocks to guide the learning of movements while retrospective judgments of time spent in a locale, which may subserve the optimization of foraging strategies, tolerate cruder measurement. Indeed, the cruder measurement is functional, as it entails a longer time-base over which the stochastic irregularities of the environment may be averaged.

There are many ways that an organism might average past events, but one of the simplest is the linear operator:

$$A_{n+1} = \beta x + (1 - \beta)A_n, \tag{10}$$

where A_{n+1} is the current average, A_n is the previous average, β is a "currency parameter," $0 < \beta < 1$, and x the new input (Killeen, 1981a). A new average is struck by iterating Eq. (10), decreasing the weight given to past events geometrically as the most recent event is entered with a weight of β. For values of β near 1 most weight is given to recent events, and the decay is very steep; for smaller values of β more weight is given to the previous history of reinforcement and the decay is more gradual. If following a period of reinforcement an animal is put into extinction, successive values of A should approximate an exponential decay function [Eq. (8)]. I have used such an *exponentially weighted moving average* (EWMA) model to describe the cumulative energization of behavior by recurrent rewards (Killeen, 1979, 1982a; Killeen, Hanson, & Osborne, 1978).

No matter what the value of β, A will be an unbiased estimator of the mean of x, μ. McNamara and Houston (1985; 1987b) showed that A contains all of the relevant information about x, and "any efficient decision-making process should be based on it." Furthermore, they showed that the weight given to past events should depend on the rate at which the environment changes. In a rapidly changing environment, the currency parameter should increase or equivalently, the animal should sample more frequently. Let reinforcements be scheduled randomly in time at intervals averaging μ, with x representing the most recently experienced interval, A the organism's estimate of μ, and β the currency parameter. Then, if rate of reinforcement is doubled, either β should increase or the organism should sample twice as often. (This is not required in order that A approach μ, which is guaranteed to happen for any β; it is required for the organism to optimally blend current with historical information.) This may be accomplished automatically if the animal strikes a new average in step with the delivery of a reinforcer, e.g., if Eq. (10) is iterated with every tick of a clock, whose speed is in turn regulated by the frequency of reinforcement (as in Fig. 5), or perhaps by the value of A itself. Although the dynamics of such a system are not necessarily simple, the basic implication— exponential approach to asymptote with rate of approach proportional to rate of reinforcement—is central to several successful models of behavior (Myerson & Miezin, 1980; Staddon & Horner, 1989). Analysis of foraging experiments shows that adjustment of β (or, equivalently, changing the rate at which an average is recalculated) is necessary to capture the behavior of organisms (Dow & Lea, 1987; Kacelnik, Krebs & Ens, 1987).

Furthermore, it is clear that updating of the average cannot occur only upon receipt of reinforcement, as then organisms would be unable to adapt to experimental extinction. Updating *must* either be continuous (and then lose the valuable feature of synchronization to the rate of reinforcement) or synchronized to the ticks of an endogenous clock calibrated to the expected time between reinforcers. In the past I have thought of the value of β as being adjusted as a function of the rate of reinforcement; however, it seems more parsimonious to expect the value of β to remain relatively constant at some base value, with the rate of iteration proportional to the rate of reinforcement. Each tick of the clock will then stimulate both the movement between behavioral states and an updating of the estimated rate of reinforcement in that context.

This adaptive relationship between clock speed and temporal horizons for integrating reinforcement is currently among the least well-understood functions of behavior's time. I now outline implications of this hypothesis for further research, while emphasizing their speculative nature.

VI. Generalizations

A. Extinction

Animals reinforced on only a percentage of the trials during acquisition will often persist longer in extinction than those reinforced on every trial; this is the *partial reinforcement extinction effect* (PREE). Whether or not the PREE is found depends on many factors, including the dependent variable [e.g., whether persistence is measured by the slope of the extinction curve or the number of responses in extinction (Nevin, 1988), by velocity or acceleration in the alley (Killeen & Amsel, 1987), and so on]. The major PRE effect is an immediate consequence of the initially faster clocks of continually reinforced subjects, as is predicted by the adaptive clock model. But there is another theoretical factor that must be part of our models for rates of responding: the accumulation of arousal at rates that depend on both the clock speed and the schedule of reinforcement. Many observed effects may be consequences of interactions of these two processes of adjustment and their starting points. There is a vast literature on this subject, and the attempt to organize it in terms of these two processes is just beginning.

B. Contingencies of Reinforcement

Reinforcement, we have argued, increases the probability of the class of responses of which the reinforced response is a member. It also shapes the characteristics of that class toward the characteristics of the reinforced instance. Thus, if the last response was forceful, or occurred with a short latency, further instances of responses from that class will come to share those properties. But it is not only the most recent response that is affected by reinforcement; clearly, the effect of reinforcement spreads to earlier responses in a sequence, whose characteristics will also be inherited (if to a lesser extent) by future members of that class (Killeen, 1969; Staddon & Zhang, 1989). What is the shape of the organism's window on the past, and how far back does it extend? Knowing that, we could optimally control behavior, neither squandering the extended effects of reinforcement by ignoring the character of earlier behavior that is still under its purview, nor insisting on qualities for earlier parts of a performance that have vanished from the organism's memory. Conversely, evidence that we have optimal control of behavior is evidence that we have defined our contingency window congruent to the animal's own window. In particular, let us reinforce pigeons for responding at a high rate for one week, a low rate for the next, and so on, taking the absolute slope of a linear regression through the resulting learning curves as a measure of how quickly the animal learns. Define our criterion for reinforcement in terms of Eq. (10), with x measuring the most recent interresponse time, and requiring that to be reinforceable, the current value of A must be above the 80th percentile (or below the 20th percentile). Every month select a different value for β. When our window coincides with the animal's window, the slope of the learning curves should be maximal. Figure 12 shows the results of this experiment for four pigeons, whose speed of learning is greatest for β values between .50 and .125.

Do these values for β vary with the rate of reinforcement, as posited above, and interpreted as synchronized updating? What is the relation of these β values to the τ values of prospective timing? Do other discount functions generate sharper optima? These are all questions for future research.

C. COMPETING CONTEXTS

Equation (10), interpreted as an estimate of the value of reinforcement associated with a stimulus, is isomorphic with the familiar Wagner–Rescorla model of associative conditioning (Rescorla & Wagner, 1972). If organisms attend more to stimuli associated with greater value of reinforcement (A), the conditioning process will be autocatalytic, with the more attended features becoming more conditioned, and thus attracting more attention (Frey & Sears, 1978). The background ("contextual, envi-

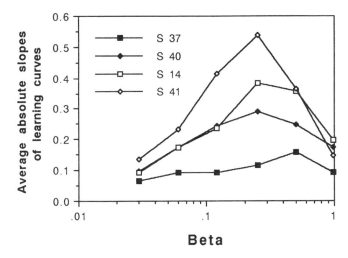

Fig. 12. Tuning curves for reinforcement for four pigeons, two of which (unfilled symbols) received an ascending sequence of values of β and two of which received a descending sequence. Reinforcement was contingent on the interresponse times, averaged using Eq. (10), being in the top 20% (or bottom 20%) of the values from the session as a whole. Linear regressions through the learning curves showed that learning was fastest (i.e., slope was greatest) for certain values of β, ostensibly those values that characterize the pigeon's own window on the past.

ronmental'') stimuli provided by the experimental chamber constitute a relevant and conditionable set of stimuli. Whereas the nature of the context will affect all conditioning processes, including extinction and control by contingency, the following phenomena can only be treated with contextual models.

1. Warm-up

To the extent an animal integrates events before an experimental session into the background rate of reinforcement (i.e., generalizes home cage stimuli to the experimental chamber), it will begin the session with low values for background value, A_B, and thus attend more closely to the trial stimuli. As conditioning proceeds, A_B will be updated and approach the value of the experimental stimuli, and thus compete more effectively with them for attention. Such a mechanism would explain the within-session decrement often found for rats, both in runways and in Skinner boxes. Figure 13 shows average response rates through a session for rats lever-pressing for pellets that they received every 100 sec (Osborne, 1977). The

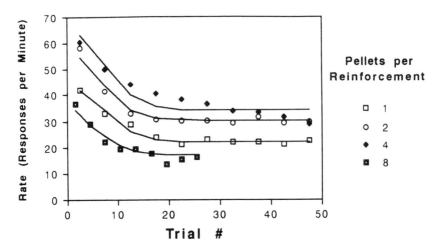

Fig. 13. Response rates for rats reinforced for lever pressing on an intermittent schedule, as a function of the time through the session. The parameter is the number of pellets delivered as reinforcement. Note the decrease in responding through the session. Note also that the decrease is not faster for larger reinforcers, or toward the end of the interval; this rules out satiation as a cause of the decline. Curves are proportional to the rate of reinforcement for lever pressing, relative to that plus the rate of reinforcement associated with the background. The latter is assumed to be low at the start of the session and increase according to Eq. (10) as the session progresses. Data are from Osborne (1977).

smooth curves are proportional to the strength of the lever as a stimulus, relative to the strength of the background plus lever. The strength of the lever stimulus is assumed constant through the session, while that of the background is increased according to Eq. (10). This process—extinction of background cues during the intersession interval, and their reconditioning during the session—may also be responsible for the warm-up normally observed in avoidance conditioning (Killeen, 1979).

2. Sign Tracking

The lower the rate of reinforcement in the chamber, the more readily a conditioned stimulus (CS) will draw the animal's attention away from the background and elicit species-typical responses, such as observation or sign tracking. The central importance of intertrial interval to such conditioning is well known (Gibbon & Balsam, 1981; Jenkins, Barnes, & Barrera, 1981; W. A. Roberts & Kraemer, 1984; Williams, 1982; Wixted, 1989), and consistent with a model for the differential accumulation of

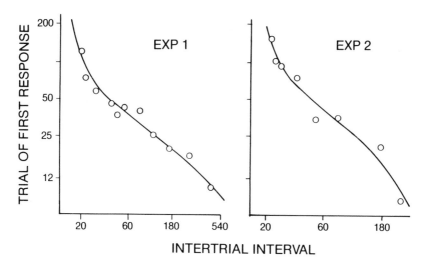

Fig. 14. Trial of the first auto-shaped response as a function of the intertrial interval. The CS was always of 10 sec duration. In Experiment 1 the response key was dark between CS presentations; in Experiment 2 it was lit with a different color. Curves come from a model of accumulation of attention to competing stimuli, the heart of which is Eq. (10). Data are from Terrace, Gibbon, Farrell, and Baldock (1975).

attention to CS and background (Killeen, 1984). That model provides a good account of the data (see, e.g., Fig. 14).

3. Foraging

How long an animal should persist in a patch depends on the quality both of that patch, and of others in the environment. Again, Eq. (10) will provide a mechanism for updating both estimates. When the value of the new patch falls below that of the larger environment, the latter will capture the animal's attention, and if it can, the animal will move on to it (Killeen, 1990). Insofar as A_B is being updated along with the average for the patch, we predict persistence in poor patches somewhat longer than predicted by the marginal value theorem (McNamara & Houston, 1987a), and persistence in rich patches for a somewhat shorter time. With updating yoked to rate of reinforcement, decisions will be made more quickly in a rich environment than in a barren one. Models based on these assumptions have had some success in accounting for foraging data (Kacelnik, et al., 1987).

4. *Contrast*

If the animal cannot immediately move on to a richer patch, response rate in the current patch will decline, a phenomenon called negative contrast. As is the case with the partial-reinforcement effect, there is a large and complex literature on the behavioral contrast, the shift in response rates in a direction opposite to the direction of a change in rate of reinforcement in alternate signalled contexts (Williams, 1988). An account similar to that given for the data of Fig. 14 will work for contrast in rats. More attention, and more species-typical behaviors such as shaped terminal responses (operants) will be directed at stimuli that are associated with greater values of A. When a higher-valued stimulus (CS) is extended in time, the value of the background will approach it, as Eq. (10) is iterated for both stimuli. Thus, long duration CS's should weaken both sign-tracking and contrast, as they do; conversely, long intertrial intervals (ITI's) should enhance both. In contexts or species with fast clocks, contrast should be found at the beginning of the CS, because continued updating will cause the relative values of the CS and background to converge: After rich contexts, the current CS is weak relative to the generalized background cues, yielding negative contrast; the reverse happens after lean contexts. This should be especially true when the CS's are indistinct, as then we may expect more generalized control by the background. But whereas this is true for rats (Williams, 1990) and pigeons (White, 1990), pigeons show in addition anticipatory contrast, increasing their response rate before an inferior component (Williams, 1981), and this is the major source of contrast for that species. McSweeney (1987) has argued that this contrast is due to inhibition by the following reinforcers. It is likely that toward the end of the interval animals search for the alternate response, just as they will readily switch out of one multiple schedule into another if that option is given them, or respond to observe stimuli correlated with the forthcoming context. Toward the end of the component, the animal becomes more highly aroused, and the forthcoming stimulus becomes more attractive and worth looking for (if it is scheduled to be a good one, or less attractive if it is associated with a poor schedule), and these diversions detract from measured response rates (Timberlake, Gawley, & Lucas, 1987). While pigeons are especially likely to make this temporal discrimination of forthcoming rewards, rats are apparently more retrospective creatures, and drag along with them an evaluation of their context based primarily on the past.

In all of these cases, the animal's context is in part defined by memories and expectations—visions of the past and of the future. Conversely, its sense of the past and future is profoundly affected by the rates of reinforcement and punishment within that context. Such dynamically interacting factors contribute to the complexity and adaptiveness of behavior, and to the necessity for couching our analysis in terms of behavior's own time.

VII. Conclusions

Time is a hypothetical construct invoked to help us understand and predict the behavior of events around us. Newton's time is the standard for measurements of the physical world. Its accuracy was increased over the centuries by the development of counters that could accurately keep pace with faster and faster pacemakers. Its utility and replicability has caused us to reify it, treating it as an entity in its own right, rather than as a tally of recurrent events. Other organisms, less needful of a universal time and lacking extremely accurate counters, keep time in a relative manner. Their most salient pacemakers are driven by the rate of reinforcement in their environment, their accuracy is relative to the speed of the pacemaker, and they are opportunistic about their choice of a counter.

The present theory of behavior's time makes the following additional assumptions: Animals switch between behavioral states at the prompting of the pulses from a pacemaker; they evaluate past intervals by noting which behaviors coterminate with them; they select forthcoming intervals as a function of the frequency with which the state of selecting them has been paired with primary reinforcement, and the strength of any immediate conditioned reinforcement for that choice. With each pulse from the pacemaker, animals also update their estimates of the frequency of reinforcement; if they keep separate accounts of these estimates for the context at large and for the experimental stimuli or operanda, then many phenomena such as foraging strategies, warm-up, contrast, and sign tracking fall into place.

Science is different from philosophy because its inferences may be tested and used to improve the theory. The means for such tests are the models that translate the force of the theory to data and measure the reactance of the data to theory. The present theory is grounded by a network of such models, cited throughout the paper. The last section is more speculative, however, and often lacks well-elaborated models; this is where the potential for a broader and more accurate theory now lies. Much work needs to be done to realize that potential. But there will always be time.

ACKNOWLEDGMENT

Preparation of this article was supported in part by NIMH Grant 1 RO1 MH43233.

References

Church, R. M., & Broadbent, H. M. (1990). Alternative representations of time, number and rate. *Cognition, 37*, 55–81.

Church, R. M., Getty, D. J., & Lerner, N. D. (1976). Duration discrimination by rats. *Journal of Experimental Psychology: Animal Behavior Processes, 2*, 303–312.

Church, R. M., & Gibbon, J. (1982). Temporal generalization. *Journal of Experimental Psychology: Animal Behavior Processes, 8*, 165–186.

Cox, D. R., & Miller, H. D. (1965). *The theory of stochastic processes.* New York: Wiley.

Dow, S. M., & Lea, S. E. G. (1987). Foraging in a changing environment: Simulations in the operant laboratory. In M. L. Commons, A. Kacelnik, & S. J. Shettleworth (Eds.), *Quantitative analysis of behavior: Vol. 6. Foraging* (pp. 89–113). Hillsdale, NJ: Erlbaum.

Dreyfus, L. R., Fetterman, J. G., Smith, L. D., & Stubbs, D. A. (1988). Discrimination of temporal relations by pigeons. *Journal of Experimental Psychology: Animal Behavior Processes, 14*, 349–367.

Falk, J. L. (1972). The nature and determinants of adjunctive behavior. In R. M. Gilbert & J. D. Keehn (Eds.), *Schedule effects: Drugs, drinking and aggression.* Toronto: University of Toronto Press.

Fantino, E. (1981). Contiguity, response strength, and the delay reduction hypothesis. In P. Harzem & M. D. Zeiler (Eds.), *Predictability, correlation, and contingency* (pp. 168–201).

Fetterman, J. G., & Dreyfus, L. R. (1986). Pair comparisons of duration. *Behavioural Processes, 12*, 111–123.

Fetterman, J. G., & Killeen, P. R. (1990). A componential analysis of pacemaker-counter timing systems. *Journal of Experimental Psychology: Human Perception and Performance, 16*, 776–780.

Fetterman, J. G., & Killeen, P. R. (1991). Adjusting the pacemaker. *Learning and Motivation, 22*, 226–252.

Fetterman, J. G., Stubbs, D. A., & MacEwen, D. (in press). The perception of the extended stimulus. In W. K. Honig & J. G. Fetterman (Ed.), *Cognitive aspects of stimulus control.* Hillsdale, NJ: Erlbaum.

Frank, J., & Staddon, J. E. R. (1974). Effects of restraint on temporal discrimination behavior. *Journal of the Experimental Analysis of Behavior, 12*, 861–874.

French, A. P., & Kennedy, P. J. (1985). *Niels Bohr: A centenary volume.* Cambridge, MA: Harvard University Press.

Frey, P. W., & Sears, R. J. (1978). Models of conditioning incorporating the Rescorla-Wagner associative axiom, a dynamic attention process, and a catastrophe rule. *Psychological Review, 85*, 321–340.

Gibbon, J. (1977). Scalar expectancy theory and Weber's law in animal timing. *Psychological Review, 84*, 279–325.

Gibbon, J. (1981a). On the form and location of the psychometric bisection function for time. *Journal of Mathematical Psychology, 24*, 58–87.

Gibbon, J. (1981b). Two kinds of ambiguity in the study of time. In M. L. Commons & J. A. Nevin (Eds.), *Quantitative analysis of behavior* (pp. 157–189). Cambridge, MA: Ballinger.

Gibbon, J. (1986). The structure of subjective times: How time flies. In G. H. Bower (Ed.), *The psychology of learning and motivation* (pp. 105–135). Orlando, FL: Academic Press.

Gibbon, J., & Balsam, P. (1981). Spreading association in time. In C. M. Locurto, H. S. Terrace, & J. Gibbon (Eds.), *Autoshaping and conditioning theory* (pp. 219–253). New York: Academic Press.

Gibbon, J., & Church, R. M. (1981). Time left: Linear versus logarithmic subjective timing. *Journal of Experimental Psychology: Animal Behavior Processes, 7,* 87–108.

Gibbon, J., & Church, R. M. (1984). Sources of variance in an information processing theory of timing. In H. L. Roitblatt, T. G. Bever, & H. S. Terrace (Eds.), *Animal Cognition* (pp. 465–488). Hillsdale, NJ: Erlbaum.

Gibbon, J. & Church, R. M. (1990). Representation of time. *Cognition, 37,* 23–54.

Gibbon, J., Church, R. M., & Meck, W. H. (1984). Scalar timing in memory. In J. Gibbon & L. Allan (Eds.), *Timing and time perception* (pp. 52–77). New York: New York Academy of Sciences.

Grier, J. B. (1971). Nonparametric indices for sensitivity and bias: Computing formulas. *Psychological Bulletin, 75,* 424–429.

Grossberg, S., & Schmajuk, N. A. (1989). Neural dynamics of adaptive timing and temporal discrimination during associative learning. *Neural Networks, 2,* 79–102.

Haight, P. A., & Killeen, P. R. (in press). Timing and the organization of adjunctive behavior. *Animal Learning & Behavior.*

Jenkins, H. S., Barnes, R. A., & Barrera, F. J. (1981). Why autoshaping depends on trial spacing. In C. M. Locurto, H. S. Terrace, & J. Gibbon (Eds.), *Autoshaping and conditioning theory* (pp. 255–284). New York: Academic Press.

Kacelnik, A., Krebs, J. R., & Erns, B. (1987). Foraging in a changing environment: An experiment with starlings (*Sturnus vulgaris*). In M. L. Commons, A. Kacelnik, & S. J. Shettleworth (Eds.), *Quantitative analysis of behavior: Vol. 6. Foraging* (pp. 63–87). Hillsdale, NJ: Erlbaum.

Killeen, P. (1969). Reinforcement frequency and contingency as factors in fixed-ratio behavior. *Journal of Experimental Analysis of Behavior, 12,* 391–395.

Killeen, P. (1975). On the temporal control of behavior. *Psychological Review, 82,* 89–115.

Killeen, P. R. (1979). Arousal: Its genesis, modulation, and extinction. In M. D. Zeiler & P. Harzem (Eds.), *Advances in analysis of behavior: Vol. 1. Reinforcement and the organization of behavior* (pp. 31–78). Chichester, England: Wiley.

Killeen, P. R. (1981a). Averaging theory. In C. M. Bradshaw, E. Szabadi, & C. F. Lowe (Eds.), *Recent developments in the quantification of steady-state operant behavior* (pp. 21–34). Amsterdam: Elsevier.

Killeen, P. R. (1981b). Learning as causal inference. In M. Commons & J. A. Nevin (Eds.), *Quantitative studies of behavior* (pp. 289–312). New York: Pergamon.

Killeen, P. R. (1982a). Incentive theory. In D. J. Bernstein (Ed.), *Nebraska Symposium on Motivation, 1981: Response structure and organization* (pp. 169–216). Lincoln: University of Nebraska Press.

Killeen, P. R. (1982b). Incentive theory: II. Models for choice. *Journal of the Experimental Analysis Behavior, 38,* 217–232.

Killeen, P. R. (1982c). A model for concurrent-chain performance. *Behaviour Analysis Letters, 2,* 305–307.

Killeen, P. R. (1984). Incentive theory: III. Adaptive clocks. In J. Gibbon & L. Allen (Eds.), *Timing and time perception* (pp. 515–527). New York: New York Academy of Sciences.

Killeen, P. R. (1985). Incentive theory: IV. Magnitude of reward. *Journal of the Experimental Analysis of Behavior, 43,* 407–417.

Killeen, P. R. (1990). Behavioral Geodesics. In D. S. Levine & J. S. Levin (Eds.), *Motivation, emotion, and goal direction in neural networks* Hillsdale, NJ: Erlbaum.

Killeen, P. R., & Amsel, A. (1987). The kinematics of locomotion toward a goal. *Journal of Experimental Psychology: Animal Behavior Processes, 13*, 92–101.

Killeen, P. R., & Fantino, E. (1990). A unified theory of choice. *Journal of the Experimental Analysis of Behavior, 53*, 189–200.

Killeen, P. R., & Fetterman, J. G. (1988). A behavioral theory of timing. *Psychological Review, 95*, 274–295.

Killeen, P. R., Hanson, S. J., & Osborne, S. R. (1978). Arousal: Its genesis and manifestation as response rate. *Psychological Review, 85*, 571–581.

Killeen, P. R., & Smith, J. P. (1984). Perception of contingency in conditioning: Scalar timing, response bias, and the erasure of memory by reinforcement. *Journal of Experimental Psychology: Animal Behavior Processes, 10*, 333–345.

Killeen, P. R., & Weiss, N. (1987). Optimal timing and the Weber function. *Psychological Review, 94*, 455–468.

Kristofferson, A. B. (1984). Quantal and deterministic timing in human duration discrimination. In J. Gibbon & L. Allan (Eds.), *Timing and time perception* (pp. 3–15). New York: New York Academy of Sciences.

Lejeune, H., & Wearden, J. H. (1991). The comparative psychology of fixed-interval responding: Some quantitative analyses. *Learning and Motivation, 22*, 84–111.

Lett, B. T. (1975). Long-delay learning in the T-maze. *Learning and Motivation, 6*, 80–90.

Lieberman, D. A., Davidson, F. H., & Thomas, G. V. (1985). Marking in pigeons: The role of memory in delayed reinforcement. *Journal of Experimental Psychology: Animal Behavior Processses, 11*, 611–624.

Luco, J. E. (1990). Matching, delay-reduction, and maximizing models for choice in concurrent-chains schedules. *Journal of the Experimental Analysis of Behavior, 54*, 53–67.

Mazur, J. E. (1984). Test of an equivalence rule for fixed and variable delays. *Journal of Experimental Psychology: Animal Behavior Processes, 10*, 426–436.

McDowell, J. J., & Kessel, R. (1979). A multivariate rate equation for variable-interval performance. *Journal of the Experimental Analysis of Behavior, 31*, 267–283.

McGill, W. J. (1963). Stochastic latency mechanisms. In R. R. Bush & E. Galanter (Eds.), *Handbook of mathematical psychology* (pp. 309–360). New York: Wiley.

McGill, W. J., & Gibbon, J. (1965). The general-gamma distribution and reaction times. *Journal of Mathematical Psychology, 2*, 1–18.

McIntire, K., Lundervold, D., Calmes, H., Jones, C., & Allard, S. (1983). Temporal control in a complex environment: An analysis of schedule-related behavior. *Journal of the Experimental Analysis of Behavior, 39*, 465–478.

McNamara, J. M., & Houston, A. I. (1985). Optimal foraging and learning. *Journal of Theoretical Biology, 117*, 231–249.

McNamara, J. M., & Houston, A. I. (1987a). Foraging in patches: There's more to life than the marginal value theorem. In M. L. Commons, A. Kacelnik, & S. Shettleworth (Eds.), *Quantitative analysis of behavior: Vol. 6. Foraging* (pp. 23–39). Hillsdale, NJ: Erlbaum.

McNamara, J. M., & Houston, A. I. (1987b). Memory and the efficient use of information. *Journal of Theoretical Biology, 125*, 385–395.

McSweeney, F. K. (1987). Suppression by reinforcement, a model for multiple-schedule contrast. *Behavioural Processes, 15*, 191–209.

Meck, W. H. (1983). Selective adjustment of the speed of internal clock and memory processes. *Journal of Experimental Psychology: Animal Behavior Processes, 9*, 171–201.

Moore, J., & Fantino, E. (1975). Choice and response contingencies. *Journal of the Experimental Analysis of Behavior, 23*, 339–347.

Myerson, J. (1990). *Formal relations between dynamic models of molar matching.* Jacksonville Conference on Behavior Dynamics, Jacksonville, AL.

Myerson, J., & Hale, S. (1988). Choice in transition: A comparison of melioration and the kinetic model. *Journal of the Experimental Analysis of Behavior, 49,* 291–302.

Myerson, J., & Miezin, F. M. (1980). The kinetics of choice: An operant systems analysis. *Psychological Review, 87,* 160–174.

Nevin, J. A. (1988). Behavioral momentum and the partial reinforcement effect. *Psychological Bulletin, 103,* 44–56.

Osborne, S. R. (1977). *A quantitative analysis of the effects of amount of reinforcement.* Doctoral dissertation, Arizona State University, Tempe.

Rescorla, R. A., & Wagner, A. R. (1972). A theory of Pavlovian conditioning: Variations in the effectiveness of reinforcement and nonreinforcement. In A. H. Black & W. F. Prokasy (Eds.), *Classical conditioning: II. Current research and theory* (pp. 64–99). New York: Appleton-Century-Crofts.

Richelle, M., & Lejeune, H. (1980). *Time in animal behavior.* New York: Pergamon.

Roberts, S., & Church, R. M. (1978). Control of an internal clock. *Journal of Experimental Psychology: Animal Behavior Processes, 4,* 318–337.

Roberts, W. A., & Kraemer, P. J. (1984). Temporal variables in delayed matching to sample. In J. Gibbon & L. Allan (Eds.), *Timing and time perception* (pp. 335–345). New York: New York Academy of Sciences.

Roper, T. J. (1978). Diversity and substitutability of adjunctive activities under fixed-interval schedules of food reinforcement. *Journal of Experimental Analysis of Behavior, 30,* 83–96.

Shull, R. L. (1970). The response-reinforcement dependency in Fixed-Interval Schedules. *Journal of the Experimental Analysis of Behavior, 14,* 55–60.

Shurtleff, D., Raslear, T. G., & Simmons, L. (1990). Circadian variations in time perception in rats. *Physiology and Behavior, 47,* 931–939.

Staddon, J. E. R. (1974). Temporal control, attention and memory. *Psychological Review, 81,* 375–391.

Staddon, J. E. R. (1977). Schedule-induced behavior. In W. K. Honig & J. E. R. Staddon (Eds.), *Handbook of operant behavior* (pp. 125–152). New York: Prentice-Hall.

Staddon, J. E. R., & Ayres, S. L. (1975). Sequential and temporal properties of behavior induced by a schedule of periodic food delivery. *Behaviour, 54,* 26–49.

Staddon, J. E. R., & Horner, J. M. (1989). Stochastic choice models: A comparison between Bush-Mosteller and a source-independent reward-following model. *Journal of the Experimental Analysis of Behavior, 52,* 57–64.

Staddon, J. E. R., & Simmelhag, V. (1971). The "superstition" experiment: A re-examination of its implications for principles of adaptive behavior. *Psychological Review, 78,* 3–43.

Staddon, J. E. R., & Zhang, Y. (1989). Response selection in operant learning. *Behavioural Processes, 20,* 189–197.

Terrace, H. S., Gibbon, J., Farrell, L., & Baldock, M. D. (1975). Temporal factors influencing the acquisition and maintenance of an autoshaped keypeck. *Animal Learning and Behavior, 3,* 53–62.

Timberlake, W., Gawley, D. J., & Lucas, G. A. (1987). Time horizons in rats foraging for food in temporally separated patches. *Journal of Experimental Psychology: Animal Behavior Processes, 13,* 302–309.

Timberlake, W., & Lucas, G. A. (1985). The basis of superstitious behavior: Chance contingency, stimulus substitution, or appetitive behavior? *Journal of the Experimental Analysis of Behavior, 44,* 279–299.

White, K. G. (1990). Delayed and current stimulus control in successive discriminations. *Journal of the Experimental Analysis of Behavior, 54*, 31–43.

Wilkie, D. M. (1987). Stimulus intensity affects pigeons' timing behavior: Implications for an internal clock model. *Animal Learning & Behavior, 15*, 35–39.

Williams, B. A. (1981). The following schedule of reinforcement as a fundamental determinant of steady-state contrast in multiple schedules. *Journal of the Experimental Analysis of Behavior, 35*, 293–310.

Williams, B. A. (1982). On the failure and facilitation of conditional discrimination. *Journal of the Experimental Analysis of Behavior, 28*, 265–280.

Williams, B. A. (1988). Reinforcement, choice, and response strength. In R. C. Atkinson, R. J. Herrnstein, G. Lindzey, & R. D. Luce (Eds.), *Stevens' handbook of experimental psychology* (pp. 167–244). New York: Wiley.

Williams, B. A. (1990). Absence of anticipatory contrast in rats trained on multiple schedules. *Journal of the Experimental Analysis of Behavior, 53*, 395-407.

Wing, A. M., & Kristofferson, A. B. (1973). Response delays and the timing of discrete motor responses. *Perception & Psychophysics, 14*, 5–12.

Wixted, J. T. (1989). Nonhuman short-term memory: A quantitative analysis of selected findings. *Journal of the Expermiental Analysis of Behavior, 52*, 409–426.

INDEX

A

Access, goal-derived categories and, 57–58
Accuracy
    spatial mental models and, 110, 121–122, 124, 126
    timing and, 303, 329
        prospective, 317–319
        retrospective, 306, 312–313
Achievement of goals, categories and, *see* Goal-derived categories
Activation
    language comprehension and, 218, 256–257
        individual differences in skill, 253–254
        suppression and enhancement, 238–244
    temporal learning and, 280, 282–283
Ad hoc categories, achievement of goals and, 1, 3, 52
    derivation of categories, 36, 38–39
    planning, 28, 30, 44
    structure, 9–10
Adjunctive behavior, timing and, 296
    prospective timing, 314–315
    retrospective timing, 306–307, 311–312
Advantage of first mention, language comprehension and, 220–227, 255
Age, distorted recollection and, 188
Amnesia, distorted recollection and, 201
Anaphors, language comprehension and, 240–243, 246, 248, 256
Antecedents, language comprehension and, 240, 242
Arousal, timing and, 312, 317, 319, 323, 328
Artificial categories
    achievement of goals and, 20
    unsupervised domains and, 100

Artificial intelligence, goal-derived categories and, 27,29, 54
Assimilation, category knowledge and, 74–75
Association, language comprehension and, 240
Associative interference, category knowledge and, 75
Asymmetry
    spatial memory and, 182–183
    spatial representation and, 164, 167, 169, 171–172
Attention, category knowledge and, 105
    biases, 105
    capacity, 69, 103
    experiments, 88, 91, 101, 103
    model, 72–73
Attribute clusters, goal-derived categories and, 24
Attribute listing, category knowledge and, 77–80, 83, 91, 104–105
    hierarchy of categories, 87, 90
Attribute norms, category knowledge and, 72, 80, 83
Attributes
    achievement of goals and, 3, 58
        ad hoc categories, 36, 38–39
        cognitive system, 51, 55, 57
        constraint, 32–37
        frame instantiation, 22, 24–30
        optimization, 31–32
        planning, 22, 24, 39–45
    category knowledge and
        experiments, 81, 85, 96, 100, 103
        hierarchy of categories, 88, 90
        memorized instances, 93–95
        model, 70–72

Attribute salience, category knowledge and, 91–93
Attribute taxonomies, goal-derived categories and, 24
Attribute values
    category knowledge and, 70–73, 80–81, 92
    goal-derived categories and, 51

B

Background categories, unsupervised domains and, 77
Background cues, timing and, 326, 328
Background goals, categories and, 31
Basic level categories, achievement of goals and, 46–47
Behavioral theory of timing (BeT), 306–307, 309
Behavior's time, *see* Timing, behavior and
Between-subject agreement, goal-derived categories and, 11–12, 14
Blocked categories, unsupervised domains and, 80–83
Blocking, distorted recollection and, 199
Brain damage, distorted recollection and, 201

C

Cataphoric access, language comprehension and, 244–246, 248, 256–257
Categories
    distorted recollection and, 202–204
    goal-derived, *see* Goal-derived categories
    spatial memory and, 163, 182–183
Categorization, time course of, 50–53
Category definition, 66
Category knowledge in unsupervised domains, 65, 104–106
    alternative approaches, 76–77
    experiments
        attribute listing, 77–80
        attribute salience, 91–93
        blocked categories, 80–83
        hierarchy of categories, 87–90
        learning of variables, 99–102
        memorized instances, 93–95
        mixed sequences, 83–87
        reliability of defaults, 102–104
        specific instances, 96–99
    model, 69–76
    theoretical issues, 66–69

Category membership
    achievement of goals and, 8, 45
    unsupervised learning and, 73, 76, 95, 99, 101–102
Category norms
    category knowledge and, 73–75, 93, 103, 105
    distorted recollection and, 204
Category priority, spatial memory and, 183
Causal attribution, timing and, 317–321
Centrality, goal-derived categories and, 25
Central tendency, achievement of goals and
    cognitive system, 50, 54, 57
    structure, 14–22
Clusters
    language comprehension and, 230
    spatial memory and, 163
Cognitive maps, spatial mental models and, 129
Cognitive processes, language comprehension and, *see* Language comprehension
Cognitive system, achievement of goals and, 1–3, 45–46, 58
    event frames, 53–57
    lexicalization, 50–53
    planning, 22
    structure, 6, 21–22
    time course, 46–50
Commitment to misinformation, 192–199, 211
Competing contexts, timing and, 324–329
Competition
    category knowledge and, 89–90, 101, 103
    distorted recollection and, 199, 211
    timing and, 299
Comprehension
    language, *see* Language comprehension
    spatial mental models and, 141
Conceptual combination, achievement of goals and, 2, 4–5
    planning, 28, 39
    structure, 9, 14, 21
Conditioned reinforcement, timing and, 315–316, 329
Conditioned stimulus, timing and, 326, 328
Conditioning
    temporal, 268
    timing and, 312–313, 324–326
Consolidation, distorted recollection and, 192
Constraint chains, goal-derived categories and, 36–37

Constraints
  achievement of goals and, 3, 26
    cognitive system, 51, 56–57
    planning, 28, 30, 32–40, 43–45
  category knowledge and, 105
  timing and, 304
Context
  category knowledge and, 66, 70, 73
  competing, 324–329
  goal-derived categories and, 46–47, 49–50
    attributes, 27
    cognitive system, 54, 56–57
  timing and, 328–329
Contextualization
  goal-derived categories and, 43–45, 51
  spatial memory and, 149–150
Contextual shift, goal-derived categories and,
    11–12, 14, 20
Context verification, language comprehension
    and, 253
Contingency, timing and, 296–297
  competing contexts, 325
  prospective timing, 314, 319
  reinforcement, 323–324
Contrast, timing and, 328–329
Convergence, goal-derived categories and, 41
Coordinate relations, spatial memory and, 182
Coreference
  language comprehension and, 229
  spatial mental models and, 113
Counter, timing and, 302–304, 312–313, 329
Counterbalancing, distorted recollection and,
    203
Cued recall
  category knowledge and, 94–95
  spatial memory and, 161
Cues
  goal-derived categories and, 41, 46
  language comprehension and, 228, 230,
    240, 256
  linguistic, 237–238
  spatial mental models and, 133, 135
  temporal learning and, 275
  timing and, 306, 311–312, 317, 326, 328
Cyclic schedules, temporal learning and, 275,
    277, 289–290, 292

D

Decay
  language comprehension and, 239
  temporal learning and, 283, 291

timing and, 301, 315, 317–318, 322
Decision making
  distorted recollection and, 201, 210
  goal-derived categories and, 1, 28
Decision rules, category knowledge and, 68
Decontextualization
  goal-derived categories and, 45
  spatial memory and, 149–150
Delay
  temporal learning and, 268, 274
  timing and, 315, 319
Delayed reinforcement, timing and, 314–315,
    317
Delay reduction theory, timing and, 315, 317
Deliberation, distorted recollection and, 210
Diffusion-generalization model, temporal
    learning and, 265, 277–284, 293
  cyclic schedules, 289–290
  failures, 291–292
  response rule, 284
  scalar timing, 284–286
  two-valued interval schedules, 286–289
Discrimination, timing and, 307, 313–314,
    318–320
Discrimination learning, category knowledge
    and, 83–84, 88
Dishabituation, category knowledge and, 80
Distorted recollection, 199–200, 211–212
  commitment to misinformation, 192–199
  implicit tests, 200–211
  misinformation effect, 187–190
  modified test, 190–192
Distractors
  category knowledge and, 100
  distorted recollection and, 191
Drugs, timing and, 307
Dynamic interaction, temporal learning and,
    266
Dynamic models
  temporal learning and, 265, 272–277,
    291–292
  timing and, 317

E

Encoding
  category knowledge and, 65, 105
    experiments, 91, 95–96, 98–99, 101–104
    model, 69, 72–73, 75–76
    theoretical issues, 67
  distorted recollection and, 189, 210–211

spatial memory and, 156–159, 164, 179–181
timing and, 304
Engrams, distorted recollection and, 189
Enhancement, language comprehension and,
218, 238, 255–257
cataphoric access, 244–246
referential access, 240–244
surface information, 247–248
word meaning, 238–240
Environment, timing and, 321–322, 327, 329
Episodic memory, distorted recollection and,
189
Equiavailability model, spatial mental models
and, 133–137
Equivalence rule for indifference, timing and,
316
Event frame, goal-derived categories and,
2–3, 46, 53–57
Evolution, timing and, 321
Excitation, temporal learning and, 291
Exemplars
achievement of goals and, 1–5
planning, 31, 39–40, 45
structure, 6–10, 15–18, 20–21
category knowledge and, 67, 76, 83, 88,
98, 102
Experience, category knowledge and, 65, 67
Expert planners, goal-derived categories and,
40–41, 56
Explicit memory, distorted recollection and,
204–206, 208–209
Exponential decay function, timing and, 322
Exponentially weighted moving average
(EWMA), timing and, 322
Extinction
distorted recollection and, 210
timing and, 322–323, 325–326

F

Facilitation, language comprehension and,
239
Fading, distorted recollection and, 188
Failure-based generalization, category knowledge and, 74
Familiarity, goal-derived categories and,
17–19
Fan effect
category knowledge and, 75, 96, 99
spatial memory and, 170
Features, category knowledge and, 70

Feedback
category knowledge and, 67
spatial mental models and, 109
Fine tuning of meaning of words, 238–240, 256
First mention, language comprehension and
advantage, 220–227, 255
functional role, 228–229
Fixed-interval (FI) schedule, temporal learning and
diffusion-generalization model, 278, 280,
283–287
reinforcement schedules, 268–269
Fixed–ratio schedule, temporal learning and,
266
Foraging, timing and, 321–322, 327, 329
Forgetting, distorted recollection and, 192,
198, 210
Frames, goal-derived categories and, 51, 53,
56
attributes, 3, 58
cognitive system, 57
planning, 22, 26–27, 30–31, 41, 43
instantiation, 22, 24–30, 32
modification, 39, 44
Free recall
distorted recollection and, 210
spatial memory and, 161
Frequency
goal-derived categories and, 17–20
temporal learning and, 279–280, 283
timing and, 314–315, 322, 329
Full-storage theory, category knowledge and,
101

G

Generalization, *see also* Diffusion-generalization model
category knowledge and, 67–69
experiments, 95, 98–99, 102
model, 74
distorted recollection and, 191
temporal learning and, 280
timing and, 300, 328
Generalized Weber's law, timing and, 303
Generate-test procedure, goal-derived categories and, 30
Goal-derived categories, 1–3, 57–58
cognitive system, 45–46
event frames, 53–57
lexicalization, 50–53
time course, 46–50

conceptual combination, 4–6
exemplar learning, 3–6
planning, 22–24
  ad hoc categories, 36, 38–39
  constraint, 32–37
  fields, 39–45
  frame instantiation, 22, 24–30
  optimization, 31–32
  structure, 6–10
  determinants, 14–22
  stability, 10–14
Guessing, distorted recollection and, 189,
  194, 200, 211

H

Habituation, category knowledge and, 73, 80,
  83
Hierarchical descriptions, spatial mental models and, 111, 113, 130–131
Hierarchy
  of categories, 87–90, 105
  spatial memory and, 157–163, 180–182

I

Ideals, goal-derived categories and, 16–17,
  19–20
Imagery, spatial mental models and, 110, 128,
  132–133, 140
Implicit memory, distorted recollection and,
  206–210
Implicit tests, distorted recollection and,
  200–211
Impulse interval, temporal learning and, 276
Incidental learning, category knowledge and,
  67
Inference
  language comprehension and, 238
  spatial memory and, 172
  spatial mental models and, 141
    statements, 118–122
    survey and route descriptions, 124, 126,
      128
  timing and, 319
Information processing, category knowledge
  and, 83, 87
Informativeness, category knowledge and,
  72–73, 75, 105–106
  experiments, 77, 80, 91–92, 103
Inhibition
  distorted recollection and, 189

mutual, 239
  spatial memory and, 149
  temporal learning and, 291
  timing and, 328
Instance generation test, distorted recollection
  and, 202
Instance storage theories, category knowledge
  and, 67
Instances
  blocked categories and, 81–83
  category knowledge and, 66–67, 76–77,
    105–106
    attribute listing, 78–80
    attribute salience, 91–93
    experiments, 96–99
    hierarchy of categories, 88, 90
    memorization, 93–95
    mixed sequences, 84
    model, 74–76
  encoding of, 73
  evaluation of, 72–73
  processing of, 68–69
Instantiation, goal-derived categories and,
  2–3, 58
  frames, 22, 24–30, 32
  frequency, 17–21, 57
  meaning, 27
  planning, 22, 28–29, 36, 38, 41, 43–44
  selection, 30–36
Interference
  category knowledge and, 75, 87, 98, 106
  distorted recollection and, 209–211
  language comprehension and, 253–254
Interfood intervals (IFIs), temporal learning
  and
  diffusion-generalization model, 277–280,
    283–292
  Markovian dynamic hypothesis, 273–277
  reinforcement schedules, 268–271
Interim behavior, timing and, 297, 299, 301,
  305, 314
Interim response, timing and, 298
Internalization, spatial mental models and,
  134
Intertrial interval, timing and, 307, 326, 328
Intervals
  temporal, 305–307
  temporal learning and
    diffusion-generalization model, 277–280,
      283–292
    Markovian dynamic hypothesis, 272–277
    reinforcement schedules, 268–271

timing and, 296, 329
  competing contexts, 326, 328
  contemporaneous effects, 296–297
  prospective timing, 314
  retrospective timing, 307, 309, 311–313
Interval schedules, two-valued, temporal
  learning and, 286–289, 291
Isodissimilarity condition, spatial memory
  and, 174–175

K

Knowledge
  category, in unsupervised domains, *see*
    Category knowledge in unsupervised
    domains
  goal-derived categories and, 4, 10, 53, 58
  spatial memory and, 176, 178

L

Labels, category knowledge and, 94
Language
  goal-derived categories and, 53
  spatial mental models and, 131–132
Language comprehension, 254–257
  individual differences in skill, 248–254
  laying of foundation, 219–229
  mapping, 229–230
  shifting, 230
    inaccessibility to information, 231–236
    linguistic cues, 237–238
  structure building, 217–218
  suppression and enhancement, 238
    cataphoric access, 244–246
    referential access, 240–244
    surface information, 247–248
    word meaning, 238–240
Laying of foundation, language comprehen-
  ˙sion and, 218–220, 255–256
  first mention, 220–229
Learning
  distorted recollection and, 201
  spatial memory and, 150, 152, 156, 165,
    168
Lexical access, language comprehension and,
  241
Lexical concepts, language comprehension
  and, 245, 248
Lexicalization, goal-derived categories and, 3,
  46, 50–53

Lexical tasks, distorted recollection and, 201,
  210
Linear waiting, temporal learning and, 276
Linguistics
  goal-derived categories and, 52
  language comprehension and, 255
    laying of foundation, 221–222, 229
    shifting, 233, 237–238
    suppression and enhancement, 238, 241,
      245
  spatial memory and, 170–172, 175, 179
  spatial mental models and, 131
Locative statements, spatial mental models
  and, 118–119, 121–122, 124, 126
Long-term memory
  category knowledge and, 71
  goal-derived categories and, 30, 54
  spatial representation and, 147, 179, 182

M

Mapping
  goal-derived categories and, 48, 56–57
  language comprehension and, 218,
    229–230, 254–256
    individual differences in skill, 251, 253
    laying of foundation, 223, 225–226, 229
  spatial memory and, 147
  spatial mental models and, 110, 112, 119,
    122, 128–131
  temporal learning and, 284, 291
  timing and, 317
Maps versus texts, spatial mental models and,
  122, 124–126
Markovian dynamic hypothesis, temporal
  learning and, 272–277
Memory
  category knowledge and, 65, 76, 105
    experiments, 90–91
    instances, 93–96, 98–99
    learning of variables, 99–101
    model, 69, 71, 73, 75–76
    theoretical issues, 67–69
  distorted recollection and, *see* Distorted
    recollection
  explicit, *see* Explicit memory, distorted
    recollection and
  goal-derived categories and, 1, 4, 57–58
    planning, 30, 39, 41
  language comprehension and, 218, 229,
    235, 238, 240, 250

long-term, *see* Long-term memory
short-term, *see* Short-term memory
spatial, *see* Spatial memory
spatial mental models and, 118, 130, 132,
141
temporal learning and, 279–281
timing and, 304, 324, 328
working, *see* Working memory
Memory impairment, distorted recollection
and, 190–192, 198, 201, 210–211
Memory nodes, language comprehension and,
218, 238
Memory traces, distorted recollection and,
188–190
Mental models, spatial, *see* Spatial mental
models
Mental rotation, spatial mental models and, 134
Mental transformation model, 133–137
Metric axioms, spatial memory and, 163–175,
179
Misinformation, distorted recollection and,
187–190, 200, 211–212
commitment, 192–199
effect, 188, 211
implicit tests, 200–211
modified test, 191–192
Misleading information, distorted recollection
and, *see* Distorted recollection
Modal properties, goal-derived categories
and, 15
Modified-modified-free recall test, distorted
recollection and, 210
Motivation, timing and, 319
Mutual inhibition, language comprehension
and, 239

N

Negative contrast, timing and, 328
Norms, category knowledge and, 74, 77
Novelty, distorted recollection and, 196–198

O

Object attributes, goal-derived categories and,
56
Ontology, spatial memory and, 157–158
Optimization, goal-derived categories and, 3,
5, 10
cognitive system, 51, 55–57
planning, 28, 30–32, 36, 38–41, 43–45

P

Pacemaker system, timing and, 302–304
selection, 312–313
speed, 307–312, 329
Paraphrased statements, spatial mental models
and, 121–123
Partial reinforcement extinction effect
(PREE), timing and, 323
Patterned interval schedule of reinforcement,
268–272
Patterns, category knowledge and, 65, 69
Perception
distorted recollection and, 201, 212
goal-derived categories and, 4
spatial memory and, 171
spatial mental models and, 110, 129, 134
Perceptual learning, category knowledge and,
91
Perceptual salience, language comprehension
and, 228
Perspectives, spatial mental models and,
141–142
experiment, 112–113, 119
survey and route descriptions, 121–122,
126, 128, 130–131
texts versus maps, 124
Planning, goal-derived categories and, 2, 5,
22–24, 58
ad hoc categories, 36–39
cognitive system, 56
constraints, 32–37
fields, 39–45
frame instantiation, 22, 24–30
optimization, 31–32
structure, 10
Point of subjective equality (PSE), timing
and, 306–307, 311
Poisson process, timing and, 301–305,
311–313
Primary categorization, achievement of goals
and, 46–48, 50, 52, 57
Primary reinforcement, timing and, 314–316,
318, 329
Priming
distorted recollection and, 201–202,
206–208, 211
language comprehension and, 230, 238
spatial memory and, 148–151, 153–156
spatial representation and, 159–160, 162,
176, 178

metric axioms, 165, 168–170, 172–175
Prospective timing, 296
    causal attributions and, 317–321
    state reinforcement model and, 314–317
Prototype structure, goal-derived categories
        and, 2, 6–10
    determinants, 14–22
    planning, 31, 38
    stability, 10–14
PSE, *see* Point of subjective equality (PSE)
Psychological space, spatial memory and,
        163, 170–171, 173–175
Psychometric function, timing and, 302–303,
        306–307

R

Random effect, distorted recollection and, 204
Rating-from-memory, category knowledge
        and, 94
Reaction time, spatial mental models and,
        118–119, 142
    spatial frameworks, 132, 134–135, 137–
        138
    survey and route descriptions, 124–125
Reasoning, goal-derived categories and, 4, 7
Recall
    category knowledge and, 94–95, 100–104
    distorted recollection and, 187, 210
    language comprehension and, 220, 228,
        230, 235
    spatial memory and, 155–156, 161–162,
        183
    spatial mental models and, 131
Recency, temporal learning and, 280, 293
Recoding
    distorted recollection and, 189
    language comprehension and, 234–236,
        256
Recognition
    distorted recollection and, 201, 203, 210
    language comprehension and, 230, 236,
        238
    spatial memory and, 149–154, 156
    spatial representation and, 159–160, 162,
        169, 176, 178
Recollection, distorted, *see* Distorted recollec-
        tion
Reference point, spatial memory and, 164,
        168
Referential suppression, language comprehen-
        sion and, 240–244, 256

Rehearsal
    category knowledge and, 99
    distorted recollection and, 210
    language comprehension and, 226
    spatial memory and, 155
Reinforcement
    category knowledge and, 69
    timing and, 296, 329
        competing contexts, 324–325, 328–329
        contemporaneous effects, 296, 300, 304
        contingencies, 323–324
        extinction, 323
        prospective timing, 313–320
        retrospective timing, 306–307, 309,
            311–312
        time horizons, 322–323
Reinforcement schedule
    temporal learning and, 265–272, 291–293
    timing and, 309, 312, 317
Renewal processes, timing and, 311–312
Repetition, language comprehension and, 229
Representation
    category knowledge and, 65, 67, 76
        experiments, 91, 98
        model, 70–71
    distorted recollection and, 188, 210
    language comprehension and, 255
        laying of foundation, 219–221, 224,
            226–227
        shifting, 235–237
        structure building, 217–218
    spatial, *see* Spatial memory
    spatial mental models and, 109, 111
        survey and route descriptions, 112, 119,
            121–122, 126, 128
        texts versus maps, 124, 126
    temporal learning and, 281, 291, 293
Response
    temporal learning and, 266–268
        diffusion-generalization model, 278,
            280–281, 283–289
        Markovian dynamic hypothesis,
            273–274
    timing and, 298, 303, 323–326, 328
        prospective timing, 314, 319–320
        retrospective timing, 306, 308
        time horizons, 320
Response-initiated delay (RID), temporal
        learning and, 274
Response rule, temporal learning and, 284
Retrieval
    category knowledge and, 75–76, 87, 96, 101

goal-derived categories and, 2, 30
impairment, 189
language comprehension and, 230
spatial memory and, 149, 156, 183
spatial mental models and, 142
spatial representation and, 159, 162, 172
timing and, 304
Retrospective timing, 296
pacemakers and, 307–313
state reinforcement model and, 314
temporal intervals and, 305–307
Route descriptions, spatial mental models
and, 111–121, 124, 126, 131
Routine activity, category knowledge and, 69

S

Salience-in-comparison, category knowledge
and, 95
Scalar expectancy theory (SET), timing and,
304, 306–308
Scalar property, temporal learning and, 280,
293
Scalar timing, 303–305, 311
temporal learning and, 284–286, 291
Schedule-induced activities, timing and, 297
Schedules, cyclic, temporal learning and, 275,
277, 289–290, 292
Schedules of reinforcement
temporal learning and, 265–272, 291–293
timing and, 309, 312, 317
Secondary categorization, achievement of
goals and, 46, 48, 50, 52, 57
Secondary reinforcement, timing and, 316
Semantics
category knowledge and, 67
language comprehension and, 255
laying of foundation, 221
shifting, 235
suppression and enhancement, 238–240,
243
spatial memory and, 162, 171
Sequences, category knowledge and, 83–88,
100
Sequential additivity, spatial memory and,
173, 175, 183
SET, *see* Scalar expectancy theory
Shaping, timing and, 296
Shared-absence effect, category knowledge
and, 95
Shifting, language comprehension and, 218,
230, 256–257

inaccessibility to information, 231–236
individual differences in skill, 251–252
linguistic cues, 237–238
Short-term memory
category knowledge and, 99, 102
language comprehension and, 234, 251
spatial memory and, 183
Sign tracking, timing and, 326–329
Similarity
category knowledge and, 92–95, 105
spatial memory and, 171, 173
Situation models, spatial mental models and,
119
SOA, *see* Stimulus onset asynchrony
Source misattribution, distorted recollection
and, 190–191
Spatial contiguity, 150–154
timing and, 319
Spatial memory, 147–148, 179–183
measures, 148–156
spatial representation, 157
hierarchical component, 157–163
integration of information, 175–179
metric axioms, 163–175
Spatial mental models, 109–111, 141–142
spatial frameworks, 131–141
survey and route descriptions, 111–112,
126–131
experiment, 112–121
texts versus maps, 122, 124–126
verbatim statements, 121–123
Spatial representation, *see* Spatial memory
Speed, spatial mental models and, 110
State reinforcement model, timing and,
314–317
Stereotypes, category knowledge and, 68, 105
Stimulus
category knowledge and, 68, 76, 105–106
attribute listing, 78, 80
attribute salience, 91–93
blocked categories, 80–81
experiments, 88, 100–102
mixed sequences, 84–85
model, 69–72, 74
distorted recollection and, 194–195
language comprehension and, 218, 222,
257
individual differences in skill, 250–251
shifting, 231, 233, 236
suppression and enhancement, 247
prospective timing and, 315, 319
retrospective timing and, 307

spatial memory and, 164, 170–172
temporal learning and, 266, 281–282
timing and, 303, 324–326, 328
Stimulus generalization, temporal learning
    and, 280
Stimulus onset asynchrony (SOA), spatial
    memory and, 149, 154
Structure building, language comprehension
    and, 217–219, 255–256
    individual differences in skill, 248, 251
    shifting, 235
    suppression and enhancement, 248
Subcategories
    achievement of goals and, 41
    unsupervised learning and, 65, 67, 76–77
        experiments, 85, 87–88, 91, 95
        model, 69, 71
Subnoding, category knowledge and, 75
Subordinate categorization, achievement of
    goals and, 46–48
Summary representation, category knowledge
    and, 67
Suppression
    distorted recollection and, 189, 199
    language comprehension and, 218, 255–257
        cataphoric access, 244–246
        individual differences in skill, 252–254
        referential access, 240–244
        surface information, 247–248
        word meaning, 238–240
        referential, 240–244, 256
Surface information, language comprehension
    and, 247–248, 257
Survey descriptions, spatial mental models
    and, 111–118, 124, 126, 131
Symmetry, spatial memory and, 163–173, 183
Synchronization, timing and, 323
Syntax
    goal-derived categories and, 25
    language comprehension and, 255
        laying of foundation, 222, 224
        shifting, 233
        suppression and enhancement, 238–239,
            247

T

Taxonomic categories, achievement of goals
    and, 2–3, 5, 58
    cognitive system, 46, 50–55, 57
    structure, 6–22

Taxonomy
    category knowledge and, 75
    goal-derived categories and, 24, 29
Temporal contiguity
    spatial memory and, 150–155
    timing and, 319
Temporal control, 293
Temporal discrimination, 280
Temporal factors, spatial memory and, 162
Temporal intervals, 305–307
Temporal learning, 265–268, 292–293
    diffusion-generalization model, 277–284
        cyclic schedules, 289–290
        failures, 291–292
        response rule, 284
        scalar timing, 284–286
        two-valued interval schedules, 286–289
    Markovian dynamic hypothesis, 272–277
    reinforcement schedules, 268–272
Temporal patterns, category knowledge and, 66
Terminal behaviors, timing and, 296, 305, 314
Text, spatial mental models and, 128
Texts versus maps, spatial mental models and,
    122, 124–126
Time, see also Temporal learning
    spatial mental models and, 121
Time marker, temporal learning and, 293
Timing, behavior and, 295–296, 329
    competing contexts, 324–329
    contemporaneous effects, 296–302
        pacemaker-counter systems, 302–303
        scalar timing, 303–305
    contingencies of reinforcement, 323–324
    extinction, 323
    prospective timing, 313–314
        causal attributions, 317–321
        state reinforcement model, 314–317
    retrospective timing
        pacemakers, 307–313
        temporal intervals, 305–307
        time horizons, 320–323
Trace, temporal learning and, 268
Trace impairment, distorted recollection and,
    188–189
Tracking, temporal learning and, 275–276,
    279, 286, 290–291
Triangle inequality, spatial memory and, 173
Tutors, category knowledge and, 67
Typicality
    achievement of goals and
        planning, 31
        structure, 6, 11–12, 15, 17–20
    category knowledge and, 72

U

Unsupervised domains, category knowledge in, *see* Category knowledge in unsupervised domains

V

Values, goal-derived categories and, 26–27
Verbal statements, spatial memory and, 176
Verbatim statements, spatial mental models and, 118–124, 126, 128, 141
Verification, spatial mental models and, 126, 128, 132, 134, 141
Visual information
  spatial memory and, 175
  spatial mental models and, 110, 124, 128

W

Waiting time, temporal learning and
  diffusion-generalization model, 279–280, 284–285, 289–290
  Markovian dynamic hypothesis, 273–276
  reinforcement schedules, 270–271
Warnings, distorted recollection and, 188
Weber fraction, timing and, 304
Weber's law, timing and, 303
Within-subject agreement, goal-derived categories and, 11–14
Working memory
  category knowledge and, 91
  goal-derived categories and, 30
World models, goal-derived categories and, 53–57

CONTENTS OF RECENT VOLUMES

Volume 17

The Structure of Human Memory
William F. Brewer and John R. Pani
A Simulation Model for the Comprehension of
Technical Prose
David Kieras
A Multiple-Entry, Modular Memory System
Marcia K. Johnson
The Cognitive Map of a City—50 Years of
Learning and Memory
Harry P. Bahrick
Problem Solving Skill in the Social Sciences
James F. Voss, Terry R. Greene, Timothy
A. Post, and Barbara C. Penner
Biological Constraints on Instrumental and
Classical Conditioning: Implications for
General Process Theory
Michael Domjan
Index

Volume 18

Nonanalytic Cognition: Memory, Perception,
and Concept Learning
Larry L. Jacoby and Lee R. Brooks
On the Nature of Categories
Donald Homa
The Recovery of Unconsious (Inaccessible)
Memories: Laboratory Studies of
Hypermnesia
Matthew Erdelyi
Origins of Behavior of Pavlovian Conditioning
Peter C. Holland
Directed Forgetting in Context
Mark Rilling, Donald F. Kendrick, and
Thomas B. Stonebraker

Effects of Isolation Rearing on Learning by
Mammals
Robert Holson and Gene P. Sackett
Aristotle's Logic
Marilyn Jager Adams
Some Empirical Justification for a Theory of
Natural Propositional Logic
Martin D.S. Braine, Brian J. Reister, and
Barbara Rumain
Index

Volume 19

Memory for Experience
Janet Kolodner
The Pragmatics of Analogical Transfer
Keith J. Holyoak
Learning in Complex Domains: A Cognitive
Analysis of Computer Programming
Richard E. Mayer
Posthypnotic Amnesia and the Dissociation of
Memory
John F. Kihlstrom
Unit Formation in Perception and Memory
John Ceraso
How Infants Form Categories
Barbara A. Younger and Leslie B. Cohen
Index

Volume 20

Recognition by Components: A Theory of
Visual Pattern Recognition
Irving Biederman
Associative Structures in Instrumental Learning
Ruth M. Colwill and Robert A. Rescorla

The Structure of Subjective Time: How Time
  Flies
    John Gibson
The Computation of Contingency in Classical
  Conditioning
    Richard H. Granger, Jr., and Jeffrey C.
    Schlimmer
Baseball: An Example of Knowledge-Directed
  Machine Learning
    Elliot Soloway
Mental Cues and Verbal Reports in Learning
    Francis S. Bellezza
Memory Mechanisms in Text Comprehension
    Murray Glanzer and Suzanne Donnenwerth
    Nolan
Index

Volume 21

An Integrated Computation Model of Stimulus-
  Response Compatibility and Practice
    Paul S. Rosenbloom and Allen Newell
A Connectionist/Control Architecture for
  Working Memory
    Walter Schneider and Mark Detweiler
The Intelligent Hand
    Roberta L. Klatzky and Susan J. Lederman
Successive Approximations to a Model of
  Human Motor Programming
    David A. Rosenbaum
Modular Analysis of Timing in Motor Skill
    Steven W. Keele and Richard I. Ivry
Associative Accounts of Causality Judgment
    David R. Shanks and Anthony Dickinson
Anxiety and the Amygdala: Pharmacological
  and Anatomical Analysis of the Fear-
  Potentiated Startle Paradigm
    Michael Davis, Janice M. Hitchcock, and
    Jeffrey B. Rosen
Index

Volume 22

Foraging as Operant Behavior and Operant
  Behavior as Foraging: What Have We
  Learned?
    Sara J. Shettleworth
The Comparator Hypothesis: A Response Rule
  for the Expression of Associations
    Ralph R. Miller and Louis D. Matzel

The Experimental Synthesis of Behavior:
  Reinforcement, Behavioral Stereotypy, and
  Problem Solving
    Barry Schwartz
Extraction of Information from Complex Visual
  Stimuli: Memory Performance and
  Phenomenological Appearance
    Geoffrey R. Loftus and John Hogden
Working Memory, Comprehension, and Aging:
  A Review and a New View
    Lynn Hasher and Rose T. Zacks
Strategic Control of Retrieval Strategies
    Lynn M. Reder
Alternative Representations
    Ruth S. Day
Evidence for Relational Selectivity in the
  Interpretation of Analogy and Metaphor
    Dedre Gentner and Catherine Clement
Index

Volume 23

Quantitative Modeling of Synaptic Plasticity
    David C. Tam and Donald H. Perkel
Computational Capabilities of Single Neurons:
  Relationship to Simple Forms of Associative
  and Nonassociative Learning in *Aplysia*
    John H. Byrne, Kevin J. Gingrich, and
    Douglas A. Baxter
A Biologically Based Computational Model for
  Several Simple Forms of Learning
    Robert D. Hawkins
Integrating Behavioral and Biological Models
  of Classical Conditioning
    Nelson H. Donegan, Mark A. Gluck, and
    Richard F. Thompson
Some Relationships between a Computational
  Model (SOP) and a Neural Circuit for
  Pavlovian (Rabbit Eyeblink) Conditioning
    Allan R. Wagner and Nelson H. Donegan
Simulation and Analysis of a Simple Cortical
  Network
    Gary Lynch and Richard Granger
A Computational Approach to Hippocampal
  Function
    William B Levy
Index

Volume 24

Dimensional Mnemonics
David S. Olton
Memory Processing by Pigeons, Monkeys, and
People
Anthony A. Wright
Short-Term Memory for Associations
Bennet B. Murdock and William E.
Hockley
Catastrophic Interference in Connectionist
Networks: The Sequential Learning Problem
Michael McCloskey and Neal J. Cohen
Fear, Stimulus Feedback, and Stressor
Controllability
Donald A. Warren, Robert A. Rosellini,
and Steven F. Maier
Semantic Context Effects on Visual Word
Processing: A Hybrid Prospective–
Retrospective Processing Theory
James H. Neely and Dennis E. Keefe
Network Structures in Proximity Data
Roger W. Schvaneveldt, Francis T. Durso,
and Donald W. Dearholt
Individual Differences in Attention
Earl Hunt, James W. Pellegrino, and Penny
L. Yee
Type A Behavior: A Social Cognition
Motivational Perspective
Nicholas A. Kuiper and Rod A. Martin
Index

Volume 25

Inferences about Word Meanings
Richard C. Anderson
Inference Generation during Auditory Language
Comprehension
David A. Swinney and Lee Osterhout
Bridging Inferences and Enthymemes
Murray Singer, Rusell Revlin, and
Michael Halldorson
The Impact of Inferences on Instructional Text
Bruce K. Britton, Lani Van Dusen, Shawn
M. Glynn, and Darold Hemphill
Integration and Buffering of New Information
Karl Haberlandt and Arthur C. Graesser

Goal, Event, and State Inferences: An
Investigation of Inference Generation during
Story Comprehension
Debra L. Long, Jonathan M. Golding,
Arthur C. Graesser, and Leslie F. Clark
Content-Based Inferences in Text
Colleen M. Seifert
Situation-Based Inferences during Narrative
Comprehension
Daniel G. Morrow, Gordon H. Bower, and
Steven L. Greenspan
Expectations, Mental Representations, and
Spatial Inferences
Monika Wagener-Wender and Karl F.
Wender
Causal Inferences and Text Memory
Jerome L. Myers and Susan A. Duffy
Causal Inferences and the Comprehension of
Narrative Texts
Paul van den Broek

Volume 26

Spatial Memory in Seed-Caching Corvids
Alan C. Kamil and Russell P. Balda
Detecting Response–Outcome Relations:
Toward an Understanding of the Causal
Texture of the Environment
E.A. Wasserman
Priming of Nonverbal Information and the
Nature of Implicit Memory
Daniel L. Schacter, Suzanne M. Delaney,
and Elizabeth P. Merikle
Metamemory: A Theoretical Framework and
New Findings
Thomas O. Nelson and Louis Narens
The New Multimodal Approach to Memory
Improvement
Douglas J. Herrmann and Alan Searleman
A Triphasic Approach to the Acquisition of
Response-Selection Skill
Robert W. Proctor, T. Gilmour Reeve, and
Daniel J. Weeks
The Structure and Formation of Natural
Categories
Douglas Fisher and Pat Langley
Index